ELIZABETHAN DRAMA

ELIZABETHAN DRAMA: MODERN ESSAYS IN CRITICISM

EDITED BY R. J. KAUFMANN
UNIVERSITY OF ROCHESTER

A Galaxy Book

NEW YORK OXFORD UNIVERSITY PRESS 1961

Library of Congress Catalogue Card Number: 61–13566

Printed in the United States of America

PREFACE

This book brings together a planned group of essays about the drama of the English contemporaries of Shakespeare. With the deliberate exception of the first and framing essays, the emphasis is on essentially critical rather than essentially scholarly writing—on writing that sharpens vision and releases sympathy rather than that designed primarily to inform. Lacking the assistance of rich biographical and social materials to inform his inquiry, and confronted by these complex and maturely ironic poetic dramas, the most gifted student and general reader needs some help to direct his intelligence in order that the pleasures others have found in these plays not be pointlessly denied him.

These essays have been chosen, then, with an eye to guaranteeing this help and assisting this pleasure. Read consecutively they constitute a virtually unified interpretation of the drama as it grew great as a whole and great in some of its parts in the plays of Marlowe, of Jonson, and of Webster. The critical modes of the essays are deliberately various; they have been chosen not only for intrinsic excellence and for their coverage of the desired works and figures, but because they manifest as well many honorable ways of approaching poetic drama—through language and image, through staging and characterization, through intellectual persuasions, and even through the distorting lens of the artist's own private vision. In its permissive and intricate attentions to all the things men do to and for each other, Elizabethan Drama well allows for all this variety of critical response.

George W. Ray of the University of Rochester assisted in the making of this anthology at every stage until his skillful services approached full-scale collaboration.

The texts included are as originally printed save for corrections requested by the authors. The footnotes have in some instances been simplified.

R. J. Kaufmann

Rochester, New York
January, 1961

CONTENTS

ELIZABETHAN DRAMA

F. P. WILSON

Elizabethan and Jacobean Drama

To EXPLAIN why English drama should have become great in the years just before and just after the close of the sixteenth century, great as never before or since, to analyse the conditions which made the soil favourable for the genius of Marlowe and Shakespeare, Jonson, Webster and Middleton, is no doubt beyond the capacity of man. Yet without any pretensions to explain what is inexplicable, let me say something, before turning to the dramatists themselves, of the theatre and audience which made their art possible.

If we survey the history of the London companies over the fifty years from about 1590 to the closing of the theatres in 1642, we shall be struck by their development in organization, in wealth, and in importance. This is particularly true of that company in which Shakespeare was the most distinguished shareholder, for it far excelled any other in the quality of its repertory, in the excellence of its acting, and in the stability of its membership. When the period begins, the company has no fixed abode; it acts now at the Theatre, now at the Curtain, now at one of the large London inns. Long before the period ends, it has acquired two theatres, and its takings at the private theatre of the Blackfriars, nearer to the Court at Westminster, had risen to perhaps twice those at the Globe. The theatre had become really fashionable, a profitable investment, the resort of 'silks and plush and all the wits.' Moreover, the fees received by the company for plays acted at Court, or for private performances ordered by the aristocracy and by wealthy citizens to entertain their guests, added more and more substantially to the company's income. As the links between Court and Parliament grew weaker, those between the

From *Elizabethan and Jacobean* (The Clarendon Press, Oxford, 1945), pp. 84–108. Reprinted by permission of the publisher and author.

Court and the theatres became stronger. In 1618 it was a matter of some comment that the Treasurer of the Household and two privy counsellors went to see a play even at the private theatre of the Blackfriars. In 1621 the Spanish ambassador Gondomar 'affably and familiarly' went to a common play at the Fortune, a public theatre. And in 1634 Charles's Queen herself visited the Blackfriars to see a play of Massinger's. It is unthinkable that Queen Elizabeth would have attended even at a private theatre: the plays she saw she saw at command performances at Court. Times had indeed changed from the days not so long ago when those 'glorious vagabonds' the actors of the sixteenth century travelled with fardels on their backs seeking permission to act in hall or inn or barn.

The patronage of the Court made the dramatic companies, or some of them, more prosperous, but did it improve the quality of the plays? Some evidence of the taste of the Court is supplied by the surviving lists of plays acted at Court, and it is not without significance that of the twenty plays acted at Court by the King's players between September 1630 and February 1631 only one was Shakespeare's—and that one *A Midsummer Night's Dream*—while ten were Beaumont and Fletcher's. Amusement and entertainment are important and essential to any theatre, but when audiences seek these alone, when the serious aspects of life are excluded, or are touched on superficially to make a mere emotional titillation, the theatre becomes their dope. In that week of October 1630 when the Court saw a performance of Fletcher's outrageous *Custom of the Country* Sir Thomas Roe wrote to Elizabeth of Bohemia that the public theatres had been closed for six months on account of the plague; 'and that makes our statesmen see the good use of them, by the want: for if our heads had been filled with the loves of Pyramus and Thisbe, or the various fortunes of Don Quixote, we should never have cared who had made peace or war, but on the stage. But now every fool is inquiring what the French do in Italy, and what they treat in Germany.' We may not attribute the decadence of early-seventeenth-century drama merely to the influence of the Court, but it was a contributory influence. The effects are more noticeable in Charles's reign than in James's, but they are to be seen already in James's reign, especially in the last decade of it, after the death of Shakespeare.

The drama is at its greatest in those years between about 1590 and 1620 when the actors were neither poverty-stricken vagabonds nor hangers-on at Court, and when the audience was most representative of City, Country, and Court. With such an audience and such actors a drama was possible that was neither coterie art nor sheer vulgarity and rant, but one that was fed by a wide range of interests. Nor is the necessity of interesting the less educated or rather the less intelligent section of the audience entirely to be deplored. The common people, says Puttenham, have their ears so attentive to the matter and their eyes to the shows of the stage that they take little heed to the cunning of the rhyme and are as well satisfied with what is gross as with what is fine and delicate. But insistence on the shows of the stage, while it may have led to an excessive use of the quaking custard, the rolled bullet, or the tempestuous drum, saved the drama from becoming academic, and attentiveness to matter saved the drama from those over-refinements of style which are the curse of much Elizabethan and some Jacobean writing. I hesitate to disturb the ghost of Ben Jonson by hinting that the groundlings may have taught him something, yet their insistence on action did no harm if it turned him from *Cynthia's Revels* and *The Poetaster,* both performed at the private theatres, to *Volpone* and *The Alchemist,* both acted at the Globe. Matter he was always ready to give them, and matter they were always ready to receive, but only if diluted with action. Moreover, as Sir John Harington and many before him said about narrative poetry, it is possible with one kind of meat and one dish to feed divers tastes. Some will feed on the pleasantness of the story, those with stronger stomachs will take a further taste of the moral sense, and 'a third sort, more high conceited than they, will digest the allegory.' *Mutatis mutandis,* this will do to suggest the different levels at which Shakespeare's plays have appealed from his day to ours. Even at the lowest level his audience was sensitive enough to the use of language and rhythm to listen even when they did not understand. Drayton writes of the poet's power

> The thick-brain'd audience lively to awake,
> 'Till with shrill claps the theatre do shake.

But it is Dekker who gives us the best contemporary account of the effect of poetic drama upon the people. He is writing for the Red Bull Theatre in Clerkenwell, near which he lived, and for a much ruder audience than that of the Globe.

> Give me that man,
> Who when the plague of an impostum'd brains

(Breaking out) infects a theatre and hotly reigns,
Killing the hearers' hearts, that the vast rooms
Stand empty, like so many dead men's tombs,
Can call the banish'd auditor home, and tie
His ear with golden chains to his melody:
Can draw with adamantine pen even creatures
Forg'd out of th' hammer on tip-toe to reach up,
And from rare silence clap their brawny hands,
T'applaud what their charm'd soul scarce understands.

We should, however, be misjudging the audience at the Globe if we supposed that it was ignorant and stupid. Webster observed in the preface to *The White Devil* that most of the audience at the Red Bull resembled ignorant asses, but he implies that at another playhouse a dramatist might find 'a full and understanding auditory.' The actor Betterton, when an old man and when the English stage had been ruined, as he maintained, 'by prodigal subscriptions for squeaking Italians and capering monsieurs,' is reported to have looked back with regret to the early days of the drama when London supported five or six playhouses and when 'the lower sort of people' frequented the theatre, discovering 'a natural simplicity and good taste when they were pleas'd and diverted with a drama so naked and unassisted by any foreign advantage.' The wealth of sermons and moral treatises available to the dramatists was available also to their audience. The sermon was the most popular form of literature of the day. Without an audience interested in serious matters tragedy is not possible. This audience at the Globe did not wholly consist of groundlings, the 'gentlemen of understanding' who were only so called because they stood under the stage. We hear so much of these because they gave the dramatists most trouble, and next to them we hear most of the foolish gulls who sat upon the stage to see and to be seen. At theatres like the Red Bull these had their way, and especially at holidays, when 'base mechanical men' were at leisure, but at the Globe there were courtiers as well, university men, Inns of Court men, gentlemen and their wives (many of them up from the country), merchants and their wives, captains and soldiers, as well as journeymen and apprentices. I will not lay stress upon Thomas Wright's view, announced in the year of the second quarto of *Hamlet,* that cities sharpen men's wits, and 'this we may daily perceive in our own country, wherein our Northern and Welshmen, when they come to London, are very simple, and unwary, but afterwards, by conversing a while, and by the experience of other men's behaviours, they become wonderful wise and judicious,' for I know that this view would be repudiated in Wales and in the North of England. Nor will I insist upon the view of Thomas Wilson, a Lincolnshire man, that 'it is much better to be born . . . in London than in Lincoln. For that both the air is better, the people more civil, and the wealth much greater, and the men for the most part more wise.' But it is indisputable that London being the seat of government and of the law and (except for the few books published by the two universities) the only publishing centre in England was the focus of the nation's intellectual as well as of its commercial life. Foreign visitors were impressed and native Puritans shocked by the handsomeness of its theatres and the splendour of the actors' costumes. When the Venetian Busino visited the theatre in 1617 he admired the sumptuous dresses of the actors, the interludes of music, dancing and singing, the nobility dressed like so many princes listening as silently and soberly as possible to the play, and the honourable and handsome ladies. It was of the Globe theatre that the chief comic actor of Shakespeare's company, Robert Armin, was speaking when in 1608 he dedicated his *Nest of Ninnies* to 'the generous Gentlemen of Oxenford, Cambridge, and the Inns of Court' from whom (he says) the glories and the livings of the actors rise and with whom he claims to have seen the stars at midnight.

One section of society, and one which was becoming increasingly powerful, never went to the theatre and did its best to suppress it. Between the theatre and those who refused to grant the moral value of the representation upon the stage of human vices, who believed that the whole business of this life was to accustom ourselves to despise it and to meditate upon the life to come, there could be no compromise. Philip Stubbes attempted a compromise in the preface to the first edition of his *Anatomy of Abuses* when he allowed that honest and chaste plays might become 'very tolerable exercises' if they were used for the avoiding of that which is evil, and learning that which is good, if they contained 'matter of doctrine, erudition, good example, and wholesome instruction,' but he withdrew this concession after the first edition, and there remained nothing to mitigate his statement that playgoers who frequented the public theatres were incurring the danger of eternal damnation except they repent. The Puritans, whether they remained in the Church of England or broke from it, supported their views by quoting many of the passages in which the Fathers had attacked the enormities of the pagan theatres and by more modern instances: the collapse of the floor of a chamber at Risley in Bedfordshire in 1607 when many were killed who had crowded to see a play on the Sabbath day, and the awful case of the young lady who, being accustomed in health to see a play a day, on her death-bed continued ever crying 'Oh Hieronimo, Hieronimo, methinks I see thee, brave Hieronimo' and 'fixing her eyes, intentively, as if she had seen Hieronimo acted, sending out a deep sigh, she suddenly died.' Puritan preachers not only attacked the theatre with *exempla* but with the syllogistic reasoning of which they were so fond: 'the cause of plagues is sin, if you look to it well: and the cause of sin are plays: therefore the cause of plagues are plays.' These preachers were honourable men, and they have left a name behind them that their praises might be reported, but those who believe that the good life is as implicit in the plays of Shakespeare as in the sermons of Perkins cannot but be thankful that London was not Geneva. The City magistrates also would have suppressed the theatres, not only for moral reasons, but for reasons of public order and public health, and because many a tradesman and worker idled away an afternoon at the theatre; and no public theatres were built on ground that came under the jurisdiction of the City. If the stage had not been protected by the Court and the Privy Council, there might have been no Elizabethan drama and no Shakespeare, only a surreptitious hole-and-corner affair such as managed to survive between 1642 and the Restoration.

It has been suggested that Elizabethan drama might have been given 'a larger scope and higher purpose' if it had been taken under the wing of that section of the Church which was prepared to allow to the natural life a richer 'freedom of movement' than that which the Puritans were prepared to allow it. The only official contact between Church and stage was in a censor's office. Plays intended for publication were licensed by ecclesiastical licensers until 1607; after that year almost all plays were licensed for publication by the Revels Office, which had always exercised the right to license plays for performance. Bacon, observing that in ancient times plays were used as a means of educating men's minds to virtue, whereas in modern states play-acting was esteemed but as a toy, regretted that the discipline of the stage in his time had been plainly neglected. But who was to exercise this discipline, he did not say. Perhaps it is as well that Elizabethan dramatists had only to do with a censorship that permitted a reasonable amount of freedom to the human mind. It curbed political and religious speculation of an unorthodox kind, but exercised no such restrictive influence over morals as the unofficial censorship of public opinion over the Victorian novelists.

If we wished to state the prevailing kinds of drama in the early fifteen-nineties with the precision of a Polonius, we should have to speak of pastoral-comical, historical-comical, tragical-historical, and even tragical-comical-historical-pastoral, but in less precise terms we may speak of the chronicle-history play, romantic comedy, and romantic tragedy. And if we ask what the prevailing kinds of drama are ten years later, we shall find that while romantic comedy and romantic tragedy persist, but with striking differences, there is a vogue for satirical comedy or 'comical satire,' and that the play whose theme is based on some episode in English history has almost disappeared. It has often been observed that the flourishing time of the chronicle-history play was for a few years before and after the Armada, and contemporary writers like Nashe and Heywood applaud this type of play on grounds of patriotism and morality: 'they shew the ill success of treason, the fall of hasty climbers, the wretched end of usurpers, the misery of civil dissension.' The moral was enforced in poetry, too, in such collections as *The Mirror for Magistrates* and in Daniel's *Civil Wars*. In the preface to the 1609 edition of the *Civil Wars* Daniel observes that his argument 'was long since undertaken (in a time which was not so well secur'd of the future, as God be blessed now it is) with a purpose, to shew the deformities of Civil Dissension and the miserable events of Rebellions, Conspiracies, and bloody Revengements . . . thereby to make the blessings of Peace, and the happiness of an established Government (in a direct line) the better to appear.' Clearly, the need for such a moral was not so great in 1609 as in 1595, yet we should go wrong if we supposed that the history play ceased to be important because of the peaceful accession of the Stuart dynasty in 1603. As I have said, epochs of literature do not wait upon the deaths of kings and queens, and two or three years before the death of the Queen it had become apparent that the vein of the history play was exhausted.

About this very time we notice a change in the temper of comedy. Henslowe's Diary is an excellent barometer to popular taste in the latter years of Elizabeth's reign. From 1592 to 1597 the titles suggest romantic comedies and tragedies and above all chronicle-history plays, but about the end of 1597 it is clear that domestic comedy is becoming popular. We notice under 1598 William Haughton's *A Woman will have her Will* or *Englishmen for my Money*, perhaps the earliest comedy now extant of which the scene is laid in London, and soon afterwards Porter's *Two Angry Women of Abingdon*, and Dekker's *Shoemaker's Holiday*. To this time also belongs Shakespeare's only English middle-class comedy, *The Merry Wives of Windsor*. At first these comedies of contemporary life are either comedies of intrigue like Haughton's and Shakespeare's or are more romantic than satirical like Porter's and Dekker's. Comedy has not here become satirical. Earlier in this decade the attempt had been made to acclimatize the Latin satire after the manner especially of Juvenal and Persius and the satirical epigram after Martial, and in the popular pamphlets of Nashe and others social types and social abuses had been attacked with great force. The drama, however, had remained on the whole untouched by this satirical force, but now at the turn of the century the drama too became satirical, and more and more comedies appeared which were not romantic but were in Marston's definition of comedy 'a spectacle of life and public manners.'

I cannot believe that it was the edicts of 1599 and 1600 calling in many satires and epigrams and ordering no more to be printed which caused this strong satirical movement in poetry and prose of the early nineties to spill over into the drama, for there were signs that the change was happening before 1599. Moreover, the way was prepared for satirical comedy by the new developments which had already become apparent in poetry and in prose; in poetry, the shaking free from many of the more formal figures of sound and the approximation of verse to the rhythms and diction of speech, accompanied sometimes, but not always, by a sceptical critical anti-romantic spirit, and in prose the anti-Ciceronian movement with its insistence on matter and succinctness. We may notice also that in the critical examination of such social types as the gull and malcontent the poets and pamphleteers were before the dramatists. In such a pamphlet as Lodge's *Wit's Misery* of 1596, social satire increasingly takes the form of characters of social types, and the influence of Theophrastus is noticeable for perhaps the first time.

Two years later, and as some say not without some indebtedness to Theophrastus, a great satirical dramatist started on the career which was to leave its mark on English comedy for generations to come. In the first version of *Every Man in his Humour*, acted at the Globe in 1598, Jonson has not quite got rid of eloquence. I do not mean such eloquence as the raptures of Volpone and Sir Epicure

Mammon—Marlowesque in their style, though raptures of earth not of 'air and fire'—for these are dramatic, but I mean the undramatic eloquence of the praise of poetry which is spoken by Lorenzo Junior. Such inconsistency of tone is never again found in Jonson, and when he came to revise his first humour play he cut the passage out. In his next play *Every Man out of his Humour* of 1599 he laid down the principles of the comedy of humours. Comedy was to be familiarly allied to the times in theme, in characters, and in language, and it was to serve for the correction of manners. It was, in short, to become what all the theorists of the Renaissance had said comedy ought to be, and what no English writer had yet made it on the popular stage. England has never produced an artist and moralist more consistent than Jonson. From *Every Man in his Humour* until 1632, when in *The Magnetic Lady* he closed the circle of his humours, he anatomized the time's deformity 'With constant courage and contempt of fear.'

'As for laughter,' wrote William Perkins, rather grudgingly, 'it may be used.' The laughter of Jonson is rarely laughter for its own sake, and it is never sympathetic laughter. It is usually laughter mixed with contempt or disapprobation. He never spends much pains upon a character that is not either a fool or a rogue. His comedy is a kind of comedy of manners, but a comedy where the manners are not perfect freedom but an object lesson in what to avoid. Etherege reports his society and makes patterns out of it and is amused to do so. He is himself a part of the society he reports. It is his Zion, and he is at ease in it. But Jonson is as uneasy and contemptuous in the society he satirizes as is Pope among his dunces. In his early comedies he seems often to be wasting his powers upon unworthy material. In his later comedies, while his themes are often of the utmost importance to man's life in society, his power of finding an adequate representation of them in dramatic form is dwindling. In his middle plays, from *Volpone* to *Bartholomew Fair,* there is a splendid equilibrium of matter and means, and while his plays are crammed with topical allusions to the London of his day—so that it is to him, not to Shakespeare, that we look for information about Jacobean London—yet their foundations are permanent and indestructible, based as they are on the rascality and credulity of human nature.

His plays are as 'moral' as the old moralities. The difference is, as he hints in *The Staple of News,* that the Vice no longer enters on the stage with a wooden dagger, but as the Vices male and female, 'attir'd like men and women o' the time. . . . Prodigality like a young heir, and his Mistress Money . . . prank't up like a prime Lady.' Vanity, blind zeal, hypocrisy, greed, stupid ignorance, these are among his constant targets. He is, if you like, intellectually arrogant, and he has a fundamental contempt for what he calls 'the green and soggy multitude.' But it is no foolish snobbery that inspires this attitude; for the fashionable gallant, spendthrift and profligate, was to him as much a caterpillar of the commonwealth as the rogues and vagabonds of the lower classes. As he grew older, the changing structure of society brought more and more into prominence the adventurers who in their greed for money and social advancement acted without moral scruple and at the expense of their fellow members of the state. Usurers, monopolists, profiteers, are always attacked by the dramatists. They inherited the attitude of the Medieval Church to usury, and the selfish exploitation of wealth which they attacked upon the stage Lancelot Andrewes and others were at the same time attacking in the pulpit. Of all the dramatists, however, Jonson attacked the unscrupulous greed for money with most force and persistence, most powerfully enforced the view that wealth and rank have obligations and responsibilities. No other seventeenth-century dramatist approached him in this respect save Massinger in *A New Way to pay Old Debts* and *The City Madam*. Jonson's attack is not blunted by sentiment and dilation, as is Dekker's. (Jonson's quarrel with Dekker was in great part the quarrel of an artist: for Dekker was 'a fellow of a good prodigal tongue.') The weight of his 'strict and succinct style,' of what Edmund Bolton calls his 'vital, judicious, and most practicable language,' the integrity of his art with its firm sense of relevance, the tough persistence of the man, make his blows effective. As he gets older, his art deteriorates, but his view of life and of society does not change. He is *fortis, et in se ipso totus, teres atque rotundus.*

Romantic drama persists, I have said, into the Jacobean age but with a difference, and the difference between the Elizabethan plays of Greene or Peele and the Jacobean plays of Beaumont and Fletcher is so great that it seems remarkable that they are separated by less than twenty years. Bacon wrote to his *alter ego* Tobie Matthew that it was both King James's and Buckingham's nature 'to love to do things unexpected'; James and Buckingham found the plays of Beaumont and Fletcher to their liking. These dramatists, and after them Massinger and Shirley, are adepts at springing surprises upon the audience. Jonson had done it in *The Silent Woman,* but these later dramatists make a habit of it. A casual clue is often provided in the first act such as

> Were the child living now ye lost at sea
> Among the Genoway galleys, what a happiness!

—a clue which the practised playgoer or reader of these later dramatists would no doubt be able to interpret with some of the satisfaction felt by the solver of a problem in a detective novel. The aim is to stimulate suspense, to give a fresh and unexpected impetus to the plot, or to provide a solution to what appears to be an insoluble tangle. We contrast the method of Shakespeare who gives us all motives, all clues, 'not surprise but expectation' as Coleridge said, and then the satisfaction of perfect knowledge. The sudden surprises of Jacobean and Caroline drama are sought after by men who lay most stress upon plot and narrative. They have a transient effect. In *Headlong Hall* Mr. Gall distinguishes between the picturesque and the beautiful in landscape gardening and adds to them a third character—unexpectedness. 'Pray, sir,' said Mr. Milestone, 'by what name do you distinguish this character, when a person walks round the grounds for a second time?'

This unexpectedness is found not merely in surprises of plot but in surprises of feeling, surprises which are encouraged by the tragi-comedy which these writers affected. How the thermometer of passion goes up and down in a single scene of Beaumont and Fletcher! In that scene in *The Maid's Tragedy* in which Aspatia dies, the alternations of hope and despair are most exciting. 'She lives,' 'She lives not,' we keep saying, and as theatre it is most effective. But when we put it beside the end of *King Lear,* or, to be fairer, beside the closing scenes of Chapman's *Bussy D'Ambois* or Tourneur's *Revenger's Tragedy* or Webster's *White Devil,* we realize what a superficial stirring of the emotions this is. It is platform pathos.

These writers have indeed their merits. Fletcher ranks high as an entertainer. The one constant principle underlying his work is the desire to amuse. He writes as if he had not a care or a conviction in the world. With no capacity for tragedy or tragi-comedy he attempts tragic passion only to suit the fashion and taste of his audience. A sceptic in morals, an observer only of the superficies of life, he mirrors faithfully the froth and bubble of the court life of his time. That is his criticism of life in so far as he offers any, and we find it not in more ambitious plays like *Bonduca* or *Valentinian* but in such comedies as *The Chances* or *The Humorous Lieutenant*. And Massinger, whose talent is as saturnine as Fletcher's is mercurial, and whose chief interests are political and social rather than tragic, does his best work not in romantic comedy or tragedy but in those two satirical comedies, *A New Way to Pay Old Debts* and *The City Madam,* which provide the most acute analysis of the abuses of the contemporary social scene to be found outside the plays of Jonson.

Beaumont and Fletcher, Massinger, Shirley held the stage when Marlowe, Tourneur, Webster, Middleton were almost forgotten. I suppose that the late seventeenth and the eighteenth centuries preferred them to their greater contemporaries for much the same reasons that William Archer praised the plays of Massinger: the story was more prominent and better-wrought, the characters clearly marked and fairly consistent, and the style clearer and more lucid. A poet of the late seventeenth century looking for easy expression and smooth composition and detesting a style that according to his standards was 'all metaphor and catachresis' would find less to complain of in Fletcher and Massinger than in Chapman or Webster. Yet this very lucidity is a symptom of superficiality and of the impoverishment of their ideas and their language. Massinger's metaphors, as Mr. T. S. Eliot has observed, are often borrowed, and they are weakened in the borrowing; his stock is limited and he uses them again and again; and they are consciously and often elaborately worked out and used as so much temporary ornament with no imaginative reverberations upon the play as a whole. The gift of thinking in images which is characteristic of the best Jacobean drama is lost, and the speech and rhythms of poetry which enable writers like Chapman and Tourneur and Webster to display serious aspects of life with power and concentration are replaced by oratory and spectacle and incident.

But for a few years—years which take in the turn of the century and the reign of James I—dramatists found the words and phrasing with which to express a tragic vision of good and evil with an insight not rivalled by English dramatists before or since. With much that is ephemeral a few wrote plays that in the analysis of civil and private behaviour are of permanent value. Marlowe was the Moses who led the way to the promised land, though he did not live to enter it. He is the first English poet using drama who possesses intellectual energy. The Jacobeans thought of him as a great primitive. They speak of his 'pure elemental wit,' of his raptures being 'All air and fire, which made his verses clear.' He was to them what Bacon seemed to be to the early members of the Royal Society. He forged the New Instrument which was to change for ever the character of dramatic verse. The suppleness and flexibility with which Spenser had transformed the rigidity of mid-sixteenth-century verse began to be made available for the stage. But Marlowe's verse has pace and resonance. He held the attention of wit and groundling alike, and was the first Englishman to make of tragedy a form of art that was both popular and serious.

Milton might not have thought Marlowe 'a better teacher than Scotus or Aquinas,' yet Marlowe's chief interest lay in morality. To say that he was more interested in moral ideas than in dramatic character is to say little, for it is true of most of these dramatists. John Hoskins says that 'he that will truly set down a man in a figured story must first learn truly to set down an humour, a passion, a virtue, a vice, and therein keeping decent proportion add but names and knit together the accidents and encounters.' He is speaking in particular of that figured story, the *Arcadia,* but he might as well have been speaking of the drama. Few dramatists, perhaps only Webster and Middleton, share some of Shakespeare's power of expressing a play's moral intention in and through characters that can be mistaken for creatures of flesh and blood. And Shakespeare puzzles at times those critics who have tried to test him by the conventions of modern naturalistic drama. Marlowe is thought of as a typical man of the Renaissance, and the famous words of Tamburlaine have often been taken from their context to serve as an emblem of the Renaissance spirit.

> Nature that fram'd us of four elements
> Warring within our breasts for regiment
> Doth teach us all to have aspiring minds.

But to expect in Marlowe's plays or in Elizabethan or Jacobean drama in general a realistic representation of human character comparable to what is found in some fifteenth- and sixteenth-century paintings is to expect what is not there and seriously to misinterpret what is there. In Marlowe there is a strong infusion of the morality play. Greedy-for-power, Insolence, Greed, Pride, are some of his characters. In Jonson, Marston, and Tourneur, also, the characters are humours or moral qualities, and any convention is considered justifiable if it subserves the moral idea. The significance of the names of Jonson's *dramatis personae,* Voltore, Corbaccio, Corvino, Volpone and the rest, is well-known, but it has not perhaps been noticed that Marston in *The Fawn* and Tourneur in *The Revenger's Tragedy* seem to have searched an Italian dictionary for words descriptive of the moral types they exhibit: *Nimphadoro* defined by Florio in 1598 as 'an effeminate, wanton, milksop, perfumed, ladies-courting courtier,' *Dondolo* 'a gull, a fool, a thing to make sport,' *Granuffo* (in Florio *Gramuffa*) 'a kind of staring, stately, stalking, puffing look,' *Nencio* 'a fool, an idiot, a natural, a dolt, a gull,' *Piato* 'squat, cowered down, hidden, close to the ground.' The moral attitudes are patent and rigid from the start. If characters change, the change is sudden, as the balloon of a character's conceit or sin is pricked by love or repentance and explodes with a bang. It is the rarest thing outside Shakespeare to find the gradual modification of character by character or experience. There remains in Jacobean as in Elizabethan drama a strong infusion of the morality play.

When Chapman says, then, that 'material instruction, elegant and sententious excitation to virtue, and deflection from her contrary' are 'the soul, limbs, and limits of an authentical tragedy,' he is giving an adequate description of important Jacobean drama. It is not so adequate a description of Shakespeare's plays, for Shakespeare stands far above his contemporaries in the power of diffusing through his works a 'soul . . . quite through to make them of a piece.' By his own principles, principles which were based on his own perceptions, Dr. Johnson was right to condemn Shakespeare for not making moral instruction more deliberate. It is never more deliberate than in the tragedies of the two most learned of Jacobean dramatists, Jonson and Chapman. For this reason we can be more certain about their private beliefs than we can about Shakespeare's. Both are profoundly influenced by the Stoic morality of Epictetus and Seneca. When through the mouthpiece of his Stoic character Clermont Chapman praises the stage and its function in society he does so in the words of Epictetus. Both writers are as much interested in the political virtues, in man's duty to the state as subject or ruler, as in the private virtues, in man's duty to himself; and both dramatists, and particularly Chapman, suffered more than any from the restrictions imposed by the censorship upon the treatment of political themes. Jonson in *Sejanus* gives us a durable examen of the corruption of tyrannical power and in *Catiline* an analysis of the career of a political firebrand; and if we wish to find Chapman at his greatest, we look to the two plays which were inspired by the career of Charles Duke of Byron. His most famous lines are those in which Byron declares his boundless ambition and contempt of danger, lines which express even more powerfully than Tamburlaine's the rugged and self-sufficient individualism known to Chapman not only in the world of contemporary politics but also in the old Greek and Roman worlds.

> Be free, all worthy spirits,
> And stretch yourselves for greatness and for height,
> Untruss your slaveries; you have height enough
> Beneath this steep heaven to use all your reaches;
> 'Tis too far off to let you, or respect you.
> Give me a spirit that on this life's rough sea
> Loves t'have his sails filled with a lusty wind,
> Even till his sail-yards tremble, his masts crack,
> And his rapt ship run on her side so low
> That she drinks water, and her keel plows air.
> There is no danger to a man that knows
> What life and death is; there's not any law
> Exceeds his knowledge; neither is it lawful
> That he should stoop to any other law.
> He goes before them, and commands them all,
> That to himself is a law rational.

The 'atheist' Byron who believes that love, fame, loyalty are 'mere politic terms' is defeated by Henry IV, the patriot king, and while Byron is presented powerfully and sympathetically, it is with Henry that victory remains. Above all, Chapman identifies himself with the two Stoics Cato and Clermont, who are contrasted with such passionate heroes as Byron and Caesar: Clermont, the 'Senecal man,' to whom

> Well or ill is equal
> In my acceptance, since I joy in neither
> But go with sway of all the world together

and Cato whose last speech before he kills himself is the Stoic paradox:

> Just men are only free, the rest are slaves.

That Cato should kill himself to preserve his integrity is in accordance with history and pagan morality; that the Christian Clermont should kill himself and justify his action is indeed a surprising departure from Christian morality. Not more surprising, however, than the imputation to the Stoic Cato of a belief in immortality and what seems very like a Christian heaven, in which

> We shall know each other, and past death
> Retain those forms of knowledge learn'd in life.

It is an unusual synthesis of Stoic and Christian morality with which Chapman presents us in his plays and in his poetry, but the synthesis seems natural to this stern and paradoxical writer, who believed that something of the spirit of Homer was infused in him and continually sings the praises of the 'ancient honour'd Romans.'

Both Chapman and Jonson write for the public theatres, but they make few concessions to popular taste. Jonson's aim was to keep tragedy 'high and aloof,' and Chapman while basing his plots mainly on contemporary French history infused into them the spirit of Stoic morality, and preserved in his use of the messenger and the long set-speech some of the technical characteristics of Senecan drama. There is, however, another line of drama, less learned and more popular, though retaining many Senecan traits, which descends from Kyd's *Spanish Tragedy* through *Hamlet* and the revenge plays of Marston to Tourneur and Webster. It is here that some critics have found the finest examples of dramatic poetry outside Shakespeare, while others, repelled by the preoccupation of these dramatists with lust and crime and death, have likened the reading of their plays to a visit to the chamber of horrors in Madame Tussaud's. I will not say with Mr. F. L. Lucas that the only answer to those who say 'But people do not do such things' as are done in the plays of Tourneur and Webster is: 'They did. . . . Read the history of the time,' especially the history of Renaissance Italy; I will not argue on these lines, for to do so might suggest that the action in these plays was naturalistic. Perhaps the modern reader has to make certain adjustments: to remember, for example, that that age believed in omens and portents, not tepidly and sporadically, but profoundly, so that the effect of the prodigious storm when Essex left London for Ireland 'with furious flashings, the firmament seeming to open and burn' was such that Florio recorded it in his Italian-English dictionary; to remember that the Jacobeans, as the Elizabethans, inherited from the later Middle Ages a preoccupation with death which seems to us abnormal. Their lives were guarded about with symbols of dissolution; the death's head and the *memento mori* were still in vogue. An illustration may make this clear. When the Duchess of Malfi is to be strangled at the order of her brothers, and the executioners enter with a coffin, cords, and a bell, the bellman is impersonated by Bosola, the half-willing, half-reluctant tool of the brothers:

> I am the common Bellman
> That usually is sent to condemn'd persons
> The night before they suffer.

The reference is to a charity presented in 1605 by a rich citizen of London to the church of St. Sepulchre's hard by the prison of Newgate. Money was given for the making of a speech outside the dungeon of condemned prisoners the night before their execution, and for another speech to be made the next morning, while the cart in which the prisoners made their melancholy progress to Tyburn was stayed for a while by the church wall. The words of both speeches are set out in the gift, as also is the refrain, accompanied by a tolling handbell, *Our Lord Take Mercy Upon You All.* Documents like these illustrate the gulf in taste between that age and this. It has not been noticed that one of the signatories to this gift is a John Webster, but the name is too common for us to be sure that he is the dramatist. Those who confuse Webster's plays with *The Police News* will say that there could be no more appropriate document for him to sign and no more appropriate church for him to worship in than St. Sepulchre's. Yet let us notice that in his play Webster says nothing to recall the speeches of the charity but gives to bellman Bosola verses which express in universal terms the desire for death after overwhelming suffering.

> Hark now every thing is still.
> The Scritch-Owl, and the whistler shrill
> Call upon our Dame, aloud,
> And bid her quickly don her shroud.
> Much you had of land and rent,
> Your length in clay's now competent.
> A long war disturb'd your mind,
> Here your perfect peace is sign'd.
> Of what is't fools make such vain keeping?
> Sin their conception, their birth, weeping,
> Their life, a general mist of error,
> Their death, a hideous storm of terror.
> Strew your hair with powders sweet:
> Don clean linen, bathe your feet,

And (the foul fiend more to check)
A crucifix let bless your neck.
'Tis now full tide, 'tween night and day,
End your groan, and come away.

There is no gulf in feeling between us and this kind of writing, and the gruesome apparatus which Tourneur and Webster find necessary should not come between us and the power of their poetry.

The gift of concentrated speech which is one of the marks of great dramatic poetry is nowhere greater than in Tourneur and Webster; but the writer who next to Shakespeare gets the profoundest effects of tragedy with the utmost plainness of speech is Middleton. Unlike Webster he keeps to verse for his most cutting irony, and he is not dependent on curiously chosen adjectives or on conceits as are Webster and Tourneur. His gift of plain statement is often spent on the superficies of contemporary manners, but he does not relinquish this plainness in his greatest writing. We recognize his quality in such spare stripped sentences as de Flores'

Push! you forget yourself;
A woman dipp'd in blood, and talk of modesty!
Can you weep Fate from its determin'd purpose?
So soon may you weep me.

An anthologist in search of pretty passages would find few in Middleton. His most decorative poetry appears in passages of searching irony. The lines in *A Game at Chess* which are said to have influenced Milton in 'Lycidas' are spoken by a lustful priest attempting a seduction:

Upon those lips, the sweet fresh buds of youth,
The holy dew of prayer lies, like a pearl
Dropt from the opening eyelids of the morn
Upon the bashful rose.

And these lines from *Women Beware Women* are spoken by a man just before he hears of his wife's infidelity:

Honest wedlock
Is like a banqueting-house built in a garden,
On which the spring's chaste flowers take delight
To cast their modest odours.

Under the flowers of Middleton's speech lurk serpents of vice and suffering.

Shakespeare founded no school, and his development is unlike that of any contemporary. Yet in seriousness of purpose, in moral imagination, and in the gift of compression by which a line becomes taut with meaning and the disturbance of the rhythm is as much a work of the imagination as the word and the image, it is these men—Tourneur, Webster, and Middleton—who come nearest to him.

HARDIN CRAIG

The Shackling of Accidents: A Study of Elizabethan Tragedy

THE RENAISSANCE was an era in which, in obedience to many complicated influences and motives, the ancient world supplied to the modern an ability to express itself in terms of something to say and in terms of forms and patterns of expression. Perhaps, indeed certainly, the ancient world also supplied to the modern what we call inspiration; that is, desire to express thought and feeling and moving interest in human life and its environment.

The process of gaining ideas and forms was begun in grammar schools by means of the study of school authors. These authors, mainly Latin, were the ones who appealed most to the western Europeans of the fifteenth and sixteenth centuries. They were happily chosen, since they were relatively simple, easily comprehended, and so picturesque and human in quality that they may be said to have suited the society to which they were presented. They were the authors who had, for the most part, been best known in the Middle Ages and those who had inherited the sanction of the schools of rhetoric and logic in the Roman empire. Among the poets were Virgil and Ovid. Among the dramatists were, first, Terence (because of the excellence of his latinity), then Seneca, then Plautus. Cicero, who was a writer on rhetoric as well as a proponent of Latin culture, stood in popularity far ahead of Livy and Sallust, who, however, were also known and read. On the philosophic side Aristotle was supreme and next him perhaps stood Plutarch, who in his philosophic and ethical influence is comparable both to Aristotle and to Cicero.

From the *Philological Quarterly,* XIX (January 1940), pp. 1–19. Reprinted by permission of the journal and author.

In the very first rank of influences was Boethius, and next him the Neo-Latin writers (Erasmus, Vives, and others), who were also great disseminators of ancient culture. This list is by no means complete; for, as we shall see if we consider the scholastic habits of the Renaissance, a large body of selected doctrine came because of these habits from the remotest corners of the ancient and the modern worlds.

Renaissance learned culture was aggregative in its practices, and as regards its corpus of study was neither consistent nor systematic. It was moralistic rather than moral, rhetorical rather than literary, and often sentimental rather than sincere. It was, however, reverent toward antiquity and relied upon the ancient world as the source of truth rather than upon its own ability to discover truth. This attitude of mind, it may be said, was in some respects a fortunate one. Both text-books and school methods reflect an attitude which was aspiring as well as docile.

The most elementary book, and possibly the text-book most widely used in the grammar schools of the Renaissance, was the famous *Disticha Moralis,* reputed to be the work of one Dionysius Cato. In the school course it was followed by or accompanied by the *Sententiae Pueriles,* a cento of simple aphoristic materials, which seems to have been used as a basis of Latin speaking; this, in turn, by Æsop's *Fables.* The first two of these books exemplify the *sententia* and the third the *exemplum,* both present in the schools since Roman times. The next layer of instruction seems to have been drawn from Terence, Cicero, or the Latin poets, and seems to have had to do, pedagogically speaking, with the art of Latin phrasing.

The particular instrument used in the schools for the mastery by students of these three fundamentals—*sententia, exemplum,* and *phrasis*—was the commonplace book. Pupils were taught from their earliest appearance in school to keep commonplace books. They were instructed as to what to record in their commonplace books and were required to keep them neatly. There was thus bred in them the habit of keeping notes, of looking out for such bits of wisdom and eloquence, wit and beauty, and for such significant anecdotes, apothegms, and apologues as would later serve their turn as writers and speakers and guide them on the road to wisdom. These commonplace books, both those made in school and in later life, exist to this day by the hundreds. Those which have perished must run into the tens of thousands. The commonplace book, which included besides quotations also translations and original compositions, was the center of the school course and is the symbol of the learned mind of the Renaissance both in its habits and its objectives.

The theory of composition which underlay the commonplace book was this: if a student had gathered the truest, wisest, and most timely things that had ever been said on every appropriate subject and had at the same time noted and memorized the best possible phraseology of every available idea from the Latin writers—Cicero, Terence, Virgil, Lucan, and their Neo-Latin exponents—he would be prepared to write with perfection on anything he chose to write about. Given his subject, he would divide it according to the technical principles of logical definition, and then apply to each division the places or *loca* of rhetoric and logic. He would then search his commonplace book for materials and phraseology. After the fundamentals had thus been accumulated, the writer's task was merely amplification. The principles of amplification were well organized for his use, and his commonplace book would again be in demand. With such a system at its base can it be wondered at that the literature of the Renaissance repeats and repeats again the ideation of the age?

In justification of this rather slavish system the Renaissance was ready to advance its doctrine of imitation. This doctrine is more than a defence of plagiarism. It rests ultimately upon the great doctrine of similitude. The Renaissance looked upon man as a universal being repeating in his life the deeds of all men. If man is a universal being, his conduct will always follow a pattern. Men's actions are always alike because their natures are always the same. Imitation was thus inherent in the fundamental concept of man's origin, nature, and relation to the universe. A modern who absorbed the ancients was rendered like the ancients. By saying their words and thinking their thoughts he became like them. He acquired their virtues. There was no other way than imitation by which he might acquire virtues. Renaissance imitation was, in a universe thus patterned, methodologically inevitable.

In addition to materials, patterns, and forms—facts, phrases, *exempla*, aphorisms, *sententiae*, and figures of speech—there was another significant practice within the same tendency. It is a larger aspect of manner which has not been so fully recognized, because it is harder to formulate and identify. I refer to the practice, particularly in drama and fiction, but also in oratory and history, of handling similar situations in similar ways; that is, of following patterns of thought and style derived from the ancients. Given a real or a fancied resemblance of the modern world to the ancient in an array of social forces, in the current of event, or in the logic of fact, the poets, dramatists, and historians of the Renaissance often tended to modify their modern situations to such a degree that they became actual parallels to those treated in the ancient classics. Polydore Vergil, for example, reshaped the English chronicles to conform them to the principles and significances he found in Plutarch, Suetonius, and Livy. This practice is to be regarded as the result of an accepted belief that life was somewhat narrowly patterned, and the models were in part at least rubrics worked out in ancient times in order to render life intelligible.

The greater authors of the Renaissance from Petrarch to Cervantes habitually began on a level of close imitation both in matters rhetorical and in those which were structural and architectonic; but usually, as their geniuses developed, they emancipated themselves, to a greater or less degree, from formalism in style and thought.[1] They thus came, by following the road of rather stupid imitation, to exemplify what we regard as true originality, so that their imitation no longer intruded itself or restricted their freedom. There is little doubt that Shakespeare himself is an example of such an emancipated genius, and in general it must be admitted, in the light of performance, that the practice of imitation worked well.

By means of the commonplace book and the habits which it engendered, as no doubt also by the practice of deliberate imitation of one author by another, Renaissance literature was permeated by classical literature, particularly by the Latin school authors.[2] Our interest in this paper will be in borrowings and imitations of Seneca, particularly as they appear in Shakespeare.[3] By what various ways these influences of Seneca came to Shakespeare has already been suggested, and we shall not concern ourselves with the question of whether Shakespeare knew Seneca and borrowed from him. Perhaps the greatest number of Senecan features came from Italian, French, and English imitators of Seneca, Shakespeare's predecessors in Renaissance drama. It is at least certain that in treating various subjects Shakespeare followed a Senecan pattern, for Seneca had taught dramatists what to say in certain serious or tragic situations and what tone or style to use.

Seneca was a principal channel through which the wisdom of the past reached the Renaissance. His understanding of the workings of human emotions commended itself to the Renaissance and was the more effective since he showed in his plays a dramatic use of the system of thought and feeling to which the Renaissance adhered. In his tragedies certain lines of action are pretty definitely worked out in accordance with his system of thought. The Renaissance was thus schooled in a method of imitation, schooled also in the belief that human behavior is universal; that is to say, that a particular line of action or a particular affection expresses itself always in accordance with the same pattern, so that the imitation of Seneca and the repetition of his ideas was inevitable.

Many bits of wit and wisdom found their way, no doubt by devious roads, into the plays of Shakespeare. Since this influence in the use of aphoristic idea has been dealt with rather adequately by Cunliffe and others, a very few illustrations will suffice here:

a) *Hercules Furens*, 735 ff.: [4]

Each for his sins of earth
Must suffer here; the crime returns to him
Who did it, and the guilty soul is crushed
By its own precedents.

Macbeth, I, vii, 8 ff.: [5]

. . . we but teach
Bloody instructions, which, being taught, return
To plague the inventor: this even-handed justice
Commends the ingredients of our poison'd chalice
To our own lips.

Cf. also *Macbeth*, III, iv, 122:

It will have blood; they say, blood will have blood;

and *Richard III*, V, i, 20 ff.:

That high All-Seer that I dallied with
Hath turn'd my feigned prayer on my head
And given in earnest what I begg'd in jest.
Thus doth he force the swords of wicked men
To turn their own points on their masters' bosoms.

b) *Phœnissæ*, 664:

A kingdom is well bought at any price.

3 *Henry VI*, I, ii, 16–17:

But for a kingdom any oath may be broken:
I would break a thousand oaths to reign one year.

c) *Agamemnon*, 142 ff.:

Cly. Where wrath, where grief, where hope shall bear me on,
There will I speed my course; my helmless ship

I've given to be the sport of winds and floods.
Where reason fails 'tis best to follow chance . . .
To stop midway in sin is foolishness.
. . . .
Nurse. Yet desperate measures no one first attempts.
Cly. The path of sin is headlong from the first.

Hamlet, IV, iii, 9 ff.:

. . . diseases desperate grown
By desperate appliance are relieved
Or not at all.

Richard III, IV, iii, 51 ff.:

. . . I have heard that fearful commenting
Is leaden servitor to dull delay . . .
Come, muster men: my counsel is my shield.

King Lear, V, i, 68–69:

. . . for my state
Stands on me to defend, not to debate.

More significant as regards extent of influence are many passages in which it is obvious that Shakespeare carried over from Seneca, either directly or indirectly, rhetorical methods of handling situations. There are in Seneca, for example, several cases in which a character emphasizes his personal daring or resolution by setting it against impossibilities in the world of nature:

And dost thou think that I would touch the hand
That is besprinkled with my father's gore,
And my two brothers blood? Oh, sooner far
Shall day's last beams go out in eastern skies,
And dawn break in the west; sooner shall peace
Be made 'twixt snow and flame, and Scylla join
Sicilia's shores with those of Italy,
And sooner shall Euripus' rushing waves
Lap peacefully upon Eubea's shores.

(*Hercules Furens*, 373 ff.)[6]

With this exaggerated manner of speaking compare the following:

You may as well go stand upon the beach
And bid the main flood bate his usual height;
You may as well use question with the wolf
Why he hath made the ewe bleat for the lamb;
You may as well forbid the mountain pines
To wag their high tops and to make no noise,
When they are fretten with the gusts of heaven. . . .

(*Mer. Ven.*, IV, i, 71 ff.)

Seneca is also fond of permitting a character to set up for himself possible tests of endurance:

> And shouldst thou bid me tread the driven snows,
> To walk along high Pindus frozen peaks,
> I'd not refuse; no, not if thou shouldst bid
> Me go through fire, and serried ranks of foes,
> I would not hesitate to bare my breast
> Unto the naked swords. (*Hippolytus,* 613 ff.)

Shakespeare turns speech of this type to account in portraying the courage of characters in perilous situations. Compare the following with the passage from Seneca:

> O, bid me leap, rather than marry Paris,
> From off the battlements of yonder tower;
> Or walk in thievish ways; or bid me lurk
> Where serpents are; chain me with roaring bears; . . .
> And I will do it without fear or doubt. . . .
> (*R. and J.,* IV, i, 77 ff.)

> Rather a ditch in Egypt
> Be gentle grave unto me! rather on Nilus' mud
> Lay me stark naked, and let the water-flies
> Blow me into abhorring! rather make
> My country's high pyramides my gibbet,
> And hang me up in chains! (*A. and C.,* V, ii, 57 ff.)

From Seneca Shakespeare inherited in one way or another much figurative language, prominent here being images contrasting the cares of high and low estate in terms of mountain peaks and valleys, ships in mid-sea and near the shore, palaces and cottages. Typical use of such imagery appears in the following:

> More soft than Tyrian couch,
> The greensward soothes to fearless sleep;
> But gilded ceilings break our rest,
> And sleepless through the night we lie
> On beds of luxury.
> . . . . Not so the poor:
> His heart is ever full of peace.
> From shallow beechen cups he drinks,
> But not with trembling hands; his food
> Is cheap and common, but he sees
> No naked sword above his head. . . .
> (*Hercules Œtæus,* 644 ff.)

'Tis not the balm, the sceptre and the ball . . .
Not all these, laid in bed majestical,
Can sleep so soundly as the wretched slave,
Who with a body filled and vacant mind
Gets him to rest, cramm'd with distressful bread. . . .
(*Henry V*, IV, i, 277 ff.)

Compare also these figurative descriptions of the effects of sleep:

Hercules Furens, 1065 ff.:
O sleep, subduer of our ills,
The spirit's rest, thou better part
Of human life, . . .

Macbeth, II, ii, 36 ff.:
. . . the innocent sleep,
Sleep that knits up the ravell'd sleave of care,
The death of each day's life, sore labour's bath,
Balm of hurt minds, great nature's second course,
Chief nourisher in life's feast, . . .

2 Henry IV, III, i, 5 ff.:
O sleep, O gentle sleep,
Nature's soft nurse, how have I frighted thee,
That thou no more wilt weigh my eyelids down,
And steep my senses in forgetfulness? . . .

One might go on to cite passages in which reaction on the part of characters follows a similar pattern:

Thyestes, 176 ff.:
O soul, so sluggish, spiritless and weak,
And (what in kings I deem the last reproach)
Still unavenged, after so many crimes,
Thy brother's treacheries, and every law
Of nature set at naught, canst vent thy wrath
In vain and meaningless complaints? By now
The whole wide world should be in arms . . .

Hamlet, II, ii, 593 ff.:
Yet I,
A dull and muddy-mettled rascal, peak,
Like John-a-dreams, unpregnant of my cause,
And can say nothing; no, not for a king,
Upon whose property and most dear life
A damn'd defeat was made. . . .
it cannot be
But I am pigeon-liver'd, and lack gall
To make oppression bitter. . . .

Or one might note the tendency on the part of both dramatists to describe emotion in terms of physiological accompaniment. For example, in *Troades* (488 ff.) Andromache says as she hides her child in the tomb,

> But at the very thought a chilling sweat
> Invades my trembling limbs, for much I fear
> The gruesome omen of the place of death.[7]

And Juliet when she is about to swallow the potion (*R. & J.*, IV, iii, 15 ff.) says,

> I have a faint cold fear thrills through my veins,
> That almost freezes up the heat of life: . . .
> Or, if I live, is it not very like,
> The horrible conceit of death and night,
> Together with the terror of the place,—
> As in a vault, an ancient receptacle,
> Where, for this many hundred years, the bones
> Of all my buried ancestors are pack't . . .

Similarity exists here in motivating image also.

There are further parallels in Shakespeare to *Phœnissae*, 295 ff., which deals with discord within a kingdom; to *Troades*, 1 ff., and *Hippolytus*, 488 ff., which praise the humble life and exalt its happiness above the lot of kings; to *Hippolytus*, 671 ff., in which vengeance is expected from heaven and night is called upon to hide the sins of men. We might mention as typical the famous parallel between *Hercules Furens*, 1325 ff., *Hippolytus*, 715 ff., and *Macbeth*, II, ii, 60 ff.:

> What Tanais or Nile,
> What Tigris, with the waves of Persia mad, . . .
> Can ever cleanse this right hand of its stains?
> Though chill Maeotis pour its icy floods
> Upon me; though the boundless sea should pour
> Its waters o'er my hands; still would they be
> Deep dyed with crime.

> What Tanais could make me clean again?
> Or what Maeotis rushing to the sea,
> With its barbaric waves? Not Neptune's self,
> With all his ocean's waters could avail
> To cleanse so foul a stain.

Will all great Neptune's ocean wash this blood
Clean from my hand? No, this my hand will rather
The multitudinous seas incarnadine,
Making the green one red.

In the lines from *Macbeth* there is obvious similarity of phrasing and situation. Elsewhere Shakespeare seems to have adapted the basic idea of these Senecan passages to suit other purposes:

Not all the water in the rough rude sea
Can wash the balm off from an annointed king.
(*Rich. II,* III, ii, 54–5.)
Is there not rain enough in the sweet heavens
To wash it white as snow? (*Hamlet,* III, iii, 45–6.)

Because of the highly formalized patterns of tragic life as they appear in Seneca, larger structural resemblances are actually too numerous to record; a few illustrations are, however, requisite. In *Œdipus* the father of Œdipus, like the father of Hamlet, appears as a ghost (625 ff.), reveals the crime, accuses the murderer, and asks for revenge. Jocasta, like Gertrude, is only secondarily guilty. Œdipus's sorrow for his own deeds is like that of King Lear. The blinding of Gloucester recalls the blinding of Œdipus, even to the tearing of the hollow sockets with the nails. The motive of incest appears in both *Œdipus* and *Hamlet*. In *Phœnissae* the relation of Eteocles and Polynices resembles both in general situation and in treatment that between Edmund and Edgar in *King Lear*. Œdipus, like Gloucester, desires to die by jumping from a high cliff. The speeches of Œdipus to Antigone are much like those of Lear to Cordelia. The choice that Jocasta is forced to make between her sons is like that which Octavia is compelled to make in *Antony and Cleopatra* between her husband Antony and her brother Octavius. Jocasta's plea for reconciliation between her sons is like that which Volumnia makes to Coriolanus. And so on in every Senecan play in large and in small.

It may, moreover, be possible to carry this discussion into a still wider realm. It is universally admitted that Seneca was the preceptor of the tragic writers of the Renaissance. One may, therefore, also inquire whether he and other stoical writers exercised special influences on the nature of Elizabethan tragedy, influences profounder than those already considered.

The Greeks had no other conception of tragedy than that it was the theatrical presentation of calamity and grief. There is nothing to show that Aristotle thought of tragedy otherwise, although undoubtedly in following his inductive method he laid special stress on the stories of those heroes who were the victims of fate. He did not regard death as a necessary culmination of tragedy. Certainly Seneca did not. On the other hand, the Elizabethans seem to have believed that a tragedy must close with death, which becomes for them an inevitable end, a symbol of the final and the terrible. In their philosophy and their morals they set a greater value upon death than did the ancients. One must not be misled by the customary infliction of death, for there are many cases in Elizabethan drama in which death is cheapened.

Seneca himself was the leader of a revival of Greek tragedy. Part of the plays which pass under his name present tragedy in the same moral and philosophic terms in which it was produced by the Greeks. These are merely Greek tragedies written in a new rhetorical style and given a certain stoical coloring. I refer to such plays as *Œdipus* and *Agamemnon*. But others of the Senecan tragedies, particularly the Hercules plays and the plays based closely on Euripides, show a different conception of tribulation and disaster from that which appears in Æschylus and Sophocles. Seneca's consolation for the blows of fate is different from that of Æschylus. It is philosophic instead of religious. The naturalistic submission of Æschylus is gone. Instead of a human behavior controlled and directed within human limits and justified by veneration to the gods, Seneca introduces a stoical remedy against the badness of man's lot, which lot he regarded as inevitably bad. Æschylus did not so regard it. With Æschylus and Sophocles and with Aristotle and wherever and as long as the mighty influence of Aristotle prevailed, man was believed to have some chance for happiness. He had some chance to escape disaster, not always and in all circumstances to be sure; but the fact remains that human life was a possible enterprise normally and for most men. Man could live the life of reason. This Aristotelian doctrine belongs to the *Ethics* rather than to the *Poetics*. According to it man might come out a victor in the struggle. In Seneca man was sure to be beaten, but Seneca proposed to build up something within the heart of man which would enable him to gain a pyrrhic victory over fate. This doctrine is inherent in the stories of Hercules and Prometheus and is closely allied with titanism. The Renaissance had thus a fatalistic theory of tragedy remotely derived from Aristotle and a stoical theory implicit in some of the tragedies of Seneca.

An important conception of tragic fate, a conception arising out of Christianity and in its typical form unknown to the ancient world, is that catastrophe is the result of guilt and is a function of character and conscience. The Renaissance was thus provided with a third way of regarding tragedy. Christianity did not deny the badness of man's lot, but it tended to see the spectacle of human calamity as a result of wrongdoing.[8] Sometimes there are attempts to reconcile the new view with the old, as in the following passage from Daniel's *Cleopatra:*

> For sencelesse sensuality, doth euer
> Accompany felicity and greatnesse,
> A fatall witch, whose charmes do leaue vs neuer,
> Till we leaue all in sorrow for our sweetnesse;
> When yet our selues must be the cause we fall,
> Although the same be first decreed on hie:
> Our errors still must beare the blame of all,
> This must it be; earth, aske not heauen why.

Of the Aristotelian, or Æschylean, kind of tragedy there are many potent and convincing artistic examples. According to this familiar view human calamity is an irresistible and sometimes inexplicable manifestation of divine order. There is nothing to be done about it. Calamity must be accepted as the will of the gods delivered through the agency of fate. There was even no pattern for its acceptance. Man sustained calamity as best he could according to the strength or weakness of his humanity. If man was sufficiently strong in his fortitude, his endurance might become so heroic as to offset the evils of his lot. It had come to be believed that those in high station were most subject to the onslaughts of evil fate; but this idea, universal though it was, is not inherent in the conception.

With Seneca the very nature of things was disastrous, and calamity was irresistible and inescapable. There was nothing left for man but to endure, and in endurance lay his only hope. He could by learning to be indifferent both to life and death rob fate of its triumph, become a victor in attitude in his ability to resist or meet courageously. There is also a positive way of saying this. If man did acquire this self-dependence, if he became the master of himself, he became also the master of his fate.

The third idea was that man is the responsible child of God. His joys are God's gift and his misery is God's punishment. Man's character and his conduct are the sources of his weal or woe, though his disasters need not be purely punitive, for whom the Lord loveth he chasteneth.

Confronted by these three doctrines of tragedy, the Renaissance, particularly the English Renaissance, made no absolutely clear choice. Elements of all three are to be met with throughout the period of the Elizabethan drama. Writers of tragedy never thought the matter through. But in practice Shakespeare and some others gave preference to the third or Christian ideal. Shakespeare invented, or perfected the tragedy of character, and to this the world has given its approval as perhaps the greatest of his achievements. Shakespeare is often said to have established modern tragedy, but nobody would contend that Shakespeare was not influenced by and does not give voice to the doctrines of both Aristotle and Seneca. If this is true of Shakespeare, it is even more true of his contemporaries; for Marston, Chapman, Jonson, Webster, and Ford are much more archaic than is Shakespeare. Senecan conceptions are often more fundamental to them than to Shakespeare. Since Seneca carries with him the Æschylean idea, what these closer followers of Seneca often give us is the spectacle of sheer fate, opposed or unopposed by stoical resistance.

The situation here described recalls the familiar modern contrast between the views of Hegel and those of Schopenhauer. The place of tragedy in Hegel's thought is suggested by Paul Elmer More's dictum, 'Vice is the gymnasium for virtue.' Even so in Hegel tragedy is the gymnasium for happiness. His unity is a unity of integrated opposites, and out of his notion of conflict and tragedy comes triumph. Of the two opposing personages in the true tragic play each is represented as in the right. The protagonist, not being able to realize what he knows to be right without the violation of another power, will and end (equally just), is drawn to commit faults notwithstanding his morality, or rather on account of it. This contradiction must be destroyed and a solution of this conflict brought about. Moral unity must be re-established by the destruction, if need be, of what has troubled its repose. Thus, according to Hegel, the real conflict is not so much between particular interests as between moral reason in its pure idea, on the one hand, and, on the other, moral reason in its concrete manifestations in the real world and in human activity.

'There is,' says Schopenhauer, 'only one inborn error, and that is, that we exist to be happy.' If we exist, he would say, we will; if we will, we are striving to be that which we are not; and if we strive and attain only to seek something more, we cannot be happy. The will is bound to no special organ, but is everywhere present as the basic ingredient of the universe, the soul of the soul, the essence of reality. It constitutes the whole organism, is the metaphysical substratum of the phenomenal world and is not, like the intellect, dependent upon the phenomenon, but the phenomenon depends upon it. Though will scorns happiness, there must be a happiness in the exercise of will. This exaltation of will alines Schopenhauer with the stoics; whereas the longing, the unrest, the strife, the will to unity which is Hegel's absolute presupposes a world in which something can be done, such as Aristotle's world, and offers denial to Schopenhauer's doctrine of the totally evil nature of all things.

This distinction may be made clearer by an examination of the well known rubric for the analysis of tragedy based, or supposed to be based, on Aristotle. It is explained in Freytag's *Technique of the Drama* and in many other works on tragedy. According to this scheme, which is in wide popular use, we are to consider the elements of tragic story in some such terms as these: an inciting force, a rising movement, a turning-point or climax (usually said to be brought about by some form of tragic guilt), a moment of final suspense, and a catastrophe. At the very end, as a final element, there is a return to the *status quo ante*, the re-establishment of a normal *Weltanschauung*. There is no doubt that, not only the majority of tragic plots, but physical action, social event, and human life itself conform themselves well to this orderly series; for we behold action followed by reaction, growth followed by decay, and youth followed by maturity, old age, and death. Consider, for example, how consistently Plutarch's *Lives* and the series of Renaissance tragedies conform to this outline. There is an actual series, beginning, let us say, with the fall of Caius Marius. In such an opening drama the fortunes of Sulla were crescent, those of Marius cadent. In the next drama of the series Pompey was crescent and Sulla was cadent; in the next Julius Caesar was crescent and Pompey was cadent; in the next Julius Caesar fell and Brutus rose; in the next Brutus fell and Antony rose; and in the final episode of the series, Antony went down before a triumphant Octavius.

In spite of the critical and pedagogical utility of the scheme we have been discussing, I confess I have long been dissatisfied with its application to certain great tragedies and tragic heroes of the Elizabethan drama. The thought underlying the sequence–inciting force, rising action, turning-point, declining action, and catastrophe–is certainly Aristotelian. It fits in well with the tragedy of character and conduct, which is also a tragedy of event. But this scheme can hardly be made to agree with the principles of stoicism, since it moves in the wrong direction and assumes that tragedy is only incidental in a world not normally calamitous. This kind of tragedy ends with calamity, shame, and death; whereas the stoical doctrine begins with these things as the inevitables of human life. The difference is one of degree, but the ideal of stoicism is not the avoidance of these things but the triumph over them. This question might therefore be asked: do any of the tragedies of the Elizabethan age show the dramatist elevating these stoical doctrines into an ideal in such a way as to subordinate change and accident to fortitude and self-command? If so, there will be found in that age two types of tragedy often lumped together under one definition, like the following from A. H. Thorndike's *Tragedy*: [9]

> The action of tragedy should represent a conflict of wills, or of will with circumstance, or will with itself, and should therefore be based on the characters of the persons involved. A typical tragedy is concerned with a great personality engaged in a struggle that ends disastrously.

This definition applies with modifications to the first and larger group, those tragedies in which we behold a man or group of men making a (typically brave) struggle against an evil fate; behold them caught in the toils of an unpropitious destiny, like Œdipus, Agamemnon, Philoctetes, Ajax, or Hecuba; or see them as victims of divine justice following in the wake of their sins, like Faustus, Othello, Macbeth, Vittoria Corambona, or Beatrice Joanna.

But is there not a second kind of tragedy in which we see a man struggling for mastery of himself, struggling in order to achieve indifference to disaster and death, struggling ultimately in order to achieve a philosophic calm? It would not be a tragedy in which event would be the important thing. Indeed, it would minimize calamity and subordinate it to the way in which calamity is borne. Such an element appears in most tragedies, since part of tragic effect comes from our admiration of the heroic fortitude which arises as a concomitant. The difference would, therefore, be one of emphasis. We might illustrate this difference by comparing the Œdipus of *Œdipus Rex* with the *Œdipus* of the *Œdipus at Colonus*. Aged Lear struggles as does Hamlet to gain mastery over self, and he ultimately also achieves a calm; but in certain plays the development is so marked as to become an artistic principle; so much so that it would seem as if here the dramatist has come close to, if he has not actually achieved, a different type of tragedy.

The admirable spectacle of human courage, brought into tragedy from the earliest times, does not constitute a criterion. But with reference to titanism the problem is somewhat more complicated. *Prometheus* is a drama of titanism, and it is not necessary to resort to later times to find an example. There is *ab initio* no relief for Prometheus; the terms of his contract call for suffering. The same thing seems to be true of such tragedies of heroes and demi-gods as *Hercules Furens* and *Hercules Œtœus*. Hercules presents the case of enforced suffering without surrender. The tragedy of the villain-hero in the Elizabethan age, with the fascination which it exercised and still exercises over audiences, is possibly best explained as a form of the tragedy of titanism. Richard III is committed to a religion of selfish ambition; Vindici to a religion of revenge; and, as we watch their pursuit of these ungodly purposes, we may fairly ask ourselves how our attitude differs in its essence from that of the Greeks as they watched rebellion against the gods. In *Octavia* Seneca presents us with a Nero who is possibly the first example of the villain-hero. Our feelings as we follow the machinations of Iago, fascinated by his adroitness, possibly have in them an element of titanism. Richard Crookback has exalted his evil ambition to a level of as complete and irrational tyranny as the will of Zeus or the jealous rage of Juno. We cannot be said to sympathize with Richard III as he preys on the lives of innocent and guilty alike; but we do, I think, sympathize with Chapman's Bussy d'Ambois. Bussy has drawn his titanism from his own character. His will to live, his passion to enjoy, are ours, and, as we see him crash, it is in some sense ourselves who fall. Since the stoic psychologists had taught Chapman that the passions within the heart of man are mighty forces, he chose to make of Bussy a proponent of passion against reason; so that *Bussy d'Ambois* presents rebellion, not only against Christian morals, but against the fundamental principle of Aristotelian ethics, namely, that reason should rule passion. Bussy d'Ambois is neither merely a villain-hero nor an Aristotelian protagonist. He is, I think, primarily a titan, and there are other such heroes in the later Elizabethan drama. In Jacobean drama Neo-Stoicism perhaps tended to express itself in terms of titanism, but this is not the form I have in mind.

All attempts to apply to *Hamlet* the Aristotelian rubric of tragedy are, to say the least, unsatisfactory. Distinguished critics have seen in Hamlet a man dominated by fate in the form of an extreme weakness of will. To do this is to rob the most representative of all fictional characters of his representative quality. It has even been said that Hamlet's failure to stab the King while at his prayers is a manifestation of tragic weakness, which idea is absurd. Hamlet's primary quality is that he is a normal man. His universal appeal is due to the breadth of his humanity. If he is weak in will, or if he is limited by a conflict between his ideals and his realities, these shortcomings are merely those of all men. He is beset with troubles, and he is a man who cares; but to say that he is abnormal in these matters is to rob him of his universality. All men are immersed in difficulties. Most men care acutely about them, as Hamlet does, and strive to throw off the shackles of grief. Hamlet's problem is merely the greatest and most typical: 'who will deliver me from the body of this death?' Hamlet is an inquiry about the validity of human existence, the fundamental query of stoicism on foot. The representative quality of Hamlet accounts for his failure to be explained away by the numerous attempts that have been made to do so.

Hamlet struggles through an existence, very full of evil and, as regards the future, disastrous. So far as one can see, there is no question of praise or blame. He has merely confronted his life. Ultimately he finds a remedy for its evils. He says to Horatio, 'I defy that augury which says that there is a special significance in the fall of a sparrow. I tell you that death, which has so long threatened me and caused me dread, has at last lost its terrors for me. It will come, and I have at last arrived at a state of mind in which I do not concern myself any longer about when it comes. "If it be now, 'tis not to come; if it be not to come, it will be now. If it be not now, yet will it come: the readiness is all."' This passage, which marks the end of a long struggle, seems to me to be the key to Hamlet's tragedy. He has reached his goal at last, and it is the end and aim of stoicism.

I was long puzzled by Brutus's statement at the end of *Julius Cæsar:*

Countrymen,
My heart doth joy that yet in all my life
I found no man but he was true to me.

Surely an odd assertion by one who has been fooled by almost everybody in the play! But when I sought a stoical interpretation of Brutus's character, the whole thing became clear to me. Brutus meant to say that, if a man such as Marcus Brutus (or Woodrow Wilson) is true to himself, all men, even his enemies, will be true to him for evermore. It is enough that he has been Brutus.

It has seemed to me also that this doctrine of ultimate self-mastery as an ideal may help us in the interpretation of the character of Cleopatra. All limitations being duly recognized, the fact remains that Shakespeare presents in her in her later hours a tragic greatness comparable to the finest of his achievements. The vain, selfish, and frivolous woman rises to a height of magnanimity which, in spite of all the critics have said, is convincing. It presents the aspect of a movement upwards like that of Hamlet and Brutus, a spiritual triumph in the face of death, which you recall was the Elizabethan symbol of catastrophe:

We'll bury him; and then, what's brave, what's noble,
Let's do it after the high Roman fashion,
And make death proud to take us. . . .
My desolation does begin to make
A better life. 'Tis paltry to be Cæsar;
Not being Fortune, he's but Fortune's knave,
A minister of her will: and it is great
To do that thing that ends all other deeds;
Which shackles accidents and bolts up change.

NOTES

1. See the author's *The Enchanted Glass* (New York, 1936) pp. 160-3; also J. M. Manly, 'Chaucer and the Rhetoricians,' British Academy, *Proceedings*, XXI, 95–113.

2. The fact of the permeation of English literature of the Renaissance by the classics becomes abundantly clear from such studies as R. K. Root, *Classical Mythology in Shakespeare* (New York, 1903); Douglas Bush, *Mythology and the Renaissance Tradition in English Poetry* (Minneapolis, Minnesota, 1932); Walter F. Schirmer, *Chaucer, Shakespeare und die Antike.*

Bibl. Warburg, *Vorträge*, 1930–1931. (Leipzig, 1932); Edgar I. Fripp, 'Shakespeare's Use of Ovid,' in *Shakespeare Studies* (Oxford, 1930); and many others.

3. John W. Cunliffe, *The Influence of Seneca on Elizabethan Tragedy* (1893; reprint, New York, 1925), *passim;* Rudolf Fischer, *Die Kunstentwicklung der Englischen Tragödie* (Wien, 1899), *passim;* J. M. Manly, 'The Influence of The Tragedies of Seneca upon Early English Drama' in *The Tragedies of Seneca.* Translated by Frank Justus Miller (Chicago, 1907), pp. 3–10; J. Engel, article in *Preussisches Jahrbuch,* April, 1903; F. L. Lucas, *Seneca and Elizabethan Tragedy* (Cambridge, 1922), pp. 121–5; T. S. Eliot, *Shakespeare and the Stoicism of Seneca,* The Shakespeare Association (Oxford, 1927) and Mr. Eliot's introduction to *Seneca, his Tenne Tragedies Translated into English.* Edited by Thomas Newton. Anno 1581. The Tudor Translations, Second Series. 2 Vols. (London, 1927), pp. v-liv; A. M. Witherspoon, *Influence of Robert Garnier on Elizabethan Drama* (New Haven, 1924), *passim; The Works of Thomas Kyd.* Edited by F. S. Boas (Oxford, 1901), pp. xxxii–xlv. As bearing closer relation to the point of view of this paper, see A. H. Gilbert, 'Seneca and the Criticism of Elizabethan Tragedy,' *Philological Quarterly*, XIII, 370–81.

4. Citations from Seneca's plays are taken from Frank Justus Miller's verse translation (Chicago, 1907) above referred to.

5. Quotations from Shakespeare are from the Globe edition.

6. See also *Hercules Œtœus*, 335 ff.; *Thyestes*, 447 ff.; *Hippolytus*, 569 ff.

7. See also *Medea*, 386 ff.

8. See Lily B. Campbell, *Shakespeare's Tragic Heroes* (Cambridge, 1930), pp. 15 ff.; Willard Farnham, *The Medieval Heritage of Elizabethan Tragedy* (Berkeley, California, 1935), 103 ff., 290 ff., *et passim.*

9. A. H. Thorndike, *Tragedy* (Boston, 1908), p. 9.

G. WILSON KNIGHT

Lyly

ELIZIBETHAN thought was more linguistically alive than ours. Perhaps the reputation of puns and word-play varies according to an age's literary strength (and is indeed rising to-day): you get them in Hebrew literature and Greek drama. Word-play sees similarity in opposites. Metaphor is a sort of pun; and Elizabethan conversation may have held, weakly, the metaphoric and allusive quality of Bacon's prose. That Elizabethan tragedy depended on a verbal joy now lost is generally allowed; that *Ralph Roister Doister* is a word-farce only slightly dependent on situation and action has not been, I think, noticed: hence its surges of doggerel absurdity rising at high moments to nonsensical word-makings of a rough syllabic music. Lyly's verbal and allusive extravagances, and their contemporary popularity, must not be too sharply dismissed: his dramatic work relates significantly to his Euphuism. Before turning to the plays I would make two points concerning *Euphues* itself.

The style is neatly balanced and heavily antithetical in word, phrase, sentence, paragraph. Complex cross-antitheses are usual. Consider this one:

> What is he, Euphues, that, knowing thy wit and seeing thy folly, but will rather punish thy lewdness than pity thy heaviness? (*Euphues*, Bond, Vol. I, p. 208.)[1]

Observe that the technical essence can be characterized—and if it can be it must be—as substance. This sentence expresses a lively awareness of opposites. Now Lyly's style plays constantly round psychological contradictions. In *Euphues* soliloquy, letters, dramatic argument

From *Review of English Studies,* XV (April 1939), pp. 146–63. Reprinted by permission of The Clarendon Press, Oxford, and the author.

regularly express mental conflict. Lyly's 'Ay, but . . .' connections in fictional self-communing serve continually to introduce battalions of opposing reasons to what precedes. Implicit in his method—which is also his matter—there is therefore dramatic conflict. The antithetic style of *Euphues* reflects that balancing of contradictions that is also the core of Elizabethan drama. However luxuriant and leisurely the book, as a whole, may seem, it has thus a dramatic immediacy and tension faintly analogous to the very different, yet also epistolary, manner of Richardson. A certain wisdom of accepted uncertainty is always at the back of the opposing parties or principles rooted in the nature of drama: this wisdom is Lyly's, pre-eminently.

Second, we have a mass of pseudo-scientific, natural, and classical comparisons. Though there is gross exaggeration, the thing exaggerated is of vital poetic importance. Lyly continually refers human and psychological issues to the natural universe. True morality must be in some sense truth to nature: it is Hooker's problem in Book I of his *Ecclesiastical Polity*. It is everybody's problem, rooted in the very structure of poetic expression. Consider this typical passage:

> The similitude you rehearse of the wax, argueth your waxing and melting brain, and your example of the hot and hard iron showeth in you but cold and weak disposition. Do you not know that which all men do affirm and know, that black will take no other colour? That the stone abeston being once made hot will never be made cold? That fire cannot be forced downward? That nature will have force after kind? That everything will dispose itself according to nature? Can the Aethiope change or alter his skin? or the leopard his hue? Is it possible to gather grapes of thorns or figs of thistles? or to cause anything to strive against nature? (*Works*, ed. Bond, Vol. I, p. 191.)

The explicit human-natural reference here is implicit throughout the multitudinous crazy similitudes of *Euphues:* a desire at once to read the human mind in terms of the living physical universe and see that universe and its properties—including inorganic matter (remember the rock in *Love's Metamorphoses*)—as a vital extension of the human mind. In Wordsworth you have the philosophy of it; in all poets the practice of it. Certainly Lyly's references smell overstrong of mediæval bestiaries and alchemy: but the Renaissance mind in wording a new consciousness of nature is often driven to expression in mediæval terms—as we shall find, too, in Marlowe. The generalized and intentional force of Lyly's comparisons blends easily into his use of a well-known proverb near the end of my quotation, followed by the transcription, similar in both substance and direction, of a famous New Testament passage. The fundamentally serious quality and profound intention is thus clear.

Lyly's numerous mythological, especially Greek, references tone with the upsurge of Renaissance Hellenism generally: and this, too, relates to my last argument, since Greek mythology is continually for Renaissance and Romantic poets the natural grammar for a consciousness that has broken the man-nature opacity. In *Euphues* the stress falls mostly on pseudo-scientific learning; in the plays, on Greek mythology.

The neat antitheses of *Euphues* recur in the balanced parties and general symmetry of design in the plays. These show vital conflicts though no powerful train of action: they are static and spatialized rather than narrative, yet their vivid immediacy never lacks excitement. The conclusions to the first two scenes of *Endimion* will illustrate this technical mastery. Scene beginnings also consistently rivet the eye. Though the action is slow to advance, its very static unrest is so emphasized at a re-entry that suspense is strong:

> No rest, Endimion? Still uncertain how to settle thy steps by day, or thy thoughts by night? (*Endimion,* II. iii. I.)

A trick Shakespeare assimilated thoroughly: soliloquy often exquisitely expands the dualized personality of a central figure, whetting your attention to the outcome. As you read, you see:

> Yonder I espy Endimion. I will seem to suspect nothing, but soothe him, that seeing I cannot obtain the depth of his love, I may learn the height of his dissembling. (*Endimion,* II. I, 47.)

You are jerked into a stage-awareness and your anxiety sharpened. All that tires in *Euphues* under strict compression ignites. Instead of listening, you see; instead of knowing, experience. Dramatic suspense adds a dimension to your receptivity: and Lyly's progress from *Euphues* to the plays miniatures neatly the movement from *The Faery Queen* to Shakespeare. Effects are narrowed and intensified under a tight dramatic technique. There is far less pseudo-science but new vital personifications of Hellenic myth.

As in Spenser different sorts of allegory or symbolism jostle each other. Lyly, like Spenser, is a court-poet: the title-page to *Euphues* says: 'Very pleasant for all gentlemen to read, and most necessary to remember.' He is even closer to court life than Spenser. He transmits the electric touch of contemporary social eroticism; somewhat like Pope. In all poetry we expect a particular event or person to be at one with a generalized significance: but in Spenser and Lyly there is the additional complication of masked contemporary meanings. If these are too organic something may be lost for future ages: the work is too closely bedded in its own birth. With Spenser I feel this, but less with Lyly. Most of his drama can, like Shakespeare's, be read without searching too exactly for such origins: and when, as in *Endimion,* such independence in reading is not possible, there is somehow a pleasing necessity about our very mystification. Lyly's plays more precisely than any others reflect the court of Elizabeth; our interest is closely involved in this; his pregnant love-analyses come hot, as it were, from knowledge of court-flirtations; and we rather like to feel there are points in the dialogue and sometimes the whole structure to which we cannot respond as directly as his first audience. The very flavour, as it were, of the plays would be different were he always transmuting, instead of reflecting, his day. Lyly is not, and is not wanted to be, Shakespeare. The conventional choice of *Endimion* as Lyly's most representative play is probably fortunate enough. It distils and intensifies his general qualities. Its various allegories are of shifting importance. There is Cynthia = Elizabeth, Tellus = Mary Queen of Scots, and the otherwise-to-be-interpreted other persons; parallel with this, and of changing importance, is Cynthia = the Moon and Tellus = the Earth, without further correspondences; and last, the more generalized sense of a hero set between a high and divine love and earthy and unscrupulous passions. Cynthia rules the action from the start and statuesquely takes charge at the close. That Cynthia-Elizabeth should so dominate Lyly's most dense and weighty single play is apt, since the Queen is necessarily the focal point of all that courtly eroticism at the back of his work. The imaginative and factual coalesce. The Queen is close-involved in the mysterious dream allegories at the play's heart; so that Lyly's most deeply imaginative, even mystic, apprehension is appropriately locked, as by a navel-string, to the age of its birth. Cynthia's particularity as Elizabeth becomes itself a universal.

Often, however, his persons and plots, and continually isolated exquisite movements of dialogue, have symbolic or poetic force of the most normal kind. There is a new strength in advance of the moralities. Those started with a rigid abstraction: poverty, good-deeds, or such like, and set it walking in human form. The resulting personality either outgrows the conception and general plan, or stays severely limited. The Elizabethan recognizes the complexity and contradictions and dramatic oppositions *within* the single personality and the baffling indecisiveness of all moral categories. So he starts with a concrete, often mythical or pseudo-historical, figure and lets his abstract thinking play round and into its growth. The ideas within his human delineation will be many and paradoxical. Where there is a seeming figure of the mediæval sort, it will shadow some vast and universal idea such as Cupid = Love: itself, in Lyly, one tissue of contradictions. The weakness of the moralities is suggested by their name. Moral categories are on a plane below that of poetic creation (which is not therefore independent of them), and, if allowed to direct autonomously the plan, tend to impose a seeming simplicity on a real complexity. 'Death' or 'love' are realities so ultimate that they hold power beyond the shifting concepts of the moral order, and can safely be personified in any age. The communistic or pacifist propagandist art of to-day might study, with profit, this problem. Of course, a Christian propaganda does not exactly incur this limitation, Christianity being itself a complex poetry first, and an ethic, if at all, afterwards. It is significant that when Lyly uses a mediæval touch in *The Woman in the Moon* his personified qualities are vast and non-ethical: Nature, Concord, Discord—the two last, under their own names or in symbols of Music and Tempest being the rooted dualism throughout Shakespeare. But generally Lyly lets his plays grow from and form about some concretely conceived story.

I pass to consider Lyly's more direct content, what the plays say to us. Love, as in *Euphues,* is his whole theme. He is as aware as Spenser of its complexities: he is more aware than Spenser of its inward contradictions. His understanding is at once purer and more realistic. He can refer to crude, and in a sense healthy, lust but seems to have little or no sense, as have Spenser, Marlowe, and Milton, of the sexual nature in subtle mental disease: in this he is with Shakespeare.

Campaspe dramatizes a typical Renaissance conflict, of soldiership and love. The whole play is redolently Elizabethan. The choice of an Alexander story is apt; since Alexander and Cæsar have here an almost Messianic authority. The Elizabethan ideal must be a soldier, yet a Christian gentleman. Shakespeare's Theseus and Lyly's Alexander are correspondent, precisely: strong and masterful, yet gentle:

> Alexander as he tendereth virtue, so he will you; he drinketh not blood, but thirsteth after honour, he is greedy of victory, but never satisfied with mercy. In fight terrible, as becometh a captain; in conquest mild, as beseemeth a king. In all things, than which nothing can be greater, he is Alexander. (I. i. 48.)

As in *A Midsummer Night's Dream* the poet shows his hero returning from conquests, not actually seen at any bloody work: so exploiting the positive while not the negative aspect of valour. Alexander is anxious to

> have as great care to govern in peace, as conquer in war: that whilst arms cease, arts may flourish, and, joining letters with lances, we endeavour to be as good philosophers as soldiers, knowing it no less praise to be wise than commendable to be valiant. (I. i. 80.)

Which is answered by Hephaestion's:

> Needs must that commonwealth be fortunate, whose Captain is a Philosopher and whose Philosopher is a Captain. (I. i. 85.)

The typically Elizabethan conception shows how close we are in this (earlier) play to the equation of Cynthia with Elizabeth in *Endimion*. The play's central problem is the age's problem, intrinsic to such a book as Castiglione's *Courtier*. What is the perfect courtly, humanistic, existence? Notice Alexander's courteous and delightful conversation with Apelles: and how exquisitely the warrior-king is balanced against the artist. The Elizabethan aims at the paradox of a Christlike warrior: Alexander, and Theseus. And when his foes are vanquished, how must he act? What is left to do? The solution is, dramatically at least, obvious: he must fall in love. Which Alexander does, shocking his soldier retainer, Hephaestion:

> What! is the son of Philip, king of Macedon, become the subject of Campaspe, the captive of Thebes? Is that mind, whose greatness the world could not contain, drawn within the compass of an idle alluring eye? (II. ii. 31.)

He reminds Alexander of Campaspe's mortality. This is Lyly's recurrent problem—if love is divine, why so brittle? and so sternly to be controlled? Yet, if it be not, then what is? Alexander is given a typically neat defence:

> My case were light, Hephaestion, and not worthy to be called love, if

> reason were a remedy, or sentences could salve, that (which) sense cannot conceive. (II. ii. 77.)

Being a king, he says, his passions are greater than others'. Hephaestion must cease

> With arguments to seek to repel that which with their deity the gods cannot resist. (II. ii. 89.)

Again, a typical thought of Lyly's—love's superb strength. Moreover, says Alexander, is it not likely and reasonable that the captive Campaspe should return an Alexander's love? But note the exquisite reply:

> You say that in love there is no reason, and therefore there can be no likelihood. (II. ii. 110.)

The light dialogue plays over psychological profundities. Alexander's arguments are turned against himself. Lyly's persons are often so tangled in the mysterious contradictions and irrationalities of their own love. Hephaestion turns out to be right, Campaspe loves Apelles, the painter:

> I perceive Alexander cannot subdue the affections of men, though he conquer their countries. Love falleth like dew as well upon the low grass, as upon the high cedar. (V. iv. 127.)

Which holds a lucid and lovely truth comparable to its New Testament original. Alexander ends the fine, generous-hearted hero, as little subdued by a selfish passion as Theseus is taken in by the seething imaginations of lunatic, lover, or poet. He leaves love to 'seamsters and scholars' and 'fancies out of books,' like Theseus; while Apelles takes Campaspe. This is not strange. The king, the soldier, man of action, is often greater than poet or philosopher to the Elizabethan; as Christ is a greater, apart from all theology, than a Dante or a Shakespeare—the man who lives, not writes, his record. So

> HEPHAESTION: The conquering of Thebes was not so honourable as the subduing of these thoughts.
>
> ALEXANDER: It were a shame Alexander should desire to command the world, if he could not command himself. (V. iv. 148.)

This touches, for an instant, something beyond both love and warriorship. But—and it is a big one—the play ends on a delightfully pregnant remark:

> And, good Hephaestion, when all the world is won, and every country is thine and mine, either find me out another to subdue, or, of my word, I will fall in love. (v. iv. 153.)

If we thought Love dethroned, we are wrong: so often a seeming conclusion in Lyly turns into its opposite. Every separate statement is, by itself, a shadow only of the profound movement of his dialogue, something bigger, heavier than his delicate phrases at first suggest. So here the problem of an ultimate good remains.

The love that rules these plays is definitely sexual and romantic. Yet Lyly distinguishes between a high and low variety in *Endimion*. Cynthia seems to inspire a somewhat platonic fervour:

> O fair Cynthia! O unfortunate Endimion! Why was not thy birth as high as thy thoughts, or her beauty less than heavenly? (II. i. 1.)

But it induces the usual lover's 'sad and melancholy moods of perplexed minds, the not to be expressed torments of racked thoughts' (II. i. 9): the unrest and perplexity to which Lyly so often refers. Eumenides is entrapped in the fairly usual Elizabethan conflict of love and friendship. First we have

> Ay, let him sleep ever, so I slumber but one minute with Semele. Love knoweth neither friendship nor kindred. (III. iv. 109.)

But soon after,

> The love of men to women is a thing common and of course: the friendship of man to man infinite and immortal. (III. iv. 114.)

Geron advises him that

> Love is but an eye-worm, which only tickleth the head with hopes and wishes: friendship the image of eternity, in which there is nothing movable, nothing mischievous. (III. iv. 123.)

Whatever precisely 'friendship' may mean here—and to an Elizabethan it meant more than to us—the issue is fairly clear. Lyly often thus, provisionally, criticizes the uncertainty and insubstantiality of purely sexual attraction, as in *Love's Metamorphoses:*

> I do not think Love hath any spark of Divinity in him; since the end of his being is earthly. In the blood he is begot by the frail fires of the eye, and quenched by the frailer shadows of thought. What reason have we then to sooth his humour with such zeal, and follow his fading delights with such passion? (I. i. 9.)

The central reality is turned round and round for continual inspection. One moment we are told that 'liking, a curtsy, a smile, a beck, and such like, are the very quintessence of love' (*Sapho and Phao,* I. iv. 16). But Eumenides in *Endimion* considers his approach to Semele in words (almost exactly repeated by Shakespeare's Troilus) that do deep intellectual justice to the riches of desire:

> I pray thee, fortune, when I shall first meet with fair Semele, dash my delight with some light disgrace, lest embracing sweetness beyond measure, I take a surfeit without recure: let her practice her accustomed coyness, that I may diet myself upon my desires: otherwise the fulness of my joys will diminish the sweetness, and I shall perish by them before I possess them. (III. iv. 96.)

That is, in the very preliminary tension something is known which in satisfaction is lost. The full possession with full enjoyment is an impossibility. As though in love there is a necessary fiction not to be actualized, or, if actualized, fatal, or, maybe, enjoyed in death: perfect love on earth being a self-annihilating paradox. So exquisitely is the delicate bright agony in all its mystery analysed, criticized, defined at every turn. And with what Shakespearian ease the complex problem of *The Bower of Bliss,* that of the essentially mental twist in human desire, is, not ignored, but assimilated, from a higher plane of reference. Love is shown as compact of contradictions and paradoxes. It is

> a heat full of coldness, a sweet full of bitterness, a pain full of pleasantness; which maketh thoughts have eyes and hearts ears . . . (*Gallathea,* I. ii. 16.)

As in Biron's long love-defence in *Love's Labour's Lost* this heightened awareness adds new powers to the senses, a thought insistently recalling certain passages from the Gospels. The impossibility-working aspect of love is reflected by the miraculous love-changes arranged by Cupid and Venus in the plays: the fanciful plot, as in *A Midsummer Night's Dream,* mirroring a psychological truth. The mysteries of love are divine mysteries:

> O divine Love, which art therefore called divine because thou overreachest the wisest, conquerest the chastest, and dost all things both unlikely and impossible, because thou art Love. Thou makest the bashful impudent, the wise fond, the chaste wanton, and workest contraries to our reach, because thyself is beyond reason. (*Gallathea,* III. i. 102.)

Again:

> Madam, if love were not a thing beyond reason, we might then give a reason of our doings, but so divine is his force, that it worketh effects as contrary to that we wish, as unreasonable against that we ought. (*Gallathea*, III. iv. 54.)

There is no hope of a logical consistency. Constancy is highly valued here; yet at *Love's Metamorphoses*, III. i. 90, we have Niobe remarking that 'the oak findeth no fault with the dew, because it also falleth on the bramble,' and 'the only way to be mad is to be constant.' Infinite are the twisting mazes and contradictions. So in the same play Silvestris speaks of

> Jealousy, without which love is dotage, and with which love is madness; without the which love is lust, and with which love is folly. (IV. i. 22.)

What other writer has so honestly put down the baffling fact? And when we are convinced of love's whimsical and perverse extravagances, Cupid himself (who should know) is found saying:

> Why, Ceres, do you think that lust followeth love? Ceres, lovers are chaste: for what is love, divine love, but the quintessence of chastity, and affections binding by heavenly motions, that cannot be undone by earthly means, and must not be controlled by any man. (*Love's Metamorphoses*, II. i. 122.)

Where chastity does not mean, of course, physical renunciation. This passage, but for the style, might have come from the marriage-service. 'Such is the tying of two in wedlock as is the tuning of two lutes in one key . . .' (*Sapho and Phao*, IV. iii. 75.) And indeed Lyly continually suggests, delicately, a Christian cast of thought: except that his main god is Cupid.

All these passages should be studied in their contexts. I merely point to the range and subtlety of the analysis. From it all Cupid emerges as a great and irrational god, 'no more to be suppressed than comprehended.' (*Sapho and Phao*, II. iv. 17.) *Love's Metamorphoses*, which most explicitly of all points by action and symbolism Lyly's philosophy, shows Cupid's victory over the would-be cold nymphs of Ceres. 'Dare they blaspheme my godhead,' asks Cupid, 'which Jove doth worship, Neptune reverence, and all the gods tremble at?' (IV. i. 60.) That is, love is the greatest of cosmic forces.

Lyly knows its cauterizing pain, its fantastic and frail joys, its godlike strength. It may be set beside some more common-sense, prosaic and rational, essence: friendship in Eumenides, warrior-government in Alexander. But its unreasoned paradoxes are never subdued to moral categories. If Alexander and Cynthia are above love, that is because they are conceived as semi-divine already and play central parts similar to Venus or Cupid elsewhere.

Lyly's love-apprehension is new and striking. His faith in the naked impulse of sexual attraction is exceptionally pure and independent of all moralizings. He is more interested in studying and projecting the impulse than in judging its results. The eros-perception is dramatically best consummated in marriage: but his analyses concern the thing itself, in which positive and negative impressions are inseparable. His conflicts are subtle and intricate with no easy black and white solutions. *The Bower of Bliss,* which is parasitic on a sin-consciousness, is to him an unknown field. The stream of romantic love welling from Provence and fertilizing mediæval allegory is locked now in the tight reservoirs of Lyly's dramatic work, forming new depths. Love has become, for the first time, dramatic, challenging the religious consciousness which, through the centuries preceding, held a monopoly over drama. This forces the creation, or borrowing, of a new, non-Christian, theology. Hellenic myth obviously fits his need. Cupid—variously projected—is his main god. In this he follows mediæval allegory, yet with a certain Hellenic kinship rather than an Ovidian latinity. Also Venus, Ceres, 'Sacred Neptune,' all have their rights. Observe that Ceres in *Love's Metamorphoses* stands for chastity, for marriage-fertility as opposed to love naked and unrelated, Cupid himself not being precisely a marriage god. Lyly's use of divine beings is a sincere mythology. The movement is intensely significant. Drama is close, by its very nature, to religion in that both hold an extra degree of shared, communal, and immediate realism over secondary sorts of literature. Both are ritualistic and involve a temporary living of the action concerned. The Puritan consciousness has always recognized this threat, and consequently opposed the stage. Lyly's work rivals Christian dogma and is itself coloured with many traditional religious tonings. Asked what he thinks of love, Diogenes, a typical sex-opposing ascetic of an extreme and unrealistic sort recalling Thersites and Apemantus, answers—'A little worser than I can of hate.' (*Campaspe,* v. iv. 58.) And observe such a movement as this from *Sapho and Phao:*

SYBIL: Why, do you love, and cannot obtain?
PHAO: No, I may obtain, but cannot love.
SYBIL: Take heed of that, my child!
PHAO: I cannot choose, good madam.
SYBIL: Then hearken to my tale, which I hope shall be as a straight thread to lead you out of those crooked conceits and place you in the plain path of love. (II. i. 33.)

Note (i) the similarity to a Christian confession—Lyly is using old implements for a new task; (ii) the theological supremacy of the god of love; and (iii) the treatment of a psychological case such as might interest the science of to-day. Which leads to another thought. The erotic adventure of Renaissance drama and literature generally is, fundamentally, the propulsive centre of the more generally observed scientific quest of the modern world, its attempt to face actuality afresh and interpret faithfully, without preconceived critical formulæ. Observe this scientific literary awareness finding place in the movement from the mediæval moralities to the dramatic *Interlude of the Four Elements:* as also in Lyly's *Euphues* itself. So, after the rigid certainties of moral theology, Lyly faces instead the mystery of human personality most intensely known in eros-perception in all its paradox and irrationality. Hence one of his plays, *The Woman in the Moon,* is concerned entirely with the creation of woman. The recognition of woman as equal to yet diverse from man is at the back of the whole sex-cult of the modern world. So this genesis-myth shows the infusing into Pandora by various gods of all wayward passions. She is the prototype of Shakespeare's Cleopatra. The limitation of mediæval theology is that it does not allow for a Cleopatra. So, breaking away from moral absolutes, Lyly writes from an original and challenging perception of the life-fire comparable not to mediæval theology but rather to the New Testament itself. He crowns Cupid, or Eros, for the first time in England as lord of dramatic ritual: a place held by him—a jealous little god—ever since, with new cinematograph realms added recently by that very science he also, if the truth were known, inspires.

It may be said I read too deadly a seriousness into a fantastic maker of pretty phrases. Certainly, Lyly can make them—no one better: 'My thoughts, Eumenides, are stitch'd to the stars . . .' (*Endimion,* I. i. 4). Or again,

EUROTA: How did it take you first, Telusa?
TELUSA: By the eyes, my wanton eyes, which conceived the picture

of his face, and hang'd it on the very strings of my heart. (*Gallathea,* III. i. 55.)

These are everywhere. But to point his more philosophic profundity, I shall note a few exquisite miniatures of compressed dialogue of a sort all his own. Here is one:

ALEXANDER: Is love a vice?
HEPHAESTION: It is no virtue. (*Campaspe,* II. ii. 15.)

Was ever intellectual richness so compacted? Love is more ultimate than the moral order, like the rain or sun, beyond praise or blame and careless of both. Yet the moral order is not indicted, far from it. Neither vice nor virtue. Is that a compliment or criticism? We are left uncertain, but supremely aware. Here is another, less pregnant but delightful:

PARMENIDES: Madam, you need not doubt it, it is Alexander that is the conqueror.
TIMOCLEA: Alexander hath overcome, not conquered.
PARMENIDES: To bring all under his subjection is to conquer.
TIMOCLEA: He cannot subdue that which is divine.
PARMENIDES: Thebes was not.
TIMOCLEA: Virtue is. (*Campaspe,* I. i. 41.)

Alexander's talk with Apelles, the painter, is crammed with suggested depths. I point to two:

ALEXANDER: When will you finish Campaspe?
APELLES: Never finish: for always in absolute beauty there is somewhat above art. (*Campaspe,* III. iv. 80.)

Alexander tries his hand at painting:

ALEXANDER: . . . But how have I done here?
APELLES: Like a king.
ALEXANDER: I think so: but nothing more unlike a painter.
(*Campaspe,* III. iv. 110.)

What perfection lies in Apelles' tiny answer, what courtly, humorous, and, finally, philosophic depths! The relative importance of art and learning to soldiership and kingship, the passive and the active life, was a vital Renaissance dualism. So, too, Diogenes' criticisms of kinship go deep:

ALEXANDER: Why then, dost thou owe no reverence to kings?

DIOGENES: No.
ALEXANDER: Why so?
DIOGENES: Because they be no gods.
ALEXANDER: They be gods of the earth.
DIOGENES: Yea, gods of earth. (*Campaspe*, II. ii. 125.)

Campaspe is uniquely strong in this sort, partly because its plot gives less scope for more concrete symbolisms. But you find them elsewhere. In *Endimion* the problem of eternal value and temporal mortality is given completely, and almost answered, in six short phrases ('immortal' is a favourite love-association in Lyly—*Endimion*, I. ii. 34; II. i. 43):

TELLUS: She shall have an end.
ENDIMION: So shall the world (*i.e. that which so argues is itself no less mortal than what it presumes to criticise; observe that Endimion addresses Tellus, the Earth*).
TELLUS: Is not her beauty subject to time?
ENDIMION: No more than time is to standing still (*i.e. it is as much beauty's nature to exist somehow in its own changeless and eternal right as it is for time to move*).
TELLUS: Wilt thou make her immortal?
ENDIMION: No, but incomparable. (II. i. 83.)

It is utterly honest, value is left facing mortality. But, where the terms are 'incomparable,' is reference involving comparison possible? See the two senses subtly held by 'incomparable': (i) excessively beautiful, and (ii) not to be compared with any mortal reasonings. Strange as it sounds, Lyly's excellences in this kind hold something of the quality of Christ's replies in the Gospels: simple and devastating at once because the speaker's mind moves above the irrelevance of the question. Here is my last example and a very pretty one:

SILVESTRIS: Sweet Niobe, let us sing, that I may die with the swan.
NIOBE: It will make you sigh the more, and live with the salamich (*i.e. salamander*).
SILVESTRIS: Are thy tunes fire?
NIOBE: Are yours death? (*Love's Metamorphoses*, III. i. 128.)

With which I close my list. Note that they are by nature dramatic, not so much proving or disproving a point, but balancing one way of thinking against another.

Lyly's mind is essentially philosophic; but it is no less essentially poetical. I offer an example of his use of gentle surprise, his way of revealing unexpected depths of exquisite symbolic artistry. The three lovers in *Love's Metamorphoses* have been rejected; and in revenge persuaded Cupid to turn their ladies respectively into a rock, a rose, and a bird. (Observe: mineral, vegetable, and animal, recalling the 'scientific' universe of *Euphues.*) As the play draws to its close and other complications are smoothed out, the lovers get Cupid to reverse his miracle. There are only a few pages left and you expect an easy conventional agreement. But the ladies still refuse: if need be, they will be metamorphosed again, but love they will not. One is at a loss as to Cupid's answer: it is perfect. If they will not love normally he will turn them next into life-forms thoroughly loathsome. Observe how the symbolism—as so often—offers opportunity for a profound psychological interpretation. Next see Lyly ring the changes on his symbols. The men are penitent and excuse their original action thus: one only wished to end his life on the rock; the next to spend his existence gazing on the rose and so die; the third, that his love might fly for ever from him, to cause his own death. The girls melt—but it is not quite over. One stipulates that her husband attributes any coldness or hardness in her to her rocky experience; the next, that if she is shrewish her husband remember roses have thorns; the third, that if she is not always at home, it is to be remembered her lover first gave her wings. Again, deep meanings are softly shadowed, meanings that involve the reciprocal antagonisms and rights of the sexes: remember Pandora. Notice, too, how the central symbols remain fixed while the author and his persons play with them, extract meanings from them. This is the way of the purest symbolism as opposed to allegory: a true symbol does not properly 'stand instead of' something else. Meanings can be found in it: it is not conditioned by any meaning.

Each play has a controlled and variably significant design. *Campaspe* is human and simple. *Endimion* is the most imaginatively compressed and involved, thick with close-enwoven suggestions, perhaps even too dense and opaque in contemporary meaning. *Love's Metamorphoses* is probably the most intellectually profound, with a beautifully transparent symbolism. The Neptune sacrifice of a maiden in *Gallathea* is interesting, 'sacred Neptune,' it may be, representing floods of violent passion to be contrasted with the love-god who sets the difficulties to rights, since love in Lyly is more æsthetic than sensual: Lyly is in his way a moralist, though under Cupid's ensign; never exactly a sensuous writer. He is 'intellectual' compared with

Spenser, or even such a work as Drayton's *Endimion.* Beneath his English pastoralism and Hellenic mythology—note the woods of Lincolnshire delightfully and characteristically made the home of a Neptune cult in *Gallathea*—there is continually meaning, though it would be unwise to pluck at it too fiercely. Behind the miraculous changes arranged by Cupid in more than one play are possible psychological significances as I have already noticed. Sometimes there are dark, almost tragic essences: the passion of Tellus in *Endimion;* the money-greedy Erisichthon's cutting of the tree sacred to Ceres and its consequent pain—a fine opportunity for symbolic interpretation—in *Love's Metamorphoses;* satire on greed again in *Midas,* with again the obvious contrast of metallic and natural values. But mainly such poisonous evils are avoided, and analysis and plot both confined to the infinite complexities of love, with a steady movement towards a ceremonious conclusion.

Shakespeare's debt to Lyly has been often emphasized; though it is as much a natural kinship as a debt. Thought-parallels bristle on page after page. I would stress a wider parallel of design, a measured and purposive working out of complications unfurling to a satisfying, often somewhat ritualistic, close. This, so beautifully executed in Lyly, is part of the Shakespearian art always. And I do not mean only Shakespeare's lighter work. Lyly's thought points the mind as much to the metaphysic of love in *Troilus and Cressida* and *Antony and Cleopatra* as to *Love's Labour's Lost* and the *Sonnets.* So, too, the central dream in *Endimion* and its recapitulation at the end forecast Posthumus' dream and description in *Cymbeline:* note the part played by the eagle in both plays. And the conclusions, and indeed the whole designs, are so ceremoniously satisfying through use especially of two sorts of *centrality,* both throwing forward to Shakespeare.

First, there are central dominating figures: Cynthia, Venus, Cupid, Alexander. All the plays reflect Elizabethan royalism in that they possess some dominant and central figure of worldly or divine authority or, as in *Endimion,* of both; persons of power on whom everything depends, and who yet do not steal the whole action like Marlowe's protagonists. This reflects, of course, the Queen-centred court-life of the plays' origin. And we see how Lyly and Shakespeare constructed admirable art-forms (remember Shakespeare always has his king or duke) partly because the Queen-centred life around Elizabeth was itself of art-form quality: they had a hub on which to revolve. Moreover, a hub that could inspire a belief—however transient—like this:

> GYPTES: They are thrice fortunate that live in your palace, where Truth is not in colours, but life, virtues not in imagination, but execution.
>
> CYNTHIA: I have always studied to have rather living virtues than painted Gods; the body of Truth, than the tomb.
>
> (*Endimion,* IV. iii. 48.)

Which shows how an earthly paradise was, or seemed, at hand to the Elizabethan imagination. The actual was eros-impregnated on a grand scale, and Elizabethan literature is one of the results. The synthesis of loyalty and eroticism in Endimion's adoration for Cynthia points ahead to the twin positive forces of Shakespeare's work: the romantic and kingly ideals, not so distinct then as now. Kindred dual feelings are blent into Shakespeare's sonnets, neither flattery nor sexual emotion quite, but something to us slightly alien, made of both.

There are, secondly, central symbols, the impregnating of some object with a central significance, such as the Well, or the sleeping figure of the hero himself, in *Endimion,* or the Tree both in *Gallathea* and *Love's Metamorphoses.* Such a symbol taking as it were the stage-centre of the play's massed area (and often it will therefore be an object central on the actual stage) lends concreteness and focal length to the action round it; serves as a heart to the organism, as the central person is its spine and head and the ceremonial conclusion its crown. Time and again art-forms of Shakespearian texture, whether in poem, play, or novel, show such central symbolisms: something both created by and reacting on, the dominant conflicts concerned; the body's heart.

Lyly's formalized and ceremonious designs enclose acts of sacrifice or other ritual and devotion to one or other of his gods. A fervent piety breathes in all these, especially in the sublimation and victory of Cupid over the chastity of Ceres' nymphs in *Love's Metamorphoses,* and the friendly exchange of sacrifices between the two divinities, Cupid and Ceres; reflecting a synthesis of naked desire and marriage fertility, perhaps of all Lyly's most significant symbolic stroke of art. Sacrifice and piety are intrinsic to Lyly's conception of love; a humble, rich, sweetly human thing. Campaspe and Apelles talk of Venus, who can, of course, almost be equated with Cupid:

CAMPASPE: How is she hired: by prayer, by sacrifice, or bribes?
APELLES: By prayer, sacrifice, and bribes.
CAMPASPE: What prayer?
APELLES: Vows irrevocable.
CAMPASPE: What sacrifice?
APELLES: Hearts ever sighing, never dissembling.
CAMPASPE: What bribes?
APELLES: Roses and kisses: but were you never in love?
CAMPASPE: No, nor love in me. (*Campaspe,* III. iii. 34.)

Notice the religious tonings. Lyly's religious feeling in the plays may recall his more specifically Christian and Biblical moralizings in *Euphues.* He was saturated in all that first before becoming an artistic devotee of his eros-cult. This is correspondingly sweetened and ennobled. It is his essential humility and purity before direct human experience that brings Lyly closest to Shakespeare and makes his humour sympathetic and kindly, the antithesis of Jonson's: compare his satire on alchemists (in *Gallathea*) with Jonson's. Lyly's comedy there with the Astronomer, who falls in a ditch whilst studying the stars, is, characteristically, a humour playing around the philosophic. Such humour (of Shakespearian sort) is, like his dialogue, dependent often on a sudden awareness of a big simplicity breaking through a slight complexity. Remember his delightful fun with Latin tags in *Endimion;* with Sir Tophas as 'three quarters of a noun-substantive'; and remember he is a schoolmaster, producing with his boys as players. A deeper wisdom puts learning in its place: yet surely no Elizabethan used learning to better purpose; nor any literary genius of the first order in English literature was more fit to be, as well, a teacher of children.

For this is, in short, his humanistic message.

> There is no man so savage in whom resteth not this divine particle, that there is an omnipotent, eternal, and divine mover, which may be called God. (*Campaspe,* I. iii. 35.)

And, yet, paradoxically—and to be true to him we must preserve a paradox:

> I cannot see, Montanus, why it is feigned by the poets that love sat upon the chaos and created the world; since in the world there is so little love.
>
> (*Love's Metamorphoses,* I. i. 1.)

That may be. But it is not the fault of Lyly's plays.

NOTE

1. The references follow R. Warwick Bond's fine and indispensable edition of Lyly's works, Oxford University Press, 1902. Spelling, and in some instances punctuation, have, however, been modernized.

WILLIAM EMPSON

The Spanish Tragedy

It seems to me that *The Spanish Tragedy* of Kyd has been underrated through misunderstanding, as I shall try to show in this article. The question may seem remote, but the play is commonly regarded as the surviving analogue to the *Ur-Hamlet* of Kyd, so has a considerable bearing on Shakespeare's *Hamlet;* or at least on what the first audience thought Shakespeare was doing when he rewrote the old favourite, a thing which they had laughed at even before they decided it was out of date.

So far as I have seen, critics always take for granted that the Ghost of Andrea has no point; Kyd was crude, and anyhow he was copying Seneca. I think the point was obvious at the time, so obvious that it did not get stated in the text. Andrea has suffered the fate of Uriah; the father and brother of Belimperia, that is, the Duke of Castile and Lorenzo, had arranged to have him killed in battle so that they could marry her to Balthazar the Prince of Portugal. Presumably they informed the enemy Prince, who killed him in the battle, where he was going to be sent and how he could be recognized. There is a reason for not mentioning this (though I agree that one would expect the Ghost to say it at the end) because the Ghost is part of the audience, and it has been arranged by the Queen of Hades that he must discover what happened to him, without being told. The culprits themselves, of course, have no occasion to mention it. If this is assumed, the audience has the interest of keeping half an eye on the Ghost, to see whether he has guessed the point yet, while the Ghost watches the actors and the actors watch the play-within-the-play. I do not think this bold conception has been given its due.

From *Nimbus,* III (Summer 1956), pp. 16–29. Reprinted by permission of the author.

The Ghost opens the play by entering with Revenge, and makes clear at once that he knows of no reason for revenging himself. His coolness all round, indeed, compared to Hamlet's Father for example, is very refreshing. (However, we cannot suppose that the Ur-Father-Hamlet was cool, since the only thing we hear about him is that he was pale and cried Revenge miserably like an oyster-wife; this would at least prevent the two plays from being absurdly similar.) When alive he was at the Spanish Court, he says, and was accepted as a lover by a lady above his social position, not that his position was bad; then he happened to get killed in a war with Portugal. The puzzle began when he got to the classical Hades; the officials there couldn't decide whether he was a lover or a soldier, so he was referred up in the administrative machine to the King and Queen. Proserpina smiled, and asked Pluto to let her settle it; then she whispered in the ear of Revenge, and the two have arrived back on earth. Revenge says Andrea will see his Belimperia kill the man who killed himself (Andrea); 'here sit we down to see the mystery.' But on the face of it there is no mystery, and no reason why the administration of Hades should be disturbed, let alone why Proserpina should grin and whisper. The Ghost also sees something else, which he is not told beforehand; Belimperia chooses another lover, Horatio, and Horatio is killed by her brother Lorenzo, so that there will again be no obstacle to her marrying the Prince of Portugal. Surely all this has only one possible point; Andrea is to guess that her family had previously arranged, in the same way, to kill himself.

We may pause at 'Here sit we down' to ask where they sit. The text as we have it seems planned for a full Elizabethan stage, and it looks as if the play-within-the-play was done on the inner stage, with the courtly audience on the balcony, rather absurdly pretending that the spectacle was in front of them. In any case, human listeners appear 'above' at II. ii, the imprisoned Belimperia appears 'at a window' in III. ix, and before the play-within-the-play Hieronymo asks the Duke to throw him down the key after the audience has gone up (this gives him a bit of time to harangue them before they 'break down the doors'). Thus Ghost and Revenge can't be 'above'; I take it they sit right out in front, each of them leaning against one of the pillars which held up the Heavens. This puts them on a rather homely footing, and makes clear that they are part of the audience, except that most of the time Revenge is asleep.

At I. iv, Belimperia hears about Andrea's death from Horatio, who captured Balthazar just after he had killed Andrea. Andrea, he says, had fought long with Balthazar, but then Fate took a hand and 'brought a fresh supply of halberdiers, Which paunched his horse and dinged him to the ground'; then Balthazar 'finished' him, 'taking advantage of his foe's distress.' Belimperia, after Horatio has gone, finds this sufficient reason to want revenge on Balthazar, and to make Horatio her lover for the purpose:

> But how can love find harbour in my breast
> Till I revenge the death of my beloved?
> Yes, second love shall further my revenge.
> I'll love Horatio, my Andrea's friend,
> The more to spite the prince that wrought his end;
> And where Don Balthazar, that slew my love,
> Himself now pleads for favour at my hands,
> He shall, in rigour of my just disdain,
> Reap long repentance for his murderous deed.
> For what was't else but murderous cowardice
> So many to oppress one valiant knight
> Without respect of honour in the fight?

However, she clearly doesn't mean to kill him for his unsporting behaviour—she assumes he will have 'long repentance'; nor would the audience think it an adequate reason for the Ghost to be sent back by Proserpina. The audience can however notice that the halberdiers arrived very opportunely; maybe they weren't sent only by Fate. By the way, on the stage Belimperia has not yet met Balthazar; it is assumed that for dynastic reasons he is already her suitor, not that he fell in love with her on meeting her after his capture. At II. i. 45, when Lorenzo is extracting the secret of Belimperia's love for Horatio from her servant Pedringano, we learn that her father was angry at her love for Andrea, and that the watchful Lorenzo then saved Pedringano from being punished as a go-between, apparently to use him later; it all helps to make the fate of Andrea look suspicious. The nearest we get to an admission of the murder is in the evasive language which Lorenzo uses to Belimperia when he is explaining why he locked her up (III. x). He says it is essential for her honour that he should protect her from herself, so when he happened to find her with Horatio—

> Why then, remembering that old disgrace
> Which you for Don Andrea had endured
> And now were likely longer to sustain

By being found so meanly companied
Thought rather—for I knew no readier means—
To thrust Horatio forth my father's way.

We learn nothing about how she interprets this; she is behaving with fierce dignity, especially because of the presence of Balthazar. We do not see her again for some time, apart from two riddling answers in public, till IV. i. where she upbraids Hieronymo for not having done his revenge, threatens to do it herself, and promises to help him (prefiguring Lady Macbeth and the Queen of *Hamlet* Q1). One might think that her brother's remark had some geographical meaning, that Horatio was banished from the town by a private gate; but she would know this to be a lie; she saw the murder, said so at the time, and told about it in her letter afterwards. Thus there seems no meaning for 'I thrust him forth my father's way' except 'I killed him, as my father did Andrea.' It is meant of course to be the more thrilling because obscure.[1]

The idea that the Duke is guilty appears again prominently at the end, though he has always kept up an innocent appearance. The last act of Hieronymo before he kills himself is to kill the Duke; this might be merely a sign of madness, or might give him a complete revenge against the son, but I do not think the audience would find that satisfying. In any case, the Ghost of Andrea is then allowed by Revenge to arrange punishments for the villains; he starts the list cheerfully with the Duke, and it is clear that Revenge thinks this proper. The reason must be (though poor Hieronymo may not have been told by Belimperia, and the audience only know it from the phrase 'my father's way') that the Duke had arranged the death of Andrea.

The reason why we have this Duke in the caste, brother to a childless King, is I take it simply to avoid revenge against a King, which would be too wicked on the separate ground of Divine Right; the King has then to be childless to make the proposed marriage of Belimperia dynastic. We gather from III. xiv. that Lorenzo has hidden his murder of Horatio from the Duke, which seems unnecessary as he must know the Duke would approve; but it adds to the mystery to make the Duke a complete hypocrite, and no doubt Lorenzo himself is merely keeping to his principles:

no man knows it was my fetching reach.
Tis hard to trust unto a multitude,

Or any one, in mine opinion,
When men themselves their secrets will reveal.

The effect of the speech (III. iv. 45) is a challenge to the audience to discover further secrets.

Going back to the scene of Lorenzo with his sister, the actors need to make clear that he is trying to break her spirit. Soon after the riddle about 'my father's way,' which she ought to receive as a horrible flash of light, she asks with her usual firm dignity whether her father has not inquired for her while Lorenzo kept her imprisoned, and he breaks the formality of their dialogue (Balthazar being present) by saying he must whisper in her ear. We heard about this before she entered; Balthazar remarked that she had better be released soon because her father was asking for her, and Lorenzo said jauntily:

Lor. Why, and my lord, I hope you heard me say
Sufficient reason why she kept away.
But that's all one. My lord, you love her?
Bal. Ay.
Lor. Then in your love beware; deal cunningly

and so forth; 'jest with her gently,' which in view of the other jokes in the play may be expected to mean something appalling. He might simply have told her father that she was prostrated by the murder of her lover, but why need such a story be whispered to her? I take it the audience presumed him to whisper, perhaps falsely, that he had told her father she was procuring an abortion. She could make this clear by a flash of horror and disgust, though she must recover at once her contemptuous grandeur towards both of them:

Too politic for me, past all compare,
Since last I saw you; but content yourself,
The prince is meditating higher things.

(i.e. 'Balthazar is too holy to have overheard you'). The play should be rather like an opera, with the end-stopped lines pronounced next door to song, so this break is a strong dramatic effect; what had to be whispered, presumably, was what could not be said in the high language of the Honour of Spain. She ends the scene with a riddle about fear in Latin, and no doubt this would easily suggest Seneca and a determination to revenge.

I think, then, that the play could be produced so as to make pretty clear to the audience that Andrea had been murdered for love, but I admit that it is peculiar for the text never to say it. A mystery is dramatic, but you expect to have an answer at the end of the play, and the Ghost could give it in one line. Perhaps he did, and it got dropped from the printed text. But there were several editions, the first probably earlier than the first dated one of 1594, and you might argue that even the Elizabethans would want to restore such an important omission. However, though the answer would need to be made clear to the first audiences (if only by the production), the first readers would know it already, not buy the quarto to find it. In any case, the Ghost at the end could not say much about himself, because the audience has rather lost interest in his story compared to what they have seen; he settles down contentedly to the administrative work of giving the villains suitable torments in his classical Hades. He is an unusual type of Ghost, and one may imagine that from the first he didn't bother to draw the moral about himself; thus perhaps recovering some of the mystery which he had otherwise so frankly thrown away.

Another peculiar thing about him is that he is entirely unjealous; to watch Belimperia giving herself to Horatio excites no complaint. He does indeed complain at the end of Act I that he is only shown 'league, love, and banqueting' instead of revenge as expected (Revenge gives him a brief appalling reassurance), but presumably he would mention the infidelity of Belimperia if he felt it as such; and at the end of Act II he combines their names without the smallest resentment:

> Broughtst thou me hither to increase my pain?
> I looked that Balthazar should have been slain.
> But 'tis my friend Horatio that is slain;
> And they abuse fair Belimperia
> On whom I doted more than all the world
> Because she loved me more than all the world.

(Revenge gives him a brief appalling reassurance). For that matter, Belimperia while imprisoned (III. ix. 9) herself appeals to the Ghost of Andrea, taking for granted that he would not mind her change to Horatio:

> Andrea, oh Andrea! That thou sawest
> Me for thy friend Horatio handled thus,
> And him for me thus causeless murdered!

By the way, this almost necessitates some reaction from the Ghost, so he may be presumed to have reacted elsewhere; I think Revenge ought to have to hush him, both here and at the words 'my father's way.' The appeal seems to get him worked up, though in a stupid manner, because after Act III (there are only four acts) he needs a longer interlude. He is distressed at finding all quarrels apparently quieted, and Belimperia agreeing to marry the prince of Portugal. The audience are to think the poor creature rather dull, because the agreement of Hieronymo is patently false, and we only hear from Belimperia three and a half lines of harsh double-talk. Revenge while trying to reassure him uses an exact echo of the riddling talk of Hieronymo in III. xiii, and prepares us for more of it in IV. i:

> Nor dies Revenge, although he sleeps a while,
> For in unquiet, quietness is feigned,
> And slumbering is a common worldly wile.

This proves to the audience that Hieronymo is a correct Revenger; and indeed a Revenger always wants to be somehow Revenge in person. It is inadequate to calm the Ghost, who is only made to shut up ('argue not') by being given a separate Dumb Show with an explanation of it. He then says

> Sufficeth me: thy meaning's understood;
> And thanks to thee, and those infernal powers
> That will not tolerate a lover's woe.

Now the combination of this grand phrase with his complete friendship to Horatio cuts out all but one interpretation; the Lover's Woe has to be the Arranged Marriage. I understand that this custom was almost universal, at least in the sense that the families were expected to come to an agreement about the money affairs of a young couple; but the theatre was always in favour cf the lovers as against the Arranged Marriage, and no doubt it was echoing a state of sentiment which often avoided harshness in borderline cases. Now, if you wanted to have a play against the Arranged Marriage, the royal marriages of Spain and Portugal gave the most impressive example you could find. It is clear that dynastic importance attaches to the marriage of Belimperia and Balthazar; as early as II. iii. 20, by way of settling the war, the King says to the Portuguese Ambassador (after referring to the dowry from the lady's father),

> in case this match go forward
> The tribute which you pay shall be released;
> And if by Balthazar she have a son
> He will enjoy the kingdom after us.

One might assume that this meant giving Spain itself to the royal family of Portugal, but he never speaks of excluding his nephew Lorenzo, and Portugal is only ruled by a Viceroy, whose failure to pay tribute has caused the war. He means that Portugal would be allowed to recover its independent sovereignty in favour of a son of this marriage. The only problem is that, if Lorenzo is the heir to both Spain and Portugal, he can hardly want to commit all these murders merely in order to make his sister produce an independent heir to Portugal. He might conceivably argue, in a statesmanlike manner, that Portugal is getting too hard to hold under the present system. Presumably the audience wouldn't bother much; they would only feel sure that the marriage somehow mattered a great deal.

The question of course was a major one of current politics. Spain and Portugal had acquired the first maritime empires, and the Pope had divided America between them. For England, the great enemy was Spain, and Spain when the play was new had recently acquired by inheritance the whole empire of Portugal. That is, Philip II took it in 1580 and made a reasonable hereditary claim; he had to send an army to Lisbon, and I gather had other grounds such as that the Portuguese had been trying to take Morocco, but the hereditary claim was an essential part. One could hardly say that he got Portugal by marriage; he got it because the more direct male heirs of that house had become too holy to produce children; but he got it by an earlier royal marriage, and that is the kind of thing the play envisages. Emanuel the Fortunate, I learn from the encyclopaedia, in whose reign the Portuguese Empire was founded, 'had pursued the traditional policy of intermarriage with royal families of Castile and Aragon, hoping to weld together the Spanish and Portuguese dominions'; as indeed he did, though sexually the wrong way round for his purpose. (The arrangement, with Portugal technically independent but happening to have as its King the King of Spain, lasted till 1640.) One might think the first audiences would be in favour of Belimperia for liking brave native lovers and refusing to unite Spain with Portugal, but politically they would have to be in favour of this marriage, because it might separate Spain from Portugal. Presumably they would also be rather shocked by her because it is made so clear that she goes to bed with her lovers (among the first words of the play are 'In secret I possessed a worthy dame.') One would assume that all the characters were a bit wicked, but the main sentiment would be against these oppressively important royal marriages (which the Queen of England had been quite right to refuse); one would take for granted that any amount of murder would be done before such a thing was arranged.

A slight suggestion that all these characters are wicked no doubt helps to bring in the idea of Fate, which gets rather unusual treatment. Some critics have called the Ghost a clumsy and undramatic device because, not only pointless, he has no effect on the action. In any case, it is dramatic to be able to glance at the Ghost in the audience, as you might at one of your friends, and wonder whether he has got on to the point yet. But I also think it is symbolically good as expressing a moral truth. Swinburne wrote about the *Hamlet* of Shakespeare that the characters 'veer sideways to their doom'; this is true in general about the Elizabethan Revenge Play, rather than making as he supposed a contrast between the First and Second Quarto. May I express here my impatience with 'Fate'; it seems both logical nonsense and harmful in its historical effects. But in the story before us we can give the word a reasonable interpretation; if this family keeps on killing the daughter's suitors, one after another, to make a grand marriage, then it does seem likely to run into trouble some time. Persephone might intelligibly smile when she told Andrea to go and see what happened next. Revengers indeed are usually presented as acting in a roundabout manner, chiefly perhaps because they dislike what they are trying to approach; and the catastrophe is usually arranged to come as much from the nature of the villains as from the loony though fascinating calculations of the Revenger. In this play, for example, Lorenzo is only discovered because he is so vainly ingenious about getting his tools to kill each other off. However, though this gives us a tolerable meaning for Fate, I must admit it is not one that a Revenger while in mental turmoil would accept. He wants to take part in Fate; he wants to show that he is acting *as* or *like* Fate, which itself evidently works in a roundabout way. Such is the doom of Old Hieronymo, but the Ghost is spared it; he sits among the audience listening with some impatience while the Revenger babbles about how clever and useful it is for him to be mad. I have come to think that this early play gave a more profound treatment of Revenge than the later ones.

It can be presumed, I think, that the *Ur-Hamlet,* with its handfuls of speeches and the Ghost crying miserably like an oyster-wife, had been written before *The Spanish Tragedy.* The French of Belleforest was an easily accessible source for Hamlet, and likely to be combed for material—it was a big collection of moral tales; whereas for *The Spanish Tragedy* no source has ever been found. None could be, if it was simply an attempt to apply the technique and atmosphere of the *Ur-Hamlet* to the highly topical theme of the royal marriages of Spain. The basic idea would be 'Take a woman who revolted against one of these shocking royal marriages, and you would get a similar case of madness and revenge.' Like so many previous critics, I am putting a lot of weight on the *Ur-Hamlet* for conjectural arguments, but to do that one need not assume it was very good (indeed, it seems plausible as well as comforting to suppose that no very good Elizabethan play failed to hit print). It was a decisively important foundation, or piece of basic engineering, for the Elizabethan drama, because it showed them how to express something they wanted to (if you like, how to adapt their Seneca to the Christian conscience and the Renaissance code of honour); but Kyd would have learned a bit by experience, the year after his initial success, when he entirely transposed his material into *The Spanish Tragedy.* This would be a good reason why only the second play got printed, though no doubt there were accidental causes as well.

I am assuming that the audiences of the first period of Elizabethan drama thought revenge wicked, and that a dramatist trying to present a revenger had to reckon with the weight of that feeling. This is handled by the structure of the play, before it advances on the serious case of Hieronymo; such is the only purpose of the rather absurd sub-plot, about events at the court of Portugal. The first time human characters speak of revenge is when the Viceroy is brooding over the fate of his son if captured in the battle; a courtier suggests that the Spaniards would not make 'a breach of common law of arms,' but he answers, in the first of the grand echoing lines of which the play is so full,

> They reck no laws that meditate revenge.

A courtier in reply calls revenge 'foul.' We then see the captured son insisting with high rhetoric (II. i. 111–133) that revenge is essential to his nature if the woman refuses the marriage which his plans demand;

Yet I must take revenge, or die myself,

he says, if she has another lover. The dramatic irony is heightened if we already suspect that he had been tipped off to kill her previous lover in the battle. In any case, he is presented early as the admittedly wicked type of man who takes revenge for granted, therefore as very unlike the final revenger Hieronymo.

Some critics have said that in a crude play like *The Spanish Tragedy* the revenger is simply mad, whereas the whole subtlety and profundity of Shakespeare consisted in introducing doubt as to whether the hero was mad or not. This sounds likely, but I believe it is now generally admitted to be wrong. It underrates the general moral background of the audience, apart from their native wits; and the questions which were being discussed in the theatre, in a theatrical manner as one might expect, had a good deal of practical importance. I want now to advance on a rather lengthy attempt to prove that Hieronymo is just like Hamlet in being both mad and not mad, both wise and not wise, and so forth.

The last action of Hieronymo, before the trick by which he secures a knife to kill the Duke and himself, is to bite out his tongue lest tortures force him to confess his secret. Many critics have complained at the 'sensationalism' of this, particularly as he seems to have no secret to tell. I think they would have discovered the point if they had allowed themselves to speak with less restraint; the incident is wildly absurd, as it was meant to be, because Hieronymo has just told the bereaved fathers everything he possibly could.

And to this end the bashaw I became
That might revenge me on Lorenzo's life,
Who therefore was appointed to the part
And was to represent the knight of Rhodes
That I might kill him more conveniently.
So, Viceroy, was this Balthazar, thy son,
That Soliman which Belimperia,
In person of Perseda, murdered,
Solely appointed to that tragic part
That she might slay him who offended her.
Poor Belimperia missed her part in this
For though the story saith she should have died
Yet I of kindness, and of care to her,
Did otherwise determine of her end;

But love of him whom they did hate too much
Did urge her resolution to be such.

Nothing could seem madder than this professorial tone, patiently explaining at length what is already obvious, with a pedantic satisfaction in making clear where there were little errors of detail. But at last, when he has finished telling everything, a great wave of revulsion comes over him; there is something he must never tell, at all costs; so he bites out his tongue. This is very imaginative, I think, and the whole point of it is that he is now completely mad. The reason why critics have not found this obvious, I suspect, is that they were ready to assume the old play would commit any absurdity, just to have some more blood splashing about, and also ready to let the development of the character be obscured by Jonson's additions. Jonson removed the incident of biting out the tongue and put in some poetical mad talk instead; no doubt it had come to seem too absurd altogether, *too* un-life-like, by 1600. But really his additions, as a whole, made the old play much *more* un-life-like, because he was going all out to satisfy 'the modern convention' of the Revenge Play. He makes Hieronymo raging mad as soon as he finds his son dead, and from then on another splendid bout of madness is inserted at each convenient point; then each time we return to the old text and find him sane enough to carry on his plot. But in the crude old play he is only gradually pushed into madness, just as he is only gradually pushed into revenge; he disapproves of both, but cannot keep them from him; a long period of grizzling over his wrong and puzzling over his duty has to be gone through, and all this time he is getting madder. Just before he gets to the deed of blood his wife kills herself because he hasn't yet done it; this ought to be enough to show that he is assumed to feel powerful resistances against it. And after he at last has done it, instead of being 'pleased and eased' as he boasts, he is for the first time completely off his rocker. Presumably the audience knew that a man would be unable to bite out his tongue unless in a highly abnormal condition. All this makes a much more human and sensible picture of revenge and its madness than you get from the play with Jonson's additions, though I confess that the old version would be very hard to put over on a modern audience, as no doubt Jonson felt about his own audience. The theatre of Kyd was presumably very formalized both in acting style and in the way the audience was meant to interpret; they were to feel that biting out the tongue symbolized something true, rather than that this individual had already convinced them he had a character likely to do it.

The contrast between the periods looks rather more definite if one considers Jonson himself. We know from Henslowe's accounts that he was twice paid to write Additions to Hieronymo, in 1601 and 1602, and it seems clear that this marks an attempt by the Admiral's Company to offer an adequate counter to Shakespeare's *Hamlet* (incidentally I think Shakespeare was also offering further 'additions' in the second year). Some critics carry their reverence for style so far that even with the accounts in front of them they refuse to believe Jonson wrote the existing Additions, because they aren't 'in Jonson's style'; so Henslowe must have paid somebody else for better Additions than Jonson's, and these are what got printed. From what we know of Henslowe it is extremely unlikely that he tossed money about in this manner, and I don't think it at all unlikely that Jonson could write in a different style if he was challenged and paid to. He was then 29, rather struggling for his position, and a very clever man. It does him great credit that he could write so wonderfully in the high Elizabethan romantic manner:

> Confusion, mischief, torment, death and hell
> Drop all your stings at once in my cold bosom
> That now is stiff with horror: kill me quickly.
> Be gracious to me, thou infective night,
> And drop this deed of murder down on me;
> Gird in my waste of grief with thy large darkness
> And let me not survive to see the light
> May put me in the mind I had a son.

(this is Hieronymo when he has just discovered the corpse); but one can understand that he did not want to print it in his collected edition. No doubt he didn't himself know quite how far his tongue was in his cheek; but in any case he was trying to satisfy a demand, he was writing to a very clear-cut 'convention.' Whereas, when Kyd wrote the old version, the convention had not yet been established; he needed to make his basic development of character much more reasonable and in accordance with serious moral opinion, even though the incidents he used could be less realistic. This view, I submit, gives a consistent explanation of the difficulties of the texts.

I must admit that Hieronymo speaks of revenge soon after he has discovered the body. He has twenty lines of lament before his wife enters, then:

Isabella. What world of grief! My son Horatio!
O, where's the author of this endless woe?
Hier. To know the author were some ease of grief;
For in revenge my heart must find relief.

He tells her that he will keep the bloody handkerchief till he takes revenge, and tells her to dissemble her sorrow for the present: 'so shall we sooner find the practice out.' It seems to be the lament of the mother which puts this practical idea into his head. Even so, they both appear to be thinking in terms of law; as when Isabella says 'The heavens are just; murder cannot be hid.' It is only when the heir to the throne is found to be implicated that normal justice is assumed to be impossible. The discovery of the body is at the end of Act II; in Act III. i. we are taken away to see the Viceroy of Portugal doing injustice because of the false witness of a villain, and the victim says

Nor discontents it me to leave the world
With whom there nothing can prevail but wrong

Then sc. ii. begins with the famous soliloquy of Hieronymo denouncing all the world, as

Confused and filled with murder and misdeeds.

The whole scene is darkening. He feels he is being dragged into revenge; both night and day, he says, are driving him to seek the murderer, and

The ugly fiends do sally forth of Hell
And frame my steps to unfrequented paths
And fear my heart with fierce inflamed thoughts.

These lines can only mean that he partly suspects the whole process of revenge to be a bad one. Next the letter falls, written by the imprisoned Belimperia in her blood to accuse her brother. Hieronymo like Hamlet is suspicious of this first evidence, and warns himself that it may only be intended to prevent his revenge by inducing him to make a false accusation against Lorenzo, which would endanger his life. In spite of this caution to himself, he immediately does excite the suspicion of Lorenzo, who enters at once, and Lorenzo therefore sets to work to cover his tracks by killing both his accomplices. This is done by getting one of them, Pedringano, to kill the other, and then having him hanged for it; Pedringano believes till the last moment that Lorenzo will get him off. We next see Hieronymo in sc. vi, acting in his function as judge; he begins by bemoaning that 'neither gods nor men be just to *me*.' The refusal of Pedringano to pray before he is hanged (actually because he can see the boy holding the box which he believes to contain his pardon) draws from Hieronymo his most splendid sentence against the revengeful mind.

> I have not seen a wretch so impudent.
> O monstrous times, where murder's set so light,
> And where the soul, that should be shrined in heaven,
> Solely delights in interdicted things,
> Still wandering in the thorny passages
> That intercept itself of happiness.
> Murder! O bloody monster! God forbid
> A fault so foul should scape unpunished.
> Despatch, and see this execution done!
> This makes me to remember thee, my son.

In a way it is dramatic irony against Hieronymo, who fails to apply this reflection to himself. But it is not heavily against him; he is speaking as a judge, and we are not meant to think him wrong for wanting justice to be done. By the way, there is evidence here that our text at any rate leaves out stage directions, because no use is made of the boy standing by with the box. When Pedringano demands life 'by my pardon from the king,' and the hangman replies

> Stand you on that? Then you shall off with this.
> *Turns him off.*

it is clear that Pedringano must point at the boy with the box, who opens it with hearty laughter showing it to be empty, before the hangman dare proceed. A critic may reasonably impute other omitted 'business' elsewhere, such as might clear up the mystery about Andrea.

In sc. vii. Hieronymo in soliloquy is a noticeable degree crazier; he has

> Made mountains marsh with spring-tides of my tears
> And broken through the brazen gates of hell,
> Yet still tormented is my tortured soul . . .

Then the Hangman brings a letter written by Pedringano in prison, begging Lorenzo to hurry up, and pleading for himself 'I holp to murder Don Horatio too.' Hieronymo is now convinced that the letter written in blood was true; and by the way he hasn't learned it by any of the subtlety he proposed—the prison letter is merely handed on to him as the officiating judge. For that matter, Hamlet's pretence of madness in Saxo does not let him find out who the murderer is (a thing universally known), and even in Shakespeare it at most only makes the king act suspiciously—what convinces Hamlet is the play-within-the-play. Hamlet in Saxo has superfine senses (like the fairy-story princess who was black and blue from the pea under the nineteen mattresses), and Belleforest makes this 'rational' by explaining he was a magician. Shakespeare may have been drawing on this tradition for the piercing and testing quality of the mad talk of his Hamlet, but I don't suppose it was much use to the Hamlet of Kyd. The main thrill about his talk was that he could tell the truth without being believed.

Hieronymo deduces from this accident that Heaven is arranging to punish the murderer by letting out the truth (ll. 50 and 58). He is still thinking as a judge, and can say as such that 'nought but blood can satisfy my woes'; indeed, not only does he still hope to get this blood lawfully, but he noticeably refuses to threaten that he will otherwise get it unlawfully.

> I will go plain me to my lord the king
> And cry aloud for justice through the court
> Wearing the flints with these my withered feet;
> And either purchase justice by entreats
> Or tire them all with my revenging threats.

There should I suppose be a dramatic pause after 'Or.' We next see him, after three more scenes, on his way to the Court for this procedure; and he is now, perhaps from reflecting on the difficulty of it, at a stage where passers-by call him mad. He goes out and comes back (a mark of folly on the stage used by Hamlet in talking both to Ophelia and the Queen). The passers-by ask him the way to Lorenzo's house, and he describes it as going to hell; this appears simply to denounce Lorenzo, but also means that his own going there puts him on the path of wickedness.

> A darksome place, and dangerous to pass;
> There shall you meet with melancholy thoughts

> Whose baleful humours if you but uphold
> It will conduct you to despair and death.

He begins the next scene by rejecting two methods of suicide as an unreliable source of revenge—this is not as stagey as it may appear, because many suicides actually are done to punish other people (institutionally among the Japanese); and it was a necessary partial justification of the Revenger that he should be willing to die. In his appearance before the king (this is sc. xii) he is too easily shuffled aside by Lorenzo; one would think the letter of Pedringano need only be shown. It would be fussy to deny that Kyd is unskilful at this crucial point of the play, unless our text has been curtailed. But the story is not absurd; Hieronymo's nervous condition might well prevent him from making his accusation except in so violent a form as to sound mad, and the first audiences might recognize more easily than we do that he had a practical danger—if he produced at once his evidence against the heir to the throne, it could simply be taken from him and destroyed. He does win the sympathy of the King, who proposes to look into his case later (l. 99). As the chief object of Hieronymo is to speak to the king away from the brother and nephew, this means that his choice of mad behaviour nearly succeeded. (Of course, in one way he can't help being peculiar, but in another way he is trying to make use of it.) But the King only says this after he has gone, and then refers the matter to the Duke, who has Lorenzo at the interview; so that Hieronymo again feels that his case is hopeless.

He next comes in (sc. xiii) 'with a book in his hand' like Hamlet, because he is grappling with the theory of revenge. I want to maintain that his arguments were meant to seem mad to the audience, or at least tragically deluded; such is the point of development he ought to have reached, and he is at least very confused about the well-known difficulties of his topic. But you may say that the audience was confused too, and I confess that there is at least one point in the play where we are inclined to think both author and audience very simple. It is at the end of Act I; to establish the position of Hieronymo as court playwright, we have him showing a masque to the King and the Portuguese Ambassador, consisting of three English knights who capture two Portuguese kings and one Spanish king. Both dignitaries accept this with high chivalry, saying that, as even little England can win, one ought to accept calmly the fortunes of war. This seems childlike unreality, but I suppose any members of the audience who thought so would be content to take it as charming; in any case, it comes early, before the play is too serious for it. I do not think we need impute the same careless effrontery to the discussion of Hieronymo about revenge. He begins with the Scripture text 'Vindicta mihi' (I will repay, saith the Lord), which meant that men must *not* do this work of God, and contrives to twist it into meaning only that a revenger ought to delay until God gives him a good opportunity. Having used Latin for this Bible text, he can move smoothly over to Seneca as if the two had equal moral authority; but his next bit of Latin has to be twisted equally violently before it will suit his purpose. The line became a stock one for the Elizabethan drama, either in quotation or in echo, but I doubt whether it was ever again so starkly misused.

> *Per scelus semper tutum est sceleribus iter;*
> Strike, and strike home, when wrong is offered thee.

Clytemnestra says this when nerving herself to kill Agamemnon, and has just remarked that her chance of taking 'the better way' has already gone; she has already behaved so badly that her only chance of safety lies in further crime. Nobody but Hieronymo ever took it to mean that a good man, when a crime is done against him, ought to commit an immediate crime in reply. Even so, his interpretation contradicts the one he has just made from the Bible text; he deduces now that he ought to revenge at once, instead of waiting till God gives him a good opportunity. He encourages this view by a baffling argument that the duty of 'patience,' which of course was prominent in medieval thought, was really a recommendation to suicide. This is supported by a third Latin quotation, about Fate; this time from the *Troiades,* when poor little Astyanax is hidden in a tomb and told that, even if the Greeks catch him there, he has at least got his tomb handy. Hieronymo manages to deduce:

> let this thy comfort be;
> Heaven covereth him that hath no burial.
> And, to conclude, I will revenge his death!
> But how? Not as the vulgar wits of men,
> With open, but inevitable ills,
> As by a secret, yet a certain mean,
> Which under kindship will be cloaked best.

'Not with open injuries, as men do, but with inevitable ones, as Fate does'—such has to be the grammar, and the effect is that he proposes to become Fate in person, so he must act by roundabout and unexpected methods, as one must agree that Fate appears to do. The lines go straight on to a solution of the problem whether to delay, and here I think the audience *must* have been meant to realize that he is talking nonsense, even if they were meant to be rather stunned by the bits of Latin.

> Wise men will take their opportunity
> Closely and safely fitting things to time.
> But in extremes advantage hath no time;
> And therefore all times fit not for revenge.
> Thus therefore will I rest me in unrest,
> Dissembling quiet in unquietness,
> Not seeming that I know their villainies,
> That my simplicity may make them think
> That ignorantly I will let all slip;
> For ignorance, I wot, and well they know
> *Remedium malorum iners est.*

In extremes advantage hath no time can only mean, I submit, 'in such a hard case as mine waiting is useless, because there will never be a safe opportunity'; and indeed all cases suited to revenge plays are 'extreme' like this, because the revenger is so desperate that he is ready to die as soon as he has succeeded—this is necessary, to make the audience respect him however much they think him wrong. But this created a difficulty for the other requirement of the theatre, that he is needed to argue and delay; and here the knot is cut (by a complete contradiction in the next line) with a bold absurdity intended to make the audience realize that he is mad. Now that he has settled his problem the poetry sounds very contented; he enjoys thinking how subtle he will be, and manages to extract a kind of cosy gloating out of a third tag from Seneca, which is again off the point. Oedipus was saying, with courageous public spirit, that the reason for the plague must necessarily be found, whatever its unpleasantness to himself; this is very remote from the idea of hiding by flattery an intention of private revenge. After thus consistently showing the informed spectator that he is hopelessly confused, he ends the speech with the one argument that the audience would respect; that he cannot work in any other way, because if he showed any 'menace' to his enemies they would 'bear him down with their nobility.'

Some petitioners now enter to see the judge, and for the first time he is violently crazy, as the speech has prepared us to find him; he rips up their expensive documents, and then patters away saying 'catch me' (Shakespeare copied this twice, separating the two elements of the madness of the revenger; we get the grim humour of the pretence in Hamlet– 'Hide fox, and all after'–and the pathos of its reality in Lear, waving his boots in his hands). It is in the next scene that we see Hieronymo fail in his last chance of getting public justice, the interview with the Duke of Castile (the audience thinks he is right in suspecting the Duke to be a hypocrite, but also that a saner man would have made some attempt); then we advance on the final Act, where he agrees on revenge with Belimperia and has only to plan the method with a lunatic and presumably unnecessary cunning.

I hope this is enough to show that the old play gives a graduated advance towards madness and revenge, taking for granted that only great and prolonged forces would have driven such a character into such a crime. It might not seem to need much proof, but a rival theory has been growing up, of a kind which I call 'neo-Christian,' that the Elizabethans considered their theology to be in favor of revenge, and that we would too if we weren't rotted with 'humanitarianism.' I find something rather alarming in this fashion for savagery among dons. Actually, I take it, the clergy regularly said that revenge was very wicked, but the soldiers tended to say that a man's honour might require it; an audience would not have only one opinion, but would broadly agree on feeling that, while revenge was nearly always very wicked, a point might come where it was almost inevitable. Indeed, so far as we still find the plays good, we do so because they reflect this breadth of feeling. As for Hieronymo, who has worried about it as much as he ought to have done, the pretence of a classical next world might leave room for doubt, but still he is definitely not damned at the end of the play by the supernatural characters who distribute punishments in Hades; indeed the Ghost calls him 'good Hieronymo.'

It could be said, however, that the second crop of Elizabethan Revenge Plays, around 1600, was itself a rather similar fashion; Marston makes a pet of a hero in a monstrous fit of sulks, in some way that Kyd does not. Shakespeare in re-writing *Hamlet* seems to have been following a trend, and, though he certainly didn't abandon himself to it, I rather suspect he cut out the 'moral' of the old play, in the course of bringing it up to date. The obvious moral, from the surviving plot, is that Hamlet ought not to have spared Claudius at prayer, at least for the reason he gave; being the rightful King, it was his duty to kill a criminal usurper, but even a King had no right to try to send a man to Hell (as by refusing absolution before he was executed). Hamlet went too far about revenge, and this was fatal to him. He is already an alarmingly tricky character in the sources, and Kyd needed to invent some crisis which would turn his story into a tragedy. If you admit that *The Spanish Tragedy* is not pointless, this moral for *Hamlet* seems one which Kyd might well have invented. Shakespeare of course would assume it to be well known, so that the chief effect of not mentioning it in his version was to raise a further mystery about the real motives of the character. Many critics of the last century, including Bernard Shaw, thought that Shakespeare couldn't say plainly what he thought about revenge because he was morally so much in advance of his coarse audience; and I should fancy they were right, except that he was about ten years behind it.

CORRECTION

1. It has since been pointed out to me that 'thrust Horatio forth my father's way' could then mean 'out of his way,' and evidently did because that makes a display of arrogance; the murder is described as removing an unsightly object from the Duke's path. I thus lose the one bit of the text which appeared to tell the secret. But Lodovico would have been unlikely to tell it anyhow, so this does not refute the theory. The arguments against it which have kindly been sent me have left me all the more convinced.

IRVING RIBNER

The Idea of History in Marlowe's Tamburlaine

At either end of Christopher Marlowe's short career stands a great historical drama. *Edward II*, perhaps his finest achievement, is one of the best of Elizabethan chronicle plays and one which, by its direct influence upon Shakespeare, indicated the highest potentialities which that dramatic genre was to reach. It is sometimes forgotten, however, that the first part of *Tamburlaine*, the play whose overwhelming success virtually ushered in a new era in the English drama, is also a history play. It is, moreover, as Tucker Brooke has emphasized, 'more than any other drama, the source and original of the Elizabethan history play.' [1] What essentially distinguishes the history play from other forms of drama is, as Lily B. Campbell has pointed out,[2] the author's purpose: in the history play it is to fulfill the function of the historian, or, following Aristotle's ancient division, to deal with politics as opposed to ethics. That historical dramatists did fulfill the function of the historian has, I believe, been amply demonstrated by Professor Campbell. If, then, *Tamburlaine* is a historical drama, and one, moreover, which served as the model for scores of later history plays, the conception of history which its author entertained becomes a matter of great importance.

Much has been written about the Elizabethan idea of history, but the subject is a vast one, and no small formula can adequately characterize it. Perhaps the most dominant trend is that which we find in the chronicles of Halle and Holinshed. It was to see history as the

From *ELH*, XX (December 1953), pp. 251–66. Reprinted by permission of the journal, the author, and the Johns Hopkins Press.

working out of God's purposes, just as the Medieval Christian historians had seen it. But the limitations of such a philosophy of history, as Dean makes clear (particularly pp. 17–24) were already clear to many Tudor historians who, although they repeated the accepted commonplaces, found it almost impossible to embody them in their actual writings. Many new and contrary notions were current. The Italian schools of Leonardo Bruni, Machiavelli and Guicciardini had made their influence felt in England, and their doctrines were to find fruit in Sir Francis Bacon's *History of Henry VII*.

Doubtless, many of the historical trends of his age combined in Marlowe, but the evidence with which we must work is scanty and incomplete. There is, moreover, evidence of much change and development between *Tamburlaine* and *Edward II*. In its general outlines, however, the concept of history in *Tamburlaine* stands apart from the dominant tradition in Elizabethan historical writing; it is quite different from that in Halle or Holinshed. In this first historical play Marlowe incorporated an idea of history which was largely classical. His models were probably the historical writings of antiquity, and perhaps chiefly those of Polybius whom he may well have read at Cambridge. Christopher Watson's English translation of Polybius, moreover, had appeared in London as early as 1565.

To separate classical from later historiography is, of course, not easy, for the lines of cleavage between cultural eras are never exact, and certainly no period in the world's history has ever failed to carry on a great part of that which preceded it. One undeniable fact, however, does separate the historical writings of the Greco-Roman world from those of later ages, and that fact is the advent of Christianity. The pre-Christian account of man's career on earth could not share the same philosophical bases as an account predicated upon Christian belief. It is thus not an oversimplification to distinguish, as Collingwood does,[3] at least two features of Greco-Roman historiography which separate it from later Christian history. These he calls *Humanism* and *Substantialism*. These features are alien to the premises of Christian history, and they are not found in most Elizabethan historical writings. Both, however, are present in Marlowe's *Tamburlaine,* although there may be much in the play which is not classical and it may not include all aspects of classical historiography. The incorporation into drama of these two elements of classical historiography did much, I believe, to make *Tamburlaine* the peculiar dramatic anomaly which it is.

Collingwood's description of the *Humanism* of classical history may well be quoted at length:

> It is a narrative of human history, the history of man's deeds, man's purposes, man's successes and failures. It admits, no doubt, a divine agency, but the function of this agency is strictly limited. The will of the gods as manifested in history only appears rarely; in the best historians hardly at all and then only as a will supporting and seconding the will of man and enabling him to succeed where otherwise he would have failed. The gods have no plan of their own for the development of human affairs; they only grant success or decree failure for the plans of men. This is why a more searching analysis of human actions themselves, discovering in them alone the grounds for their success or failure, tends to eliminate the gods altogether . . . The ultimate development of this tendency is to find the cause of all historical events in the personality, whether individual or corporate, of human agents. The philosophical idea underlying it is the idea of the human will as freely choosing its own ends and limited in the success it achieves in their pursuit only by its own force and the power of the intellect which apprehends them and works out means to their achievement. This implies that whatever happens in history happens as a direct result of human will; that some one is directly responsible for it, to be praised or blamed according as it is a good thing or a bad. (p. 41)

Rarely in classical history is there any indication that historical events may be the product of anything other than human action based upon human will in a world ruled only by fortune, a female and fickle fortune whom the hero of history can master and bend to his will. Such a historical philosophy, of course, is based upon the same primitive psychology which could produce a philosophy like Stoicism: the characteristically Greek idea that man is a rational animal who can live by the dictates of his reason.

The *Humanism* of classical historiography was, of course, incompatible with Christian doctrine which held that human will alone could never lead man to noble ends; only the grace of God could do so. The clouding of human reason, which was the fruit of original sin and had accompanied the fall of man, made it inevitable that human action should be blind, impulsive and unperceiving of ultimate ends. To early Christians even that which led man to desire the good and to accept God was not his reason, but the grace of God guiding his reason and causing it to embrace God's purposes. The wisdom displayed in man's actions is never his own wisdom; it is that of God.

The events of history thus do not occur because men have decided upon them, but simply because men, while following their own blind courses of action, have nevertheless executed the purposes of God.

Just as classical history had been concerned with human reason and human purposes, Christian history, perhaps best exemplified in the work of Eusebius, became concerned with the purposes of God. Its great task became to chart the influence of divine providence in human affairs, to display in human events the unfolding of a divine plan. The moral purpose of the classical historians was continued in Christian history, but it took on a new shape. Whereas for men like Polybius it had consisted of observing the deeds of earlier men and learning from them the probable results of future action, for Christian moralists it consisted of observing the will of God in the universe, accepting that will and learning submission to it. The duty of man, they taught, was to become a willing instrument for God's purposes.

It is obvious that this attempt to find a divine plan in history, to see man as the agent of divine will, runs through the Medieval chronicles, and it persists in England well into the seventeenth century. There is a tremendous difference, of course, between Edward Halle and Ranulph Higden, but like his Medieval predecessors Halle also sees history as the working out of God's plan, although that plan might not be for him exactly what it was for them. His school of Tudor historiography, for the most part, did not discard the philosophical bases of Medieval Christian historiography, although it made great improvements in historical method, and it approached its subject with peculiarly sixteenth-century political biases.

Marlowe found his chief source for *Tamburlaine* in Thomas Fortescue's *The Forest,* a translation of *Silva de Varia Lection* of Pedro Mexia, but he used other sources as well, perhaps most notably George Whetstone's *The English Mirror* and the *Magni Tamerlanis Scythiarum Imperatoris Vita* of Petrus Perondinus. The story of the Scythian conqueror was widely known in Elizabethan England, and it may be found in many places. By the time it reached Marlowe, the character of Tamburlaine had thus pretty well been moulded by literary and historical tradition. This tradition had two facets. On the one hand, Tamburlaine had been glorified in the writings of Italian humanists, beginning with Poggio Bracciolini in his *De varietate fortunae libri quattor* (Paris, 1713, pp. 25 ff.) as the perfect prince, the symbol of Renaissance *virtù.* Although a pagan himself, Tamburlaine was glorified as the defender of Christian Europe against the Turks.

Marlowe's play carries on this picture created by the Italian humanists. Alongside this apotheosis of the Mongol conqueror, however, had grown up a parallel tradition: Tamburlaine was regarded as 'a scourge of God,' a tyrant sent to earth by God to punish both evil rulers for their tyranny and wicked people for their sins.[4] Tamburlaine's actions on earth, thus seen, were entirely in line with God's plan; he forwarded God's purposes, and a history of his life might be written with a strong Christian point of view. As a 'scourge of God' Tamburlaine would have certain sinful traits himself, and like all scourges he must inevitably be destroyed by God when the divine purpose is fulfilled and he is no longer needed. This idea appeared, as Battenhouse points out, in Marlowe's most immediate source, Fortescue's *The Forest.* Marlowe thus inherited an account which was already cast for him in conventional Christian terms.

F. S. Boas, Paul H. Kocher, and Willard Thorp have all demonstrated the unChristian framework of Marlowe's play.[5] Tamburlaine certainly does not execute God's purposes; he defies and contradicts them and is successful in spite of them. And there is certainly nothing of divine retribution in the death of Tamburlaine; nor is there any moral castigation of Tamburlaine's ideals by the dramatist. 'His career closes at last,' writes F. S. Boas (p. 100), 'because all that lives must die, and he looks forward to its continuation by his sons.' There is, in fact, a reaffirmation by Tamburlaine before his death of all that he has been and has accomplished:

> Giue me a Map, and then let me see how much
> Is left for me to conquer all the world,
> That these my boies may finish all my wantes.[6]

There is nothing here of Christian recognition of sin and repentance before death. If there is any tragedy in the play it is in the tragedy of man himself, the recognition that all men, no matter how great or noble, must inevitably die. Marlowe's Tamburlaine is a victorious hero. Unless we regard him as such the play has no meaning, for it is certainly not a morality play illustrating the sins of ambition and pride, although that suggestion has been made. And Tamburlaine is a hero not because of any Christian virtues, but because of a Machiavellian *virtù* which enables him to master fortune and win success in his enterprises. The theme of the play is a glorification of *virtù,* and this theme places *Tamburlaine* outside the Christian world of divine providence which rewards man for good and punishes him for evil.

As history it belongs in the A-Christian world of Machiavelli which considers not what should be but what is, and which does not study the path to virtue, but rather the path to success.

The idea of history implicit in *Tamburlaine* thus becomes immediately apparent. Throughout both parts there is a strong and direct denial of the role of providence in the affairs of man. History, for Marlowe, is created by two things: fortune and human will. Fortune is not conceived of in the Medieval Christian manner as the instrument which executes God's providence; Marlowe's is a classical fortune, the capricious, lawless element in the universe which can be controlled and directed only by human wisdom and power.[7] His hero, like the heroes of Machiavelli and Guicciardini, is the man who can master fortune and bend her to his will, for the classical fortune, it must be remembered, is a woman who can easily be swayed. Marlowe's emphasis upon fortune is particularly close to Polybius who perhaps gave a greater place to fortune in human affairs than did the other classical historians. Polybius is probably the ultimate source of what was to become the *virtù* and *fortuna* of Machiavelli.

It is not God who makes kings, says Marlowe in defiance of the entire body of Tudor political doctrine; it is fortune and human will. Menaphon emphasizes fortune in his speech to Cosroe at the beginning of *Part I:*

> This should intreat your highnesse to reioice,
> Since Fortune giues you opportunity,
> To gaine the tytle of a Conquerour,
> By curing of this maimed Emperie. (I, i, 131–34)

The first great description of Tamburlaine is as a man whose human worth combines with fortune to make him what he is:

> Nature doth striue with Fortune and his stars
> To make him famous in accomplisht woorth:
> And well his merits show him to be made
> His Fortunes maister, and the king of men.
> (II, i, 487–90)

Tamburlaine, throughout both parts, is a figure who controls completely his own fate. History is created by his strength and will, and even by his whim, as witness his sudden removal of the crown from Cosroe (*Part I*, II, vi). Fortune's wheel, the fatalistic symbol of Medieval Christianity, with its emphasis upon submission to divine power over which man has no control, holds no terrors for Tamburlaine:

I hold the Fates bound fast in yron chaines,
And with my hande turn Fortunes wheel about.
(I, ii, 369–70)

Tamburlaine does not unify the world under his command because heaven wills that he do so; he conquers the world in opposition to the Gods. He defies them, sets himself up against them as an opposing power. When he has taken the crown from Cosroe, he says:

Though *Mars* himselfe the angrie God of armes,
And all the earthly Potentates conspire,
To dispossesse me of this Diadem:
Yet will I weare it in despight of them. (II, vi, 909–11)

That which is attained by human will and power, moreover, is surer than anything which the gods may grant:

So, now it is more surer on my head,
Than if the Gods had held a Parliament:
And all pronounst me king of Persea. (II, vi, 916–18)

There is throughout an emphasis upon human power, and a de-emphasis upon the power of God:

Ioue viewing me in armes, lookes pale and wan,
Fearing my power should pull him from his throne.
(V, vi, 2234–5)

Nor is this merely the vaunting of an over-ambitious braggart destined for divine punishment, for with this attitude Tamburlaine does accomplish his ends. *Part I* ends upon a note of great triumph, and *Part II* ends with the promise that his sons, embodying the philosophy of their father, will continue his conquests. Throughout both parts of the play, the classical *Humanistic* conception of history is vindicated and triumphant. The greatest statement of it occurs at the end of *Part II* when, after burning the Alcoran, Tamburlaine mocks Mahomet. This, in the words of F. S. Boas, represents Marlowe himself speaking, 'in realistic derision of direct divine intervention in human affairs.' (p. 98)

It is thus evident that *Tamburlaine* embodies the first element of classical historiography; it is *Humanistic*. The events of history are not conceived of as parts of a divine plan; they are created by fortune and the human strength and will which can control it. In this Marlowe stands apart from much of the historical thought of his age. In denying the role of providence in history, however, Marlowe is very close to the Italian humanist historians, for, as Eduard Fueter emphasizes, this is probably the most important single characteristic of their work. It is what most distinctly, aside from matters of style, distinguishes the history of Leonardo Bruni from those of Dino Campagni and Giovanni Villani. Marlowe is thus allied also with the stream of English humanist history which stems from Bruni, (Fueter, pp. 199 ff.) beginning with Thomas More and Polydore Vergil and reaching its full growth with Francis Bacon.

The Italian humanists did not, however, borrow the other great characteristic of classical historiography, and it is significant that we do find this order characteristic in Marlowe's *Tamburlaine*. Collingwood has termed it *Substantialism*, and he has accounted for it in terms of Greco-Roman metaphysics, whose chief category was that of substance. For want of a better term, we may use Collingwood's, and whether or not one accepts the metaphysical explanation of its origins, *Substantialism* is a definite and immediately observable attribute of classical history.

Collingwood's explanation is as lucid as it is subtle. A metaphysics whose chief category is substance implies that only the unchanging is knowable, since substance, by definition, is fixed in form and cannot change. Since the subject matter of history, however, is not unchangeable and eternal, but transitory events, it must ultimately be unknowable. A dichotomy thus arose in classical times between history, which was regarded as transitory and unknowable and the agents of history, which were considered substantial, unchanging in form, and thus knowable. The result was that for classical historians history itself, the passing train of events, became unimportant in itself. This in turn gave rise to the pragmatic conception of history, so markedly present in Polybius: history's chief importance lay in the lessons which could be learned from it, not in the events themselves. For classical historians, events were important for the light they might throw upon the agents of history, although the agents themselves were not a part of history. Collingwood puts it thus:

> A distinction is now taken for granted between act and agent, regarded as a special case of substance and accident. It is taken for granted that the historian's proper business is with acts, which come into being in time, develop in time through their phases and terminate in time. The agent from which they flow, being a substance, is eternal

> and unchanging and consequently stands outside history. In order that acts may flow from it, the agent itself must exist unchanged throughout the series of its acts: for it has to exist before this series begins and nothing that happens as the series goes on can add anything to it or take away anything from it. History cannot explain how any agent came into being or underwent any change of nature; for it is metaphysically axiomatic that an agent, being a substance, can never have come into being and can never undergo any change of nature. (p. 43)

For Livy, thus, Rome is an agent, a substance, changeless and eternal; the events of history are only important in so far as they throw light upon this agent. Such history has no place for the evolution of institutions, and perhaps more important for our purposes, it has no place for development and change in human character. Man, as a substance, is fixed and changeless.[8] His actions can have no influence upon his nature. Such a concept, of course, is basically hostile to the very notion of drama, and it is what helps to set *Tamburlaine* and its followers apart from the main current of Elizabethan drama.

Whether or not the classical historians approached their tasks with the metaphysical assumptions which Collingwood attributes to them we cannot say, but certainly their work is such as would proceed from such assumptions. Thus, whether or not one accepts Collingwood's explanation of this peculiar characteristic of classical historiography, we must nevertheless recognize that the characteristic exists, account for it as we may. The agents of classical history are fixed and unchanging. When human character appears to be changing, new facets of it merely are being revealed. Every action which a historical character ever performs he is capable of when first we meet him. Thus classical history could not depict a man like Shakespeare's King Richard II, who attains maturity and wisdom through suffering, or like Lear, who goes through the same process on an infinitely grander scale. Such characters are the products of long Christian tradition.

The notion that anything on earth might be fixed and changeless was, of course, incompatible with Christianity. Nothing, according to Christian belief, is eternal and unchanging except God. All else has been created by God, and what God has created he can change. He can change human character by grace; he can turn the evil man into the good. The very doctrine of salvation presupposed the possibility of change in human character, and history was a long record of such changes. Christian history, moreover, abandoned the division between act and agent in history. Since all history was the working out of

God's will, the agents of history, as vehicles of God's will, became a part of the historical process.

The emphasis upon human character development became an important part of all post-classical history, and it continued through the writings of both the Italian humanists and the English humanists. There was a place in post-classical history for recognition of error, repentance and alteration of character. In England we find it both in the old style chronicles of Halle and Holinshed and in the humanistic history of Sir Thomas More. It is basic in the *Mirror for Magistrates* as in all *de casibus* narrative. It is also a basic element in the greater Elizabethan historical drama, in the anonymous *Woodstock*, in Shakespeare's Lancastrian plays and in Marlowe's *Edward II*. But we do not find it in *Tamburlaine*.

Not only are the events of both parts of this drama entirely the products of human agents, but those agents themselves are fixed and changeless. They appear upon the stage full drawn; there is no development, and when the play ends, they are no more or no less than they had been at the beginning. It is this essential feature of classical historiography in the play which has led critics to call Tamburlaine poorly motivated, incredible, almost a caricature. Everything he will ever be, he already is at his first appearance in the second scene of the first act of *Part I*, when, as a mere brigand with almost no following, he has captured Zenocrate and her train. It is in his speech to her:

> I am a Lord, for so my deeds shall proove,
> And yet a shepheard by my Parentage:
> But Lady, this faire face and heauenly hew
> Must grace his bed that conquers *Asia:*
> And meanes to be a terrour to the world,
> Measuring the limits of his Emperie
> By East and west as *Phoebus* doth his course.
>
> (I, ii, 230–6)

And his followers are almost a chorus as they foretell the future greatness which is already completely implicit in his character:

> Techelles: Me thinks I see kings kneeling at his feet,
> And he with frowning browes and fiery lookes,
> Spurning their crownes from off their captiue heads.
> Usumcasane: And making thee and me *Techelles,* kinges,
> That euen to death will follow *Tamburlaine.*
>
> (I, ii, 251–5)

Techelles and Usumcasane are just as fixed and static as their master. They are prototypes of loyal followers, and they never can be anything else. They are the static agents of *Substantialist* history; they cannot be changed by their actions, and their actions are such as could only proceed from such agents. This is true also of Theridamas; all of the potentialities of his nature are clear when we first meet him. It is inevitable that he should desert Cosroe and follow Tamburlaine to the death. Bajazeth and Zabina cannot change; they can only learn, like the unfortunate characters in Polybius, a Stoic resignation to fate.

The successes of Tamburlaine have no effect upon him whatsoever. This is particularly apparent in the second scene of the fifth act of *Part I,* when the virgins of Damascus come to Tamburlaine to plead for mercy. There is a potentiality for mercy in Tamburlaine; it is his custom to be merciful to a city which yields on the first day of his siege, when his army is encamped in white tents. But on the third day of his siege, when his black tents are out, nothing can move him to mercy. The potentialities of his nature are fixed and cannot change; no virgin tears can move him. For their pleading he gives the virgins death. And he sums up his own unalterable character:

> And know my customes are as peremptory
> As wrathfull planets, death, or destinie (V, ii, 1908–9)

Nothing can move Tamburlaine from the course of action for which his nature calls: the conquest of the world and the ruthless destruction of all opposing kings. Not even his love for Zenocrate can deter him from the conquest of her father's army and the destruction of her native city. And in Tamburlaine's death, as has been indicated, there is none of the Christian recognition of sin and repentance, the self-awareness and self-understanding, which we find in the closing scenes of *Richard II* and *Edward II.*

Zenocrate is never more than a passive symbol of beauty whose nature it is to follow Tamburlaine. Like the others, she is a wooden figure, cut in a fixed pattern which cannot vary. Thus also, the three sons of Tamburlaine in *Part II* are fixed and changeless. Amyras and Celebinus are small copies of their father, to whose glory they aspire; Calyphas scorns the glory of battle. Nothing that happens can alter the essential characters of these three sons. Calyphas dies without change or recognition of error, although he is clearly portrayed as a symbol of sloth, one of the most distasteful of all vices to an Elizabethan audience.[9]

Marlowe's first historical drama thus embodies two basic qualities of classical history: *Humanism* and *Substantialism. Tamburlaine,* moreover, is particularly close to the history of Polybius, both in its emphasis upon fortune and in its theme. For just as the theme of Polybius is the conquest and unification of the world by a complete and fully established national spirit called Rome (see Collingwood, p. 34 ff.) the theme of Marlowe's play is the conquest and unification of the world by an initially complete and fully established spirit called Tamburlaine. In both works the expanding force is complete in all respects at the beginning, and the material of history is merely a series of events to show its expansion. It is essentially this theme which creates in *Tamburlaine* the almost plotless episodic structure, barren of dramatic conflict, which was to become so characteristic of the early English history play, and which W. D. Briggs has called its most distinguishing feature. Both Polybius and the author of *Tamburlaine* portray history as a series of episodes, each of which serves to augment the greatness of a complete and initially established central force, and this is an important similarity.

The *Substantialism* of classical historiography further helped to make of *Tamburlaine* the peculiar dramatic anomaly which it is, for *Substantialism* is basically incompatible with the needs of drama. Not only was the play's action episodic and motivated solely by the requirements of physical expansion, but there could be no character development. One of the important requirements of tragedy was thus lacking: the pattern of self-awareness and repentance which occurs at the end of Shakespeare's greatest tragedies, and which has its probable source in the Christian framework of the Medieval morality play. The philosophical bases of classical historiography thus contributed much to the form of a play which was to exert a great influence upon the course of English drama.

For because of its tremendous popularity the play had many followers. The imitators of *Tamburlaine,* for the most part, had not Marlowe's genius, and it is not likely that they shared his classical and pagan predilections. But one nevertheless wonders to what extent elements of classical historiography found their way into such plays as Peele's *Battle of Alcazar,* Greene's (?) *Selimus,* and the first English chronicle plays such as *The Troublesome Reign of King John,* where *Tamburlaine* is referred to in the prologue, *The Famous Vic-*

tories of Henry V, The Life and Death of Jack Straw, and perhaps Shakespeare's *Henry VI* plays.

As Marlowe developed, both as a thinker and a dramatist, his philosophy of history was to change, until in his final play, *Edward II,* we find a historical sense and understanding much altered from that which underlies *Tamburlaine.* It is difficult to trace the forces which moulded Marlowe's later idea of history, but perhaps among them was his experience in the theater and the lessons he must have learned from *Dr. Faustus.* The philosophy of history to which he finally came, and which he embodied in *Edward II,* was to have an effect upon the course of English historical drama perhaps even more profound than that of *Tamburlaine.*

NOTES

1. *The Tudor Drama* (Boston, 1911), p. 302. This is less true of *Part II.* Whereas in *Part I* Marlowe fulfilled the function of the historian, drawing his material from historical sources which he followed fairly closely, these source materials were exhausted when he came to write his continuation, and Marlowe was forced both to invent material and to incorporate material from sources unrelated to the Tamburlaine story. Thus, although *Part II* carries on the form and pretense of history, it is actually a work of fiction.

2. *Shakespeare's Histories: Mirrors of Elizabethan Policy* (San Marino, 1947), p. 10.

3. *The Idea of History* (Oxford, 1946), pp. 40–45. On classical history, see also James T. Shotwell, *The History of History* (New York, 1939), I, 161–321; M. L. W. Laistner, *The Greater Roman Historians* (Berkeley, 1947).

4. See Roy W. Battenhouse, *Marlowe's Tamburlaine: A Study in Renaissance Moral Philosophy* (Nashville, 1941), particularly pp. 129–33.

5. Boas, pp. 76 ff., 98 ff., Kocher, pp. 79–88; Williard Thorp. 'The Ethical Problem in Marlowe's *Tamburlaine,*' *JEGP*, XXIX (1930), 385–89.

6. *Part II,* V, iii, 4516–18. All *Tamburlaine* references are to *The Works of Christopher Marlowe,* ed. C. F. Tucker Brooke (Oxford, 1910).

7. For classical and Christian concepts of fortune, see Howard R. Patch, *The Goddess Fortuna in Medieval Literature* (Cambridge, Mass., 1927), particularly pp. 8–34.

8. The psychology implicit in a substantialist conception of history appears very markedly in the *Annals* of Tacitus: 'When Tacitus describes the way in which the character of a man like Tiberius broke down beneath the strain of empire, he represents the process not as a change in the structure or conformation of a personality but as the revelation of features in it

which had hitherto been hypocritically concealed. Why does Tacitus so misrepresent facts? . . . It is because the idea of development in a character, an idea so familiar to ourselves, is to him a metaphysical impossibility . . . Features in the character of a Tiberius or a Nero which only appeared comparatively late in life must have been there all the time. A good man cannot become bad.' (Collingwood, p. 44.)

9. There is some departure from the pattern of classical history in the sub-plot in *Part II* of the treachery of King Sigismund of Hungary, which Marlowe adapted from a source completely unrelated to the Tamburlaine story. Here Sigismund, although he is not naturally inclined to treachery, is moved to it by the arguments of Fredericke and Baldwine. His treachery involves no character change, for it is a simple matter of falling into an error of which he had always been capable. After the destruction of his army, however, Sigismund dies with a recognition of his own perfidy and a repentance which actually involves a Christian alteration of character:

O iust and dreadfull punisher of sinne,
Let the dishonor of the paines I feele
In this my mortall well deserued wound,
End all my penance in my sodaine death.
(II, ii, 2925–28)

The appearance of this entire episode in the play is curious, and it has been much commented upon, for it has no relation to the Tamburlaine legend, and in its Christian moral emphasis it is out of keeping with the tone of the rest of the play. Marlowe, running out of material and eager to fill his five acts, probably adapted a Christian moral tale and incorporated it into his play with the traditional death lament which accompanied such exempla.

M. M. MAHOOD

Marlowe's Heroes

THE WHOLE story of Renaissance humanism is told in four Elizabethan tragedies: the two parts of *Tamburlaine the Great, Doctor Faustus, The Jew of Malta* and *Edward II*. To claim so much for Marlowe's plays is not, I think, to fabricate a Renaissance summer from one swallow. Undoubtedly it is true that Marlowe, if he is to be identified with his Promethean heroes, is less representative of the Elizabethan Renaissance than is, for example, Hooker.[1] But such identification is dangerous guesswork. It implies that the dramatist wholeheartedly approved Tamburlaine's career of massacre and rapine, penned the last scene of *Doctor Faustus* as a sop to the pious, and intended the Jew of Malta for a valiant Enemy of the People. This is to appoint Nietzsche as Bankside critic; and recent writers on Marlowe have rightly protested against such an anachronism.[2] Marlowe had enough mastery of his art to accomplish an objective portrayal of character. In his tragic heroes he has embodied the spiritual adventures of his own generation, as he observed them.

This observation, however, if it was to be complete, had to include the observer. So there is perforce some subjective element in Marlowe's heroes, since he is himself involved in the intellectual and spiritual revolutions of his time. Marlowe is not to be identified with Tamburlaine and the rest; but he describes their revolt with imaginative understanding. For this reason, the view that his dramas represent the protest of traditional ethics against Renaissance individualism [3] seems to me no more tenable than the view that they are so many self-portraits. If Marlowe's dramas were simply Morality plays,

From *Poetry and Humanism* (London: Jonathan Cape, 1950), pp. 54–86. Reprinted by permission of the publisher and author.

their chief characters would be monsters of villainy, with none of the complexity which he has bestowed upon them. Even in Tamburlaine's wildest rant there is much more than a mere out-Heroding Herod; and although the problems before Faustus also confront Everyman and Mankind, Marlowe's hero is master of his fate in a different way from the Morality figure who cries, 'As wynde in watyr I wave.'[4] Marlowe is a moralist; but he does not invent character to fit his moral judgements. Instead he portrays, with a kind of objective sympathy, the Renaissance intellectual as he found him, at Cambridge or the Inns of Court. To the figures thus drawn from the life he applies the moral insight which enables him to trace the inevitable impoverishment of Renaissance humanism. Through the course of the four great tragedies, the Marlowe hero shrinks in stature from the titanic to the puny, and his worship of life gives place to that craving for death which is the final stage of a false humanism's dialectic. A similar intellectual process is reflected in the half-century of the Elizabethan and Jacobean drama as a whole. But Marlowe's acumen made it possible for him to diagnose and describe the times' disease in the half-dozen or so years between the first part of *Tamburlaine* and *Edward II*.

Marlowe's place in the literary histories is with the University Wits; but he shows kinship with Greene, Peele, Lyly and Kyd only in his non-dramatic work and in the first part of *Tamburlaine*. Before that two-part tragedy is completed he has far outgrown Kyd's relish for a Stygian gloom or that pleasure in the discovery of classical legends which makes Lyly import the whole of Olympus into the English countryside. Like them, Marlowe delights in Greek and Roman mythology, but he puts it to a finer and more symbolic use than could these lesser writers. The presence of so many classical similes in a play about a Tartar emperor of the fourteenth century cannot be explained away by reference to the happy-go-lucky Elizabethan acceptance of anachronisms. Each of these similes contributes something to the total effect, and in studying them we may be able to come a step nearer to the play's real meaning.

Tamburlaine's speeches, and those of other characters who labour to describe him, abound in allusions to the rebels and the usurpers of classical legend: the Olympians in their strife against the Titans, the Giants rebelling in their turn against the rule of Zeus, Phaethon in the chariot of Apollo, Hercules in his madness defying the gods out of heaven. Theridamas's exclamation at Tamburlaine's first appearance to the Persians in the opening act, recalls Hercules:

> His looks do menace heauen and dare the Gods,
> His fierie eies are fixt vpon the earth,
> As if he now deuis'd some Stratageme:
> Or meant to pierce *Auernas* darksome vaults,
> To pull the triple headed dog from hell.[5]

But although this *motif* is introduced so early in the play, another mythical figure whose intrusion into Hades was very different from that of Hercules is suggested by Tamburlaine's words and behaviour in the first act—the musician Orpheus, who overcame death through the enchantment of his art. The Tamburlaine of these opening scenes is essentially Orphic, winning whole armies to his cause by eloquence alone, and compelling Theridamas to declare that

> Not *Hermes* Prolocutor to the Gods,
> Could vse perswasions more pathetical. 405–6

This implicit Orpheus *motif* makes it difficult to see in Tamburlaine's courtship of Zenocrate a villainous tyrant's passion for a 'plainly reprehensible' pagan queen; [6] which is the interpretation we must give to the scene if the play is to be considered primarily as a Morality. Rather does it suggest Marlowe's lyrical self-idealisation in this orator whose dazzling apostrophe to Zenocrate reveals the artist's power to make beauty the lover's gift. At the beginning of the second act, when Menaphon describes the hero in lines summarising the euphuistic theory of physical and mental perfection, Tamburlaine is still the embodiment of Marlowe's own creative vitality. So far, the hero has been presented as the Renaissance *uomo universale*, soldier, courtier, philosopher and poet; and his aspirations have been Marlowe's own.

Here the day-dream of self-glorification seems to stop. After displaying in his hero that Orphic sense of creative power which he himself shared with many of his generation, the dramatist turns to study the misdirection of such desire. As different critics have shown, the germ of the tragedy is Tamburlaine's choice of an earthly crown as his sole felicity; all the events of this second act lead, with an acceleration of dramatic effect, to the point at which Tamburlaine announces this goal of his ambitions and is crowned King of Persia. But since the play is not a medieval Morality, its theme is not simply that of a man preferring an earthly treasure to a heavenly one. So commonplace a happening would have little of the heroic magnitude required of true tragic action. If the pomp and opulence granted to Tamburlaine at his coronation were the end of his desire, the whole scene would be a clumsy piece of bathos. A clue to the real significance of Tamburlaine's choice lies in the imagery of this second act, in which the Titan *motif* is persistent. Before the battle against Mycetes, Tamburlaine defies the gods and threatens to chase the stars from heaven with the sun-bright armour of his forces. Cosroe, when he falls victim to Tamburlaine's counterplot, cries

What means this diuelish shepheard to aspire
With such a Giantly presumption,
To cast vp hils against the face of heauen:
And dare the force of angrie *Iupiter*. 812–15

Tamburlaine also alludes to the Titanic wars, but sees himself as the Olympian pitted against the elder tyrants:

The thirst of raigne and sweetnes of a crown,
That causde the eldest sonne of heauenly *Ops*,
To thrust his doting father from his chaire,
And place himselfe in the Emperiall heauen,
Moou'd me to manage armes against thy state. 863–7

Such passages, by aligning Tamburlaine with the legendary rebels, suggest that his satisfaction with an earthly crown does not lower his ambition to a mundane level, but rather lifts it to superhuman heights. His desire equals that of Phaethon, of Croeton, of Lucifer himself: it is to sit in the seat of the gods and to have power over life and death. Because, to Tamburlaine's way of thinking, kings already possess this power on earth, his strongest aspiration finds its goal in kingship. To the incantatory repetitions of

Is it not braue to be a King, *Techelles*?
Vsumcasane and *Theridamas*,
Is it not passing braue to be a King,
And ride in triumph through *Persepolis*?

Usumcasane replies, with significant stress on superhuman powers,

To be a King, is halfe to be a God,

and Theridamas adds:

A God is not so glorious as a King:
I thinke the pleasure they enioy in heauen

Can not compare with kingly ioyes in earth.
To weare a Crowne enchac'd with pearle and golde,
Whose vertues carie with it life and death. 756–66

Even before the victory over Mycetes which gains Tamburlaine his throne, Menaphon sees him as an uncrowned king, already wielding this authority:

His lofty browes in foldes, do figure death,
And in their smoothnesse, amitie and life. 475–6

The godlike power to spare or slay is therefore the summit of Tamburlaine's desire—a misdirected desire, because it makes the royal prerogative an end in itself rather than the means to justice.

Although Marlowe's use of Titan images shows that he condemns rather than condones his hero's ambition, he continues to portray that ambition as the misuse of impulses which in themselves are far from blameworthy. Thus even Tamburlaine's exultation in the power to destroy is caused by a perversion of the impulse to create. He still displays an Orphic control over another's mind when he drives Agydas to slay himself—an incident which appears to have been added to the story from Marlowe's own imagination—and the siege and destruction of Damascus in Acts IV and V are a further proof of this close affinity between the Orphic and the titanic elements in Tamburlaine's nature. The pageantry of the three tents, as full of colour and symbolical import as a Renaissance triumph, leads to the moment which, for Tamburlaine, represents the full satisfaction of his desires. With the virgins of Damascus trembling before him, he balances life and death, with godlike authority, upon the point of his sword:

Tam. Behold my sword, what see you at the point?
Virg. Nothing but feare and fatall steele my Lord.
Tam. Your fearful minds are thicke and mistie then,
For there sits Death, there sits imperious Death,
Keeping his circuit by the slicing edge. 1889–93

'Circuit' is perfect; by its scimitar-sound it decapitates the unfortunate virgins, and by its identification of Death with a justice going his inevitable rounds it ironically foreshadows the play's ending. Because this impulse to destroy is a misdirection of the impulse to create, there is nothing incongruous in the praise of inexpressible and unattainable beauty spoken by Tamburlaine after the virgins have been massacred. Nor is the conqueror out of character when he ends this speech with a tribute to virtue, since by the word Marlowe means *virtù*, the essential human energy whose strength the Scythian has put to such disastrous use in giving it a goal beyond the rights of man.

Magnificent as is Tamburlaine's praise of beauty, its persuasiveness cannot silence the critical undertone running through the play. Although the catastrophe is postponed until Part II, both its inevitability and the form it will take are suggested in Part I by an often-sounded note of foreboding. This undertone, heard in the Titan images and in the dying curse of Cosroe, grows insistent with the introduction of Bajazeth and Zabina in the third and fourth acts. In the scene in which Tamburlaine, by his brutal exultation over the fallen emperor, Bajazeth, loses in the eyes of the audience some of his aura of spiritual ascendancy, there occurs the clearest rebel image in the play. The conqueror compares himself to '*Clymenes* brain-sicke sonne' (l. 1493), scattering meteors in his mad career across the sky. At this stage in Tamburlaine's ascent, the idea that he is the Scourge of God becomes prominent. Even while the tyrant triumphs in his seeming usurpation of the judgement-seat of the gods, the reader and hearer feel the presence of that Divine Justice of which Tamburlaine is the mere tool and not, as he himself imagines, the guiding hand. But the strongest note of warning, the clearest indication that Tamburlaine's power is far from superhuman, is in the deaths of Bajazeth and Zabina. When his captives elude his cruelty by suicide, they point the way towards Tamburlaine's ultimate discovery that, although he can destroy, he cannot keep alive, and that the real power over life and death lies beyond human reach.

Tamburlaine the Great is the only drama I know in which the *death* of the hero constitutes the tragedy. The heroes of Shakespeare's tragedies die because their life has been drained of its experience, and the poet can no longer bear to see them stretched upon the rack of this tough world; but Tamburlaine's voyage of self-discovery takes him as far as death before he finds the limits set to his ambition. Despite his immortalising art, Orpheus must lose both Eurydice and his own life. In the second part of the play the death of Zenocrate, coming abruptly after an opening which shows Tamburlaine at the zenith of his power, marks the beginning of the conqueror's disillusion.

Important new *motifs* appear in the imagery of this second part. The Titan theme remains, but more interesting here is the repeated use, to great poetic and dramatic effect, of images of light and darkness. Zenocrate, in the character given her by her lover—largely by transference of his own vitality—is surrounded in Part I by a dazzling light-imagery. Tamburlaine pictures her in clear mountain air, jewel-spangled in the glitter of ice and snow. This association with light is renewed at Zenocrate's first appearance in Part II:

> Now, bright *Zenocrate,* the worlds faire eie
> Whose beames illuminate the lamps of heauen,
> Whose chearful looks do cleare the clowdy aire
> And cloath it in a christall liuerie,
> Now rest thee here. . . . 2570–4

The scene of her death opens with a deliberate and striking contrast:

> Blacke is the beauty of the brightest day,
> The golden balle of heauens eternal fire,
> That danc'd with glorie on the siluer waues:
> Now wants the fewell that enflamde his beames
> And all with faintnesse and for foule disgrace,
> He bindes his temples with a frowning cloude,
> Ready to darken earth with endlesse night. 2969–75

Such images of darkness, which appear in the first part of the play at the deaths of Bajazeth and Zabina, become more numerous and intense throughout the sequel. Sometimes the afterworld is imagined as a celestial Heaven, but much more frequently the characters picture it as Hades; in the closing scenes Marlowe surpasses Kyd in the infernal gloom of his imagery. In thus making his characters portray life and death as light and darkness, he is causing them to express the Renaissance view of existence. To the medieval mind earlier, as to the Baroque imagination later, life appeared a shadow cast by eternity's ring of light; but to the men of the Renaissance (and Bede has long before shown this to be a fundamentally pagan view) it resembled a sparrow's flight through a brightly-lit hall on a winter's evening, out of darkness and into darkness again at the last. In the second part of *Tamburlaine* these images of darkness are used with a forceful dramatic irony, since they recall the sable pomp with which Tamburlaine prepared for the sack of Damascus; the power to spare and slay which there brought thousands to their deaths is not able now to keep Zenocrate alive. Her own quiet reply to the tyrant's rant—'I fare my Lord, as other Emperesses'—is more than a repetition of the age-old commonplace that

> Brightness fall from the air;
> Queens have died young and fair,[7]

for it is also a specific reply to Tamburlaine's denial of human limitations. But the conqueror has already advanced too far in his aberrations to accept even this refutation of his error; at Zenocrate's death he breaks into a passion which builds up a barrier of rant between himself and the unwelcome truth. He continues this self-deception when he tries to perpetuate Zenocrate's beauty by embalmment; and the impotence of Tamburlaine's creative will, once he has deflected it from its true aim, is revealed in his senseless destruction of the town where Zenocrate has died. Unable to give or retain life, he can be revenged on Death only by forestalling him with massacre and fire.

The death of Zenocrate represents the first major defeat of Tamburlaine's will to power. It is the fall of the lightbearer into an inner darkness. From this point in the play onwards, it is evident that even while Tamburlaine's conquests have enlarged his seeming power, his greatness of mind has been lost. His cruelty nauseates, and mechanical repetition finally renders it absurd. The intellectual strength which, in Part I, made him a half-legendary figure whose human birth was in question and whose conquests were achieved with almost magical ease, has given place, in Part II, to brute force and commonplace strategy—a mere matter of quinque-angles and counterscarps.

Marlowe dealt more freely with his sources in the second part of *Tamburlaine;* and all his chosen incidents heighten the tragedy by showing the failure of Tamburlaine's trust in his own creative will. Death must check the conqueror's power, yet he might still make defence against Time's scythe by perpetuating his greatness in his three sons. But once again Tamburlaine's creative instinct is perverted by a fatal egotism. Not content to witness the development of three new personalities, he insists that his sons become replicas of himself. Calyphas alone resists this conditioning and supplies a Falstaffian commentary, blended of cowardice and common sense, to the Hotspur rant of his father. Calyphas has the most character of the three sons; but, by the sharpest irony, Marlowe causes Tamburlaine to kill the only being he has endowed with some measure of his own vitality, and to leave his kingdom to his other two sons, pale and sketchy replicas of their father and quite incapable of maintaining his conquests.

The episode of Olympia and Theridamas is also chosen deliberately for its bearing on the main theme of the play. This improbable story, taken from Ariosto, gives wider significance to the theme that earthly authority, although it enables the wielder to take away life, does not empower him to bestow or preserve it. Tamburlaine and Theridamas are a simple form of the Lear and Gloucester parallel. Although Theridamas strives with all the force of his eloquence to keep Olympia from suicide, he is himself trapped into becoming her executioner, and sees her elude him in death just as Bajazeth and Zabina elude Tamburlaine.

Death wins every trick against Tamburlaine's bid for the power to spare or slay, and in the final scene of the play he answers the challenge with which Tamburlaine ends the preceding blasphemy scene—'Sicknes or death can neuer conquer me.' The irrefutable truth which overwhelms the tyrant at the last is in part the timeless commonplace that 'Death lays his icy hands on kings.' But it is also a truth particularly apparent to the more thoughtful of Marlowe's own generation: that a creative joy in living, perverted to a sterile pride of life, can end only in life's negation. Tamburlaine's own death is the last in a series of events which have shown him that man cannot usurp power over life and death for his own ends. Like Shakespeare's heroes, Tamburlaine grows great in the moment of self-discovery. The truth once grasped, the long-obliterated artist reasserts himself in the hero's character. With his last breath he sums up the fatal contradiction of his career in a magnificent line, worthy of Zenocrate's lover:

For *Tamburlaine*, the Scourge of God, must die.

One disastrous result of the humanist disintegration was that man's refusal to understand or accept his 'middle state,' by depriving his nature of its equilibrium, left him helpless between the extremes of rationalism and fatalism. At first, in the stage of thought represented by *Tamburlaine,* man asserts his self-sufficiency with a pride which is loth to allow God any part in his existence. But we have already seen, in that play, how the insatiable mind, 'Still climing after knowledge infinite,' seeks a superhuman virtue even in terrestrial power. Natural man, growing aware of his insufficiency, likewise begins to crave the completion of his experience in the knowledge of spiritual worlds. Here he runs his head against a wall erected by himself; his vaunted self-sufficiency prevents him from putting any faith in that interpenetration of the natural and spiritual worlds which is implicit in Christian doctrine. Deprived of his self-esteem, he swings rapidly from his assertion of man's greatness independent of God to the other blasphemy of denying human greatness altogether. The titanic hero shrinks to the plaything of malignant powers which are more capricious than just. Some of the greatest Elizabethan and Jacobean tragedies depict this ebb and flow of exultant individualism and despairing fatalism in the minds of their heroes.

No play isolates this conflict more clearly than *Doctor Faustus.* That this is the main theme of the play becomes even more apparent if we strip the action of its playhouse accretions.[8] There then remain six episodes in which the tragedy of Renaissance humanism is told with a swift simplicity paralleled only in Greek tragedy and in *Samson Agonistes.* Of course, what remains after these textual prunings is not the play as Marlowe wrote it. The Wagner scenes suggest that he intended the work to be a typical Elizabethan blend of high tragedy and ironic fooling; one must regret the loss of Wagner, who has the making of a real Shakespearean clown. He might have been the little man shrewdly commenting on the vagaries of the great, *l'homme moyen sensuel* always at hand to deflate the bombast of fanatics. But Wagner disappears early in the printed play, and the comic scenes are botched by less skilful pens. So this tragedy of the Renaissance mind survives as a play of almost Hellenic intensity, unrelieved by that Shakespearean comedy which relaxes the tragic tension only to increase it the next instant.

While Faustus's character is complex by contrast with Tamburlaine's, it is evolved from it, since Marlowe continues to draw on his and his contemporaries' experience of the humanist fallacy. The opening speech by the Chorus, although it contrasts Tamburlaine's 'prowd audacious deedes' with Faustus's retired life, suggests many points of similarity between the two heroes. Like Tamburlaine, Faustus is lowborn, but endowed with the natural gift of a brilliant mind. The mention of Icarus, a prey like Phaethon and the Titans to a fatal ambition, prepares us for the appearance of a second Promethean hero:

> . . . swolne with cunning, of a selfe conceit,
> His waxen wings did mount aboue his reach,
> And melting heauens conspirde his ouerthrow, 20–2

and the speech ends with the clear statement that once again we are to hear the story of misdirected desire:

> Nothing so sweete as magicke is to him
> Which he preferres before his chiefest blisse. 26–7

It is worth noting that the Titan *motif* appears in Marlowe's source, the *English Faust Book,* where the magician is stated to be 'worse than the Giants whom the Poets feign to climb the hills to make war with the Gods: not unlike that enemy of God and his Christ that for his pride was cast into Hell.' [9]

This theme of misdirected desire is sustained all through Faustus's opening soliloquy. His ambition to become a great physician is directed only by the craving for present wealth and posthumous fame:

> Be a physition *Faustus,* heape vp golde,
> And be eternizde for some wondrous cure. 42–3

But neither wealth nor fame can satisfy an aspiration which transcends mortal limits. Like Tamburlaine, Faustus desires a godlike power over life and death:

> Yet art thou still but *Faustus,* and a man.
> Wouldst thou make man to liue eternally?
> Or being dead, raise them to life againe?
> Then this profession were to be esteemed. 51–4

'But a man': in this phrase the self-contradiction of a false humanism is already seen at work. Pride in man's potentialities is swiftly reversed to despair at his limitations. The cave of Despair lies at no great distance from the castle of Orgoglio; and in the absence of conclusive evidence for a late date of *Doctor Faustus,* this natural kinship of the two states of mind suggests that the play was successor to *Tamburlaine.*[10] Here again Marlowe found in the *English Faust Book* a parallel to the humanist experience: 'Dr. Faustus was ever pondering with himself how he might get loose from so damnable an end as he had given himself unto, both of body and soul: but his repentance was like to that of Cain and Judas, he thought his sins greater than God could forgive and here upon rested his mind.' [11] Already in this opening soliloquy Faustus is a prey to such spiritual despondency, and it proves his undoing when, with the words 'When all is done, Diuinitie is best,' he turns to the one learning which might slake his thirst of mind. Faced by the barrier which a false humanism has erected between God and man, he discovers as the sum of all theology nothing but the threat of doom. With the superstitious fatalism of the High Renaissance, he flings open the Vulgate in order to force two random texts—*Stipendium peccati mors est* and *Si peccasse negamus, fallimur et nulla est in nobis veritas*—into a syllogism which, if it did in fact comprise all divinity, would undoubtedly make it 'Vnpleasant, harsh, contemptible and vilde.' The action represents both contemptuous pride and credulous despair—the extreme swings of the pendulum.

The main crisis of the drama is reached in this first soliloquy when Faustus bids 'Diuinitie, adieu.' Divinity to God—and Faustus to the devil. Despair deflects Faustus's natural and rightful thirst for knowledge from divinity to magic, which alone seems to offer a way of escape from human insignificance:

> But his dominion that exceedes in this,
> Stretcheth as farre as doth the minde of man. 88–9

This theme of despair dominates the play, and the word itself recurs with a gloomy, tolling insistence. Faustus, at the beginning of the third episode, his conveyance of his soul to the devil by deed of gift, soliloquises upon 'Despaire in God, and trust in Belsabub'; and his words

> I [Ay] and Faustus wil turne to God againe.
> To God? he loues thee not, 441–2

voice a despondency which is deepened by the Evil Angel's insistence that 'God cannot pitty thee.' The intervention of the Old Man in the fifth episode suggests that Faustus's soul might be regained if only his despair could be overcome. As Mephistophilis gives Faustus a dagger that he may confirm his desperation by killing himself, the Old Man pleads with him to 'call for mercie and auoyd dispaire,' and leaves him

> with heauy cheare,
> Fearing the ruine of thy hopelesse soule. 1298–9

The ill-success of the Old Man's mission is clear from Faustus's next words: 'I do repent, and yet I do dispaire.' In this despondent state he is easily made to cower under Mephistophilis's threats. He summons Helen to help him to forget the heritage he has lost; but his tongue betrays him into a pathetic reminder of the price he has paid—'Sweete *Helen,* make me immortall with a kisse.'

All through the play, the triumphs of Faustus's magic are accompanied by such chilling undertones; the delights he seems to enjoy serve only as drugs to alleviate the pain of loss. Wrenched from their setting, the famous lines upon Greek poetry and legend appear to express the heady excitement of the humanists over the New Learning.

In their context, they have a querulous tone, as if Faustus were struggling hard and painfully to justify his choice:

> And long ere this I should haue slaine my selfe,
> Had not sweete pleasure conquerd deepe dispaire.
> Haue not I made blinde *Homer* sing to me
> Of *Alexanders* loue and *Enons* death,
> And hath not he that built the walles of *Thebes*,
> With rauishing sound of his melodious harp
> Made musicke with my *Mephastophilis*?
> Why should I dye then, or basely dispaire? 635–42

The questionings of a brilliant mind cannot long be silenced by such diversions. Faustus's intellectual vigour drives him on to seek some resolution of the conflicting views of man as god and as nonentity, some balance between pride and despair.

After a fashion, he solves the problem; but his solution is yet another tragic error. Like the heroes of Chapman and Webster, he makes a virtue of his despair, turning it into a stoical indifference to his fate and confounding Hell in Elysium, since there he may be with the old philosophers who have led him to this view of life. In his pride at finding such a solution, he even dares to lecture Mephistophilis on the attainment of a stoical detachment: 'Learne thou of *Faustus* manly fortitude' (l. 321). There is not only a grim humour here in the choice of epithet, but characteristic irony as well; this flimsy philosophy of self-reliance is destined to final collapse, and he is to meet death with none of the stoicism which distinguishes the Jacobean tragic heroes.

The main crisis of *Doctor Faustus* comes at the forty-seventh line of the opening speech. Thus the end of the play is made inevitable before it is well begun. Marlowe hereby sets himself a difficult problem which he solves in a manner that not only preserves the dramatic tension of the play, but also deepens its philosophical meaning. In this opening speech, Faustus has turned from God; God has not turned from him. In the ensuing scenes we are continually made aware of the presence of a Divine Mercy which Faustus will not allow himself to trust. Just as Tamburlaine's pride blinds him to the Divine Justice whose existence is kept before the audience throughout the earlier play, so Faustus's stoical despair renders him insensible to the Divine Mercy which surrounds him—whose presence, indeed, is felt even at the moment he makes his disastrous choice. For there is a clear message of hope in the two texts which appear to Faustus to counsel despair. '*Stipendium enim peccati mors*' has as its corollary '*Gratia autem Dei, vita aeterna, in Christo Jesu, Domino nostro*': while the sorrow of St. John's words is dispelled by those which follow: '*Si confiteamur peccata nostra, fidelis est et justus, ut remittat nobis peccata nostra, et emundet nos ab omni iniquitate.*'[12] The Good Angel, in his first appearance, reproaches Faustus for this wilful blindness when he begs him to 'Reade, reade the scriptures.' But his appeal is overborne by the Evil Angel's words:

> Go forward *Faustus* in that famous art
> Wherein all natures treasury is containd:
> Be thou on earth as *Ioue* is in the skie,
> Lord and commaunder of these Elements. 102–5

No longer is the hero to scale the crystal battlements and usurp divine authority. There is now to be a division of power, and provided man is absolute lord of everything beneath the sun, God may keep whatever is beyond it. Such is the arrangement in this second stage of the humanist revolt; that in which a dividing wall has been built between the two worlds, and built by man alone.

Throughout the tragedy, the obstacles to Faustus's salvation are raised only by him. He is always at liberty to repent and return, since Marlowe softens and almost erases the idea found in the *English Faust Book*, that the devils withhold him by brute strength from such a course. On the contrary, when Faustus has rejected both revelation and reason—the words of Scripture and the Good Angel's warnings—the speeches of Mephistophilis himself begin to contain warnings which would be clear to any ears less deafened by a stoical pride. At his first conjuration of the fiend, Faustus questions Mephistophilis about his master, Lucifer. The replies which he receives point a clear likeness between his own case and that of the rebel angel. It is a comparison implied all through the play, by many seemingly chance references such as Mephistophilis's promise to bring Faustus a courtesan 'as beautiful As was bright *Lucifer* before his fall' (l. 589). Mephistophilis's powerful words upon the Hell that encompasses him should likewise remind Faustus of the existence of worlds other than the visible. But these warnings go unheeded, and the hero sells his soul.

Even at this juncture, the idea of Divine Mercy is presented to the unresponsive Faustus by the fact that the deed of gift has to be signed in blood: for another deed of blood—the Crucifixion—is the crowning pledge of that Mercy. The words '*Consummatum est*' with which Faustus hands the parchment back to Mephistophilis imply that the comparison is there, in some recess of that 'perplexed, labyrinthicall soule.' But the bargain is made; the words which were perhaps prompted by some stirrings of remorse, are spoken as a satanic parody.

The deed once sealed and delivered, Mephistophilis's task is to confirm Faustus in his despair. He is not wholly successful; sometimes he finds himself acting as God's advocate in his own despite. At the beginning of the next episode, Faustus cries, 'When I behold the heauens, then I repent.' The fiend tries to dissuade him from such thoughts, with the question,

> Thinkst thou heauen is such a glorious thing?
> I tel thee tis not halfe so faire as thou,
> Or any man that breathes on earth. 616–18

The words are intended as a bait at which the humanist pride of Faustus may rise. But they do not quite repeat Tamburlaine's claim that heavenly joys cannot compare with those of kings on earth. For when Mephistophilis replies to Faustus's quick challenge, 'How proouest thou that?' with 'It was made for man, therefore is man more excellent,' Faustus for the first time comprehends the full dignity of man which previously his despair had forced him to deny; and his logician's mind leaps to the only possible conclusion:

> If it were made for man, twas made for me:
> I wil renounce this magicke, and repent. 621–2

This moment of inner crisis is externalised by a contention between the Good and the Bad Angels. The Bad Angel wins and Faustus seeks to escape from his uneasy thoughts by disputing of astronomy with Mephistophilis. The replies to his questions do not satisfy his thirsty intellect; they are all 'slender trifles *Wagner* can decide.' Besides which, they bring his thoughts back to the 'heavens'—to the magnificent order in the universe which at the beginning of the scene prompted his desire for repentance—and he faces Mephistophilis with the defiant question: 'tell me who made the world?' (l. 678).

He gives the answer himself. At this critical moment of the play, Faustus comes near to understanding that the one thing which can overcome his despair is the love of God who made the heavens for man, made the earth for man, and at last sent His Son to redeem man fallen, like Faustus, through the misdirection of his desire for knowledge. At the first faint recognition of this truth, Mephistophilis vanishes, a brief contest gives the Good Angel the victory over the Bad Angel, and Faustus is on the verge of recovery in his cry

> Ah Christ my Sauiour,
> Seeke to saue distressed Faustus soule. 695–6

But the moment represents a true peripeteia; no divine messenger, but the Arch-fiend Lucifer, appears to drive all thought of salvation out of the hero's mind. One last effort is made to reclaim Faustus. The Old Man is moved to the attempt by a share of the love of which Faustus has become dimly conscious in the preceding episode. The theme of redemption is made explicit as the Old Man pleads with the conjuror to trust in—

> . . . mercie Faustus of thy Sauiour sweete,
> Whose bloud alone must wash away thy guilt. 1283–4

This last effort also fails. Faustus even seeks the destruction of this one remaining means whereby grace might reach him; henceforth he is lost. The utter finality of his despair is conveyed by the flat tone of his prose conversation with the scholars, which also forms an area of neutral colour to isolate the sharp brilliance of the last soliloquy. In this final hour, the fact of redemption to which Faustus has closed his eyes for so many years becomes apparent to him with a terrifying clarity, since now it is a vision of the unattainable: 'See see where Christs blood streames in the firmament.'

Thus, despite the confusion of the extant texts, the philosophical structure of the play is perfect and more than justifies Goethe's exclamation: 'How greatly it is all planned!' As James Smith has shown, far from this last soliloquy being a *volte face* to appease the pious, it is an integral part of the play.[13] Themes taken from earlier scenes recur in almost every line, but all are transposed into an ironic key. It has long been acknowledged a master-stroke of irony that this Renaissance Everyman should quote Ovid's '*Lente currite, noctis equi*' in the hour of his downfall; nothing could be more aptly bitter than the contrast between Faustus's present position and that of the contented lover who first spoke the words. There is a further irony in Faustus's dread of an inescapable anger, to escape which the once titanic hero would heap Pelion and Ossa upon himself; it is in forcible contrast with his earlier indifference to an after-life:

Thinkst thou that Faustus is so fond, to imagine,
That after this life there is any paine? 565–6

It is supremely ironic that the interpretation of two worlds, made possible by the Divine Mercy which Faustus has repudiated, is now at last effected by the Divine Justice. In the closing phrases of the soliloquy, the crowning irony is achieved. It is not just the indomitable strain of speculation in Faustus's nature which makes him babble of metempsychosis at such a moment; Marlowe is drawing a deliberate contrast between his hero's present envy of 'brutish beasts,' whose 'soules are soone dissolud in elements,' and his earlier pride in an individuality which could not be destroyed. As the clock strikes, this craving for annihilation becomes frantic:

O it strikes, it strikes: now body turne to ayre,
Or *Lucifer* wil beare thee quicke to hel:
O soule, be changde into little water drops,
And fal into the *Ocean*, nere be found. 1470–3

Such irony is not limited to the last scene, but is found throughout the play. It shows itself in the way Faustus gains nothing whatever from his bargains with the devils. The information they give him is trifling, mere 'freshmens suppositions.' The material pleasures are undistinguished and even trivial; a soul is a high price to pay for admission to a conventional masque of the Seven Deadly Sins. But Faustus did not sell his soul for such diversions; he turns to them for consolation or escape when he is disappointed in the replies given to his questions by Mephistophilis. All these questions he could himself have answered—this is the central irony of the play—without selling his soul at all, but by attaining his 'chiefest bliss' in the study of that divinity from which he turned aside in the opening scene.

Doctor Faustus is Marlowe's one complete tragedy. *Tamburlaine* had little dramatic conflict and was more a chronicle play than a tragedy—the chronicle, not only of external events, but also of the Renaissance discovery that human nature, cut off from its divine source, was not emancipated, but impoverished. In Faustus we see man struggling against this sense of impoverishment, but himself blocking the only way of return, and consequently driven to despair. The experience of despair in itself gives the opportunity for recovery, and the play's suspense consists in this; but Faustus's despair is pagan and stoical rather than Christian. With Renaissance man, he asserts his self-sufficiency and rejects the grace which is offered him. The separation of the natural from the spiritual man is hereby completed, and in *The Jew of Malta* Marlowe portrayed this third stage in the humanist dialectic.

The Jew of Malta is a tragic farce,[14] at once both terrifying and absurd. The world it exhibits, by its wide dissimilarity to life as we know it, is ludicrous beyond the bounds of comedy; yet it frightens by reason of a certain logical relationship with reality. If certain conditions governed the world as we know it, it would be exactly like the Malta ruled by Ferneze and terrorised by the Jew Barabas. Chief among these conditions would be the conviction, acknowledged or concealed, of all such a world's inhabitants, that the material order comprised the whole of existence. Throughout his first two tragedies, Marlowe never lets us forget the existence of worlds other than the visible—the Heaven which Tamburlaine's pride impels him to defy, the Hell into which Faustus is plunged by his despair. In *The Jew of Malta* there is no such impingement of one order of being upon another. The play depicts a world which has cut itself off entirely from the transcendent. The God invoked by Barabas is a 'Prime Motor,' who has set the machine in motion and left it to run as best it may. There is no possibility here of intervention by the Divine Justice that pursues Tamburlaine or by the Divine Mercy offered to Faustus.

Such contraction of the drama's scope to mundane, social matter, almost unparalleled in tragedy, imparts a feeling of constriction to the opening scene. Tamburlaine and Faustus are both physically and mentally restless; the one marches over great areas of the eastern hemisphere, the other, 'to prooue *Cosmography*,' moves invisible over the length and breadth of Europe. In contrast, *The Jew of Malta* has for its setting an island of the land-locked Mediterranean; and Barabas is content to remain in his counting-house where the wealth of many lands is compressed into the 'little room' of his jewels. By comparison with Marlowe's earlier plays, *The Jew of Malta* shows an impoverishment in the character of the hero, as well as in the play's setting. Where Tamburlaine and Faustus sought to control, the one by conquest and the other by knowledge, Barabas is satisfied to plunder:

> What more may Heauen doe for earthly man
> Then thus to powre out plenty in their laps,

Ripping the bowels of the earth for them,
Making the Sea their seruant, and the winds
To driue their substance with successefull blasts? 145–9

The Jew turns his back upon the coloured splendours of his Mediterranean world, content with the reflection of fire and sea and sky in the precious stones which comprise his wealth. If any of an artist's delight in form and hue remains in Barabas's praise of his treasure, it has been contaminated by the worldly sense of values which is inimical to art. And although he holds a king's ransom in his hand when the play opens, Barabas is soon forced to admit that he has no hope of a crown; no principality awaits this Machiavellian. Thus in comparison with Tamburlaine and Faustus, the Jew appears a shrunken figure, withered in body and mind. The earlier heroes try to embody, in Zenocrate and Helen, their scarcely attainable ideal of love's perfection. For Barabas there remains only the memory of old lust, recalled in lines of flat indifference:

Friar. Thou has committed–
Barabas. Fornication? but that was in another Country:
And besides, the Wench is dead. 1549–51

Tamburlaine's aspirations and Faustus's fears impart a sense of the transcendental to the earlier tragedies; and because their deaths reveal certain truths about this immaterial world, they are made the occasions of great poetry. Barabas never makes any discovery of this kind. He is merely exterminated, and Marlowe does not waste good verse on his ending.

The ruling philosophy of this constricted and materialist world is 'each man for himself and the devil take the hindmost.' In the Jew's monstrous egotism, this philosophy is carried to its logical extreme. Barabas is prepared to sacrifice his one natural affection, his love for his daughter Abigail, to his principle—if anything so unprincipled deserves the name—of '*Ego mihimet sum semper proximus*' (l. 228). Natural affections, he instructs his slave Ithamore, are mere encumbrances in such a society:

First be thou voyd of these affections,
Compassion, loue, vaine hope, and hartlesse feare,
Be mou'd at nothing, see thou pitty none. 934–6

This cynical opportunism was accredited by the Elizabethans to Machiavelli, whose philosophy they knew chiefly through the adverse comments of Gentillet and others.[15] The Prologue of Marlowe's play is spoken by 'The Ghost of Machivel,' who claims the Jew for his disciple. Such pronouncements as

> in extremitie
> We ought to make barre of no policie, 507–8

and

> And since by wrong thou got'st Authority,
> Maintaine it brauely by firme policy 2136–7

identify Barabas as a Machiavellian, since a 'politician,' on the Elizabethan stage, was always an admirer of Machiavelli's opportunist doctrines. Allusions to the Borgias and other Italian poisoners add to an atmosphere of transalpine villainy calculated to send a shiver down every English Protestant spine.

The Jew is not, however, the only villain in the piece. In a world where love, justice, honesty have all lost their validity, no character is fundamentally better than the frankly opportunist Barabas. The Christians among whom he lives have long since diverted their worship from God to Mammon. Practices and phrases which once were the expression of spiritual experiences linger amongst them as 'ideals' in the Shavian sense—truths which are outworn from a materialist viewpoint, but which are retained for the commercial value of their respectability. Commercial values are, indeed, the only standards of the society which Marlowe has imagined in *The Jew of Malta*. 'What wind drives you thus into *Malta* rhode?' Ferneze asks the Basso; and the Turk's reply sets the mood for the whole play:

> The wind that bloweth all the world besides,
> Desire of gold. 1422–3

Time and again Barabas is able to excuse his actions on the grounds that the Christians, for all their pretended horror of usury, are just as rapacious as he:

> Thus louing neither, will I liue with both,
> Making a profit of my policie;
> And he from whom my most aduantage comes,
> Shall be my friend.
> This is the life we Iewes are vs'd to lead;
> And reason too, for Christians doe the like. 2213–18

He prepares for one of his crimes with the words: 'Now will I shew my selfe to haue more of the Serpent Then the Doue; that is, more knaue than foole' (ll. 797–8). Since the world of *The Jew of Malta* is one into which ethical considerations do not enter, intelligence alone counts. Characters are not good or bad; they have fewer or more wits about them. As in Jonsonian comedy, the rogue who deceives everybody except himself is far more acceptable than the self-deceiving hypocrite who flatters himself that his own shady deeds are directed by the highest motives. Or, as Barabas puts it,

> A counterfet profession is better
> Then vnseene hypocrisie. 531–2

This contrast of self-confessed opportunism with self-concealed greed is most marked in the scene between Ferneze and Barabas, in which the Governor deprives the Jew of all his possessions in order to obtain tribute money for the Turks. When the Jew asks if he and his fellow-Jews are to contribute 'equally' with the Maltese, Ferneze replies in words which are both unctuous with hypocrisy and fierce with superstitious hatred:

> No, Iew, like infidels.
> For through our sufferance of your hatefull liues,
> Who stand accursed in the sight of heauen,
> These taxes and afflictions are befal'ne. 294–7

To this the First Knight self-righteously adds:

> If your first curse fall heauy on thy head,
> And make thee poore and scornd of all the world,
> 'Tis not our fault, but thy inherent sinne. 340–2

There is no doubting Marlowe's ironic intention in the Governor's next speech:

> Excesse of wealth is cause of couetousnesse:
> And couetousness, oh 'tis a monstrous sinne. 355–7

Again, Ferneze's use of the word 'profession' in

> No, *Barabas,* to staine our hands with blood
> Is farre from vs and our profession, 377–8

recalls the 'profession' of the Puritans, whose hypocrisy was so often the butt of Elizabethan stage satire. Barabas several times uses the word in his contemptuous allusions to the Christians. Through such subtle direction of their feelings, the audience are driven to sympathise with Barabas; and when Ferneze, having despoiled the Jew of all his possessions, adds insult to injury by saying, in sanctimonious tones,

> Content thee, *Barabas,* thou hast nought but right,

the audience must feel itself compelled to applaud Barabas's retort:

> Your extreme right does me exceeding wrong. 385–6

Ferneze's dealings with the Turks display the same hypocrisy. As in the Sigismund scenes of *Tamburlaine* (Part II), Marlowe made use of the current notion that a promise made to a heretic need not be kept, to expose the double-dealing of those who thus justified their treachery on religious grounds. At del Bosco's persuasion, Ferneze breaks his undertaking to pay the Turkish tribute (presumably he retains for his own treasury the money which he has exacted from Barabas), and justifies his action with some high-sounding phrases about honour (l. 791). Barabas supplies the obvious comment that if Christians thus deceive those who are not of their own faith, a Jew has as good a pretext for cheating a Gentile:

> It's no sinne to deceiue a Christian;
> For they themselues hold it a principle,
> Faith is not to be held with Heretickes;
> But all are Hereticks that are not Iewes. 1074–7

The acquisitive passion directs not only all the actions of Ferneze and his court, but also those of the other groups of characters. There is nothing to commend the predatory gallants, Lodowick and Mathias; the tone for their wooing of the Jew's daughter is set by the scenes between Lodowick and Barabas in which Abigail is alluded to, in a series of innuendoes, as a diamond which Lodowick wishes to buy. Abigail herself is the one character in the play who is not ruled by greed, and her conversion represents an attempt to break free from the limitations of the narrow, materialistic society which surrounds her. The attempt is rendered pathetic by the fact that the religious, amongst whom she hopes to find release, are as mercenary as the outside world which they pretend to shun. Barabas's sneer,

> And yet I know the prayers of those Nuns
> And holy Fryers, hauing mony for their paines
> Are. wondrous; *and indeed doe no man good* 843–5

is substantiated by the behaviour of the 'two religious Caterpillers,' the friars of rival orders who come to blows over Barabas's announcement that he will enter into religion and bestow his fortune on the monastery of his choice. Lastly, the 'low-life' group of characters—Ithamore, Pilia-Borza and the Courtesan—are shown, in their blackmailing of the Jew, to be as rapacious as the rest. Turk, Moor, Christian and Jew are all as bad as each other, and in these circumstances a cynical 'policy' is to be preferred to a hypocritical 'profession' which cloaks greed in a false devotion:

> Rather had I a Iew be hated thus,
> Then pittied in a Christian pouerty:
> For I can see no fruits in all their faith,
> But malice, falshood, and excessiue pride,
> Which me thinkes fits not their profession. 152–6

There is something strangely prophetic of the mercantile society of later times in this Mammon-worshipping world of Marlowe's invention. Barabas has much of the sardonic clear-sightedness of those who have made it their work to reveal the sham values of such a society. Were the same theme to be treated by a twentieth-century dramatist, Barabas might be shown as a kind of Undershaft, exposing the low motives behind the high-sounding phrases of those around him, and the curtain would come down upon Ferneze in the cauldron. But shrewd and sensitive as was Marlowe's grasp of the humanist problem, he was no prophet of a future society; and even while he felt the Machiavellian realist to be superior to his hypocritically idealist victims, he understood the impoverishment entailed by Barabas's materialistic outlook. Humanism progressed backward. Barabas's cynicism lacks the tragic dignity of Tamburlaine's aspiration or of Faustus's despair; and by the end of the play the Jew has become a monster and not even a sinister monster.

Barabas is a diminished figure, but he is still a vital one. Life may be limited for him to a single plane of existence; nevertheless, he finds the tooth-and-claw struggle for wealth highly enjoyable. Deprived of all he held dear, he can still say, 'No, I will liue; nor loath I this my life' (l. 501). But in Marlowe's *Edward II,* the final stage of the humanist's self-destruction is portrayed: the denial, not only of human spirituality and greatness, but of life itself.

The opening act of *Edward II* presages a repetition of the theme stated in *The Jew of Malta*. The play bids fair to become another drama of the Biter Bit, in which a cunning Machiavellian politician will outwit weaker and simpler minds. The king's favourite Gaveston is a model for the Machiavellian usurper, inferior in birth, but far superior in intelligence, to those he defrauds. Not only is his cunning equal to Barabas's, but the Phaeton image recurs to suggest that he also has the overweening pride of Marlowe's earlier heroes; in Warwick's eyes he is an—

> Ignoble vassaile that like *Phaeton*,
> Aspir'st vnto the guidance of the sunne. 311–12

Then at the beginning of the third act (in the modern editors' division of the play), this incipient tyrant vanishes from the scene. Marlowe is here concerned with a further stage in humanist experience than that represented by the cynical realism of Barabas or of Gaveston. The centre of interest shifts to the king, who so far has been little more than treasurer to the usurping favourite. Stung by Gaveston's slaying, he asserts his regality, and his defeat of the barons imparts some air of authority to this 'brain-sick king'—'*Edward* this day hath crownd him king a new' (l. 1570). But the opposition is worsted, not destroyed, and the king's partiality for other favourites kindles it into new strength. We see little of Edward during the fourth act, while the faction of the Queen and of Young Mortimer is gathering head against him. At the Abbey of Neath, he reappears in disguise, exhausted and defeated, a very different figure from the crowned monarch of a few scenes before. He is seized and forced to abdicate; and once his crown has been wrested from him, life has nothing more to give. Death offers him a release, a defeat of the defeat he has already suffered.

In *Edward II*, Marlowe's imagination was more bounded by an historical source of the action than it had been in his earlier plays. But the general outline of Edward's reign, as related by Holinshed, served him well as the symbol for that final state of disillusion which Marlowe at this time felt impelled to portray. With the rejection of a cynical realism, here represented by the death of Gaveston, the human mind has the chance to achieve reintegration or, in Marlowe's favourite symbolic image, be crowned afresh. But the opportunity is lost. No such revitalising takes place, man abdicates from the humanist throne, and the pride of life crumbles into the death-wish which is voiced by many of Ford's characters (since the Caroline drama also reflects this ultimate stage) for whom life has been 'a long and painful progress.'[16]

On the removal of Gaveston, recovery becomes possible for Edward, but it is scarcely probable. From its opening scene onwards, the play makes it clear that the king's character is too weak to attain the reintegration which lies open to him. Edward is insignificant beside Marlowe's other heroes, a Mycetes in the throne of Tamburlaine. There is a magnanimous quality in Tamburlaine's love-making, whereby he bestows beauty upon the rather shadowy Zenocrate. Edward's nature has not the resources which make such generosity possible. His love demands rather than bestows and, in claiming Gaveston's affection, he is trying to fortify his shaky self-esteem. To the question, 'Why should you loue him, whome the world hates so?' his reply is, 'Because he loues me more then all the world' (l. 372). This weak possessiveness makes Edward an easy prey to jealousy and thus estranges him from the Queen. She understands his nature less perfectly than does Gaveston, who plays deftly upon the king's craving for admiration and approval, deflecting it to a perverted and barren affection for himself.

Edward is also a sharp contrast to the earlier heroes in his taste for the histrionic and the tawdry. The classical mythology which stirs the imagination of Tamburlaine and Faustus as it did that of Marlowe himself, only provides in this later play the characters and properties of masques and pageants: such are the pages clad as sylvan nymphs, the supposed satyrs dancing their antic hay and the show of Actaeon and Diana with which Gaveston plans to divert the king. Whereas Tamburlaine's ambition flares up at tales of war in heaven, Edward is well satisfied with anything of a salacious turn that he can glean from classical legend. Tamburlaine seeks by his actions to turn titanic fable into fact; Edward reverses this process and tries to make his life an interminable masquerade. His first action upon learning that Gaveston is to be recalled is to proclaim a 'generall tilt and turnament' (l. 673). His love of pretence is, however, injured by the intrusion of a harsh reality into this make-believe. The rebel barons have prepared contemptuous devices for the tourney; and lest this should not suffice to dispel the king's illusions, they bait him openly with indulging in mock battles and the pageantry of arms while his realm suffers the brutal actuality of oppression and invasion:

Mortimer. The idle triumphes, maskes, lasciuious showes
And prodigall gifts bestowed on *Gaueston,*
Haue drawne thy treasure drie, and made thee weake,
The murmuring commons ouerstretched hath.
Lancaster. Looke for rebellion, looke to be deposde.
Thy garrisons are beaten out of Fraunce,
And lame and poore, lie groning at the gates.
The wilde *Oneyle,* with swarmes of Irish Kernes,
Liues vncontroulde within the English pale,
Vnto the walles of Yorke the Scots made rode,
And vnresisted, draue away riche spoiles.

. . . . .

The Northern borderers seeing the houses burnt,
Their wiues and children slaine, run vp and downe,
Cursing the name of thee and *Gaueston.*
Mortimer. When wert thou in the field with banner spred?
But once, and then thy souldiers marcht like players,
With garish robes, not armor, and thy selfe,
Bedaubd with golde, rode laughing at the rest,
Nodding and shaking of thy spangled crest,
Where womens fauors hung like labels downe. 959–89

In keeping with the character here given him by his barons, Edward makes his abdication a very histrionic affair. Even when he faces death, life's sweetest memory is of a martial game:

Tell *Isabell* the Queene, I lookt not thus,
When for her sake I ran at tilt in Fraunce,
And there vnhorste the duke of *Cleremont.* 2516–18

Compared with the triumphs and tournaments he devises, life as it is has little meaning for Edward. His state of mind is one of romantic *ennui,* the feeling that life is less real than art. In his previous tragedies, Marlowe had depicted the human person as lord of the earth, conquering its territories, controlling its phenomena, plundering its wealth. But the stage of self-knowledge represented by Edward is the realisation that natural man, for all his skill and strength, is the plaything of natural forces and the victim of necessity. Edward attempts to escape this subjection by denying the reality of that life whose symbol he laid aside when he gave up his crown. Henceforth the world appears to him as 'perfect shadowes in a sun-shine day' (l. 2013), and there runs through the play's last act a craving for a death which will bring complete annihilation:

> Come death, and with thy fingers close my eyes,
> Or if I liue, let me forget my selfe. 2096–7

> . . . I know the next newes that they bring,
> Will be my death, and welcome shall it be.
> To wretched men death is felicitie. 2112–14

Even when the murderer Lightborn appears, Edward's animal instinct of self-preservation is quickly suppressed by the thought of his lost crown; that gone, life is valueless and not worth the preserving:

> Know that I am a king, oh at that name,
> I feele a hell of greefe: where is my crowne?
> Gone, gone, and doe I remaine aliue? 2537–9

In these despairing words, the king sums up not only his own failure, but also that of all the heroes through whom Marlowe has displayed the self-destruction of a false humanism. The process is here complete, from pride in life to rejection of life; from the visualising of death as the only unconquerable enemy to the welcoming of it as a tardy friend.

In this interpretation of Marlowe's chief tragedies I do not, of course, mean to suggest that he consciously thought out 'the problem of humanism' and then wrote four plays to illustrate the successive stages in the downfall of the humanist ideal. But I do think that Marlowe was acutely aware that he was living in an age of revolt, whose intellectuals were making the claim of self-sufficiency in innumerable ways. Marlowe may have shared in that revolt; but he had a clearer understanding than any of his contemporaries of its disastrous effects, and for this reason his tragedies record the disintegration of humanism. Had he lived, he might have experienced and portrayed the seventeenth-century reintegration. Chapman, whose analysis of the time's disorders is almost as clearly defined as Marlowe's, gives us the beginning of such a reintegration in the character of Clermont. But to find the struggle towards a new synthesis consciously attempted, we need to turn from the drama to the religious poets at the beginning of the new century.

NOTES

1. 'It is a *cliché* of English literary history that Marlowe is the very incarnation of the pagan Renaissance. But is Marlowe's half-boyish revolt against traditional faith and morality more, or less, typical and important than Hooker's majestic exposition of the workings of divine reason in divine and human law?' Douglas Bush, *The Renaissance and English Humanism*, pp. 34–5.

2. Such a criticism of the conventionally 'Romantic' interpretation of Marlowe's plays has been made by Leslie Spence in 'Tamburlaine and Marlowe,' P.M.L.A., XLII, 1927; by James Smith in his study of *Dr. Faustus* in *Scrutiny*, June, 1939; and by Roy Battenhouse in his book, *Marlowe's Tamburlaine*. The studies of Marlowe by Una Ellis-Fermor, F. S. Boas, and Paul Kocher represent the opposite viewpoint of the dramatist as a highly subjective artist.

3. See especially Battenhouse's final chapter, 'A Summary Interpretation.'

4. *The Castle of Perseverance*, l. 380.

5. This and the ensuing quotations from Marlowe's plays are from C. F. Tucker Brooke's edition of his *Works*.

6. Battenhouse, *op. cit.*, p. 167.

7. *Works of Thomas Nashe*, ed. R. B. McKerrow, Vol. III, p. 283 (*Summers last will and testament*).

8. See P. Simpson, 'The 1604 Text of Marlowe's *Doctor Faustus*,' *Essays and Studies*, Vol. VII. P. Kocher (M.L.Q., III, 1942) makes out a very strong case for 'Nashe's Authorship of the Prose Scenes in *Faustus*.'

9. *The Historie of the damnable life, and deserued death of Doctor John Faustus*, ed. W. Rose, p. 75.

10. F. S. Boas, in the Introduction to his edition of *Doctor Faustus*, argues for a much later date for the play, which he considers to be Marlowe's most mature work. But see P. Kocher, 'The Early Date for Marlowe's *Faustus*' (M.L.N., XVI, 1941).

11. *Ed. cit.*, pp. 92–3.

12. Rom. 6: 23; I John 1:8.

13. 'Marlowe's *Dr. Faustus*,' *Scrutiny*, June, 1939.

14. T. S. Eliot, *Elizabethan Essays*, p. 28.

15. Battenhouse, *op. cit.*, pp. 41–9.

16. *The Broken Heart*, V, ii.

SAMUEL SCHOENBAUM

The Precarious Balance of John Marston

IN THE FIRST act of *The Malcontent,* the best known play of John Marston, Pietro is informed that his wife is engaged in an adulterous relationship with the usurping duke, Mendoza. Pietro's informant is Malevole, who is not content with a simple presentation of the facts. Instead, he taunts the foolish old man with a brutal account of the infamy of cuckoldom, tortures him with a lurid description of the wife's lascivious thoughts, suggests, finally, the possibility of unwitting incest:

> *Mal.* Nay thinke, but thinke what may proceede of this,
> Adultery is often the mother of incest.
> *Piet.* Incest.
> *Mal.* Yes incest: marke, *Mendozo* of his wife begets perchance a daughter: *Mendozo* dies. His son marries this daughter. Say you? Nay tis frequent, not onely probable, but no question often acted, whilst ignorance, fearelesse ignorance claspes his owne seede.
> *Piet.* Hydeous imagination. (I.iii, pp. 149–150)[1]

Malevole's procedure would be appropriate for a Machiavellian villain, but Malevole is in reality Giovanni Altofronto, the rightful duke of Genoa, now deposed and forced to assume the role of court railer. He wanders about the palace, jesting bitterly with the parasites and fools, commenting outspokenly on the enormities of Genoa and the world's wickedness.

As we follow his movements, we soon realize that Marston's hero is not simply a virtuous nobleman earnestly combatting an evil force which has temporarily triumphed. He is rather a strangely tortured individual whose activities are often perversely unpleasant. And he is

From *PMLA,* LXVII (December 1952), pp. 1069–78. Reprinted by permission of the author and the Modern Language Association of America.

much more than the central figure in a melodrama of court intrigue. For the dramatist has lavished all his satirical and rhetorical powers on the acid speeches of the Malcontent; he is Marston's spokesman. Malevole, like Marston, is the satirist drawing forth the core of imposthumed sin, lighting up the hiding places and dark corners where evil lurks, repelled and fascinated at once by the spectacle of human depravity. His asides, comments, and soliloquies reflect the unrest of the Jacobean age, are, indeed, an expression of that skeptical outlook on life which pervades the plays of Middleton, the two great tragedies of Webster, and the early poems and satires of Donne.

But, more important perhaps, the remarks of the Malcontent constitute an intensely personal utterance, the anguished expression of a troubled spirit. For Malevole's 'hydeous imagination' is also Marston's. This personal note is perhaps the most striking feature of the dramatist's work; Marston is an artist noteworthy not so much for what he has to say about the world around him, as for what he manages to reveal of the world within him. If his work lacks high intrinsic merit, it is nevertheless a fascinating document of the divided soul of a man.

Perhaps what most immediately impresses the reader is the essential incongruity of Marston's work. It is bizarre—more eccentric than the art of any of his contemporaries. *Antonio and Mellida,* one of his earliest plays, affords startling illustrations of this quality. At times the dramatist is inarticulate, occasionally he is incoherent, and quite frequently he is hysterical. Marston's hero enters in a state of frenzy and manages to remain in that unhappy condition for the greater part of the play. Here is Antonio mourning his separation from Mellida:

> Breath me a point that may inforce me weepe,
> To wring my hands, to breake my cursed breast,
> Rave, and exclaime, lie groveling on the earth,
> Straight start up frantick, crying *Mellida,*
> Sing but, *Antonio* hath lost *Mellida,*
> And thou shalt see mee (like a man possest)
> Howle out such passion, that even this brinish marsh
> Will squease out teares, from out his spungy cheekes. (IV.i, p. 47)

But he is not always so articulate:

> I have beene—
> That Morpheus tender skinp—Cosen germane
> Beare with me good—
> Mellida: clod upon clod thus fall.
> *Hell is beneath; yet heaven is over all.* (IV.i, p. 43)

The exasperated annotator is forced to admit, 'These ravings are unintelligible.' [2] The fundamental incongruity lies, however, in the peculiar fusion of romantic melodrama with satirical comedy. The meeting of the estranged lovers on the marshes could, in other hands, have been an affecting scene. But, at the very climax, Antonio and Mellida suddenly break into an extended dialogue in Italian which is as disconcerting as it is unexpected. Marston, discerning, with the keen eye of a satirist, the preposterousness of the situation, comments on the proceedings with amused unconcern. It is Lucio, a bystander, who speaks: 'I thinke confusion of Babell is falne upon these lovers, that they change their language. . . . But howsoever, if I should sit in judgment, tis an errour easier to be pardoned by the auditors, then excused by the authours; and yet some private respect may rebate the edge of the keener censure' (IV.i, p. 49). The romantic elements in the plot are further obscured by a whole gallery of eccentrics, a group of courtiers who belong to the Jonsonian school of fops and gulls. The duality of the author's attitude can be seen even in the characterization of the villain of the piece. Piero is the cause of the lovers' sufferings; yet at the most crucial moments he behaves in a manner that can be regarded only as deliberately comic. Marston managed later to learn the essentials of his craft, to purge his style of the grossest absurdities, but moments of hysteria and obscurity re-appear even in *Sophonisba,* a later and more disciplined play. The dramatist was never able to exercise complete control over his material; for Marston literary activity remained fundamentally an outlet for his conflicting emotional energies, and, consequently, the classical principles of order and restraint could have little significance for him.

This lack of consistency and restraint is most striking in the sequel to *Antonio and Mellida.* In the induction to his first play Marston had promised a second part in which the characters 'that are but slightly drawen in this Comedie, should receive more exact accomplishment.' As these minor figures represent primarily satirical types, he apparently had intended a satirical play, perhaps in the Jonsonian vein. *Antonio's Revenge,* however, has even less satirical material than the earlier drama. Nor does the playwright attempt to continue in the romantic vein; he turns from 'the comick crosses of true love' to create a tangled melodrama crammed with intrigue, brutality, and murder. In the prologue he paints a harsh and barren winter landscape, invites the attention only of those possessed of a 'true sense of misery.' Thus he establishes the mood for the 'sullen tragick Sceane' to follow.

From the instant the play opens with the entrance of duke Piero, 'unbrac't, his armes bare, smeer'd in blood, a poniard in one hand bloodie, and a torch in the other, *Strotzo* following with a corde,' until the final torture scene, the reader is treated to a succession of gratuitous horrors, excessive even by Elizabethan standards. On one level it is pure sensationalism, and panders to the most elementary tastes. But the grisly piece was executed with obvious gusto; in its frank delight in sheer brutality *Antonio's Revenge* takes on the quality of a prolonged sadistic fantasy. At the climax Piero is bound and his tongue plucked. A dish is opened, revealing the severed limbs of his son, a 'prettie tender childe' sacrificed by Antonio for the purpose of tormenting Piero. The revengers taunt the duke, call him foul names, stab him one by one, and, finally, run all at once upon him with drawn rapiers. The scene owes much to Seneca, but exceeds even the Roman in violence. It is noteworthy that the author's sympathies lie entirely with the revengers; there is no suggestion that they have proceeded beyond the proper limits of retribution. After the bloody interlude has ended, the avengers clamor for recognition, until all finally agree that they are equally worthy of 'the glorie of the deede.' They are congratulated and offered generous rewards, but choose to

> live inclos'd
> In holy verge of some religious order,
> Most constant votaries. (v.vi, p. 131)

This odd conclusion, so contrary to the conventional denouement, wherein the contaminated revenger must also perish, shows the playwright identifying himself with the forces of violence, enjoying vicariously the piling up of horrors.

Indeed the distinguishing characteristic of Marston's work is violence. In *Antonio's Revenge* it appears in its most obvious form as the core of the action. But it manifests itself also when Marston assumes the pose of the satirist lashing the follies of the age. There is a savage exuberance about Marston's invective, a pulsating emotional energy that—aside from considerations of quality—puts it in a class apart from the brooding cynicism of a Webster or the metaphysical wit of a Donne. Violence is apparent also in Marston's language—in the strained diction and mutilated syntax, in the discordant sound combinations and grotesque imagery. The violence of expression may be symptomatic of the clash of conflicting emotional currents in the deeper levels of his consciousness. Perhaps the nature of these divided emotional attitudes may best be understood by an examination of Marston's imagery, which is stamped with the peculiarities of his temperament.

Images of physical torment are common. In the prologue alone to *Antonio's Revenge* he writes of the 'snarling gusts' which 'pils the skinne / From off the soft and delicate aspectes,' of breasts 'nail'd to the earth with griefe,' of panting hearts 'Pierc't through with anguish.' Marston's imagery reveals a fascination with man's body and its functions. His verse is rich in references to various parts of the anatomy—to heart and stomach, to ribs and breasts, to veins and arteries. A few illustrations will suffice:

(As from his birth, being hugged in the armes;
And nuzzled twixt the breastes of happinesse)
(Prol., *Antonio's Revenge*, p. 69)

I tell you bloods
My spirit's heavie, and the juyce of life
Creepes slowly through my stifned arteries.
(*Antonio's Revenge* I.iii, p. 77)

Unbendst the feebled vaines of sweatie labour;
(*Malcontent* III.ii, p. 178)

'*Sweet breath from tainted stomacks who can suck.*'
(Prol. *What You Will*, p. 235)

He is equally concerned with physiological processes. Thus he describes the arrival of spring in terms of sexual intercourse:

The wanton spring lyes dallying with the earth,
And powers fresh bloud in her decayed vaines.
(*What You Will* I.i, p. 238)

But his biological interests extend beyond the sexual; he is preoccupied with the waste products of the body, with vomit and spit, sweat and excrement, abscesses and putrefaction:

Now had the mounting Suns al-ripening wings
Swept the cold sweat of night from earths danke breast,
(*Malcontent* IV.iii, p. 189)

Why tainst thou then the ayre with stench of flesh,
And humane putrifications noysome sent?
(*Antonio's Revenge* II.ii, p. 87)

> . . . the sea grewe mad,
> His bowels rumbling with winde passion, . . .
> Downe fals our ship, and there he breaks his neck:
> Which in an instant up was belkt againe.
> (*Antonio and Mellida* I.i, p. 19)

> Dog, I will make thee eate thy vomit up.
> Which thou hast belk't gainst taintlesse *Mellida.*
> (*Antonio's Revenge* I.iv, p. 80)

In the comparatively innocuous little comedy, *What You Will,* there is, at one point, a whole succession of such images:

> Shall he be creast-falne, if some looser braine,
> In flux of witte uncively befilth
> His slight composures? shall his bosome faint
> If drunken *Censure* belch out sower breath,
> Nay say some halfe a dozen rancorous breasts
> Should plant them-selves on purpose to discharge
> Impostum'd malice on his latest Sceane . . .
> (Induction, p. 232)

Such imagery permeates the Malcontent's most eloquent utterance of despair and revulsion: 'this earth is the only grave and *Golgotha* wherein all thinges that live must rotte: tis but the draught wherein the heavenly bodies discharge their corruption, the very muckhill on which the sublunarie orbes cast their excrement: man is the slime of this dongue-pit, and Princes are the governours of these men' (IV.v, p. 197). Man has a soul, but he has a body as well. He is a creature of superior faculties, but he is also a biological entity. Marston cannot bring himself to accept this duality; it is at the core of his disgust with mankind. And yet, if the body is a source of revulsion, it exerts nevertheless a peculiar fascination. Marston is unable to countenance what is physical in man, but he cannot avoid contemplating it. This divided response of attraction and revulsion reaches its culmination in the desecration motif, in images of noble or lovely things besmirched and reviled:

> Hast thou a love as spotlesse as the browe
> Of clearest heaven, blurd with false defames?
> (*Antonio's Revenge* I.v, p. 82)

> Sticke candells gainst a virgin walles white back,
> If they not burne yet at the least theile blacke,'
> (*Malcontent* II.v, p. 173)

> ... I ha seen a sumptuous steeple turned to a stinking privie: more beastly, the sacredst place made a Doggs kenill: nay most inhumane, the ston'd coffins of long flead Christians burst up, and made Hogs-troughs. (*Malcontent* II.v, p. 173)

Perhaps the most striking example occurs in *Sophonisba,* when Erictho describes 'a once glorious temple rearde to *Jove*':

> there the daw and crow,
> The ill voic'de Raven, and still chattering Pie
> Send out ungratefull sound, and loathsome filth,
> Where statues and *Joves* acts were vively lim'd
> Boyes with blacke coales draw the vaild parts of nature,
> And leacherous actions of imaginde lust,
> Where tombes and beauteous urns of well dead men
> Stoode in assured rest, the shepheard now
> Unloads his belly: Corruption most abhord
> Mingling it selfe with their renowned ashes,
> Our selfe quakes at it. (IV.i, p. 48)

This ambivalent attitude extends beyond imagery to permeate Marston's view of external reality; it is, in a large measure, responsible for the incongruous nature of his art. Conflicting emotions can be seen in operation in his reaction against his own *Metamorphosis of Pygmalion's Image,* a conventionally erotic poem in the tradition of *Hero and Leander* and *Venus and Adonis.* This youthful work is frankly sensual in its approach, showing a delight in feminine beauty and amorous impulses. Although the poem is no more outspoken than others of its type, Marston apparently felt disturbed and needed to justify himself. In the sixth satire of his *Scourge of Villainy* he insists that the *Pygmalion* is satirical, that its purpose is to discredit erotic poetry:

> Hence, thou misjudging censor! know I wrote
> Those idle rhymes to note the odious spot
> And blemish that deforms the lineaments
> Of modern poesy's habiliments. (23–26)

The apology does not ring true, and Marston has been accused of insincerity. It is more likely, however, that the poet, at first attracted to the erotic theme, underwent a change of heart. His statement reflects, perhaps, the need for rationalizing and self-justification as feelings of guilt and revulsion succeeded the original impulse toward sensual delight.

What originated perhaps as an inability to overcome an infantile repugnance to elementary biological facts becomes the key to the fantasy world that is his drama. In his plays Marston creates a nightmare world of lust and viciousness, intrigue and violence. His setting is usually 'an *Italian* lascivious Pallace' peopled with villains and fools. The time is generally night; Marston delights in descriptions of the darkness which conceals shame and wickedness. The atmosphere is charged with eroticism, brutality, and cynicism. 'I would sooner leave my ladie singled in a *Bordello*,' remarks Malevole, 'then in the *Genoa* pallace.' Women become symbols of sheer animalism, a tendency culminating in the ferocious Franceschina of *The Dutch Courtezan* and Isabella, *The Insatiate Countess*—fantastic embodiments of insatiable sexuality. Innocence is tainted or destroyed, while evil and malice flourish. The old harmony has been replaced by universal discord. Pandulpho wants no song for his dead son:

> *Pan*. No, no song: twill be vile out of tune.
> *Alb*. Indeede he's hoarce: the poor boyes voice is crackt.
> *Pa*. Why cuz? why shold it not be hoarce & crackt,
> When all the strings of natures symphony
> Are crackt, & jar? why should his voice keepe tune,
> When ther's no musick in the breast of man?
>
> (*Antonio's Revenge* IV.V, p. 121)

The dramatist has conceived a monstrous and distorted world, but one animated with extraordinary relish and energy. Having created such a world, he seeks to destroy it. He introduces the satiric commentator who rails upon it savagely; his plays are punctuated with tirades against courts and women, fools and parasites. Attraction and repulsion meet and are held in precarious balance. Sometimes this balance is destroyed, and we have those baffling excursions into obscurity or hysteria.

Marston is divided against himself even in his attitude toward his own work. He longed, quite naturally, for a literary reputation. At times he adopts an air of affected nonchalance. *Antonio and Mellida*, 'the worthless present of my slighter idleness,' is dedicated to '*the most hono*rably renowned No-body,' while *What You Will* is 'a slight toye, lightly, to swiftly finisht, ill plotted, worse written, I feare me worst acted, and indeed *What You Will*.' Such self-conscious modesty is the product of solicitous concern. Marston regarded his craft with high seriousness; he provided his plays with elaborate inductions and unusually full stage directions. But, at the same time that he strove after recognition, he yearned for oblivion:

> Let others pray
> For ever their fair poems flourish may;
> But as for me, hungry Oblivion,
> Devour me quick, accept my orison,
> My earnest prayers, which do importune thee,
> With gloomy shade of thy still empery
> To veil both me and my rude poesy

These lines, which give the impression of complete earnestness, appeared in the dedication 'To everlasting Oblivion,' at the close of his first publication. The year before his death he was apparently endeavoring to remove all traces of his authorship from a collection of his plays about to be issued, and on the stone above his burial place is carved, 'Oblivioni sacrum.' Perhaps it was an obscure sense of guilt that led to the desire to efface any memory of his work; perhaps he regarded his plays with the same mixed emotions that he felt toward the world he created within them.

Such conflicts exerted a crippling influence on Marston's art. He has no objective, or even consistent, view of reality, and consequently his work lacks relevance. Although he has much to reveal, he has little to say. T. S. Eliot feels, however, that Marston conveys 'the sense of something behind, more real than any of his personages and their action,' and thus 'establishes himself among the writers of genius.' [3] Eliot discerns in *Sophonisba* 'a pattern behind the pattern into which the characters deliberately involve themselves; the kind of pattern which we perceive in our own lives only at rare moments of inattention and detachment, drowsing in sunlight.' The critic's language is vague; he never reveals clearly the elements of which this pattern consists. But if Eliot wishes to imply that he sees in the play a significance beyond the merely literal, a philosophical or psychological validity that transcends the interplay of character, an expression, in other words, of a vision of humanity that is full and yet individual—then Eliot is reading into the plays a breadth of understanding which Marston gives no indication of possessing. For, in order to present a view of life which goes beyond the purely personal expression of mood or feeling, the artist must possess a certain degree of insight and stability. These are precisely the qualities which Marston lacks. There is too much of the turbulent and irrational in Marston's temperament for writing to have served as anything more than a means of expressing the disordered fancies and half-acknowledged impulses that rankled within him.

And so, although his plays contain many dramatically effective situations and isolated passages of genuine poetry, they are on the whole unsatisfactory. There is little genuine characterization, because Marston had little real understanding of or interest in people. He succeeds best with a figure like Malheureux in *The Dutch Courtezan.* 'A man of Snowe,' he regards lust as the deadliest of sins, cautions his friend to desist from the pleasures of a lascivious bed, warns him of the dangers to his health and good name. But Malheureux's imagination dwells on the loose sensuality he abhors, and he is at once repelled and fascinated by the sordidness of sexual license. Assuring himself that 'the most odious spectacle the earth can present is an immodest vulgar woman,' he accompanies his friend to the brothel to view a whore, Franceschina. 'Ile go to make her loath the shame shee's in,' he says—but he remains to become enamoured himself. At first startled that a creature of such moral degeneracy can be beautiful, he soon falls hopelessly in love. He is driven almost to distraction by the physical charms of Franceschina; he is tormented by the guiltiness of his passion. So complete is his fall that he consents to murder his best friend in order to possess a whore. Only when faced with the gallows does he fully comprehend the moral abyss into which he has fallen, and not until then is his frantic yearning transformed into horrified revulsion. It is easy to see why such a character would appeal to Marston, and why the dramatist should succeed in his portrayal. But his range of emotional experience is so limited and his ambitions so grandiose that he fails far more frequently than he succeeds. On the whole his fools are repellent, his villains preposterous, and his heroes uninteresting or inconsistent.

He was fortunate in that his own maladjustment coincided with the malaise of his age, and that he was temperamentally suited to gratify the tastes of his spectators. Marston's plays were written for the exclusive patrons who attended performances at the private theatres. In much the same manner as the dramatists of the Restoration, he stimulated the jaded tastes of his frivolous and sophisticated aristocratic audience—an audience that lacked a feeling for true tragedy, an audience that was pleased with sensationalism, satire, exaggerated emotions, and sententious declamation. Marston was able to satisfy these needs; he included, moreover, a gratuitous display of his own morbid tendencies, for he found his audience receptive to the cynical, the tortured, and the perverse. For the modern reader Marston remains interesting primarily for his self-revelation. Eventually he abandoned the stage and entered the church, but we do not know whether he resolved in his new surroundings the conflicts that are evident in his writings. All that remains is the work of his earlier years—a testimonial of the turbulent emotions of a distressed spirit.

NOTES

1. The H. Harvey Wood edition of Marston's plays (Edinburgh, 1934–39) has been used throughout for quotations. The text is not satisfactory; but a definitive edition of Marston is yet to be issued, and meanwhile the Wood volumes are the most generally available. As there is no line numbering, page references have been supplied instead. The Bullen text (London, 1887) has been used for the non-dramatic works.
2. Bullen, I, 63.
3. 'John Marston,' in *Elizabethan Essays* (London, 1934), pp. 190, 194. One may, indeed, remark that there has been a tendency in recent years possibly to overestimate the artistic and historical importance of Marston's work. The dramatist has been romanticized, perhaps even sentimentalized. To Theodore Spencer he became the attractive symbol of the thwarted idealist. In *Criterion*, XIII (July 1934), 581–599, Spencer wrote: 'The secret of Marston's temperament is that he was an idealist whose idealism was built on insufficient facts. When the facts hit him in the face the blow was severe, and in order to conceal how much he was hurt, he pretended that he had known about them all along, that he enjoyed them' (p. 597)

ROY W. BATTENHOUSE

Chapman and the Nature of Man

I

Study of Chapman's doctrine of man offers interesting illustration of one aspect of the sixteenth-century 'revival of the classics.' For Chapman's teachers were Plato, Plutarch, and Epictetus—along with such antiquarians as Comes and Ficinus; and steeping himself in these Hellenists, the poet acquired a nostalgia for the world of 'old humanity.' His models of virtue are Homer the mystic seer and Cato the serenely self-controlled. Christ upon the Cross is, indeed, also a hero—but a hero fitted to accord with Stoic and Platonic morality. Like the Florentine Platonists, Chapman is a syncretist of classical and Christian thought, assimilating the two in such a way as generally to blur over historical and theological distinctions. He makes his Cato argue, most un-Stoically, for the immortality of the soul, and even for a resurrection of the body; and, on the other hand, he has Christ propound the dubiously Christian doctrine that 'As we are men, we death and hell controule.' [1] Ranging Christian story side by side with pagan myth, Chapman interprets both in terms of Plotinian philosophy. In this respect he represents a recrudescence of that 'religion' of Classicism which Athanasius and Augustine had with difficulty conquered. The religious concepts of Hellenistic philosophy rather than the definitions of Christian orthodoxy furnish Chapman the premises of his view of man.

The distinction is an important one; and to see it clearly it will be profitable to recall quickly a few of the points particularly urged by the two Church Fathers just mentioned. Philosophic wisdom, Augus-

From *ELH*, XII (June 1945), pp. 87–107. Reprinted by permission of the journal, the author, and the Johns Hopkins Press. The article is reprinted as published but amplifying footnote material has been excised.

tine had remarked in his 13th Book *On the Trinity*, enables men not to be blessed but to be 'bravely miserable.' Unable to be what they would wish, they counsel themselves to will only what they can—thus binding themselves under 'nature' rather than freeing themselves under God. They desire immortality, for such is implied in the universal will to be blessed, but they fail to see that immortality is for 'the whole man, who certainly consists of soul and body.' This insistence on the integrity of the whole man, and on his genuine freedom within the realm of nature, is what distinguishes Augustine and Athanasius from their Classical opponents.

Equally important is Christianity's emphasis on the essential goodness of the created world. Against Arius, whose intellectual affiliations were Neoplatonic, Athanasius declares that the world has not been made, as Plato teaches, by some mere mechanic out of a pre-existent stuff, but by a genuine Creator, out of nothing; [2] and hence evil does not reside in matter but in the perverted choice of the soul which has shut its eyes against God.[3] Arius must be instructed on this point: that our Lord's putting on of human flesh in no way disqualified him for equal status with God the Father, for the Son 'was not lessened by the envelopment of the body, but rather deified it and rendered it immortal.' [4] Augustine, a century and a half later, is equally careful to establish the point that 'in its own kind and degree the flesh is good.' He censures the Manichees for detesting our present bodies, and the Platonists for holding the view that the diseases of desire which affect the soul arise from the soul's association with an earthly body. A Christian, he says, does 'not desire to be deprived of the body, but to be clothed with its immortality.' [5] The Platonists, though we may call them the wisest among the philosophers of antiquity, were yet blinded by the absence of two fundamental doctrines: that of the Incarnation and that of the Resurrection of the Body.[6]

With this necessarily very brief account of the important points of cleavage between Christian and Classical thought as it bears on the problem of the nature and destiny of man, I turn now to an examination of Chapman's views.

II

Let us give attention, first, to the constitution of man as Chapman conceives him. The words of the 'Senecal' Clermont as he stands on the threshold of deifying himself by suicide are generally supposed, I think, to represent the dramatist's own view. Clermont says:

The garment or the cover of the mind,
The human soul is; of the soul, the spirit
The proper robe is; of the spirit, the blood;
And of the blood, the body is the shroud.
With that must I begin then to unclothe,
And come at th' other.
(*Revenge of Bussy*. 5. 5. 170–75)

The picture here is of 'layers' of being, increasingly material and crude in nature, encasing and imprisoning an intellectual being whose homeland is 'beyond.' Plainly, the body is not viewed as good, nor is the soul the 'form of the body' as for Aristotle and St. Thomas; instead, man is a Neoplatonic spirit imbedded uncomfortably in nature. The interpretation is made the more vivid in certain of Chapman's non-dramatic verses, where man's soul is spoken of as a ray from heaven dwelling in a dunghill body; or again, man's flesh is said to be a Shirt of Nessus.[7] In *Eugenia* man is defined as 'all mind,' the body being merely the mind's 'instrument' (633–34). The body's 'passionate affects,' we are told in *Andromeda*, never can display satisfactorily 'what the soul respects'—just as the shadow of a man 'never can Shew the distinct, the exact Forme of Man'

For how can mortall things, immortal shew?
Or that which false is, represent the trew? [8]

In Chapman's tragedies the characters repeatedly elaborate this depreciatory view of the body. 'Our bodies,' says Tamyra, 'are but thick clouds to our souls, Through which they cannot shine when they desire.' [9] The Guise, in a speech justifying suicide, calls his body 'this imperfect blood and flesh,' 'this mass of slavery,' 'this same sink of sensuality,' 'this carrion'; and he determines to 'set my true man clear' by springing up to the stars! [10] Byron blames his ultimate misery on the 'bond and bundle of corruption' to which his soul is linked. 'I know this body but a sink of folly,' he says. At the same time Epernon, an onlooker, exclaims over the 'impossible mixtures' of 'corruption and eternnesse' of which man consists.[11]

The sources for Chapman's negative view of the body obviously go back as far as Pythagoras' suggestion that the body is a prison-house, Plato's theory that it is at best a 'principle of limitation,' and Plutarch's picture of it as a mere 'receptacle' susceptible of affection and mutation.[12] But Chapman could have encountered the same views closer at hand. From Ficinus he might have learned that man's 'immortal soul is always miserable in the body,' and from Landinus that life on earth participates in gloom and perturbation because tied to matter.[13] Abraham Fraunce stood ready to tell him that

> The *Platonists* call the body a *Hell,* in respect of the minde . . . for, being bereaft of celestial ornaments, it sorroweth and greeueth, and therefore compast with Stygian waues, displeaseth itselfe, hateth and abhoreth his owne acts, howles, and makes pitiful lamentation; and that is *Cocytus,* of *κοκένω,* to howle and crie out, as Plato expoundeth it.[14]

Among Chapman's own English contemporaries Sir John Davies was speaking of man's body as a prison, and Davies of Hereford was calling it a 'Clog.'

Chapman's view of the world parallels his view of man, for they are related as macrocosm to microcosm.[15] As body is to soul, so earth is to heaven a shadow as compared with substance. Felicity is definitely not to be found on earth. 'Hath any man been blessed, and yet liv'd?' Byron asks.[16] And Pompey wonders 'did the state Of any best man here associate?' [17] It is wisdom, he thinks, 'to turn one's back to all the world, And only look at heaven.' [18] Athenodorus concurs: 'for this giant world,' he says

> Let's not contend with it, when heaven itself
> Fails to reform it: why should we affect
> The least hand over it in that ambition?
> A heap 'tis of digested villany;
> Virtue in labour with eternal chaos
> Press'd to a living death, and rack'd beneath it.
> (*Caesar and Pompey.* 5. 2. 76–82)

Cato, joining the chorus of scorn, prepares for suicide with the words: 'The next world and my soul, then, let me serve.' [19] As for this world, Chapman's wisemen agree in condemning it as a realm of infirmity and change, depravity and flux: not until man is 'above All motion' can he be 'fix'd and quiet.' [20] Such a view, let me point out, implies that time has significance only as a Platonic 'moving image of eternity,' and history no meaning but as a period of exile.

III

Having thus made clear the way in which Chapman construes the character of the world and of man, let us now explore its implications. What is the destiny of man, assuming a definition of his nature in Neoplatonic terms? Here Chapman enters on complex territory and paradoxical answers. The multiple aspects of his answer can perhaps best be disentangled in terms of several classical myths which have a key prominence in his thinking. Particularly worth examining are the myths of Ganymede, Prometheus, the 'Senecal man,' and Hercules. Each exhibits a part of Chapman's view as to the destiny of man.

The myth of Ganymede, as interpreted by Renaissance allegorists, teaches that man's most glorious destiny is to be found in the cultivation of his intellect. According to Comes and Landinus, Ganymede stands for the human mind, beloved by the Supreme Being, and abducted from the body by the 'divine fury' of enraptured contemplation.[21] Abraham Fraunce explains that the ravishing of Ganymede by Jupiter stands for 'the lifting up of mans minde from these earthly toyes, to heauenly conceipts.'[22] The destiny here held out for man is that he may transcend the realm of misery associated with his body and earthly life and be caught up into the beatitude of heaven, if he will but concentrate his activity in the exercise of his intellect, disregarding the lure of the senses. Chapman employs the myth thus in his *Hymnus in Cynthiam.* The sense-world, he there argues, is but a shadow of the real world: it is, to use his phrase, only a 'Shadow of Night' obscuring the true Divine Dark in which man, if he be virtuous, can come to dwell like a bright star. Ganymede was snatched out of earth's noisome gloom and stellified as the great Aquarius in heaven's healthful dark, because he cultivated intellectual beauty. His story teaches that the mind 'nearest comes to a Divinity' when it 'furtherest is from spot of Earth's delight.' To be carried off by the Eagle of contemplation is to become a shining light of virtue. Chapman, believing this with all his heart, regarded scholarship as a 'holy trance' and an avenue to saving truth; unless it was that, it was worthless. What he sought in Homer was a 'flood of soul' and those 'doctrinal illations of truth' which might conduct him, and other readers, to a peace passing all understanding.[23]

But Platonic and Stoic thought has to face the fact also that man is earth-bound. He has a term to spend in the world of flux or nature. Even though his true and proper destiny be to rest in eternity as a Plotinian pure spirit, or to ascend to the fiery heavens as a spark of Stoic logos, yet the economy of the universe has imposed on him a period of struggle in the world. His plight is symbolized by the wrestling Jacob [24] or, more commonly, by the figure of Prometheus. As Prometheus was bound to a pillar, says Abraham Fraunce, so 'The minde is bound fast to the body, and there chained for awhile'; and the Eagle which devoured Prometheus' heart stands for the meditations which every day consume the wiseman's mind—which only the night (of contemplation?) can restore again.[25]

Erwin Panofsky has pointed out that the agonizing Prometheus was a favorite symbol in Renaissance art, expressing the price mankind has to pay for its intellectual awakening—the price of being tortured by profound meditation, and recovering only to be tortured again.[26] Chapman seems to express this mood in some verses addressed to his friend Harriot:

O that my strange muse
Without this bodies nourishment could vse,
Her zealous faculties, onely t'aspire,
Instructiue light from your whole Sphere of fire:
But woe is me, what zeale or power soeuer
My free soule hath, my body will be neuer
Able t' attend.

His soul's 'genuine formes,' he says, 'struggle for birth, Vnder the clawes of this fowle Panther earth'; for his body is constantly betraying its 'crown,' the soul.[27] Like Prometheus, Chapman is ill at ease in the terrestrial order; but he believes, as a passage in *The Shadow of Night* indicates, that a 'Promethean' poet serves his fellowmen by making them likewise ill at ease. His task is to picture the subhuman character of their degenerate lives, thus illuminating their predicament and stirring them up to reform.[28] Further, Chapman says elsewhere, poetry has a 'Promethean facultie' to 'create men.' [29] Here he would seem to be reflecting the notion, popularized in the Renaissance by Boccaccio, that man is not fully 'created' until given spiritual Form by the culture-bringer Prometheus. At any rate, such interpretation accords closely with Chapman's theory that man is incomplete unless ruled by 'soul,' and that the soul itself is 'a blank' until 'informed' by Learning or Art:

So when the Soule is to the body giuen;
(Being substance of Gods image, sent from heaven)
It is not his true Image, till it take
Into the Substance, those fit forms that make

> His perfect Image; which are then imprest
> By Learning and impulsion.[30]

Poetry, in Chapman's view, is the mediator of this Learning, the conveyor of this Art. So also was Christ, who endured pains to bring about the 'perfecting' of the form infused in man's creation.[31] Chapman's Christ is, in other words, a Promethean poet; and Chapman's self-dedication to Christ is an embracing of the rôle of suffering light-bringer.

IV

In accord with his understanding of man's misery and of the poet's instructional function, Chapman composed tragedies in which the protagonists are moral types.[32] They represent in the main two forms of human nature: the degenerate and the ideal. That is, Chapman's heroes are either slaves-of-passion or exemplars of calm. In the first category come Byron, Bussy, and Tamyra—'headless' and headlong men and women; in the second we find Clermont the 'complete' man and Cato his double. The one series illustrates what Chapman calls 'the body's fervour'; the other, 'the mind's constant and unconquered empire.'

These two categories, supposed by Chapman to derive from Homer, actually reflect Neoplatonic theory as to the two divergent courses in life open to man.[33] A man's destiny, according to this theory, is determined by whether he rests in reason or gives rein to passion; by whether he trusts in things inward or covets things outward. He may, to use Chapman's language, 'direct Reason in such an Art, as that it can Turne blood to soule, and make both, one calme man,'[34] or he may let his thoughts take fire from his blood, become enamoured like Narcissus of his shadow-self, and progressively drown himself in his own lower nature. Either he will use the soul's 'beams' to disperse the body's vapors, or the body will be allowed to choke the soul.[35] In giving pattern to these antithetical careers Chapman invokes two myths of opposite purport: that of the 'Senecal man' and that of Hercules.

Analysis of the Senecal man need not detain us long. He is a static figure, essentially undramatic. Cato is at his height in declaring

> I'll pursue my reason,
> And hold that as my light and fiery pillar
> (*Caesar & Pompey*, 5. 2. 42–43)

or when he is raising such queries as

> is not our free soul infus'd
> To every body in her absolute end
> To rule that body?...
> And being empress, may she not dispose
> It, and the life in it, at her just pleasure?
> (*Ibid.*, 4. 5. 74–79)

But his acting in accord with such logic makes of tragic catharsis a mockery. To put a sword to one's own heart and cry 'Now I am safe' is to deny the value of all history and make all heroism a pompous prelude to retreat. Cato is a tedious character parading an immobile virtue. His drama, being all character and no plot, is decidedly un-Aristotelian.

Clermont's principles are equally 'correct,' and his demise equally insipid. He is a protagonist 'fix'd in himself,' with a 'most gentle and unwearied mind, Rightly to virtue fram'd.' [36] We are told also that he has the 'crown of man,' which is 'learning,' to supplement and rule his natural valor. This means that he wisely abhors all those things which a merely 'natural' man like Byron glories in—change, violence, perjury, self-seeking, and outward greatness. For he has learned from Homer's story of Achilles that men endowed with nature's best gifts can come to destruction unless they set down 'Decrees within them, for disposing these.' [37] Wisely he understands nature 'with enough art' and therefore sees the Universe as a divine frame which it would be gross impiety to attempt to subject to his private will: instead, he will go 'cheek by cheek' with Necessity in 'glad obedience To any thing the high and general Cause . . . hath ordain'd.' [38] So, when he is arrested unjustly he resigns himself philosophically; when a 'Christian' ghost lets him know that God ordains the revenge of Bussy, he obeys; and when the laws of Platonic friendship urge him to join the slain Guise, he again complies. He is a curious mixture of Christian, Stoic, and Platonic morality. He commits suicide like a Stoic, but he fulfills an act of vengeance which, as several commentators have pointed out,[39] no Stoic would have considered worth performing.

But let us now examine the alternative explanation of human tragedy set forth in Bussy and Byron. A. S. Ferguson is the latest of several commentators to agree in the statement that Bussy is for the dramatist 'the classical Hercules born anew, accomplishing similar feats, and lured to a similar tragic doom.' [40] Bussy is a hero committed to the pursuit of virtue but betrayed by his 'great heart [that] will not down.' His passion, though ardently set on 'honest actions,' is presently serving the black-magic of the Friar and the adulterous will of Tamyra. His valor declares itself in the Herculean pattern when he offers himself as a cleanser of the court and is given by the King the rôle of scourge. Bussy has, however, what one of his epithets announces, a 'Passion of death!,' and we watch him trapped into death by the call of Tamyra's blood. He then meets his fate with the fortitude of a Hercules—chastened, however, by his Shirt-of-Nessus experience into an astonishing piety of quasi-Christian tone. The ending is quite un-Senecan when Bussy forgives his enemies, acknowledges his own 'worthless fall,' and proclaims his fate a warning to express the 'frail condition of strength, valour, [and] virtue.' If we ask what Bussy's tragic flaw was, there is the hint of an answer in the words of Monsieur, who tells us that Bussy is 'like other naturals That have strange gifts in nature, but no soul Diffus'd quite through.' [41] Or we may explain it as the Guise does in *The Revenge of Bussy,* a play written six years later: Bussy's valor, he says, lacked 'learning,' so that he 'was rapt with outrage oftentimes Beyond decorum' (2. 1. 89–90).

The pattern is similar, but more elaborately moralized, in the Byron plays. Byron, like Marlowe's Tamburlaine, thinks it 'immortality to die aspiring'; he wants to be 'like the shaft Shot at the sun by angry Hercules.' [42] Like Hercules and Bussy, he is a man of valor with great accomplishments: he has 'Alcides-like gone under th' earth, And on these shoulders borne the weight of France.' [43] But he is a man 'broken loose From human limits,' who is easily 'taken in affection' by the black-magic of La Fin, as Bussy was by that of the Friar. Indeed, Byron attempts later to excuse his crime by blaming it on 'this damn'd enchanter,' but one of his judges replies that 'worthy minds witchcraft can never force.' The Prologue explains Byron's tragedy as a yielding to 'policy,' so that he thirsts no longer for his country's love but Narcissus-like for 'the fair shades of himself.' There is reference, at the beginning of the second play, to the 'fatal thirst of his ambition' which is carrying Byron 'quite against the stream of all religion, Honour, and reason.' A Shirt-of-Nessus overtakes him in the form of an inward fire arising from 'adust and melancholy choler' of the blood and issuing in hysteria.[44] His virtue has now degenerated into a kind of Machiavellian virtù; so that Soissons is right in remarking 'O Virtue, thou art now far worse than Fortune.' Another observer, the Vidame, sees the true meaning of 'this angry conflagration': it is a purgatorial fire blasting Byron's earthly hopes so that 'piety [may] enter with her willing cross.' Presently piety begins to appear, phoenix-like, out of the ashes, as Byron asks

> Why should I keep my soul in this dark light,
> Whose black beams lighted me to lose myself?
> (*Byron's Tragedy*, 5. 4. 69–70)

The play's protagonist has become a chastened moralizer by the time he says

> Farewell, world!
> He is at no end of his actions blest
> Whose ends will make him greatest, and not best;
> (*Ibid.*, 5. 4. 143–45)

and he ends the play like a preacher:

> Fall on your knees then, statists, ere ye fall,
> That you may rise again: knees bent too late,
> Stick you in earth like statues: see in me
> How you are pour'd down from your clearest heavens.

Significantly, Byron now regards death as an 'eternal victory' by which his soul is freed to take her flight. Such an ending is quite in line with the Neoplatonic interpretation of Hercules' pyre as a burning of the dross of mortality by which he purged himself to become divine.[45] More importantly, the ending agrees with a long tradition of 'homiletical tragedy,' from W. Wager to John Ford, in which the 'chain of vice' theme and the 'scaffold speech' are standard features.[46]

Chapman's way of ending the Bussy and Byron dramas depends on the paradoxical theory that a display of evil forwards the good. The fire in Byron, says the King, 'not another deluge can put out';[47] consequently we see it putting itself out by exhaustion so that Byron can be reborn—and so that others may be converted by the awful spectacle. The view accords closely with that set forth in *The Shadow of Night*. The world of the senses, the poet there says, is a great smoking altar of human passions which must either be drowned by the deluge of our tears or cleansed by the fury of a Hercules; 'lust's fire' must either be quenched by intellectual love or expended in hot and noisy pursuits whose miseries may beget contrition. 'Weepe,

weepe your soules, into felicitie,' says Chapman, for sorrow is the only way to beatitude. In other words, if we do not embrace religion through repentance we will be driven to it through grievous 'justice' and fiery trial.

V

The view we have just discriminated implies an apology for violence in the name of piety, and is one of the most curious and significant aspects of the thought of the Jacobean age. I wish there were space here to develop adequately the close parallel of Chapman's theory with that of Fulke Greville, who deciphers his own name as 'Greiv-Ill' because of his gloomy view of life.[48] According to Greville, the flesh must die before grace can be born; 'The earth must burne, ere we for Christ can looke.'[49]

For God comes not till man be ouerthrowne;
Peace is the seed of grace, in dead flesh sowne.[50]

God meant not Man should here inherit,
A *time-made* World, which with time should not fade;
But as *Noes flood* once drown'd woods, hils, & plain,
So should the fire of *Christ* waste all againe.[51]
First let the law plough vp thy wicked heart
That *Christ* may come, and all these types depart.[52]

In other words, man is a rebel who must be broken by the law before he will look for grace—must feel the hot fires of justice in his own world and his own blood before he will welcome the cool of God's firmament and of Christ's red blood streaming. Our 'falne nature,' says Greville, follows 'streames of vanity' until 'For'd vp to call for grace':

Whence from the depth of fatall desolation
Springs vp the height of his [man's] Regeneration.[53]

For

When Gods All-might doth in thy flesh appeare,
Then Seas with streames aboue thy skye doe meet.[54]

Here is a hope indeed Promethean, creating (if I may quote Shelley) 'From its own wreck the thing it contemplates.'

What is particularly worth noting, I think, is that in Greville's world view, as in Chapman's, we find parading under the same banner of piety both idealism and cynicism, a theoretical humanitarianism and 'pacifism' side by side with a practical approval of violence [55] —a combination such as characterized politics in the late Roman empire, and is not wholly absent among our contemporaries. There is in Greville, as Miss Ellis-Fermor has lately pointed out, a curious crossing of a 'hard vein of Machiavellian pragmatism with the almost mystical rejection of the seen in favor of the unseen.' [56] 'Proceed in Furie,' Achmat says in *Mustapha,* for 'Furie hath Law and Reason, Where it doth plague the wickedness of Treason.' And again: 'Nothing [is] thy way vnto eternall being; Death, to saluation; and the Graue to Heauen.' [57] This may be compared with Chapman's advice to the Furies in *The Shadow of Night* to

Thunder your wrongs, your miseries and hells,
And with the dismall accents of your knells,
Reuiue the dead, and make the liuing dye
In ruth, and terror of your torturie. (306–309)

and with his invocation, in the name of justice:

Fall Hercules from heauen in tempestes hurld,
And cleanse this beastly stable of the world. (255–56)

Chapman's Bussy and Byron both think of themselves as 'scourges' and seem to receive from Chapman a kind of justification in the rôle, as if their violence, for all its intemperance, were being accommodated by Necessity to a providential function. Byron, who has brought France peace and made his own name glorious as 'Scourge of the Huguenots,' [58] gives this justification for extending his activities as scourge:

The world is quite inverted, Virtue thrown
At Vice's feet, and sensual Peace confounds
Valour and cowardice, fame and infamy;
The rude and terrible age is turn'd again,
. . . .
We must reform and have a new creation
Of state and government, and on our Chaos
Will I sit brooding up another world.
I, who through all the dangers that can siege
The life cf man, have forc'd my glorious way
To the repairing of my country's ruins,
Will ruin it again to re-advance it.
(*Byron's Tragedy,* I. 2. 14–35)

That these are indeed an aspect of Chapman's own sentiments is made clear if we compare passages in the non-dramatic *Shadow of Night:* for there we find the notion that man is in a degenerate Iron age of 'sensual' peace, that he wallows in a moral chaos from which it would be blessed to return to the physical chaos of 'the old essence and insensive prime,' and that torture advances this cure of man's diseases. The conclusion we must draw, if I interpret aright, is that such Herculean figures as Bussy and Byron advance morality even while illustrating depravity, for in their scourging of others and eventually of themselves they teach all men to despise our life in time and covet a 'second life' in eternity.

Chapman and Greville can make room at the same time for transcendentalism and Machiavellianism because they have received from Platonic teachers a 'two-story universe' and a two-story man. From Ficinus had come the doctrine that man is created 'double' with two 'lights,' one innate and the other infused, and two 'loves,' one Profane and the other Sacred.[59] This means a bifurcation of man between his secular or 'natural' life, which is under Fate, and his divine or rational life, which is under Providence. It means that man 'in nature' only is 'fallen' and miserable. For nature is of itself irrational and needs constantly to be rationalized. 'What nature gives at random,' says Chapman, must be ordered by our 'divine part.' [60] Or again, Chapman regarded Nature as 'at her heart corrupted . . . euen in her most ennobled birth,' so that 'she must neede incitements to her good'; [61] left to herself, she is brutish for lack of Reason.[62] By this perspective Chapman could declare through Monsieur in *Bussy* that 'Nature is stark blind herself.' But at the same time he could say through the Guise that Nature does not actually work 'at random,' however it may seem so to the superficial eye.[63] Nature has, indeed, an end: her own dissolution. The man who serves her is like the sea, destined to bristle with surges until 'crown'd with his own quiet foam.' Nature, in other words, is continually wasting herself by an inner law of defection. Greville was to see in this very fact of nature's failure a pious purpose:

Nature herselfe, doth her own selfe defloure,
To hate those errors she her selfe doth giue.
For how should man thinke that, he may not doe
If Nature did not faile, and punish too? [64]

Nature, let us take note, teaches negatively, warning man to flee from her to God.

The logic of Chapman and Greville is thus the logic of despair, moving dialectically from nature to grace—nature being understood in more or less Machiavellian terms, and grace being equated with Platonic and Stoic idealism. Between these two opposites lies a chasm, and there is no reconciling principle. Nature and 'fallen man' are considered so depraved, the world and the times so out of joint, that only violence can effect a cure. Chapman's Clermont, who is supposed to be the very opposite of 'your Machiavellian villains,' nevertheless sanctions violence: (*Revenge of Bussy*, 4. 4. 49)

> When truth is overthrown, his laws corrupted;
> When souls are smother'd in the flatter'd flesh,
> Slain bodies are no more than oxen slain;
>
> (*Ibid.*, 2. 1. 217–19)

and he excuses the St. Bartholomew's Day massacre:

> Had Faith and true Religion been preferr'd
> Religious Guise had never massacred.
>
> (*Ibid.*, 2. 1. 233–34)

On the other hand, Chapman seems to sanction also the violence of passion which causes religious duty to be overturned and souls to be smothered. Tamyra in *Bussy D'Ambois* says her offence is forced upon her by 'urgent necessity' and by the 'strong finger' which nature has in each of us.[65] The Friar backs her up with the doctrine that 'our affections' storm, Rais'd in our blood, no reason can reform.'[66] The dramatist presents us thus with two contradictory attitudes: on the one hand, Clermont's ruthlessness toward the body, since it is so bound up with our corruption and 'fall'; and, on the other hand, Tamyra's indulgent excusing of the body's fervors, since passion is natural to life in 'this world.' Puritan rigorism and libertine laxness are the respective horns of this dilemma. It represents, as any historian will recognize, a revival of the well-known 'paradoxes' of ancient Gnosticism and Manicheeism. The root-cause is a pessimistic view of the world, well expressed by the Ghost in *Bussy* when he says that misery is 'the just curse of our abus'd creation, Which wee must suffer heere and scape heereafter.'[67]

On one side of his thinking, therefore, Chapman has much in common with Machiavelli. For Machiavelli, as Pierre Mesnard has said, has a 'pessimisme décidé et résolu, aussi bien pour l'individu que pour L'Etat.' [68] This is because Machiavelli, like Chapman, makes a sharp distinction between the cosmos, represented by the starry heavens, an invariable and eternal realm, and our lower world, which is suspended from the heavens and participates only imperfectly in their inflexible harmony. Our earthly globe, according to Machiavelli, is determined in the mass. Its total energy, physical and moral, given once and for all, remains constant; but its aspects vary incessantly. History is nothing else than the succession of transformations of detail which inform differently this malleable matter including man. Force, industry, virtue—all is submitted to the same laws of evolution and dissolution. Man is prey to a persistent mobility. If he lets himself go, submitting to nature's influences, he accelerates the perpetual process of disintegration; and he is always inclined to do this, because matter has put in him the germ of instability which makes him desire change. Nature has endowed him with a desire for all things, while fortune permits him to attain only a few, with the result that there is in the human heart a perpetual discontent. The task of government is to restrain and guide this discontent, to collaborate with fortune and limit its effects—as a man might prepare dikes to limit the ravages of flood.

Chapman's belief in the indomitability of passion when once aroused, and his acquiescence in a necessitarian view of nature's processes, puts him in close accord with Machiavelli. He can deny the Florentine's logic, therefore, only by a leap of faith, in which Machiavellianism is allowed a dialectical status as one aspect of the truth, requiring constantly to be transcended by mystical idealism. Chapman's heroes 'overcome' nature by leaving it behind. They either stay aloof, with Clermont, until forced to flee nature's challenge by suicide; or they submit to nature's cycle, with Byron, until dissolution fits them for piety's wings. The trouble with Chapman's world view is that, having accepted a description of nature in line with Machiavelli's, he can avoid Machiavelli's principles only by avoiding nature, by repudiating wholesale the world of observed fact. In so far as he is compelled to take this world of evil into account, he knows no way of dealing with it except in terms of a 'natural law' which is Machiavellian.

VI

The point that deserves stressing is the radical difference between such a version of human nature and destiny and the Christian version. Christian theory agrees with Aristotle in believing that man has some chance for happiness in this world. Chapman, on the other hand, reverts to Senecan theory, which believes man sure to be outwardly beaten, since worldly calamity is irresistible and inescapable. Chapman's Bussy, as Hardin Craig has lately said, is no Aristotelian protagonist but a Senecan titan.[69] Seneca, says Craig,

> proposed to build up something within the heart of man which would enable him to gain a pyrrhic victory over fate. This doctrine is inherent in the stories of Hercules and Prometheus. (p. 12)

Since I have in this paper given considerable attention to these stories, let me add merely that the reader who wants to pursue further the significance of their cleavage from Christian story will find illuminating commentary in Charles N. Cochrane's recent book. Cochrane describes the history of Classical Culture's warfare with Christianity as a long contest tween two kinds of faith—the Promethean and the Trinitarian.[70] Promethean faith, Cochrane explains, is built on the notion of an opposition between man and his environment; between 'character' and 'circumstance'; between 'virtue' and 'necessity' or 'chance.' The prospect here held out for man is that of an endless struggle for the supremacy of mind over matter so long as the soul is 'in the body'; while 'beyond' there is release for the mind from all that is susceptible of death and destruction.[71] Trinitarian faith, on the other hand, denies any antithesis between human liberty and natural necessity. It affirms that God has created both man and nature, between whom there is no necessary opposition, since nature is not a closed system determined by its own laws. Prometheus therefore is but the victim of his own obsessions. He is self-frustrated.[72] I would suggest that the mental agonies of the Promethean Chapman might be thus largely explained.

Chapman's man, if I may now summarize, is split by the Platonic dichotomy between sense and intellect. He is by constitution half mortal and half celestial, with a body in nature and a soul from God. Through the sense world he is enmeshed in the tumults of fate, while through the intellectual world providence opens a path to peace.

Destined to God as his ideal end, man must yet accommodate to nature, master it so long and so far as possible, but failing this, take from nature's very gifts a precious bane. Thus man's destiny may be multiple: by aspiration a Ganymede enrapt in the ecstasy of contemplation; by intention a Senecal man ruling his earthly activities through reason; by default a Hercules chastening the world and himself through passion; and by necessity a Prometheus agonizing after transcendence. Such interpretation means introducing the settled melancholy of the Classical perspective in place of Christianity's sober cheer.

NOTES

1. See *The Tragedy of Caesar and Pompey*, 5. 5. 123 ff. and 5. 2. 140 ff.; *A Hymne to Our Saviour*, 200. All references in this paper are to the plays as edited by T. M. Parrott (London, 1910–14) and the poems as edited by Phyllis Bartlett (Oxford University Press, 1941).

2. *On the Incarnation*, 2–3.

3. *Against the Heathen*, 6–7.

4. *Defense of the Nicene Definition*, 3. 14.

5. *City of God*, 14. 3–5.

6. See *Confessions*, 7. 14; *City of God*, 8. 5–8; 22. 26–28.

7. See *The Teares of Peace*, 981 ff. (cf. *De Guiana*, 81), and *Eugenia*, 828.

8. *Andromeda Liberata*, 63–68. Bartlett points out that the doctrine, taken by Chapman from Ficinus, is elaborated also in *A Hymne to Our Saviour*, 221–48. Note that line 205 of this latter poem defines the human soul as a 'mortal celestiall'—implying that man is essentially a divinity but handicapped by mortality.

9. *Bussy D'Ambois*, 3. 1. 78–79.

10. *Revenge of Bussy*, 5. 4. 7–19.

11. *Byron's Tragedy*, 5. 4. 32 and 5. 3. 189–91. With Epernon's comments compare those of the 'Chorus Sacerdotum' in Fulke Greville's *Mustapha*.

12. See Charles N. Cochrane, *Christianity and Classical Culture* (Oxford, 1940), esp. pp. 79–80, 169–71.

13. See Erwin Panofsky, *Studies in Iconology* (Oxford University Press, 1939), pp. 135–38; also Kristeller, *op. cit.*, p. 332.

14. *The Third part of the Countesse of Pembrokes Yuychurch* (1592), fol. 28r.

15. See, e.g., *Eugenia*, 723, and *Andromeda*, 129.

16. *Byron's Conspiracy*, 1. 2. 26.

17. *Caesar and Pompey*, 4. 3. 80–81.

18. *Ibid.*, 5. 1. 216–217.
19. *Ibid.*, 5. 2. 131.
20. *Ibid.*, 5. 1. 195–96; cf. *Eugenia*, 467 ff.
21. See Panofsky, pp. 214–15.
22. *Op. cit.*, fol. 33r.
23. See *Teares of Peace*.
24. See *Eugenia*, 608–09 and gloss.
25. *Op. cit.*, fol. 9v.
26. *Op. cit.*, pp. 50–51. Elsewhere Panofsky remarks that Prometheus was 'a favorite humanistic symbol of the artist' and Hercules 'a favorite humanistic symbol of man in general.' See his 'Renaissance and Renascences,' *Kenyon Review*, 6 (Spring, 1944), 233.
27. *To Harriots*, 19–20, 31–37, 45–46.
28. *Hymnus in Noctem*, 131 and gloss.
29. *To Prince Henrie*, 137.
30. *Teares of Peace*, 352 ff.; cf. *Eugenia*, 953 ff. and 1152–59.
31. *A Hymne to our Saviour*, 135–36.
32. James Smith in his 'George Chapman,' *Scrutiny*, 4 (1935), 61, points out that the dramatist tells us very little about the physical appearance of his characters and fails to distinguish them by their speech. 'Chapman, having decided that his characters are primarily moral beings, confines them as much as possible to the moral world.'
33. See Kristeller, pp. 357–59.
34. *Teares of Peace*, 557–59.
35. *Teares of Peace*, 986–90; *De Guiana*, 106.
36. *Revenge of Bussy*, 4. 4. 14–15, 46.
37. *Ibid.*, 3. 4. 14–20.
38. *Ibid.*, 4. 1. 131 ff.
39. E. g., U. M. Ellis-Fermor, *The Jacobean Drama* (London, 1936), p. 69; R. H. Perkinson, 'Nature and the Tragic Hero in Chapman's Bussy Plays,' *MLQ*, 3. 275.
40. See 'The Plays of George Chapman,' *MLR*, 13 (1918), 10, citing with approval Professors Boas and Parrott.
41. *Bussy*, 3. 2. 435–37. Note that he is called 'The man of blood' in 3. 2. 373.
42. *Byron's Conspiracy*, 1. 2. 31 and 40–41.
43. *Byron's Tragedy*, 3. 1. 151–52.
44. See *Byron's Conspiracy*, 2. 2. 43, and 5. 2. 83–84; *Byron's Tragedy*, 5. 2. 296–98, and 5. 3. 207–09.
45. So Ficinus had interpreted in his Preface to Plato's *Symposium*. And so also Abraham Fraunce, *op. cit.*, fol. 47r: 'At length . . . he burnt himselfe on the mount *Oeta:* that is to say, his terrestrial body being purged and purified, himselfe was afterwards deified and crowned with immortality.'
46. See the excellent survey in Henry H. Adams, *English Domestic or Homiletic Tragedy, 1575–1642* (Columbia University Press, 1943), esp. pp. 82, 118–22.
47. *Byron's Conspiracy*, 5. 2. 83–84.
48. See *Caelica*, 83. I cite from G. Bullough's edition of *The Poems and Dramas of Fulke Greville*, 2 vols. (Edinburgh, 1939).

49. *Caelica,* 89.
50. *Caelica,* 96.
51. *A Treatie of Warres,* stanza 48.
52. *Caelica,* 88.
53. *Caelica,* 96.
54. *Caelica,* 88.
55. For a discussion of this dualism in Greville, see Bullough's Introduction, esp. pp. 14–15.
56. U. M. Ellis-Fermor, *The Jacobean Drama* (London, 1936), p. 194.
57. *Mustapha,* 5. 3. 96; and 'Chorus Quintus,' lines 19–20.
58. The title is twice pointed out: *Byron's Tragedy,* 1. 3. 3, and 5. 1. 79.
59. See Nesca A. Robb, *Neoplatonism of the Italian Renaissance* (London, 1935), pp. 79–83.
60. *An Anagram on Henry,* 6–10.
61. See *De Guiana,* 117–23.
62. See *Andromeda Liberata,* dedicatory lines *To Sommerset,* 129–44.
63. See *Bussy D'Ambois,* 5. 2. 4 and 21 ff.
64. *Mustapha,* Chorus Sacerdotum, 9–12.
65. *Bussy D'Ambois,* 3. 1. 61–67.
66. *Bussy D'Ambois,* 2. 2. 140–41.
67. *Bussy D'Ambois,* 5. 4. 15 ff., reading in 1607 quarto.
68. *L'Essor de la Philosophie Politique au XVIe Siècle* (Paris, 1936), p. 19. My paragraph, from here on, rests on translation and paraphrase from Mesnard, pp. 19–21.
69. See 'The Shackling of Accidents: A Study of Elizabethan Tragedy,' in this volume.
70. *Op. cit.*, pp. 368, 410–14.
71. *Ibid.*, pp. 167–71.
72. *Ibid.*, p. 411.

L. C. KNIGHTS

Tradition and Ben Jonson

I hate traditions;
I do not trust them. (*Ananias*)

RECENT revivals of *Volpone* and *The Alchemist* occasioned some surprise—surprise that they were such good 'theatre.' The general impression seems to have been that in these plays Jonson had, somehow, triumphed over his 'weight of classical learning,' had in fact forgotten it, and had provided some very good fun instead of his usual pedantries. It may not be quite fair to the dramatic critics to suggest that their delight at being entertained instead of bored showed how little Jonson is read, but certainly the reception given to those plays implied a still widespread misconception both of Jonson's intrinsic merits and of the extent and kind of his indebtedness to the Classics.

Ben Jonson is a very great poet—more finely endowed, I think, than any who succeeded him in the seventeenth century—and he read deliberately and widely. It was to be expected, therefore, that the effects of his reading would be in some manner present in his verse. Dryden said of him that he was a learned plagiary of all the ancients: 'you track him everywhere in their snow.' But this, the common view, violently distorts the sense in which Jonson is 'traditional'; it not only makes him appear to owe to the Greek and Latin writers a mere accumulation of thoughts and phrases, it completely hides the native springs of his vitality. The aim of this chapter is to correct the perspective, to show that Jonson's art is intimately related to the popular tradition of individual and social morality.

From *Drama and Society in the Age of Jonson* (Chatto and Windus Ltd., 1937), pp. 179–99. Reprinted by permission of the publisher and author.

A study such as this lies largely outside the field of strict literary criticism; but without a background of criticism to refer to it is impossible to say anything at all, and I propose to begin (without more apology for the indirect approach) by selecting one play and merely trying to explain why I find it admirable.

Sejanus is chosen not only because it is commonly underrated, but because it is the first play in which Jonson finds his proper scope: the early 'Humour' plays were mere experiments. Although here the typically Jonsonian method is deployed with less subtlety and richness than in, say, *Volpone*, the parallels between this 'tragedy' and the later 'comedies' are obvious and important.

The stuff of the play is the lust of political power and the pettiness that so often accompanies political greatness. The world with which we are presented is completely evil. Tiberius and Sejanus are equal in cruelty and cunning; Macro, the agent of Sejanus' overthrow, is, like others besides the principals, explicitly 'Machiavellian'; the satellites and senators are servile and inconstant; the mob tears the body of the fallen favourite,

> And not a beast of all the herd demands
> What was his crime, or who were his accusers.
>
> V, x (III, 147)[1]

The 'good' characters are choric and denunciatory merely, representing no positive values. How carefully anything that might bring into play sympathetic feelings is excluded is seen in the treatment of Agrippina; the meeting of her adherents, for example, is described (II, ii) in terms that reduce it to a gathering of fractious gossips. And this exclusion operates in the smallest details—in Tiberius' remark about dedicating

> A pair of temples, one to Jupiter
> At Capua; th'other at Nola to Augustus,
>
> III, iii (III, 86)

or in Sejanus' contempt for 'all the throng that fill th' Olympian hall.' V, i (III, 113).

But in drama substance and criticism of that substance are inseparable, and the world of *Sejanus* exists only in the light of a particular vision. The most obvious device for determining the angle of presentation is found in the vein of farce that runs throughout: there is a violent juxtaposition of contrasts. After the heroics of Sejanus' 'lovemaking' Livia turns to her physician:

How do I look to-day?
Eudemus. Excellent clear, believe it. This same fucus
Was well laid on.
Livia. Methinks 'tis here not white.
Eudemus. Lend me your scarlet lady. 'Tis the sun
Hath giv'n some little taint unto the ceruse. . . .
(*Paints her cheek.*) II, i (III, 41)

Here, and in the other scenes of stylized farce (for instance, V, iii, or V, vii, where the secret is passed round) there are obvious theatrical possibilities. Perhaps the most effective scene would be the last, where the senators first cluster round Sejanus—indicating by their verbal *feu de joie* the kind of stylization demanded—then edge away as the drift of Tiberius' riddling letter becomes clear, leaving only Haterius, kept 'most miserably constant' by his gout. But the whole of the last act, with its controlled confusion leading swiftly to an exciting climax, would act well; and for more subtle dramatic play we can turn to the scene (III, ii) where Tiberius and Sejanus manœuvre against each other under cover of friendship; the variations gain from the surface rigidity of the characters.

The essential Jonsonian mode, however, is determined by something more fundamental than the separable elements of farce: it is determined by the verse—a dramatic medium in which exaggeration is controlled by a pervasively implicit sardonic mood. The exuberance of 'Swell, swell, my joys . . .' (V, i) is followed by

. . . 'Tis air I tread;
And at each step I feel my advanced head
Knock out a star in heaven.

It is 'knock out'—the slight twist given to 'sublimi feriam sidera vertice'—that finally determines our attitude. But a longer quotation is in place here. In Act II, scene ii, Sejanus addresses Drusus in soliloquy:

Thy follies now shall taste what kind of man
They have provoked, and this thy father's house
Crack in the flame of my incensed rage,
Whose fury shall admit no shame or mean.—
Adultery! it is the lighest ill
I will commit. A race of wicked acts
Shall flow out of my anger, and o'erspread
The world's wide face, which no posterity
Shall e'er approve, nor yet keep silent: things
That for their cunning, close, and cruel mark,

Thy father would wish his: and shall, perhaps,
Carry the empty name, but we the prize.
On then, my soul, and start not in thy course;
Though heaven drop sulphur, and hell belch out fire,
Laugh at the idle terrors: tell proud Jove,
Between his power and thine there is no odds:
'Twas only fear first in the world made gods.

In the sentiments, and in the vigorous development of a single dominant impulse, there is an obvious resemblance to *Tamburlaine*. But the attitude of sophisticated detachment towards the words, present in those words, suggests what Jonson had learnt from *The Jew of Malta* (a relationship first stated in *The Sacred Wood*): with that play in mind we are not likely to accept Coleridge's verdict of 'absurd rant and ventriloquism'—or not as he intended it. It is equally obvious that the speech is not by Marlowe, that in its combination of weight and vigour it looks forward to the finer poetry of *Volpone* and *The Alchemist*.

The means by which Jonson achieves that combination are here immediately apparent. The alliteration not only adds to the general critical-exaggerative effect, it secures the maximum of direct attention for each word:

Sleep,
Voluptuous Caesar, and security
Seize on thy stupid powers.

More generally, we may say that whereas the auditory qualities of Shakespeare's verse arouse a vibrating responsiveness, help to create a fluid medium in which there is the subtlest interplay, the corresponding qualities in Jonson cause the words to separate rather than to coalesce. ('Separate,' of course, is only a way of laying the stress.) Everything is said deliberately—though there is no monotony in the varying rhythm—and, following Jonson's own precepts for 'a strict and succinct style,' [2] with the greatest economy. The economy of course is not Shakespeare's. There are no overlaying meanings or shifts of construction; the words gain their effect by their solidity, weight and unambiguous directness of expression. How poetically effective that weighted style can be is demonstrated again and again in the present play.

There be two,
Know more than honest counsels; whose close breasts,

Were they ripp'd up to light, it would be found
A poor and idle sin, to which their trunks
Had not been made fit organs. These can lie,
Flatter, and swear, forswear, deprave, inform,
Smile, and betray; make guilty men; then beg
The forfeit lives, to get their livings; cut
Men's throats with whisperings. . . . I, i (III, 14)

Jonson's metaphors and similes tend to fall into one of three classes. Many, perhaps the majority, are straightforwardly descriptive. ('Metaphors far-fet,' he said, 'hinder to be understood.')

The way to put
A prince in blood, is to present the shapes
Of dangers greater than they are, like late
Or early shadows.

Did those fond words
Fly swifter from thy lips, than this my brain,
This sparkling forge, created me an armour
T'encounter chance and thee? [3]

A second class is formed by those metaphors that, like the 'race of wicked acts . . .' in Sejanus' soliloquy, heighten the effect of caricature. But Jonson's most striking figures are magnificently derogatory.

Gods! how the sponges open and take in,
And shut again! look, look! is not he blest
That gets a seat in eye-reach of him? more
That comes in ear, or tongue-reach? O but most
Can claw his subtile elbow, or with a buz
Fly-blow his ears?

Jonson's triumph, we have been told, is a triumph of consistency, and the habit of mind behind this last quotation provides the dominant tone of the play. I have already commented on the exclusion of irrelevant moods and associations, and there only remains to notice the characteristic linking together of words that usually invite sympathy or admiration with those demanding an exactly contrary response.

Like, as both
Their bulks and souls were bound on Fortune's wheel. . . .

He . . . gives Caesar leave
To hide his *ulcerous and anointed* face. . . .

One does not need to look up the various suggestions of weight and clumsiness under 'cob' in the Oxford Dictionary to feel the effect of 'a cob-swan, or a high mounting bull' in the most famous speech from *Catiline*.

It should be plain by now that the appreciation of Jonson starts from the appreciation of his verse: it could start from nothing else; but it does not seem to be realized how clogging are the discussions of 'humours' which, in histories of English literature, fill up the pages on Jonson. His plays have the tightness and coherence of a firmly realized purpose, active in every detail, and a commentary on Jonson's technical achievements—the weight and vigour of his verse, the intensive scrutiny that it invites—is only one way of indicating his essential qualities.

Sejanus, like the other greater plays, is the product of a unique vision; but in stressing the uniqueness one has to avoid any suggestion of the idiosyncratic. It is not merely that the matter on which the poet works is provided by the passions, lusts and impulses of the actual world, the firmly defined individual spirit which moulds that matter springs from a rich traditional wisdom; it relies, that is to say, on something outside itself, and presupposes an active relationship with a particular audience.

The point can be made by examining a passage that is commonly recognized as 'great poetry.'

See, behold,
What thou art queen of; not in expectation,
As I feed others: but possess'd and crown'd.
See, here, a rope of pearl: and each more orient
Than that the brave Ægyptian queen caroused:
Dissolve and drink them. See, a carbuncle,
May put out both the eyes of our St. Mark;
A diamond, would have bought Lollia Paulina,
When she came in like star-light, hid with jewels,
That were the spoils of provinces; take these,
And wear, and lose them: yet remains an ear-ring
To purchase them again, and this whole state.
A gem but worth a private patrimony,
Is nothing: we will eat such at a meal.
The heads of parrots, tongues of nightingales,
The brains of peacocks, and of estriches,

> Shall be our food: and, could we get the phœnix,
> Though nature lost her kind, she were our dish.
>
> *Volpone,* III, vi (III, 249)

Mr. Palmer, supporting a general thesis that Jonson 'wrote for a generation which had still an unbounded confidence in the senses and faculties of man. England had not yet accepted the great negation . . . ,' remarks: 'In the figure of Volpone Jonson presents the splendours of his theme. Was ever woman so magnificently wooed as the wife of Corvino?'[4] This is to miss the point completely. The poetic force of Volpone's wooing has two sources. There is indeed an exuberant description of luxury—'Temptations are heaped upon temptations with a rapidity which almost outstrips the imagination'—and the excited movement seems to invite acceptance. But at the same time, without cancelling out the exuberance, the luxury is 'placed.' We have only to compare passages (from the early Keats, for example) in which the imagined gratification of sight, taste and touch is intended as an indulgence merely, to see how this placing is achieved. It is not merely that the lines quoted have a context of other swelling speeches (compare *Sejanus*), so that by the time we reach them the mode is established, the exaggeration, which reaches a climax at 'phœnix,' is itself sufficient to suggest some qualification of Mr. Palmer's 'splendours.' The verse demands the usual scrupulous inspection of each word—we are not allowed to lapse into an impression of generalized magnificence—and the splendours, in 'caroused,' 'spoils of provinces,' 'private patrimony,' are presented clearly enough as waste. 'Though nature lost her kind,' at least, implies a moral judgement; and the references to Lollia Paulina and Heliogabalus (Gifford quotes 'Comedit linguas pavonum et lusciniarum'), which would not be unfamiliar to an Elizabethan audience, are significant.

The manner of presentation (relying on a response which later criticism shows is neither obvious nor easy) suggests that the double aspect of the thing presented corresponds to a double attitude in the audience: a naïve delight in splendour is present *at the same time as* a clear-sighted recognition of its insignificance judged by fundamental human, or divine, standards. The strength of this attitude is realized if we compare it with a puritanic disapproval of 'the world' on the one hand, or a sensuous abandonment on the other. It is the possession of this attitude that makes Jonson 'classical,' not his Greek and

Latin erudition. His classicism is an equanimity and assurance that springs—'here at home' [5]—from the strength of a native tradition.

For Jonson's knowledge, and use, of the native literary tradition there is, I believe, evidence of the usually accepted kind. One could consider his references (explicit and otherwise) to earlier poets and prose-writers from Chaucer onwards; his avowed interest in the *Vetus Comoedia;* the obvious 'morality' influence in such plays as *The Devil is an Ass* and *The Magnetic Lady;* [6] the popular source of the jog-trot rhythms used for Nano, Androgyno and the Vice, Iniquity. But when we are dealing with a living tradition such terms are hopelessly inadequate, and exploration can be more profitably directed, in the manner suggested by the analysis above, towards Jonson's handling of his main themes, lust and the desire for wealth and their accompanying vanities.

In *The Devil is an Ass* the satire is more than usually direct. But the play provides more than a succession of satiric comments on the first period of intensive capitalistic activity in England; it formulates an attitude towards acquisition. The word 'formulates' is used advisedly. The outlook is a particular one, is Jonson's own; but it is clear that the satire presupposes certain general attitudes in the audience, and that it builds on something that was already there. Fitzdottrel, immersed in his schemes for making money, believes that he has surprised his wife making love with Wittipol, and (II, iii) reproaches her:

O bird,
Could you do this? 'gainst me! and at this time now!
When I was so employ'd, wholly for you,
Drown'd in my care (more than the land, I swear,
I have hope to win) to make you peerless, studying
For footmen for you, fine-pace huishers, pages,
To serve you on the knee. . . .
You've almost turn'd my good affection to you;
Sour'd my sweet thoughts, all my pure purposes. . . .

Fitzdottrel is an ass and it is quite unnecessary to say that there is not a hint of pathos, though it is easy to imagine the temptations of a nineteenth-century novelist in such a scene. (Compare the exaggerated significance that is given to Mrs. Dombey's jewels—'She flung it down and trod upon the glittering heap,' etc.) The point is that Jonson evidently relies upon his audience immediately despising those 'pure purposes'; what these are—the way in which the money acquired would be employed—is magnificently brought out in the Tailbush-Eitherside scene (IV, i: 'See how the world its veterans rewards . . .'). It is, of course, the tone and manner of presentation that is commented on here. As one learns to expect, that tone is consistent throughout and one has to be alive to its implications even in the smallest particulars. The 'Spanish lady' is

> such a mistress of behaviour,
> She knows from the duke's daughter to the doxy,
> What is their due just, and no more.

Here the scornful alliteration acts as a leveller (we have seen something similar in *Sejanus*): Jonson, that is, takes his stand on a scheme that shows duke's daughter and doxy in proper perspective. It was not merely that Jonson as an individual 'never esteemed of a man for the name of a Lord'; [7] his values were a part of the national life. We have only to turn up Bunyan's account of By-End's ancestry and connexions: 'My wife . . . came of a very honourable family, and is arrived to such a pitch of breeding, that she knows how to carry it to all, even to prince and peasant.' The tone and method are identical. [8]

In *The Devil is an Ass*, in *Volpone* and *The Alchemist* Jonson is drawing on the anti-acquisitive tradition inherited from the Middle Ages. But this account is too narrow; the tradition included more than a mere distrust of, or hostility towards, riches. Understanding is, perhaps, best reached by studying (with Volpone in mind) the speeches of Sir Epicure Mammon. Each of them, it seems to me, implicitly refers to a traditional conception of 'the Mean.' Mammon, wooing Doll, describes their teeming pleasures:

> and with these
> Delicate meats set our selves high for pleasure,
> And take us down again, and then renew
> Our youth and strength with drinking the elixir,
> And so enjoy a perpetuity
> Of life and lust! And thou shalt have thy wardrobe
> Richer than nature's, still to change thy self,
> And vary oftener, for thy pride, than she.
>
> *The Alchemist*, IV, i (IV, 120)

The reference to 'nature,' which give the proper angle on 'a perpetuity of life and lust,' is important. The accepted standard is 'natural,' and although exact definition would not be easy we may notice the part played by that standard throughout Jonson's work. An instance from *Volpone* has been quoted. Mammon's folly is that he expects Subtle to

> teach dull nature
> What her own forces are. (IV, 116)

Similarly in the masque, *Mercury Vindicated*, the alchemists 'pretend . . . to commit miracles in art and treason against nature . . . a matter of immortality is nothing'; they 'profess to outwork the sun in virtue, and contend to the great act of generation, nay almost creation.' The obviously expected response is similar to that given to the description of Mammon's jewels whose light shall 'strike out the stars.' Who wants to strike out the stars, anyway?

The Staple of News, that odd combination of morality play and topical revue, is generally spoken of as a 'dotage'; but, apart from the admirably comic Staple scenes, it contains passages of unusual power, and all of these, we notice, are informed by the same attitude. In a speech of Pennyboy Senior's the anti-acquisitive theme (the play is mainly directed against the abuse of 'the Venus of our time and state, Pecunia') is explicitly related to the conception of a natural mean:

> Who can endure to see
> The fury of men's gullets, and their groins?
> . . . What need hath nature
> Of silver dishes, or gold chamber-pots?
> Of perfumed napkins, or a numerous family
> To see her eat? poor, and wise, she requires
> Meat only; hunger is not ambitious:
> Say, that you were the emperor of pleasures,
> The great dictator of fashions, for all Europe,
> And had the pomp of all the courts, and kingdoms,
> Laid forth unto the shew, to make yourself
> Gazed and admired at; you must go to bed,
> And take your natural rest: then all this vanisheth.
> Your bravery was but shown; 'twas not possest:
> While it did boast itself, it was then perishing.
> *The Staple of News*, III, ii (V, 244)

We have seen something of the background that all these passages imply. That a sense of the mean, an acceptance of natural limitations, was a part of the inheritance of Jonson and his contemporaries, can be demonstrated from medieval and sixteenth-century sermons and the writings of moralists. But it was not something imposed from above; it sprang from the wisdom of the common people, and it was only indirectly that it found its way into writing.[9] The anti-acquisitive attitude had been more explicitly formulated. It was not only a part of the life of the small local communities of the Middle Ages, it was the basis of the Canon Law on such subjects as usury. And although the age of Jonson was also the age of Sir Giles Mompesson and Sir Arthur Ingram it was still, we remember, a commonplace, accepted by the worldly Bacon, that 'The ways to enrich are many, and most of them foul.'[10]

In a well-known passage in *Discoveries* Jonson speaks of following the ancients 'as guides, not commanders': 'For to all the observations of the ancients, we have our own experience; which, if we will use, and apply, we have better means to pronounce.'[11] That this was not a mere assertion of independence (or a mere translation—see M. Castelain's learned edition) is shown by every page on which he seems to draw most directly on the classics. Wherever the editors suggest parallels with Horace or Catullus, Tacitus or Suetonius, the re-creation is as complete as in—to take a modern instance—Mr. Pound's *Propertius,* so complete as to make the hunt for 'sources' irrelevant. When Fitzdottrel is gloating over the prospect of obtaining an estate on which his descendants shall keep his name alive, Meercraft, characteristically speaking 'out of character,' reminds him of the revolution of the times:

Fitzdottrel. 'Tis true.
DROWN'D LANDS will live in drown'd land.
Meercraft. Yes, when you
Have no foot left; as that must be, sir, one day.
And though it tarry in your heirs some forty,
Fifty descents, the longer liver at last, yet,
Must thrust them out on't, if no quirk in law
Or odd vice of their own not do it first.
We see those changes daily: the fair lands
That were the client's, are the lawyer's now;
And those rich manors there of goodman Taylor's,
Had once more wood upon them, than the yard
By which they were measured out for the last purchase.

Nature hath these vicissitudes. She makes
No man a state of perpetuity, sir.
The Devil is an Ass, II, i (V, 58)

Here is the passage in Horace (*Satires,* II, 2) that the speech 'derives' from:

nam propriae telluris erum natura neque illum
nec me nec quemquam statuit: nos expulit ille,
illum aut nequities aut vafri inscitia iuris,
postremo expellet certe vivacior heres.

Even in the lines that come nearest to translation there is a complete transmutation of idiom: 'nequities' has become 'some odd vice,' and 'ignorance of the subtle law,' the sardonically familiar 'quirk in law.' But as Horace is left behind the presence of everday life is felt even more immediately, in 'daily,' 'those rich manors there' and 'goodman Taylor's,' followed as these are by a kind of country wit about the yardstick. The strength of the passage—it is representative—lies in the interested but critical inspection of a familiar world.

In pointing to the idiom we are of course noticing very much more than 'local colour'; we are noticing ways of thought and perception. Jonson's idiom—his vocabulary, turns of phrase and general linguistic habits—might form a study in itself. It was Coleridge who spoke of 'his sterling English diction' [12]—which seems a sufficient rejoinder to the description, 'ponderous Latinism,' applied by a recent anthologist of the seventeenth century. It is easy, as Gifford pointed out, to exaggerate the extent of Jonson's latinized formations when we forget the similar experimenting of his contemporaries. (And it was not Jonson who tried to introduce 'lubrical,' 'magnificate,' 'ventosity' and the rest.) But whereas these have had too much attention, a more striking characteristic had had none. Important as Jonson was as a formative influence on the Augustan age, his English is not 'polite'; it is, very largely, the popular English of an agricultural country. It is not merely a matter of vocabulary—'ging' (gang), 'threaves,' 'ding it open': one could go on collecting—his inventive habits are of a kind that can still be paralleled in country life. There is the delighted recognition of those elements of caricature that man or nature supplies ready made: 'It is now such a time . . . that every man stands under the eaves of his own hat, and sings what pleases him.' (*Pleasure Reconciled to Virtue,* VII, 300.) There are those derisive compounds:

'Honest, plain, livery-three-pound-thrum.' There is a predilection for alliterative jingles:

> You shall be soaked, and stroked, and tubb'd and rubb'd,
> And scrubb'd, and fubb'd, dear don.

And if this kind of clowning is thought unworthy of serious criticism we can point to the easy alliterative run of 'the tip, top, and tuft of all our family,' or half the speeches quoted from *Sejanus*. But even the pleasantries reveal a natural bent, and the boisterous coining of nicknames—'His great Verdugoship'—was more than a rustic habit; 'old Smug of Lemnos,' 'Bombast of Hohenhein' (Vulcan and Paracelsus) indicate an attitude, similar to Nashe's,[13] of familiar disrespect towards text-book worthies. And the amazing fertility that reveals itself now in a popular fluency

> —our Doll, our castle, our cinque port,
> Our Dover pier—

now in Volpone's mountebank oration, now in Mammon's description of luxury, is an index of a native vigour that we recognize as 'typically Elizabethan.' The more we study Jonson in minute detail the more clearly he appears both intensely individual and—the paradox is justifiable—at one with his contemporaries.

The speech last quoted from *The Devil is an Ass* has a further significance; it represents an outlook that is present even in such pure entertainment as *The Silent Woman* (See Truewit on Time in I, i), and that combines easily with hilarious comedy, as in Volpone's ludicrously inadequate modesty:

> *Mosca.* That, and thousands more,
> I hope to see you lord of.
> *Volpone.* Thanks, kind Mosca.
> *Mosca.* And that, when I am lost in blended dust,
> And hundred such as I am in succession—
> *Volpone.* Nay, that were too much, Mosca.
>
> I, i (III, 178)

Meercraft's speech, that is, forms part of the permanent sombre background of which we are made aware in all of Jonson's comedies. But the insistence on mortality has the very opposite effect of the introduction of a death's head at a feast; it is not for the sake of a gratuitous thrill.

> Nature hath these vicissitudes. She makes
> No man a state of perpetuity, sir.

It is the tone—the quiet recognition of the inevitable—that is important; and the clearly apprehended sense of mutability heightens, rather than detracts from, the prevailing zest.

It is here, I think, that a genuine 'classical influence,' or at least the influence of Horace, can be traced.

> iam Cytherea choros ducit Venus imminente luna,
> iunctaeque Nymphis Gratiae decentes
> alterno terram quatiunt pede . . .
>
> pallida Mors aequo pulsat pede pauperum tabernas
> regumque turris. *Odes,* I, iv

The potency of the evocation of the nymphs' flying feet is not lessened because they are also the feet of Time. But even here it is plain that the Jonsonian attitude is not acquired but inherited. There is no need to stress the medieval and sixteenth-century insistence on wormy circumstance (a good deal of it was pathological), but we need to keep in mind the way in which, in the popular literature of those periods, death and life are vividly juxtaposed.

And the ability to see life under two opposed aspects simultaneously was part of the natural equipment of the poets of the seventeenth century before the Restoration. It is expressed in Marvell, in the recognition of conflicting claims in the *Horatian Ode,* in the concluding lines of the *Coy Mistress:*

> And tear our pleasures with rough strife
> Through the Iron gates of Life.

The aspects of experience represented by 'the Iron gates' would hardly be present in a nineteenth-century 'love poem,' or, if present, would have a totally different intention and effect. It was in connexion with Marvell, we remember, that Mr. Eliot defined Wit: 'It involves a recognition, implicit in the expression of every experience, of other kinds of experience which are possible.' [14] Jonson had not a metaphysic wit and he was not Donne, but it is a similar recognition, implicit or explicit, of the whole range of human life, that explains his tough equilibrium.

How little a mere classicizing can produce that equilibrium a final comparison may show. When Jonson's verse seems to catch an Horatian inflexion it is not because he has assumed it:

dum loquimur, fugerit invida
aetas *Odes,* I, xi

becomes, quite naturally,

think,
All beauty doth not last until the autumn:
You grow old while I tell you this.
The Devil is an Ass, I, iii (V, 31)

On the other hand there is Landor:

occidit et Pelopis genitor, conviva deorum,
Tithonusque remotus in auras. . . .

. . . sed omnis una manet nox
et calcanda semel bia leti. Horace, *Odes,* I, xxviii

Laodameia died; Helen died; Leda, the beloved of Jupiter went before. . . . There is no name, with whatever emphasis of passionate love repeated, of which the echo is not faint at last.[15]

In this affected mimicry the Horatian tone ('durum: sed levius fit patientia'), all, in fact, that gives value to the recognition of a common night, has completely evaporated, and we are left with as orotund a piece of self-indulgence as ever found its way into anthologies. Jonson's tone is that of a man who has seen many civilizations, and is at home in one.

I have tried to show that, in Jonson's audience, we may postulate a lively sense of human limitations. When Mammon declared of the elixir that, taken by an old man, it will

Restore his years, renew him, like an eagle,
To the fifth age; make him get sons and daughters,
Young giants; as our philosophers have done,
The ancient patriarchs, afore the flood,
But taking, once a week, on a knife's point,
The quantity of a grain of mustard of it, II, i (IV, 46)

they had a right to laugh as our modern seekers after youth have not.[16] But it was not a sense that incapacitated from living in the present. One does not need to search for illustration of Jonson's lively interest in every aspect of his environment. Meercraft's speech comes from a play which, as we shall see, forms the most striking indictment of the newer forms of economic parasitism. It would be good to see *The Devil is an Ass* acted; it would be good to see *Sejanus*—which has a contemporary relevance not merely because it is a study of tyranny ('We shall be marked anon, for our not Hail' V, viii (III, 132)), but it would be better if one could feel assured that they were widely read. Jonson's permanent importance is beyond question, but the discipline that a thorough assimilation of his work imposes is an especial need of the present day. It is not merely that poets might profitably study his verse as well as Donne's and Hopkins', Skelton's and *The Seafarer* (I am not suggesting anything so foolish as direct imitation); not merely that practitioners of 'the poetic drama' might learn something of effective stylization (the result of an emotional discipline) from his plays: these matters, in any case, are best left to poets. But for all of us he is one of the main channels of communication with an almost vanished tradition. That tradition cannot be apprehended in purely literary terms, but we can learn something of it through literature, just as to feel our way into the technique of Jonson's verse is to share, in some measure, that steady, penetrating scrutiny of men and affairs.

NOTES

1. The references in brackets are to the volume and page of the Gifford-Cunningham edition of Jonson's *Works,* 1875.

2. *Discoveries,* cxxix.

3. This second image is bright and clear, but its surface quality is emphasized if we put beside it the line from *Henry V,*

> In the quick forge and working-house of thought,

where the rhythm, the double meaning of 'quick' and the fused impression of swift movement and ordered labour evoke a far more complex activity of the mind.

4. *Ben Jonson,* pp. x and 175.

5. And make my strengths, such as they are,
Here in my bosom, and at home.
(*A Farewell to the World*)

6. An influence that was active in other playwrights. It is some time since Sir Arthur Quiller-Couch suggested that Henry IV was Shakespeare's

rehandling of a morality play ('Contentio inter Virtutem et Vitium de Anima Principis'). The subject generally is of more than academic interest; those who are interested can consider such different plays as *Troilus and Cressida* (Pandarus is demonstrably 'the Pander'), *Old Fortunatus, Michaelmas Term* or any of Middleton's comedies.

7. *Conversations,* 14. I know that Jonson was capable of writing fulsome dedications: but before we make much of that charge we need to enquire, in each instance, the grounds of his praises. Many of the Elizabethan aristocracy had a decent sense of responsibility, literary and other.

8. Dr. G. R. Owst's *Literature and Pulpit in Medieval England* (pp. 97–109) gives an admirable account of the long popular and religious tradition behind Bunyan, reinforcing the conclusions that one would draw from reading *The Pilgrim's Progress* itself.

9. An essay by John Speirs on 'The Scottish Ballads' (*Scrutiny,* June 1935) is relevant here. There it is remarked, for example, that in the Ballads, 'The images of finery . . . possess a symbolical value as profound as in Bunyan ('. . . he that is clad in Silk and Velvet'). That finery is associated with folly, pride and death. It is Vanity.'—The relation between popular thought and medieval sermon literature is brought out by Dr. Owst.

10. *Essays,* 'Of Riches.'

11. *Discoveries,* xxi, *Non nimium credendum antiquitati.*

12. *Lectures on Shakespeare* (Bohn edition), p. 397.

13. 'The gods and goddesses all on a row, bread and crow, from Ops to Pomona, the first applewife, were so dumpt with this miserable wrack . . .' (*Nashe's Lenten Stuff*).

14. *Selected Essays,* p. 289.

15. *Imaginery Conversations,* 'Aesop and Rhodope.'

16. Gifford quotes Hurd (IV, 180): 'The pursuit so strongly exposed in this play is forgotten, and therefore its humour must appear exaggerated.' It would have pleased Gifford to refute Hurd by quoting from our newspapers and upper-class periodicals, with their appeals to 'Banish middle age,' etc.

RAY L. HEFFNER, JR.

Unifying Symbols in the Comedy of Ben Jonson

CRITICS since the seventeenth century have agreed that Ben Jonson is a master of comic structure, but there has been serious disagreement as to just what kind of structure it is in which he excels. To Dryden, Jonson was preeminent among English dramatists because he obeyed the neoclassic rules of unity of time, place, and action. Of the three, unity of action is fundamental, and it is Jonson's plotting that Dryden found most praiseworthy. He preferred *The Silent Woman* above all other plays because he found it an ideal combination of the scope, variety, and naturalness of the English drama with the control and careful organization of the French. And the *examen* of that play in the *Essay of Dramatic Poesy* emphasizes that there is immense variety of character and incident but that the action is 'entirely one.' [1] Critics in recent years, however, have disputed Dryden's picture of a regular, neoclassic Jonson, especially in the matter of plot structure. Freda L. Townsend, for example, argues persuasively that none of Jonson's great comedies has the unified action characteristic of Terentian comedy and enjoined by neoclassic precept.[2] She compares Jonson's art with that of Ariosto and the baroque painters, and she sees *Bartholomew Fair* rather than *The Silent Woman* as the culmination of his development away from a simply unified comedy towards one which involves the intricate interweaving of as many different interests as possible. T. S. Eliot perhaps best sums up this 'modern' view of Jonson's technique when he says that his 'immense dra-

From *English Stage Comedy* (New York: Columbia University Press, 1955), 74–97. Reprinted by permission of the English Institute, the publisher, and the author.

matic constructive skill' is not so much in plot as in 'doing without a plot,' and adds:

> The plot does not hold the play together; what holds the play together is a unity of inspiration that radiates into plot and personages alike.[3]

The views of Eliot and Miss Townsend seem to me substantially more correct than that of Dryden on this matter. In this paper I shall try to define more precisely the 'unity of inspiration' which Eliot and others have found in Jonson's comedy and to describe the dramatic devices by which it is expressed. Briefly, I believe that the essential unity of Jonson's comedy is thematic. In each of his major plays he explores an idea or a cluster of related ideas through a variety of characters and actions. And the central expression of the unifying idea is usually not in a fully developed plot but in a fantastic comic conceit, an extravagant exaggeration of human folly, to which all of the more realistically conceived characters and incidents have reference.

For such an investigation the crucial cases are *The Silent Woman* and *Bartholomew Fair,* Dryden's ideal 'regular' comedy and Miss Townsend's ideal 'baroque' comedy. If I can show that, despite the very evident differences in superficial structure, a similar kind of thematic unity underlies each of these and that it is expressed in similar symbolic devices, my analysis may have some claim to inclusiveness.

In the case of *The Silent Woman,* I must first undertake to show that it is not, even at the level of action, held together by the 'noble intrigue' as Dryden analyzes it. Dryden's spokesman Neander, accepting the definition of unity of action given earlier in the debate by Crites, tries to show that at least one English comedy adheres to the rule. Crites's principles are those derived by Renaissance and neoclassic criticism mainly from the practice of Terence. The emphasis is on the single, clearly defined aim of the action, which should be announced in the *protasis* or beginning of the play, delayed by all sorts of complications and counter-intrigues in the *epitasis* or middle, and finally brought to completion by the *catastrophe* or denouement. Neander discusses *The Silent Woman* as if it follows exactly this formula. 'The action of the play is entirely one,' he says, 'the end or aim of which is the settling of Morose's estate on Dauphine.' And he continues:

> You see, till the very last scene, new difficulties arising to obstruct the action of the play; and when the audience is brought into despair that the business can naturally be effected, then, and not before, the discovery is made.[4]

If we consider the play in retrospect, after we have seen or read the last scene, we may agree with Neander that the securing of Morose's estate is the central aim of the whole. Dauphine's sensational revelation of the true sex of Epicoene does indeed finally and irrevocably secure for him the estate, and after the play is over we can see that all the intrigues of Truewit and Clerimont, no matter what their intended purpose, have aided Dauphine's scheme by exhausting his uncle's patience and thus making the old man desperate enough to sign the settlement. But the fact that the true nature of Dauphine's scheme is concealed until the very end makes a great difference in the kind of unity which can be perceived by the audience during the course of the play. The settling of Morose's estate on Dauphine is not the ostensible aim of the action after Act III, for the audience as well as the other characters have been led to believe that Dauphine's purposes have been fully accomplished by the marriage of Morose and Epicoene. No new difficulties arise to obstruct this action in Acts IV and V: we assume it has already been settled and our attention has turned to other matters. Even in the early acts the course of Dauphine's intrigue is remarkably smooth, and little suspense of the kind Dryden describes is generated. By the last scene, far from being brought into despair that the business of the estate can naturally be effected, we have forgotten all about it and are surprised to see it reintroduced.

As the play unfolds, the settling of Morose's estate upon Dauphine is but one among several aims which give rise to action, and it is dominant only in Act II. It is much more accurate to consider *The Silent Woman* as consisting not of a Terentian plot depending upon the delayed completion of a single, well-defined objective but of a number of separable though related actions which are initiated and brought to completion at various points in the play and which are skillfully arranged to overlap and interlock. Each of these actions is essentially a trick played on a dupe or a group of dupes, and each has four fairly well-defined stages: (1) the exposition of background material, including the characterization of the dupe; (2) the planning of the trick by the intriguer; (3) the actual execution of the trick; and (4) the reminiscence of the trick as a source of continued laughter. The general plan is that a different major action occupies the center of attention in each act except the first, which consists of exposition of material for all the actions to follow. Act II is thus centered on Dauphine's scheme to marry his uncle to Epicoene, Act III on Truewit's scheme to torment Morose by moving Sir Amorous La Foole's dinner party to Morose's house, Act IV on the double scheme to discredit the foolish knights and make all the Collegiate Ladies fall in love with Dauphine, and Act V on the tormenting of Morose through the mock discussion of marriage annulment by the pretended canon lawyer and divine.

This basic plan is complicated by the introduction of several minor actions, notably the one precipitating the disgrace of Captain Tom Otter, and by the overlapping previously mentioned. At almost every point at least three actions are under simultaneous consideration: one is at the peak of fulfillment, a second has passed its climax but is still producing laughter, and the groundwork for a third is being carefully prepared.

These sundry intrigues are connected in a number of different ways. The peculiarities of the various dupes which make them fit objects of ridicule are all described in the course of an apparently aimless conversation in Act I, so that the jokes played on them later in the play, though they seem to arise spontaneously out of particular situations, nevertheless are not unexpected. All the tricks are planned by the same group of witty companions, most of them by Truewit, and every character has some part in more than one intrigue. Often one intrigue depends on the completion of another, as the transferring of the banquet on the completion of the marriage. And the final revelation of Epicoene's sex, as Miss Townsend points out, has some relevance to all the major actions; [5] it not only accomplishes Morose's divorce and gains the estate for Dauphine, it also shows the foolish knights to be liars and discomfits the Collegiate Ladies, who have had to depend on a despised male for the vindication of their honors.

Such an elaborate intertwining of episodes demonstrates great technical skill in what Renaissance criticism called *disposition* and *economy*.[6] But we are still entitled to ask, is this the only kind of structure the play possesses? Are there no more fundamental relationships among these various characters and actions, of which the mechanical interconnections we have been discussing are but the external evidences? The thematic structure of the play will be clearer if we consider that its real center is not in any of the tricks or schemes but in the ridiculous situation in which Morose finds himself. My argument is not genetic, but a brief look at the probable sources of the play may help to confirm this impression. The sources of the separable parts are extremely varied. Passages of dialogue come from Juvenal and Ovid; many of the characters belong in the series of satiric portraits stretching back through Jonson's early plays and through contemporary nondramatic satire; the aborted duel between the two knights seems to come from *Twelfth Night;* the conflict between Dauphine and his uncle bears some resemblance to *A Trick to Catch the Old One;* and the device of trickery through concealed sex may come from Aretino's comedy *Il Marescalco.*[7] But the center around which all this material is arranged is clearly the comic conceit which Jonson took from a declamation of Libanius—the ludicrous plight of a noise-hating man married by fraud to a noisy woman.

Herford and Simpson observe that, 'The amusing oration of Libanius offered but slender stuff for drama.'[8] This is true enough, in that it contained only a situation and not a complete plot, and the implications of that situation were but little developed. The Morosus of Libanius merely describes the horrors of his noise-ridden existence and pleads with the judges for permission to commit suicide. The oration could not simply be translated to the stage without the addition of much extra material. But it is, nevertheless, an admirable idea for a comedy. For one thing, it epitomizes the eternal battle of the sexes for supremacy, including the hypocrisies of courtship and the wrangling after marriage. And then also, in its opposition of noisy people to noise haters, it suggests another eternal theme, the debate between the active and the quiet life. In constructing a play around the conceit of Libanius, Jonson greatly complicates both these latent themes, through his interpretation of the Morose-Epicoene relationship and through the addition of other characters and actions.

Jonson's interpretation of the central situation is summarized in the scene in which Morose interrogates his intended bride. (II.v.) There we learn that the old man's hatred of noise is the outward manifestation of two allied character traits. First, he has been at court and has recoiled in horror from all forms of courtliness. He tests his bride-to-be by pointing out to her that if she forbear the use of her tongue she will be unable to trade 'pretty girds, scoffes, and daliance' with her admirers; she cannot, like the ladies in court, 'affect . . . to seeme learn'd, to seeme judicious, to seeme sharpe, and conceited'; and she will be manifestly unable to 'have her counsell of taylors, lineners, lacewomen, embroyderers, and sit with 'hem sometimes twise a day, upon *French* intelligences' so as 'to be the first and principall in all fashions.' The meaning of the play's central symbol of noise is thus considerably developed in this scene; a noisy woman is a woman given over to all the vanity, hypocrisy, and affectation to which her sex and the courtly society of her age are prone. Morose can concentrate his hatred of all these things by hating the inclusive and concrete symbol, noise itself.

The second important aspect of Morose's idiosyncracy is his passion for having his own way in all things. In his first soliloquy he admits that 'all discourses, but mine owne, afflict mee.' (II.i.) He admires the absolute obedience which oriental potentates command from members of their households; and the silence of his own servants indicates their complete subservience to his will, for they can answer perfectly well by signs so long as their judgments 'jump' with his. Epicoene thus throws him into ecstasies of happiness when she answers to all his questions, 'Judge you, forsooth,' and 'I leave it to wisdome, and you sir.'

Morose's attitude towards his nephew illustrates both these aspects of his character. After putting his intended bride successfully through the test, he breaks into a scornful tirade at the notion of Sir Dauphine's knighthood:

> He would be knighted, forsooth, and thought by that meanes to raigne over me, his title must doe it: no kinsman, I will now make you bring mee the tenth lords, and the sixteenth ladies letter, kinsman; and it shall doe you no good kinsman. Your knighthood it selfe shall come on it's knees, and it shall be rejected. (II.v.)

By the coup of his marriage, Morose hopes to express his contempt for all the world of lords, ladies, and courtly society, as well as his complete dominance over all members of his family. The comic irony in his situation is that he inevitably brings all his troubles on himself, because his two desires, to command and to live apart, though so closely related, cannot both be fulfilled on his terms. An ascetic hermit might live apart and rail against the court; a great lord might command absolute obedience from all around him. But Morose will make no sacrifice; he will be the ultimate of both at once. In seeking to extend his circle of dominance beyond his servant and his barber to include a wife, he brings in upon himself the torrent of courtly commotion from which he has fled. In seeking to make his power over his nephew absolute, he loses all. When Dauphine says to him at the end of the play, 'Now you may goe in and rest, be as private as you will, sir,' his sarcastic words may seem more than a little cruel, but it is the logic of the world that decrees Morose's sentence. He can be 'private' only when he gives up all pretense of being an absolute autocrat, and this he has just done by submitting himself humbly to his nephew's will and judgment.

The other material in the play consists largely of a set of mirrors which, by reflecting various aspects of this central situation, extend its significance. The Collegiate Ladies, for example, are embodiments of all the courtly vices and affectations which Morose lumps under the heading of 'female noise.' The most prominent feature of their composite portrait is, in Morose's words, that they 'affect to seem judicious.' As Truewit says in the first act,

> [They are] an order betweene courtiers, and country-madames, that live from their husbands; and give entertainement to all the *Wits*, and *Braveries* o' the time, as they call 'hem: crie downe, or up, what they like, or dislike in a braine, or a fashion, with most masculine, or rather *hermaphroditicall* authoritie. (I.i.)

The Collegiates are thus an appropriate part of the flood of noise that pours in upon Morose after the wedding through which he had hoped to assert his masculine dominance and to declare his independence from all courtliness. The ladies' pretense to authority is just as absurd as Morose's. This is demonstrated in Act IV by the disgrace of the two knights whom they had cried up as wits and braveries, and especially by the ease with which the ladies can be turned from one opinion to its exact opposite, from idolizing the two knights to despising them, from despising Dauphine to being infatuated with him. As Truewit says, his tricks prove that

> all their actions are governed by crude opinion, without reason or cause; they know not why they doe any thing: but as they are inform'd, beleeve, judge, praise, condemne, love, hate, and in aemulation one of another, doe all these things alike. (IV.vi.)

Sir John Daw and Sir Amorous La Foole are the male representatives of the affected courtliness which Morose despises. In contrast to the three ladies, these two have separate identities at the beginning, though they are merged into a composite portrait as the action progresses. Sir John is the 'wit' or fool intellectual, Sir Amorous the 'bravery' or fool social. Jonson had treated varieties of both in earlier plays, but he fits these into his present scheme by emphasizing in both cases the noisiness of their folly. Sir John is the 'onely talking sir i'th' towne' whom Truewit dares not visit for the danger to his ears. His conversation is noise not only because it is verbose but also because it is inopportune and disorderly. He insists upon reading his wretched verses, whether or not the company desires to hear them; he pours out the names of authors in an undisciplined stream. The garrulity of Sir Amorous has similar characteristics though different subject matter. Clerimont emphasizes that this knight's pretentious courtesy respects neither place, person, nor season:

> He will salute a Judge upon the bench, and a Bishop in the pulpit, a Lawyer when hee is pleading at the barre, and a Lady when shee is dauncing in a masque, and put her out. He do's give playes, and suppers, and invites his guests to 'hem, aloud, out of his windore, as they ride by in coaches. (I.iii.)

When Sir Amorous appears on the scene, he does, as Clerimont has predicted, 'tell us his pedigree, now; and what meat he has to dinner; and, who are his guests; and, the whole course of his fortunes,' all in one breath.

The two knights thus give a wider meaning to the notion of a noisy man in much the same way as the Collegiates and Morose's interrogation of Epicoene widen the meaning of a noisy woman. Noise is ungentlemanly boasting about one's poetic and critical powers, about one's family, friends, and hospitality, and, towards the end of the play, about one's sexual powers and conquests. The one gentlemanly attribute to which the two do not conspicuously pretend is courage on the field of battle. We may therefore be somewhat puzzled when the main trick against them seems to turn on their cowardice, and we sympathize with Mrs. Doll Mavis when she defends her judgment of them by saying, 'I commended but their wits, madame, and their braveries. I never look'd toward their valours.' (IV.vi) But what has been exposed in the mock duel is not only cowardice but pliability. Like the ladies who admire them, the knights have no real standards for judging either books or men, but are governed entirely by rumor and fashion. Therefore it is ridiculously easy for Truewit to persuade each knight that the other, whose pacific disposition he should know well, is a raging lion thirsting for his blood. If either knight had been made more on the model of the swaggering *miles gloriosus,* the point about how easy it is to make a fool believe the exact opposite of the obvious truth would have been blunted.

The themes of courtly behavior, the battle between the sexes, and the pretense to authority are intertwined with that of noise versus silence wherever one looks in the play, even in the foolish madrigals of modesty and silence written by Sir John Daw. In the action involving Captain and Mrs. Tom Otter, all these subjects are invested with an atmosphere of comedy lower than that of the rest of the play. For the salient fact about the Otters is that they are of a lower social class than any of the other main characters. Mrs. Otter is a rich China woman struggling for admission to the exclusive Ladies' College; Captain Tom is at home among the bulls and bears but unsure of himself in the company of knights and wits. Here again the citizen-couple who welcome instruction in the courtly follies are familiar figures from Jonson's early comical satire, but the portraits are modified to fit the thematic pattern of this play. The Collegiate Ladies may pretend to a nice discernment in brains and fashions, but Mrs. Otter comprehends fashionable feminism rather differently and expresses her 'masculine, or rather *hermaphroditicall* authority' more elementally by pummeling her husband. And Captain Tom's noises are his boisterous but rather pathetic drinking bouts, accompanied by drum and trumpet, by which he hopes to gain a reputation among the gentry and to assert his independence from his wife. This is the comic realm of Maggie and Jiggs, the hen-pecked husband sneaking out to the corner saloon to escape his social-climbing wife, but the relationships between this farcical situation and the central one of Morose and Epicoene are clear and are emphasized at every turn. Like the characters in most Elizabethan comic sub-plots, the Otters burlesque the main action while at the same time extending its meaning toward the universal.

As the clumsy, middle-class Otters contrast with the more assured aristocrats, so all the pliable pretenders to courtliness contrast with the true gentlemen and scholars, Truewit, Clerimont, and Dauphine. Within this group of intriguers, however, there is a further important contrast. Clerimont is relatively undeveloped as a character, but the differences between Truewit and Dauphine are stressed. Truewit is boisterous and boastful about the jokes he contrives. He must have the widest possible audience; as Dauphine tells him, 'This is thy extreme vanitie, now: thou think'st thou wert undone, if every jest thou mak'st were not publish'd. (IV.V.) Dauphine, on the other hand, moves quietly about his purposes and keeps his own counsel. Truewit characteristically invents his fun on the spur of the moment, out of the materials at hand, and is apt to promise to do something (like making all the Collegiates fall in love with Dauphine) before he has the slightest idea how it can be brought about. Dauphine's plans have been months in preparation, and he betrays little hint of his purposes until they actually have been accomplished.

The rivalry of these two for the title of master plotter runs as a subdued motive through all the action. It is most prominent in the first two acts, when Truewit's rash and suddenly conceived scheme to dissuade Morose from marrying almost upsets Dauphine's carefully laid plot. It might seem that the contrast is all in favor of the quiet, modest, but in the end more effective Dauphine. Truewit assumes too readily that he can read the entire situation at first glance, and that he can easily manipulate the stubborn Morose. He becomes almost a comic butt himself when he ridiculously tries to pretend that he has foreseen from the first the really quite unexpected consequence of his action. The denouement especially would seem to prove that Dauphine is the real master at playing chess with characters and humors, and Truewit just the bungling amateur. But Jonson is not writing a treatise after the manner of Plutarch on the virtue of silence and the folly of garrulity. Dauphine and Truewit share the honors in the closing scene, and there is more than a little to be said throughout the play for Truewit's engaging love of good fun for its own sake as against Dauphine's colder, more practical scheming. Instead of arguing a simple thesis, Jonson is investigating another aspect of his central symbol of noise. Just as he holds a brief neither for the noise of courtly affectation nor for Morose's extreme hatred of it, so he argues neither for the noisy wit nor for the quiet wit but is content to explore the differences between them.

The essential movement of *The Silent Woman*, then, is the exploration of themes implicit in the central comic conceit of a noise-hating man married to a noisy woman. Noise and the hatred of noise take on the proportion of symbols as they are given ever-widening meanings by the various particulars of social satire. The play's realism and its fantastic caricature can hardly be disentangled, for they are held together firmly in the same comic structure.

Much the same things can be said of *Bartholomew Fair*, despite its even greater complexity and its different kind of surface plan. In this play, characters, actions, interests are all multiplied. If in *The Silent Woman* there are usually three separable intrigues in motion at the same time, they all have a similar pattern of development and are under the control of no more than three intriguers. But in *Bartholomew Fair* five or six actions seem always to be ripening simultaneously, there are more than a dozen intriguers, and no single pattern of development will fit all the kinds of action which the fair breeds. Jonson, however, adheres to a firm if complicated plan in devising the apparent chaos of his fair, and this play has a thematic structure much like that of *The Silent Woman.* Here again Jonson is not arguing a thesis but is investigating diverse aspects of a central problem; here again the various parts of his play are used to mirror each other; and here again the 'unity of inspiration' is best expressed by a character who is a fantastic caricature, in an extremely absurd situation which is reflected by all the more 'realistic' figures in the play.

The central theme is the problem of what 'warrant' men have or pretend to have for their actions. The problem touches both epistemology and ethics—the questions of how we know what we think we know, and why we behave as we do. Stated thus, it is very broad indeed, but it is brought into focus by several concrete symbols of legal sanction. The Induction, for example, is built on the device of a formal contract between the playwright and the audience, giving the customers license to judge the play, but only within specified limits. The play itself opens with Proctor John Littlewit discussing a marriage license taken out by Bartholomew Cokes and Grace Wellborn, and the possession of this document becomes of central importance not only in gulling the testy 'governor' Humphrey Wasp but also in the 'romantic' plot involving Grace, the two witty gallants, and Dame Purecraft.

The most important symbol of this basic theme, however, is the 'warrant' which the madman Troubleall demands of almost all the characters in the fourth act. This demented former officer of the Court of Pie-Powders, who has neither appeared nor been mentioned earlier in the play, is obsessed with the necessity of documentary sanction for even the slightest action. As the watchman Bristle explains, Troubleall will do nothing unless he has first obtained a scrap of paper with Justice Overdo's name signed to it:

> He will not eate a crust, nor drinke a little, nor make him in his apparell, ready. His wife, Sirreverence, cannot get him make his water, or shift his shirt, without his warrant. (IV.i.)

In Troubleall's absurd humor we have the same kind of grand, extravagant comic conceit as that provided by Morose's hatred of all noise. It is the ultimate extreme, the fantastic caricature of the widespread and not unnatural human craving for clearly defined authority, and it serves as the most significant unifying device in the play. Troubleall intervenes crucially in several of the threads of plot, settling the dispute between Grace's lovers, freeing Overdo and Busy from the stocks, and enabling Quarlous to cheat Justice Overdo and marry the rich widow Purecraft. But beyond his service as a catalyst of action, Troubleall's main function is, as his name suggests, to trouble everybody as he darts suddenly on and off the stage with his embarrassing question, 'Have you a warrant for what you do?' This leads to a reexamination of the motives of all the characters, a new scrutiny of what warrant they really have and what they pretend to have for their beliefs and their deeds.

Neither the outright fools nor the outright knaves are much troubled by the great question. The booby Cokes, who has never sought a reason for anything he did, exclaims scornfully, 'As if a man need a warrant to lose any thing with!' And Wasp, who pretends to 'judgment and knowledge of matters' but who really is just as much motivated by irrational whim as his foolish pupil, cries out during the game of vapours, 'I have no reason, nor I will heare of no reason, nor I will looke for no reason, and he is an Asse, that either knowes any, or lookes for't from me.' (IV.iv.) Among the knaves, Edgeworth the cutpurse is jolted for a moment by Troubleall's question, thinking that his villainy has been found out, but he quickly returns to planning his next robbery. Most resolute of all is the pimp Knockem, who immediately sits down and *forges* Troubleall a warrant for whatever he may want. As Cokes is motivated by sheer whim, so the sharpers of the fair are motivated by sheer desire for gain, and neither feels the need for further justification.

The watchmen Haggis and Bristle, however, who are on the fringes of the fair's knavery, are led to reflect that Justice Overdo is 'a very parantory person' who can get very angry indeed when he has a mind to, 'and when hee is angry, be it right or wrong; hee has the Law on's side, ever.' (IV.i.) In other words, 'warrant' for the watchmen is contained entirely in the unpredictable personality of the judge whom they serve; they have no concern with the guilt or innocence of those whom they incarcerate, and if there is ethics behind the law, they do not comprehend it.

Justice Overdo himself has a double function in the play. For the watchmen and for Troubleall, his name stands as a symbol for the ultimate authority which requires no rational understanding. But as a character in the action, Overdo has his own 'warrants' for his conduct, and they are neither irrational nor hypocritical. His motives—to protect the innocent and reprehend the guilty—are beyond reproach; nor is his reliance for his general ethics upon Stoic philosophy as expounded by the Roman poets in itself anything but admirable. And he has the further laudable desire to base his judicial decisions on exact information; he will trust no spies, foolish constables, or sleepy watchmen, but will visit the fair in disguise, to search out enormities for himself at first hand. But for all this the Justice is completely ineffectual, because he cannot interpret correctly what he sees, and because he fails to differentiate between the minor vanities and major iniquities of the fair. Many are the yearly enormities of the place, as he says, but he concentrates on the evils of bottle-ale, tobacco, and puppet shows and fails to see the robbery and seduction going on under his nose. Even when he taxes the right knaves, it is for the wrong crimes. Through the characterization of Justice Overdo, Jonson seems to me to add the warning that even the best of warrants is not in itself sufficient to insure right action; Overdo is reminded at the end that his first name is Adam and he is but flesh and blood, subject to error like the rest of us. Even such admirable principles as reverence for the classics and reliance upon the facts of evidence can, if adhered to blindly, become fetishes almost as ludicrous as Troubleall's trust in a signature.

The application of the theme of warrant to Rabbi Zeal-of-the-Land Busy, who pretends to find authority for everything he does in the words of scripture but who really is motivated by the most elemental greed and gluttony, and whose ingenious discovery of theological reasons for the consumption of roast pig by the faithful is perhaps the funniest scene in the entire play, need not be further elaborated. The most interesting *effects* of Troubleall's persistent questioning are those upon Dame Purecraft and upon Quarlous. The Puritan widow is seized with a frenzied desire to reform; the witty gentleman comes close to becoming an outright knave.

For Dame Purecraft, Troubleall's madness seems the only possible alternative to the life of double dealing she has been leading. She exclaims:

> Mad doe they call him! the world is mad in error, but hee is mad in truth. . . . O, that I might be his yoake-fellow, and be mad with him, what a many should wee draw to madnesse in truth, with us. (IV.vi.)

'Madness in error' in the specific case of Dame Purecraft means reliance upon the Puritan interpretation of Biblical authority. In the first scene of Act IV she had replied confidently to Troubleall's question, 'Yes, I have a warrant out of the word.' But now she admits freely that her adherence to scriptural authority was but subterfuge for wicked self-seeking, and she wants to exchange her hypocritical Puritanism for the absolute and ingenuous madness which Troubleall represents. The final irony is that she gains for a husband not a real madman but a gentleman-rogue disguised as a lunatic, Quarlous tricked out for his own selfish purposes in the clothes of Troubleall. Even the search for pure irrationality thus turns out to be futile; Dame Purecraft is yoked with the image of her former self, and her glorious repentance and conversion have been in vain.

Quarlous comes to a similar conclusion that the only choice is between knavery and madness, but he has little hesitation in choosing knavery. As he stands aside to deliberate Dame Purecraft's proposal, he reasons thus:

> It is money that I want, why should I not marry the money, when 'tis offer'd mee? I have a *License* and all, it is but razing out one name, and putting in another. There's no playing with a man's fortune! I am resolv'd! I were truly mad, an' I would not! (V.ii.)

And so he proceeds not only to marry the rich widow but also to extract money by fraud from Justice Overdo, from his erstwhile friend Winwife, and from Grace, the girl for whom he has so recently declared his love. The warrant which Quarlous abandons is the code of a gentleman, including the chivalric ideals of loyalty to one's friend and undying devotion to one's mistress. But the movement of the play here as elsewhere is towards the discovery of true motives rather than towards change of character, for though Quarlous has loudly protested both love and friendship, he has never really been governed by either.

Quarlous' mode of thinking and of acting approaches more and more closely that of those absolute rogues, the inhabitants of the fair. And Quarlous is just as loud in protesting his difference from the fair people as Humphrey Wasp is in protesting his difference from his foolish pupil. Quarlous resents being greeted familiarly by such rascals as Knockem and Whit, and in a very revealing passage he first lashes out at the cutpurse Edgeworth for treating him like one of 'your companions in beastlinesse.' He then proceeds to find excuses for having been accessory before and after the fact to a robbery:

> Goe your wayes, talke not to me, the hangman is onely fit to discourse with you. . . . I am sorry I employ'd this fellow; for he thinks me such: *Facinus quos inquinat, aequat.* But, it was for sport. And would I make it serious, the getting of this Licence is nothing to me, without other circumstances concurre. (IV.vi.)

This is a piece of rationalization worthy of the master, Rabbi Busy; and we observe with some amusement that Quarlous immediately starts taking steps to *make* the other circumstances concur through fraud.

The emphasis in *Bartholomew Fair* is thus on the narrow range of motives that actually govern men's actions, in contrast to the wide variety of warrants which they pretend to have. Notable prominence is given to primitive motivations: Busy scents after pork like a hound, both Mrs. Littlewit and Mrs. Overdo are drawn into the clutches of the pimps by the necessity for relieving themselves, and the longing of a pregnant woman is the ostensible reason which sets the whole Littlewit party in motion towards the fair. As the many hypocrisies are revealed, the only distinction which seems to hold up is that between fools and knaves, between Cokes and the rogues who prey on him. The other characters are seen as approaching more and more closely to these extremes, until all search for warrant seems as absurd as Troubleall's, since all authority is either as corrupt as the watchmen or as irrational as Wasp or as blind as Justice Overdo. Whim, animal appetite, and sordid greed have complete sway over men's actions without as well as within the fair; the fair merely provides the heightened conditions under which disguises fall off and the elemental motivations become manifest.

In both the plays we have been considering then, fantastic exaggerations like Morose's hatred of noise and Troubleall's search for a warrant provide the lenses through which the behavior of more realistically conceived characters can be observed and brought into focus. It is chiefly in his grand comic conceits that Jonson's 'unity of inspiration' resides, for in them the interplay of realistic satire and fantastic caricature is most highly concentrated, and from them it does truly 'radiate into plot and personages alike.'

It is this interplay between realism and fantasy which seems to me the very essence of Jonson's comedy. To decry, as Herford and Simpson do, the prominence of the 'farcical horror-of-noise-motive' in *The Silent Woman*, and to regret the 'deep-seated contrarieties in Jonson's own artistic nature, where the bent of a great realist for truth and nature never overcame the satirist's and humorist's weakness for fantastic caricature' [9] is, I believe, seriously to misunderstand Jonson's art. His purpose was always to hold the mirror up to nature, but not simply to present the world of common experience, uncriticized and unstructured. Without the extravagant caricatures which he develops into organizing symbols, Jonson's comedy would lack not only the unity but also the universality of great art.

If Jonson's comedy is of the sort here suggested, then a comparison with Aristophanes may not be amiss. Here again we have a mingling of fantasy and realism, and here again we have a comic structure centered not on a plot but on the exploration of an extravagant conceit. Jonson has almost always been discussed as if he belonged in the tradition of Menander, Plautus, and Terence—of New Comedy. I believe that we might gain more insight into his art if we considered him instead in the quite different tradition of Old Comedy. Perhaps Jonson meant more than we have given him credit for meaning when he said of the comedy he was working to develop that it was not bound by Terentian rules but was 'of a particular kind by itself, somewhat like *Vetus Comoedia*.' [10]

NOTES

1. *Essays of John Dryden*, ed. by W. P. Ker (Oxford, 1926), I, 83.
2. *Apologie for Bartholmew Fayre: the Art of Jonson's Comedies* (New York, Modern Language Association, 1947), *passim*, especially pp. 91–97.
3. 'Ben Jonson,' *Elizabethan Essays* (London, 1934), p. 77.
4. Ker, *Essays of Dryden*, I, 88.
5. Townsend, *Bartholmew Fayre*, p. 64.
6. In his *Discoveries* (lines 1815–20 in the Herford and Simpson edition) Jonson speaks slightingly of Terence's skill in these matters, though it was much praised by most Renaissance critics. For the meaning of the terms, see Marvin T. Herrick, *Comic Theory in the Sixteenth Century* ('Illinois

Studies in Language and Literature,' Vol. XXXIV, Nos. 1–2 [Urbana, 1950]), pp. 94–106.

7. For these and other sources see C. H. Herford and Others, *Ben Jonson* (Oxford, 1925–52), II 72–79 (1925), and notes in Vol. X (1950); also the edition by Julia Ward Henry ('Yale Studies in English,' No. XXXI [New York, 1906]), pp. xxviii–lvi, and O. J. Campbell, 'The Relation of *Epicoene* to Aretino's *Il Marescalco*,' *PMLA*, XLVI (1931), 752–62.

8. *Ben Jonson*, II, 76 (1925).

9. *Ben Jonson*, II, 76–78 (1925).

10. Induction to *Every Man out of His Humour*.

ROBERT ORNSTEIN

The Moral Vision of Ben Jonson's Tragedy

TIME has not reversed the Jacobean verdict on Jonson's tragedies, nor is it likely that any vagary of taste will ever bring *Sejanus* and *Catiline* into general favor. They bored Jonson's audiences and they do not excite modern readers, who expect in Jacobean tragedy the vitality and variousness of Shakespeare and Webster. *Sejanus* undoubtedly deserves more readers than Jonson's reputation as a tragedian will allow, but *Catiline* remains a trial for the most sympathetic.

The truth may be that Jonson's tragedies are more interesting to discuss than to read, because artistic failure is a fascinating subject for critical analysis, more so in some respects than artistic success. If nothing else, it allows the critic a brief moment of superiority over the creative artist and affords a rare opportunity to dictate the terms of literary creation. Jonson's failure in tragedy is particularly interesting because his dramatic genius is beyond cavil and because he wrote *Sejanus* and *Catiline* at the height of his powers. To say that he could not write tragedy because his talent, like Greene's or Dekker's, lay in comedy is not even to beg the question convincingly. For Jonson was not by temperament a lighthearted satirist or a whimsical romantic. His comic muse was harsh and bitter, too bitter, in fact, for many tastes. His satire probed beneath the surface of human folly to uncover the sordid joke of inhuman vice. And in *Volpone*, we are often told,

From *The Moral Vision of Jacobean Tragedy* (Madison: The University of Wisconsin Press, 1960), pp. 84–104. Reprinted with permission of the copyright owners, the Regents of the University of Wisconsin, the publisher, and the author.

he shattered the decorums of comedy by creating a protagonist who possessed an almost tragic magnificence. We cannot say that the qualities which made Jonson triumphant in comedy were unsuited to tragedy. We can only say that these qualities (the lightning flash of wit, the pungent realism of characterization and dialogue, and the subtle understanding of the psychology of evil) are not strikingly evident in *Sejanus* or *Catiline.* If we agree with Herford and Simpson that Jonson lacked Shakespeare's depths of compassion and understanding, we merely acknowledge that he could not have written *Hamlet* or *King Lear.* If we agree that his Roman plays were the tragedies of a satirist,[1] we may still wonder why he could not have equalled, in his own fashion, the satiric tragedies of Webster and Tourneur.

Jonson was the first of many critics to explain the failure of his tragedies on the stage. The fault, he assumed, lay in the vulgarity of the unlettered, unwashed multitude, who had no appreciation of classical art. Modern critics have somewhat maliciously taken Jonson at his word. They agree that *Sejanus* and *Catiline* are too 'classical' for the popular stage, but they mean by this that Jonson sacrificed his living genius at the dreary altar of neoclassical form. We should not, however, place too much significance on the failure of *Sejanus* and *Catiline* to win popular approval. It is hardly likely that Chapman's *Caesar and Pompey* was more successful (if it was ever performed), but whereas Chapman ignores his audience, Jonson's scornful attack on the common, swinish, mole-like torturers 'that bring all wit to the Rack' calls vivid attention to the reception of his plays. No doubt Jonson hoped to reform the vulgar errors of the stage through the example of *Sejanus,* and no doubt his idea of tragic style derived less from popular dramatic practice than from his scholarly study of the classics and from the neoclassical literary theory of the Renaissance. Yet if we can believe the preface to *Sejanus,* he did not—or at least he thought he did not—place classical decorum above 'popular delight.' Nor was his view of tragedy narrowly bound by the neoclassical 'laws' of tragic art. One could argue, in fact, that *Sejanus* is much more directly influenced by the popular dramatic tradition than is *Caesar and Pompey.* The portrait of Sejanus looks back to the Machiavellian hero-villains of the Elizabethan stage, and particularly to Marlowe's overreachers. The web of ironic intrigue and counter-intrigue in *Sejanus* recalls the archetypal plotting of *The Spanish Tragedy* even as the use of the revenge motive and design imitates the patterning of history in Marlowe's *Edward II*, in *Richard III*, and in *Julius Caesar*.

Unfortunately, however, Jonson's ill-success as a tragedian has made *Sejanus* and *Catiline* the classical stalking-horses of critics who defend less tutored Jacobean dramaturgy. Those who lament that 'Aristotle was little thumbed on the Bankside,' remarks F. L. Lucas, 'might with poetic justice be condemned to read *Catiline* once a week for life.' [2] At the risk of taking Mr. Lucas' casual thrust too seriously, I would point out that an attention to classical unities did not stultify Jonson's comic genius, nor is there any evidence that the demands of logic precluded the spontaneous flight of his dramatic imagination. Actually Jonson pays far more attention to conventional unities in his greatest comedies than he does in his tragedies, and yet the elaborate designs of *Volpone* and *The Alchemist* are breathless works of the imagination.

Because we are unduly impressed by, or scornful of, Jonson's 'labored art,' we may draw the wrong inferences from the massive structures of his tragedies. The solid characterizations, the compact verse, and the sheer weight of classical literary apparatus suggest a scholarly detachment, a firm if not throttling grasp on the subject at hand. We think of Jonson as a playwright who clearly perceived and tenaciously executed an essentially undramatic artistic intention. It is possible, however, that appearances in *Sejanus* and *Catiline* completely belie the facts. I would suggest that Jonson was unsuccessful not because his idea of tragedy was rhetorical, but because he could not come to terms with his own view of politics. Despite his careful attention to classical decorums, he could not with a divided mind achieve in tragedy the superb unity of form and vision that characterizes *Volpone* and *The Alchemist*.

To begin with, we must bury the notion, based on Jonson's pedantic documentation of his texts, that the tragedies were antiquarian exercises, works of classical scholarship completely unrelated to the Jacobean scene or to Jacobean problems. In the more sophisticated historiography of the Renaissance (Bacon's, for example) there was no contradiction between accurate, objective recreation of the past and the use of history as a guide for the present. If *Julius Caesar* is history for art's sake, *Sejanus* and *Catiline* are not history for history's sake. Like Chapman's dramatic studies of French history, they mirror in a foreign setting political and moral issues of the time. We should not casually dismiss the fact that Jonson was called before the Star

Chamber to explain the 'treasonous' matter in *Sejanus*, for there are many aspects of the play that might arouse legitimate bureaucratic suspicions. He was, moreover, a friend and colleague of Chapman, who very probably was the 'happy genius' mentioned by Jonson as a collaborator in the stage version of *Sejanus*.[3] The two men were kindred spirits; they shared similar humanistic interests and ideals and similarly disillusioned views of politics. Their first tragedies[4] were written within a year of each other and present comparable scenes of political decadence. The opening passages of *Sejanus* inform us that the Roman state (like Bussy's society) has fallen from its original 'noblesse,' that lawless ambition and intrigue have become the norms of political life. The aristocrats, once pillars of the state, have been reduced to marble-warming sycophants or ineffectual malcontents. The New Men of imperial favor grow wealthy and powerful by terrorizing Roman citizens who once enjoyed traditional privileges of law and freedom.

Although concerned with the same issues as Chapman, Jonson seems to approach the problem of political immorality from an opposite direction. Whereas Chapman's attacks on Machiavellianism presuppose specific ideals of liberty and of monarchical authority, Jonson seems to have no political theories. The only comment on forms of government in his tragedies (and in *Timber*) is the ubiquitous Renaissance commonplace that the rule of a good Prince is an ideal polity. Unlike Chapman, Jonson does not specifically challenge the absolutist claim to all-encompassing authority except in a single unimportant passage.[5] And unlike Chapman he offers no personal ideological message. If Chapman had written a play on the reign of Tiberius, his tragic hero would very likely have been, not Sejanus, but the Clermont-like Silius, who commits suicide to escape the coils of tyranny. I do not mean that Chapman admired nobility and Jonson was fascinated only with the criminal mind. (Jonson had his Cicero and Cato; Chapman, his Byron.) I mean rather that while Chapman seems a disillusioned idealist, Jonson is in tragedy as in comedy a moral realist, an ironic observer and pitiless recorder of vices and vanities.

It may not be completely accidental, therefore, that Jonson came close to tragic grandeur in comedy and achieved a primarily satiric effect in his tragedies. For the comic spirit presumes a moral security, an ineffable sense of the futility of vice, and an assurance that inhuman intent will be thwarted by human fallibility. Creating his own comic world, Jonson can delineate, through selection and emphasis, a universal moral pattern in a singular dramatic situation. Convinced of the ultimate vanity of insatiable desire, he can boldly depict the sordid comedy of greed and venality. The pattern of history, however, may not conform to ethical assumptions. Its drama may provide an apt subject for moral commentary, but its tragic events may lack moral significance or resolution.

In *Volpone* the helplessness of Celia and Bonario is inconsequential because avarice, lechery, and overreaching ambition are self-defeating. In historical drama, however, when the issues are bloody and the consequences of villainy catastrophic, the helplessness of virtue is not inconsequential. The fact that criminal ambition eventually overreaches itself does not erase the corrupting stain of tyranny. When the fate of the commonwealth hangs in the balance, the ineffectuality of decent men (the impotent gestures of the aristocracy in *Sejanus*, for example) is bitterly disillusioning. In place of the comic spirit which rules in *Volpone*, the presiding genius of *Sejanus* is the depraved Emperor Tiberius, who toys with the fates of Romans as if he were a god. Whereas *Volpone* reveals the ultimately moral pattern of psychological cause and effect, *Sejanus* implies that the ultimate reality of politics is the amoral struggle for power in which the fittest survive.

If Jonson lacked an intuition of personal tragedy—of the ruin of a noble human being—he did not lack insight into the eternal tragedy of political life. What he lacked was the nerve to present that tragedy with all the artistic powers at his command. Even more than Chapman he could accept Machiavelli's realistic appraisal of politics; but he could not share Machiavelli's appreciation of the heroic evil in politics. Although his depiction of Roman decadence makes Chapman's studies of policy seem genteel and amateurish, his Machiavellian portraits are curiously timid and unconvincing. It is almost as if he cannot admit that a politician might be heroic in stature or driven by ordinary instincts. Exaggerating the inhumanity of his villainous protagonists, he consistently denies them any redeeming traits. As Herford and Simpson point out, Tacitus' Sejanus is a credible political adventurer who stops at nothing in pursuit of his goal.[6] Jonson's Sejanus, however, is scarcely distinguishable psychologically from the Elizabethan stage Machiavels. He has a crude appetite for villainy; his arrogant brags are grandiose but uninspired. Lacking Volpone's wit or Mosca's imagination, he carries to the summit of power the contemptible venality and vulgarity of the parvenu. His ambitions are vast but his spirit is mean; he collapses with a whimper before the Senate. All in all it is not surprising that the imitations of *Sejanus* in *The White Devil* are far more effective than the original passages, for Webster's willingness to create and admire 'glorious villains' quickens the suppressed fire and brilliance of Jonson's dramatic situations.[7]

A tragedy, especially a political tragedy, can succeed even though its main figure lacks heroic stature. One thinks of Marlowe's *Edward II,* in which the weakness of the protagonist is offset by the variety and vitality of the supporting characters. But no play can succeed if the audience feels that its dramatic action centers about the wrong protagonist. And Jonson, it would seem, had a knack for creating tragedies with the wrong protagonists. The nominal hero of *Catiline* literally disappears from sight in the fourth act. Sejanus remains on stage until the final scene but as the play proceeds he is increasingly dominated by Tiberius, who even *in absentia* controls the situation. Actually Tiberius is not Sejanus' foil; he is a rival Machiavel, more psychologically convincing and more directly relevant to Machiavelli's description of the Prince. Whereas Sejanus is descended from the Elizabethan pseudo-Machiavel, Tiberius is a realistic portrait of a politician who cunningly manipulates other men's fears and desires.

Of course it is Jonson's prerogative to make Sejanus (who is a minor figure in Tacitus) his tragic hero and to relegate Tiberius (who is Tacitus' central figure) to a minor role. Unfortunately, however, Jonson leaves the impression that the inversion is arbitrary, that he has mistakenly cast a minor character in the lead while the genuine hero lurks in the wings. One could, for example, write a tragedy on the reign of Richard III in which Buckingham is the hero. But the play would be morally and aesthetically unsatisfying if when Buckingham finally ascends the scaffold, Richard continues his career of triumphant villainy. Buckingham would not seem a tragic hero to the audience; he would appear a politic dupe who failed to match wits with the more diabolical and fascinating Richard. In *Sejanus* Jonson wrote a 'Roman' version of *Richard III* in which a Buckingham-like Sejanus plays the leading role even though the hero of the Machiavellian struggle for power is the more astute Tiberius.

This is not to say that Jonson deliberately avoided making Tiberius his hero. We can well believe that *Sejanus* was Jonson's attempt to rival the tremendous success of Shakespeare's drama of Roman conspiracy, *Julius Caesar*. The opening speeches of *Sejanus* indicate that Jonson, like Shakespeare, is going to present a conflict between the ancient aristocracy and the New Man of Roman politics. It is soon evident, however, that the aristocrats are no match for Sejanus' party and that the moral conflict for control of the state is an illusion nurtured in aristocratic minds. When Drusus dares to slap Sejanus' face, the Senators exclaim 'A Castor, a Castor,' but we already know that Sejanus has begun to seduce Drusus' wife and has plotted his murder. Arruntius, the acid-tongued moral chorus, seems, like the censors of Jonson's comedy, a spokesman for the dramatist's own sentiments and ideas. Yet his moral anger is shadowed by his wordy futility and by the fact that he is licensed by the politicians to provide a harmless source of information. Although he blusters about taking action, his gestures remain verbal. When Sabinus mentions Sejanus' imperial ambitions, Arruntius exclaims:

By the gods,
If I could gesse he had but such a thought,
My sword should cleave him downe from head to heart,
But I would finde it out: and with my hand
I'ld hurle his panting braine about the ayre,
In mites, as small as *atomi,* to'undoe
The knotted bed——(I. 252–58)

Nevertheless his sword does not leave his scabbard, and he is content with a vicarious act of defiance. When Silius takes his life before the Senate, Arruntius crows that *his* thought prompted the deed.

The noble sentiments of the aristocrats provide a moral facade for the real struggle for power, which is totally amoral. Scene by scene Jonson's drama moves from moral illusion to amoral reality, gradually focusing on the deadly game of deception and pretense that absorbs Sejanus and Tiberius. At first we share Sejanus' contempt for the doting, enfeebled Emperor, who seems completely infatuated with and dependent upon his favorite. Tiberius' first address to the Senate is commonplace, couched in sententious clichés, hesitant and circuitous in movement—the expression of an apparently vapid and timorous mind. We note, however, that after acknowledging the conventional pieties, Tiberius warns his listeners not to take his professed humility too seriously:

No man, here,
Receive our speeches, as *hyperbole's;*
For we are far from flattering our friend [Sejanus],
(Let envy know) as from the need to flatter.

Nor let them aske the causes of our praise;
Princes have still their grounds rear'd with themselves,
Above the poore low flats of common men,
And, who will search the reasons of their acts,
Must stand on equall bases. (I. 532–40)

The doting Emperor weaves his way through a maze of idealistic platitudes only to arrive at a pointed expression of absolute prerogative.

We hear of Tiberius' unnatural lusts; we witness only his political sins: his conspiracy with Sejanus to degrade and enslave the Romans. Foreshadowing the entente of Baligny and his king in Chapman's *Revenge,* Jonson dramatizes the link between tyranny and opportunism—between despotic jealousies and politic ambitions—when favorites rule. Like Baligny, Sejanus confesses that he exploits Tiberius' anxieties by exaggerating the danger of conspiracy. He gloats that he has alienated Tiberius from the Roman populace by perpetrating acts of savagery in his name:

The way, to put
A prince in bloud, is to present the shapes
Of dangers, greater than they are (like late,
Or early shadowes) and, sometimes, to faine
Where there are none, onely, to make him feare;
His feare will make him cruell: And once entred,
He doth not easily learne to stop, or spare
Where he may doubt. This have I made my rule,
To thrust TIBERIUS into tyrannie,
And make him toile, to turne aside those blockes,
Which I alone, could not remoove with safetie.
(II. 383–93)

On the other hand, Sejanus' ambition provides Tiberius with an unscrupulous henchman to cut down those men who have 'grown fast/ Honor'd, and lov'd':

'Tyrannes artes
'Are to give flatterers, grace; accusers, power;
'That those may seeme to kill whom they devoure.'
(I. 70–72)

Thus fear and treachery poison the wellsprings of Roman life. No man is secure against the malice of spies or the coercions of a police state. As Chapman also suggests (in *Chabot*), the claims of absolute authority make all issues political and all dissent treasonous. Silius is accused of disloyalty because he dares to imagine that his patriotic service deserves imperial thanks. History must be revised and authors silenced to maintain the 'security' of the state.

Against the grim procession of public crimes, the private drama of tyrant and favorite slowly unfolds, each interview between Sejanus and Tiberius removing another veil of ambiguity and clarifying another aspect of their relationship. In their first meeting Sejanus appears the master. His fustian soliloquy introduces the scene; his politic acumen and decisiveness contrast with the quaking fears which Tiberius admits. It is only on restudy that we realize that the interview is a Socratic dialogue on Machiavellian 'necessity' conducted by a fearful Emperor, who shudders at every crime he suggests. Using Sejanus as his damned soul, Tiberius raises pious objections while Sejanus lectures by the Machiavellian card on the ends and means of policy. Tiberius makes no commitment to evil until Sejanus has pledged his villainy; then, feebly suggesting that they consult about the measures to be taken, he leaves the execution of the crimes entirely in Sejanus' hands.

Even as the aristocrats meet to voice their ineffectual sentiments, the net closes upon them. The fruits of policy begin to mature as Silius is trapped by false accusation in the Senate. Again Sejanus dominates the scene, pressing home the attack as both prosecutor and judge. Tiberius, seemingly ignorant of the proceedings, enters after Silius has been charged. He remains silent except to announce his magnanimous decision to adopt Germanicus' sons and to insist that customary legal procedure be followed in Silius' trial, which ensures his judicial murder. As in the deposition scene of *Richard II,* the henchman does the devil's work. The master politician watches silently, interrupting only with gracious gesture of justice or mercy. Bolingbroke orders the mirror and allows Richard to leave—to prison. Tiberius laments the 'sad Accident' of Silius' death that 'thus hath stall'd and abus'd our mercy.'

Blinded by success to the ironies of his relationship with Tiberius, Sejanus pursues his career until the only let between him and imperial power is the Emperor himself. The populace is cowed; the nobility is bought or intimidated. Nothing remains for Sejanus but to ally himself with the royal family before making his final bid for supremacy. The request for Livia's hand is, of course, the fatal act of presumption, the clear warning to Tiberius that his willing cutthroat now aims too high. Tiberius refuses the request with paternal kindness. Warning Sejanus not to arouse envy by overreaching, he promises recognition of his merit at the appropriate moment. Tiberius exits and Sejanus, irritated but not enlightened, soliloquizes on the 'dull, heavie CAESAR.' Here is the incredible blindness of clear-sighted policy, the fundamental unrealism of Machiavellian realism, which Webster was later to dramatize so brilliantly. Sejanus has no illusions about the ephemerality of power or the danger of rivalling princes; he knows that the passions and ambitions which he incites for politic purposes will be directed against himself when he nears the pinnacle of success. He assumes, however, that he is so much the master of the political universe that he will repeal its immutable laws of cause and effect.

Sejanus' insensitivity robs his crucial interview with Tiberius of its dramatic potentialities, but the succeeding flurry of scenes releases the suppressed tensions of the meeting. No sooner does Sejanus end his contemptuous reflection on Tiberius than the Emperor appears, his mask of indecision dropped, his mind vigorous and poised; he has already settled Sejanus' fate. The time has come not to reform the Roman polity but to change favorites, to pit the poison of ambition against itself. Summoning Macro, Tiberius assumes again his role of dotard. Again his method is an ambiguous hesitancy:

. . . we have thought on thee,
(Amongst a field of *Romanes,*) worthiest MACRO,
To be our eye, and care, to keepe strict watch
On AGRIPPINA, NERO, DRUSUS, I,
And on SEIANUS: Not, that we distrust
his loyaltie . . . (III. 679–84)

The inclusion of Sejanus' name seems almost an afterthought, until we see (with Macro) how Tiberius fastens upon it. True to his nature, Tiberius refuses to commit himself. He orders Macro to spy,

Informe, and chastise; thinke, and use thy meanes,
Thy ministers, what, where, on whom thou wilt;
Explore, plot, practise . . . (III. 702–4)

with impunity. He will take no answer 'but in act.' Again Tiberius shrewdly chooses his tool. Drunk with the first heady wine of imperial favor, Macro is a 'ready engine' to pull down Sejanus. When he learns that Sejanus has regained the Emperor's favor through the accident at Spelunca, Macro's decision is instantaneous. He cannot rise unless Sejanus falls.

While Sejanus and Macro maneuver for position, building and securing alliances, the absent Tiberius commands the political situation in Rome. Having set in motion the forces which will ruin Sejanus, he now psychologically prepares the Roman populace for their role in Sejanus' catastrophe. A series of contradictory letters perplex and divide their loyalties; Sejanus is praised and then censured; his followers rewarded and punished. Swayed by uncertainties, afraid to commit themselves one way or another, the people lose all will to action. Dependent upon imperial caprice, hypnotized by the sinuous weaving of Tiberius' favor, the Roman citizen hungers for a decision —any decision—to be made:

> Would he tell us who he loves, or hates,
> That we might follow, without feare, or doubt.
>
> (IV, 424–25)

It is not surprising that the flame of Jonson's dramatic genius burns most brightly in the last act of *Sejanus*. The moralizing choric commentators have served their function and disappear until the final scene; the stage is cleared, as it were, for the fascinating amoral maneuvers that determine political success and failure. The swiftly moving events release for the first time a ripple of comedy in the counterpoised scenes of Sejanus' and Macro's intrigues. The fluid Elizabethan stage becomes the perfect medium for expressing vivid contrasts and ironies of plot and counterplot. If Sejanus' bombast still falls short of the heroic, he reacts swiftly and courageously to the calamity of the statue. Macro's return to Rome, however, shakes his confidence, and the averting of the god's face brings a hysterical defiance. At this anxious moment Macro's announcement of the 'tribuniciall dignity' is a shattering psychological coup. The ever-wary Sejanus succumbs completely to relief and lowers all defenses: the sacrificial wolf has been prepared for the slaughter.

Like *Volpone*, *Sejanus* ends with a scene of judgment. The hero-villain is denounced, condemned by the Senate, and executed by the populace whom he oppressed. The perpetrator of inhuman outrages is at last punished in a fearful measure for measure. But 'justice' in Sejanus' instance means only that one cutthroat annihilates another while the master criminal goes free. Moreover Sejanus' fall brings no moral resolution. His ruin does not herald the end of political corruption, nor does it positively counterbalance the portrait of decadence developed throughout the play. On the contrary, Sejanus' execution is a final revelation of the hopeless decay of the state. When he walks into Macro's trap, the fawning Senators scramble to flatter him. Spineless, perfectly conditioned sycophants, they sit bewildered by Tiberius' last and most brilliant letter, which (for the audience) recapitulates his Machiavellian use of Sejanus. Under the pretense of considering rumors, which are not to be believed, Tiberius thrusts all guilt for their coöperative villainies on Sejanus, lamenting that Sejanus' 'loyal fury' would make Tiberius' intended mercy seem like 'wearied cruelty.' Hinting the vaguest doubt of Sejanus' innocence, motivated only by concern for the common good, Tiberius orders Sejanus stripped of position and authority, until the Senate can investigate the malicious charges. The Senators turn and twist with every calculated contradiction in the letter. As they waver Macro enters on cue to fire the tinder which Tiberius has prepared. While the ruined Sejanus moans that it has 'beene otherwise, betweene you, and I,' Macro leads the Senators in the officially sanctioned direction of mob violence. Their passions inflamed, their reasons lost in a hysteria of fear and hatred, they condemn Sejanus without evidence or trial. Then the crowd, following Macro and shouting 'Liberty, liberty, liberty,' butchers and mutilates Sejanus' body. Piling horror on horror, the 'wittily and strangely-cruell' Macro devises the rape and murder of Sejanus' innocent children. As the play ends, choric commentators exclaim against the many-headed multitude and the wanton caprice of Fortune. They warn the insolent statist

> Not to grow proud, and carelesse of the gods:
> It is an odious wisedome, to blaspheme,
> Much more to slighten, or denie their powers.
>
> (V. 899–901)

This pious moralizing, like the tags which punctuate the close of Webster's tragedies, is not without point; still we know that Sejanus' catastrophe was neither a turning of Fortune's wheel nor an act of divine retribution. Behind the insensate fury of the mob lay the calculating ambition of Macro; behind Macro's witty cruelty, the genius of Tiberius, the secular god in the empire of Rome who rigs Fortune's wheel and punishes overreaching ambition when it threatens his own security. The spasm of brute passion purges nothing except the pent-up anger of the populace, who, in high Roman fashion, have been given a spectacle and a scapegoat, and who have been made partners in crime with their oppressors.[8] At the end of *Sejanus* the players change but the political drama remains the same. As one favorite falls, another rises who bids fair to become 'a greater prodigie in *Rome,* then he/That now is falne.' The Senators compete in their flattery of the 'Newest Man.' The absent Tiberius wallows in his unnatural lusts and the present crisis forebodes an even more terrifying issue because the 'hope' of Rome lies in the sons of Germanicus, whom Tiberius has adopted: Nero and Caligula.

Only if Jonson had been willing to sacrifice historical fact for didactic purpose could he have contrived a naïvely moralistic drama out of his chosen materials. And yet a deeply moral interpretation of the relationship between Sejanus and Tiberius was possible without falsifying history. For Tacitus describes Tiberius as a tormented, superstitious criminal, who lashed out at Sejanus in a frenzy of terror.[9] Jonson's Tiberius is no less complex, but his 'anxieties' are calculated poses of a masterful politician; his 'ayenbite of inwit' is only one of many superb Machiavellian hypocrisies.

If, as has been suggested,[10] Jonson sought to portray in *Sejanus* the tragedy of civic decadence, then he could have given that tragedy a personal poignancy by depicting the fall of a Silius rather than a Sejanus. If he sought to portray the tragedy of overreaching ambition, then he should have allowed Sejanus some of Volpone's grandeur and accepted Tacitus' characterization of Tiberius. As it is, the play is neither a tragedy of civic decadence nor one of insatiable ambition. We are not allowed to pity and we are not moved to fear. Because Jonson does not clarify his tragic theme, the smoldering intensity of emotion that lies beneath the surface of *Seianus* never bursts into flame.

Catiline his Conspiracy (1611)

The Jacobean public, which did not especially admire *Sejanus,* had even less stomach for Jonson's second essay in tragedy when it appeared eight years later. Whether this surprised Jonson we do not know, but his venomous address to the 'Reader in Ordinarie' indicates that despite his contempt for the mob he was not willing to accept its displeasure. Obviously he made no attempt to woo the groundlings in *Cataline.* Its style is more rhetorical and sententious than that of *Sejanus;* it has an even greater proportion of oratory to dramatic action and an even more deliberate dedication to a 'classical' mode. Thus it is easier to admire Jonson's convictions than to read his play. He had the courage to be deliberately and terribly wrong, which by artistic canons is not a redeeming virtue.

Had he been content merely to force the gruesome story of Catiline's conspiracy into a five-act structure adorned with ghosts and choruses his play might have rivalled the most lurid contemporary melodrama, for Catiline was born to play the lead in a Jacobean revenge tragedy. According to Sallust he was guilty of almost incredible crimes of sensuality and violence; he was infatuated with murder and revenge as well as with power. He plotted with a desperate band of malcontents a Wagnerian immolation of Rome, on whose ruins he planned to build a personal empire. Here was a subject that could have made *Volpone* seem like a Sunday-school pageant, but significantly Jonson could not rise (or descend) to it. Although his conspirators seal their pact with a draught of human blood, they lack the first fine careless rapacity of the Jew of Malta. Their hunger for destruction produces only a stale hyperbole; their very inhumanity is dull. And their braggadocio merely accentuates their hollowness of spirit that in crisis borders on sheer cowardice. We cannot thrill to conspirators plotting the ruin of their city who crumble at the first opposition. The would-be assassins run when Cicero names them. Catiline is ruined, as Caesar shrewdly observes, by words alone, by his inability to outbrave Cicero's eloquent accusations.

If all the characterizations in *Catiline* were as crudely melodramatic, the inadequacies of the conspirators would be less noticeable. But unfortunately Catiline and his fellow cutthroats inhabit a bizarre Senecan demimonde in a larger, more realistically conceived Roman society. Their crude psychologies jar against the more sophisticated portraits of Cicero and Cato, even as their theatrical Machiavellianism clashes with the more astute policy of Caesar and Crassus. Whereas the contrast of Machiavel and pseudo-Machiavel in *Sejanus* serves to define the relationship between Sejanus and Tiberius, the disparate modes of characterization in *Catiline* actually threaten the unity of the play. It is as if by some strange mishap the villains of *The Revenger's Tragedy* had stumbled into a performance of *Chabot*.

The diversity of characters and of threads of plot in *Catiline* creates the impression that Jonson faced an overwhelming task in shaping diffuse historical materials into a unified fable. It is disillusioning to discover, therefore, that just the opposite was true—that

Jonson's tragedy blurs Sallust's lucid, coherent narration and interpretation of Catiline's career. To Sallust the conspiracy is a symptom of the inner rot which afflicted an overprosperous Republic. He explains Catiline's hunger for power and wealth as an extreme criminal manifestation of the vicious appetites nurtured by luxury. He makes it clear that many of the noblest sons of Rome rallied to Catiline's cause. Jonson also attempts to identify the conspiracy with civic decadence. Cicero and the Choruses recite the Polybian theory of cyclical decay; they lament the extravagance and sloth that are sapping the once virile Roman spirit. Nevertheless Jonson's conspirators seem more like the spawn of *The Spanish Tragedy* than Roman decadents. Their thirst for destruction is purely instinctive; they are not so much fallen aristocrats as psychological and moral aberrations.

Jonson, it would seem, was willing to moralize about Roman decadence but not to drive the moral home by uniting choric commentary, characterization, and dramatic action. He allows Catiline to dominate only the first half of the tragedy; thereafter Catiline plays an increasingly minor role until he finally disappears in the fourth act. Only the first half of *Catiline* dramatizes the inner rot of conspiracy; the second half portrays the patriotic struggle to preserve the state and introduces a second hero, the noble Consul Cicero. Possessing two heroes in one play, Jonson is content to drop Catiline before the last act, especially since unity of place demands that the dramatic action remain in Rome after Catiline has fled. With the experience of *Sejanus* behind him, Jonson now seems intent upon emphasizing a moral resolution which history provides; he has found in Cicero a political hero worthy of admiration and he makes much of him.

In casting Cicero as the protagonist of the latter half of *Catiline*, Jonson dramatizes an essentially Chapmanesque conflict between Stoic hero and corrupt society. Indeed, Cicero is in many respects a near relative of Clermont, Chabot, and Pompey. From his earliest appearance he is wrapped in the spiritual loneliness that haunts Chapman's heroes. He has, like Chabot, risen to high position through merit alone, but that very fact isolates him from the aristocracy, to which Catiline, Caesar, and Crassus belong. Cicero, not Catiline, is the upstart. His own brother lacks faith in him and suspects that he is exaggerating the danger of the conspiracy. Only a few men about him understand the mortal danger that faces Rome; the city as a whole is indifferent to the infection that is raging within it.

In Chapman's drama, moral victory does not depend upon public success; it resides in a private philosophical triumph over the temptations and adversities of a disordered world. In Jonson's tragedies, however, the moral issues are public and the moral resolution must also be public. Evil must be defeated upon the stage as well as in the mind. We can therefore understand why Jonson chose to divide his play between two protagonists and why he amplified the role of Cicero, who is a minor figure in Sallust. But it is hard to see why he sacrificed dramatic unity to achieve a moral resolution that is at best tentative if not completely illusory. In an excellent study of Jonson, J. A. Bryant, Jr. describes *Catiline* as the tragedy of a state that is 'spiritually doomed.'[11] Its action, he remarks, 'is roughly analogous to a sick man's detection and treatment of an annoying symptom while the fatal cancer eats patiently away at a vital organ' (p. 272). Cicero, 'naïvely comforted at the destruction of Catiline' palliates the disease but does not cure it, for though the immediate threat to the Republic is annihilated, Caesar and Crassus, the guiding spirits of the conspiracy, are free to continue their subversion of the state (pp. 269–72).

Although I agree in the main with Professor Bryant's interpretation of *Catiline* I see no evidence of naïveté in Cicero's handling of the conspiracy. On the contrary, the deepest irony in the play is the total lack of naïveté in Cicero's motives and in his acceptance of a partial victory over the forces that threaten Rome. A political realist, he willingly accepts the disparity between moral ends and political means—between his high ideals and the ambitions of those who help him to destroy the conspiracy. Cicero does not shatter Catiline by eloquence alone; he uses spies and informers, bribes and threats; he appeals to greed as well as to altruism. How strange in fact is the confederacy of motives that defeats Catiline: Cicero's and Cato's selfless patriotism, Fulvia's vanity, ambition, and envy of Sempronia, Curius' prodigality, lust, and unscrupulousness. The scene in which Cicero convinces Curius to turn his coat a second time is a quaint emblem of a society in which the expedient sham of patriotism must be accepted at face value. Fulvia urges Curius to take the safer way to advancement by becoming Cicero's spy. Cicero outlines 'what thanks, what titles, what reward' will be heaped on the true patriot. While Cicero follows virtue for its own reward, he unhesitatingly buys the 'loyalty' of Fulvia, Curius, and the wavering Antonius, who receives Cicero's province. Shrewd, disillusioned, and disingenuous, he 'anticipates' Machiavelli in his basic premise:

'Tis well, if some men will doe well, for price:
So few are vertuous, when the reward's away.
(III. 479–80)

It is not naïveté that keeps Cicero from accusing Caesar and Crassus, even though they are obviously part of the conspiracy and potentially more dangerous than Catiline. When Cato suggests that Crassus and Caesar would ring hollow if tested, Cicero agrees but adds 'if that we durst prove 'hem.' Although he suspects Caesar, Cicero would not have the Senate at this perilous time dare

an unprofitable, dangerous act,
To stirre too many serpents up at once.
CAESAR, and CRASSUS, if they be ill men,
Are mightie ones; and, we must so provide,
That, while we take one head, from this foule *Hydra*,
There spring not twentie more.
. . . .
They shall be watch'd, and look'd too. Till they doe
Declare themselves, I will not put 'hem out
By any question. There they stand. Ile make
My selfe no enemies, nor the state no traytors. (IV. 528–37)

We cannot tax Cicero's policy and call it cowardice. He agrees with Machiavelli that it is wiser to temporize with evil ambitions, 'instead of violently attacking them; for by temporizing with them they will either die out of themselves, or at least their worst results will be long deferred. And princes or magistrates who wish to destroy such evils must watch all points, and must be careful in attacking them not to increase instead of diminishing them, for they must not believe that a fire can be extinguished by blowing upon it. They should carefully examine the extent and force of the evil, and if they think themselves sufficiently strong to combat it, then they should attack it regardless of consequences; otherwise they should let it be, and in no wise attempt it.' [12]

Cicero would not aggravate the present danger to the state by forcing Caesar and Crassus into open rebellion. He prefers the mockery of allowing them to debate with the Senate the most judicious way of punishing traitors. When the full scope of the conspiracy is bared, however, he is confronted with actual evidence of Caesar's complicity. The serpents have already stirred, they are coiled to strike; the question now is whether to attack them or to turn one's back upon them for the moment. Turning his back, Cicero buys time for Rome by suppressing the evidence of Caesar's guilt. He prevents the incriminating letters to Caesar from being read before the Senate. He dismisses (to prison) as a 'lying varlet' the messenger who implicates Crassus. Praising the enemies of Rome, he refuses to believe the accusations of his own trusted spy, the twice-turned Curius. Such 'prudence' is not wholly voluntary; it is enforced by Caesar's shrewd criticism of Cicero's use of spies and informers. When Curius' 'libell' against him is announced, Caesar responds:

> It shall not [trouble me], if that he have no reward.
> But if he have, sure I shall thinke my selfe
> Very untimely, and unsafely honest,
> Where such, as he is, may have pay t'accuse me.
>
> (V. 361–64)

Under the surface mockery of this speech lies a deeper irony: the very methods Cicero employs to purge the state limit the scope of his action. His Machiavellian means of intelligencing and bribery qualify his moral ends; and, as in *Byron's Tragedy*, the preservation of the state against unlawful conspiracy is tainted by moral compromise.

If we assume that Jonson's controlling purpose in tragedy was a scrupulously faithful reproduction of history, then it is difficult, if not impossible, to account for his Machiavellian portrait of Caesar. Sallust's attitude towards Caesar is completely favorable. He brands the charges of Caesar's complicity in the conspiracy as false and views Caesar and Cato as pillars of the tottering state.[13] Even Plutarch, who condemns Caesar's political ambitions and methods, acknowledges that his part in the conspiracy was only rumored.[14] Thus we face the curious fact that Jonson undercuts the moral resolution of his tragedy, not through a stern dedication to historical truth, but through a deliberate revision of his sources. Like Sejanus, Catiline gloats over his mastery of the political situation, even though he is another politician's tool. It is Caesar who delivers the brilliant Machiavellian oration on the techniques of conspiracy. And after Catiline is denounced, it is Caesar who brazens out his Iago-like claim to honesty, keeping himself free for the future thrust towards empire which was to destroy the republic which Cicero temporarily shored. Again we are left with the impression that Jonson chose the wrong protagonist. Depicting Caesar as the intellectual leader of the conspiracy, he takes as his ostensible hero Caesar's dupe. Again we watch the 'tragedy' of a Roman Buckingham while the Roman Richard lurks in the background.

To point out Jonson's crucial alterations of his sources is not to ridicule his claim to 'truth of Argument.' No other contemporary sought or achieved so authentic a reproduction in art of the classical world. And when Jonson departed from his sources he sacrificed a recorded fact or opinion in order to clarify what seemed to him a larger truth of political history. He sacrificed the opportunity to impose naïve moralistic interpretations on his subject matter in order to convey, implicitly at least, the fundamental amorality of political conflict, in which success is not to the virtuous but to the cunning and the strong. The weaker politician goes to the wall; the Sejanuses and Catilines fail but the Tiberiuses and Caesars achieve, if only temporarily, political mastery.

I do not mean to offer too simple an explanation of the unique qualities and failings of Jonson's tragedies. No theory of moral vision will account for the frequent shallowness of his characterizations, for the staggering burden of his rhetoric, for the narrowness of his sympathies, and for the sheer monotony of his portrayal of evil. Nevertheless it does seem to me that there is a void of ethical meaning at the heart of Jonson's tragedies which the great bulk of moralizing commentary only emphasizes. The body politic is stretched out upon Jonson's dissecting table; an expert scalpel lays bare the inner rot and metastasized corruption. But the lesson in anatomy offers in the end only a Machiavellian understanding of who's in and who's out. The light of the spirit gleams fitfully in *Sejanus* and *Catiline* and is gone. Cicero, who was to the Renaissance the noblest and most eloquent moral instructor of antiquity, must descend into the market place of political loyalty to chaffer for the security of Rome.

Even had they been more successful on the stage, it is doubtful that Jonson's tragedies would have inspired imitation. Political tragedy as a form distinct from the conventional history play or tragedy required an intellectual motive and insight that was rare in the drama of the period. Only Marlowe and Shakespeare among the Elizabethan playwrights had the genius to explore the hidden realities of political conflict. Lesser talents were content to exploit patriotic themes, spectacle, and the grandeur or romantic adventure of popular history. It is quite possible, as we shall see, that the ironic technique of *Volpone* left its impress on Tourneur's imagination and that Jonson's comic vision of respectability was an indirect influence on *Women Beware*

Women. But because interest in historical drama waned rapidly in the Jacobean theaters, Jonson's Roman plays could have had little effect on the further development of tragedy. It is curious that the one great tragedian who admired Jonson enough to borrow some of the lines and dramatic situations of *Sejanus* is, by all appearances, the least likely son of Ben–John Webster. Yet the romanticism of *The White Devil* and the classicism of *Sejanus* have, as we shall see, certain common grounds, and there is good reason to believe that Jonson's tragedies provided some of the inspiration for *Appius and Virginia*.

Of course Jonson's closest affinities in tragedy were with Chapman, whose artistic journey led to a more positive conclusion than *Catiline*. Indeed, had Jonson been more like Chapman he might have felt the need to write yet a third Roman tragedy in which the jarring tensions of *Sejanus* and *Catiline* are harmoniously resolved. But he was not driven to 'reconstruct philosophy' in art, partly because he did not see his tragic theme steadily, and partly because, like the Cicero he admiringly characterizes, he could accept the eternal divorce of moral ideals and political realities. His disillusioned awareness of the many stages on which the Machiavellian drama has unfolded attenuates rather than deepens his sense of outrage. His 'detachment' is not that of a playwright dramatizing remote political issues but that of a Jacobean intellectual who perceives, almost against his will, that contemporary attacks on policy are protests against history itself.

NOTES

1. See the discussion of *Sejanus* in *Ben Jonson*, ed. C. H. Herford and Percy Simpson (Oxford, 1925–52; 11 vols.), II, 21 ff. All citation from Jonson use this edition.
2. *The Complete Works of John Webster*, ed. F. L. Lucas (London, 1927), I, 19.
3. Herford and Simpson, *Jonson*, II, 4.
4. I refer, of course, to Jonson's extant tragedies.
5. *Sejanus*, IV, 167–170.
6. Herford and Simpson, *Jonson*, II, 21.
7. Cf. *Sejanus*, IV. 1–5, with *White Devil*, III.ii. 280 ff.; *Sejanus*, I. 270 ff., with *White Devil*, II.i. 290 ff.
8. I find support for my reading of *Sejanus* in K. M. Burton's 'The Politi-

cal Tragedies of Chapman and Ben Jonson,' *Essays in Criticism,* II (1952), 397–412.

9. Herford and Simpson, *Jonson,* II, 25.
10. Burton, *op. cit.,* 404.
11. '*Catiline* and the Nature of Jonson's Tragic Fable,' *PMLA,* LXIX (1954), 276.
12. *Discourses* (Modern Library Edition), 200.
13. Bryant, *op. cit.,* 269.
14. *Ibid.,* 270.

L. G. SALINGAR

The Revenger's Tragedy and The Morality Tradition

TOURNEUR'S plays have too often been described as if they were texts for illustration by an Aubrey Beardsley. They have suffered as a result. Symonds read *The Revenger's Tragedy* as a melodrama with agreeable thrills and some needless moralizing; and, on this reading, it was not difficult for William Archer, applying the standards of naturalism, to make the play appear ludicrous. Though Mr. Eliot has supplied a corrective by pointing out that the characters are not to be taken as studies in individual iniquity, but as figures in a pattern with a poetic life of its own, his essay on Tourneur again misrepresents him. He is made 'a highly sensitive adolescent with a gift for words . . .'

> The cynicism, the loathing and disgust of humanity, expressed consummately in *The Revenger's Tragedy,* are immature in the respect that they exceed the object. Their objective equivalents are characters practising the grossest vices; characters which seem merely to be spectres projected from the poet's inner world of nightmare, some horror beyond words. So the play is a document on humanity chiefly because it is a document on one human being, Tourneur; its motive is truly the death motive, for it is the loathing and horror of life itself. (*Selected Essays,* p. 189.)

This is the reading of the 'nineties again. Tourneur's poetry, however, unlike the Romantic poetry of decadence, has a firm grasp on the outer world. Cynicism, loathing, and disgust there are in *The Revenger's Tragedy;* but if Tourneur were merely giving expression to a

---

From *Scrutiny,* VI (March 1938), pp. 402–24. Reprinted by permission of the author.

neurotic state of mind, he would hardly have written successful drama at all. The 'object' of his disgust is not the behavior of his characters, singly or together, so much as the process they represent, the disintegration of a whole social order. It is this theme, particularized and brought to life by the verse, that shapes the pattern of the play; and it is developed with the coherence, the precise articulation, of a dramatist assured that his symbols are significant for his audience as much as for himself. Tourneur is writing in the contemporary Revenge convention; but behind the Revenge plays is another dramatic influence, working in harmony with Tourneur's narrowly traditionalist outlook, that of the Moralities. *The Revenger's Tragedy* is a logical development from the mediaeval drama.

The Moralities had been the staple of popular drama when Marlowe began writing, and their methods were absorbed into the blank verse narrative play. That they were absorbed, not abandoned, is clear from *Faustus;* and Mr. Knights has pointed out that their influence on Jonson and his contemporaries was considerable and varied.[1] They offered the Elizabethans a group of stock situations, types, and themes which had been utilised for the representation of social and religious problems throughout the changes of a century;[2] and the later drama could rely on their familiarity in presenting fairly complex situations simply and effectively on the stage. The Morality influence makes itself felt, under the Senecanism and the literary satire, through the conventions of the Revenge plays themselves, and in *The Revenger's Tragedy* most strongly of all. The characters in the Moralities are personified abstractions and moral or social types, representing the main forces making for or against the salvation of the individual and social stability; they have no dramatic functions outside the doctrinal scheme. The actions on the stage are symbolic, not realistic, and the incidents are related to each other logically, as parts of an allegory, or as illustrations of the argument. *The Revenger's Tragedy* is constructed on closely similar lines. Miss Bradbrook has analysed the narrative into 'a series of peripeteia,' representing 'the contrasts between earthly and heavenly vengeance, and earthly and heavenly justice'[3]—linked as the parts of an allegory rather than as a natural sequence of events. The characters are exclusively the instruments of this movement, and it is from this point of view that they explain themselves to the audience; their speeches reveal their world, rather than individual minds. The Duke and his court are simply monstrous embodiments of Lust, Pride, and Greed; Vendice and the other revengers, despite the intensely personal tone of their speeches, are portrayed in the same way. The characters' motives are generalized and conventional—Lussurioso, for example, is an extreme case of Pride and Lust—and many of the speeches are general satiric tirades, spoken in half-turn towards the audience. This is a narrower dramatic pattern than Marston's, and more like those of the Moralities; but Tourneur gains in dramatic coherence from the earlier examples. With Jonson, he was the last writer to apply them successfully.

'I see now,' says Ambitioso in the underplot—the traditional comic underplot in which the Vices are confounded—'there's nothing sure in mortality, but mortality.' The contrast between the skeleton and the specious overlay provided by wealth and sensuality is fundamental to Tourneur and the Morality-writers alike. When Pride, in Medwall's *Nature,* leads Man to debauchery, he prepares for him 'a doublet of the new make':

> Under that a shirt as soft as silk,
> And as white as any milk
> To keep the carcase warm.

These lines might have provided Tourneur with his text. Medwall, however, writes with an equanimity, a sense of security in the values of Nature, that Tourneur has lost. His sense of decay, of the skull, is overpowering:

> Advance thee, O thou terror to fat folks,
> To have their costly three-piled flesh worn off
> As bare as this; for banquets, ease, and laughter
> Can make great men, as greatness goes by clay;
> But wise men little are more great than they.

The Stoical conclusion is feeble beside the savage intensity of the first lines. Death has triumphed, and the only course left open to Vendice is to convert a horrified recoil into a grim acceptance, turning the forces of death against themselves. Nevertheless, the fascination of physical decay has not corrupted Tourneur's satiric purpose; there is nothing mechanical in Vendice's wielding of the lash. The changes of tone in this first soliloquy with the skull imply an attitude active and controlled:

> When two heaven-pointed diamonds were set
> In those unsightly rings—then 'twas a face
> So far beyond the artificial shine

Of any woman's bought complexion,
That the uprightest man (if such there be
That sin but seven times a day) broke custom,
And made up eight with looking after her.
O, she was able to ha' made a usurer's son
Melt all his patrimony in a kiss;
And what his father fifty years told,
To have consumed, and yet his suit been cold.
But, O accursed palace!
Thee, when thou wert apparelled in thy flesh,
The old duke poisoned . . .
O, 'ware an old man hot and vicious!
'Age, as in gold, in lust is covetous.' (I, i.)

The contrasts between life and death, between natural virtue and the effects of lust and greed, are not merely presented—they are shown as a unified process in Vendice's mind, a process which extends through the whole world of the play. The imagery associated with the skull is concrete, exact, and dramatically useful; Tourneur builds up a system of relationships between images and situations which gains in cumulative effect—these lines, for example, have a bearing on the ironic undertones of the scene where the Duchess tempts Spurio, who is wearing her jewel in his ear ('had he cut thee a right diamond . . .'), and, again, on the second appearance of the skull, poisoned with cosmetics. The pun in the first line is flat, but not extraneous; it emphasizes the way in which the symbols are to be taken—the physical world is treated, in a peculiarly direct and consistent manner, as emblematic of the moral order, man in relation to the divine will. This moral order is rigidly identified with the traditional social hierarchy of ranks and obligations; but the narrowness of Tourneur's outlook makes for concentration, and his poetic material is ranged and ordered by reference to the experience of society as a whole. In this passage, the physical contrast between the 'diamonds' and their sockets, visible on the stage, prepares for, and supports, the crude cynicism of the parenthesis, which marks the change of tone. The complete degeneration of virtue is represented by placing the 'usurer's son' on the same footing of sensuality as 'the uprightest man,' the mock inflation overturning any protest from respectability. Here, however, the tone changes again: the 'patrimony,' by implication the ill-gained result of greed, is itself 'melted' away, and, though virtue cannot be reinstated, divine justice is vindicated in the rhyme.

Vendice's tone mounts again as he reverts to the palace; but the Duke, with the 'infernal fires' burning in his 'spendthrift veins,' has already been paralleled with the usurer's son—the two types of social disintegration are juxtaposed throughout the play—so that Vendice's exultant determination on revenge appears as part of an inevitable cycle of feelings and events.

The trite 'sentences' at the end of Tourneur's most passionate speeches are meant to enforce this sense of inevitability by lowering the tension and appealing to the commonplace. Tourneur himself calls them 'conceits,' and continually draws attention, in Marston's manner, to his virtuosity in using them. The resemblance to Marston, however, is only superficial; they are more closely akin to the popular moralists and the Morality writers. Vendice's emblem is an example:

> 'A usuring father to be boiling in hell, and his son and heir with a whore dancing over him':

Again:

> O, you must note who 'tis should die,
> The duchess' son! she'll look to be a saver:
> 'Judgment, in this age, is near kin to favour.' (I, iv.)
>
> Could you not stick? See what confession doth!
> Who would not lie, when men are hanged for truth? (V, i.)

These popular aphorisms and tags of Seneca Englished gave Marston and Tourneur a large part of the raw material from which their more ambitious speeches are developed. But while Marston works up his material as a self-conscious litterateur, Tourneur adheres to the Morality mode. The language of the latter is plain and colloquial, but adequate, as a rule, to the simple didactic purpose; a speech to the audience from Lupton's *All for Money* is typical:

> Is not my grandfather Money think ye of great power
> That could save from hanging such abominable whore,
> That against all nature her own child did kill?
> And yonder poor knave that did steal for his need
> A few sort of rags, and not all worth a crown,
> Because he lacks money shall be hanged for that deed,
> You may see my Grandsire is a man of renown:
> It were meet when I named him that you all kneeled down.

Nay, make it not so strange, for the best of you all,
Do love him so well, you will come at his call.

The audience is included in the framework of the play, the function of the speeches being to expound the theme to them from their own point of view. Marston's sophisticated railing has quite a different effect; it draws attention to itself:

Pietro: Tell me; indeed I heard thee rail—
Mendoza: At women, true; why, what cold phlegm could choose,
Knowing a lord so honest, virtuous,
So boundless loving, bounteous, fair-shaped, sweet,
To be contemn'd, abused, defamed, made cuckold!
Heart, I hate all women for't; sweet sheets, wax lights, antique bed-posts, cambric smocks, villanous curtains, arras pictures, oiled hinges, and all the tongue-tied lascivious witnesses of great creatures' wantonness. (*The Malcontent*, I, vii.)

The lively phrasing here is at odds with the ostensible moral purpose—it is true that Mendoza is gulling Pietro, having cuckolded him himself, but his speech is in the same style as the Malcontent's own speeches;—the literary exhibitionism accompanies a confusion of dramatic motives. Tourneur's railing is more surely realized; it is presented in the older and simpler dramatic mode:

Vendice: Now 'tis full sea abed over the world:
There's juggling of all sides; some that were maids
E'en at sunset, are now perhaps i' the toll-book.
This woman in immodest thin apparel
Lets in her friend by water; here a dame
Cunning nails leather hinges to a door,
To avoid proclamation.
Now cuckolds are coining apace, apace, apace, apace!
And careful sisters spin that thread in the night
That does maintain them and their bawds i' the day.
Hippolito: You flow well, brother.
Vendice: Pooh! I'm shallow yet;
Too sparing and too modest; shall I tell thee?
If every trick were told that's dealt by night,
There are few here that would not blush outright.

The direct appeal to the audience, as Miss Bradbrook remarks, is bathetic (*op. cit.*, p. 173); but it is significant of the condition of success for the first speech, Tourneur's single-minded attitude towards subject and audience together. The shaping influence is that of the Moralities, transmitted directly through Jonson.

It was this influence which enabled him to use the Revenge conventions so successfully. His main preoccupations appear in his first work, *The Transformed Metamorphosis*, clumsily set forth in the form of a vision. The institutions of church and state, and even the objects of the physical world, are perverted from their original and proper functions; Pan, for example, the church, has become a 'hellish ill o're-mask'd with holiness'—'Pan with gold is metamorphosed.' The Prologue describes the poet's bewilderment at the Cimmerian darkness in which he finds himself:

> Are not the lights that Jupiter appointed
> To grace the heav'ns, and to direct the sight,
> Still in that function, which them first anointed,
> Is not the world directed by their light?
> And is not rest, the exercise of night?
> Why is the sky so pitchy then at noon,
> As though the day were govern'd by the Moon?

This has the naivety, the misplacement of emotion, that finds its counterpart in the cynicism of *The Revenger's Tragedy*. The conceits are painstakingly clumsy because Tourneur is genuinely bewildered; he treats them as if they were literal statements of fact. It is evident, however, that they are not affectations of style, as with many of his contemporaries, but organic parts of his thought. The symbolism of the poem reappears in the play, in the pervasive imagery of metamorphosis, falsification, and moral camouflage. It has been thoroughly assimilated to the rhythms of dramatic speech:

> Last revelling night,
> When torch-light made an artificial noon
> About the court, some courtiers in the masque,
> Putting on better faces than their own,
> Being full of fraud and flattery . . . (I, iv.)

> Ha, what news here? is the day out o' the socket,
> That it is noon at midnight? the court up? (II, iv.)

The details are worked out in relation to a central group of metaphors, repeated, on the level of action, in the disguises and deceptions which compose the plot. Here again, the method is derived from the Moralities.

These disguises and deceptions are symbolic, not naturalistic—an occasion is even created for making Castiza herself appear in a falso character. Vendice is disguised three times—when, as Piato, he enters 'the world' and becomes 'a man o' the time,' a court pander; a second time, then he appears as a fantastic 'character' of himself, a melancholy, litigious scholar; and finally, as a masquer. The disguises are distinguished from the disguiser; what Vendice does in his assumed roles affects his character as Vendice, but the relationship is circumscribed and conventional; no provision is made to render it plausible, realistically, that Vendice would or could have sustained his roles.[4] When he tempts his sister, he is not Vendice in disguise, he is Vendice-become-Piato; Piato and Vendice are sharply distinguished. Nevertheless, Vendice suffers from what Piato has to do; and the separate roles, moreover, are complementary to each other. At first, Vendice is the honest malcontent, the nobleman wronged and depressed by poverty; then he becomes a member of the society that has wronged him. He is sardonically aware of himself in his role, as if necessity, not policy, had changed him, just as it threatens to change his mother—(this is the way in which Flamineo and Bosola fuse the roles of villain and critic). He is morally involved in his actions as Piato; and when he appears in the conventional fatal masque, he is justly the victim as well as the instrument of heavenly vengeance. The second disguise is a caricature of his original position. Thus the different roles are not linked together by reference to circumstantial probability, but by reference to the dramatic and social functions of the original character, as with Edgar in *Lear*. The disguisings are related symbols of a transformation within the moral and social order.

Symbolic disguising with a similar dramatic purpose was a stock convention of the Moralities; sometimes there is a change of dress, sometimes only of name. This was not merely a convention of the stage; it embodied popular beliefs about the methods of the Deceiver —'the devil hath power To assume a pleasing shape.' Thus, in Medwall's *Nature*, Pride and Covetise beguile Man under the names of Worship and Worldly Policy, the other Deadly Sins being disguised in the same way. Moreover, the disguisers, besides their attributes as moral types, are usually given, more specifically than any other figures in the play, the attributes of a particular social class. Man, in *Nature*, is a noble, but he is made representative of humanity in general; it is emphasized, on the other hand, that Pride is a knight, and the Deadly Sins only appear as officers of the household. In the later Moralities, social themes, as distinct from theological, become more prominent; and the moral role of the disguisers is often completely merged into their role as the agents of social change. In the Marian play, *Respublica*, for example, the Reformation is engineered by the profiteer Avarice, disguised as Policy; and the characters with aliases in *The Tyde Taryeth No Man* are the broker, Hurtful Help, who operates under the deceptive title of Help, and his accomplices.

The disguisers are contrasted with the other characters in that the latter represent the permanent and unequivocal moral standards which maintain social stability. Even in the middle-class Moralities of the sixteenth century, the disguisers—and the vices in general—frequently stand for 'usury' in its various forms; [5] the other characters, for its opponents and victims. Traditional ethics under the Tudors subsume social and economic questions directly under moral categories; the system rests on the belief that the social order has been established by Nature in accordance with the divine will. This is expounded by Nature herself at the beginning of Medwall's play:

> Th' almighty God that made each creature,
> As well in heaven as other place earthly,
> By His wise ordinance hath purveyed me, Nature,
> To be as minister, under Him immediately,
> For th' enchesoun (*the reason*) that I should, perpetually,
> His creatures in such degree maintain
> As it hath pleased His grace for them to ordain.

This is the ethic of a society predominantly agricultural, in which 'everything . . . seemed to be the gift of nature, the obvious way of life, and thus the result of the Divine ordering, whether as a good gift or as a penalty.' [6] In order to enjoy the divine bounty, to maintain each individual in the sufficiency appropriate to the station in which he was born, it was necessary to observe the conditions on which it was given; and the satisfaction of the profit-motive, of 'greed,' or, equally, the wasteful gratification of selfish pleasure, whether on the part of knight, burgher, or peasant, interfered with this primary necessity. They were 'against nature,' contrary to the obvious expression of the divine will. Opportunities for personal aggrandisement, by means of capital investment, organizing ability, or technical innovation, were, relatively, too few and unimportant, before the sixteenth century, seriously to disturb this traditional order; and it seemed evident that they could only be taken at someone else's expense. By the end of the century, as commercial enterprise, money power, and new industrial techniques began to dominate economic life, they seemed to involve a change in the whole relationship between man and nature, between the individual and his vocation. To conservative minds, it meant the substitution of appearance for realities.

Hence, while the Elizabethans applied the Morality conventions of disguise to a variety of new purposes, the earlier associations were not lost. The tradition of dramatic allegory, with disguising as an essential part, was also maintained by the court masque; and *Cynthia's Revels,* in particular, with its satire on the social climbers and rootless adventurers infesting the court, is avowedly a combination of masque and Morality. 'The night is come,' says one of the Children in the Induction, explaining the plot, 'and Cynthia intends to come forth . . . All the courtiers must provide for revels; they conclude upon a masque, the device of which is . . . that each of these Vices, being to appear before Cynthia, would seem to be other than indeed they are; and therefore assume the most neighbouring Virtues as a masquing habit.' Here Jonson turns the popular ethic against the courtly, the Morality against the masque; for it was the convention of the masques that the courtiers who came to dance as virtues or deities were in fact the incarnations of the qualities they assumed; the masque itself was a social institution, representing the court as the magnificent embodiment of the virtues by right of which it claimed to govern *The Malcontent, Women Beware Women,* and *The Revenger's Tragedy* make ironic use of this function of disguisings in the masque. In Tourneur's case, especially, the masque, as a symbol of courtly riot, is treated from the point of view of the Morality. The courtiers in the masque described by Antonio are Morality Vices—

> Putting on better faces than their own
> Being full of fraud and flattery;

and,—throughout the play, descriptions of revels form the nucleus of the satire, leading up to the fatal masque at the end. They are associated with the references to bastardy and prostitution, and to 'patrimonies washed a-pieces,' and with the images of cosmetics and of justice 'gilt o'er' with favour. Against the 'forgetful feasts' is set the image of the skeleton. The corruption of the court by wealth and luxury, and its violation of the moral order which justifies high rank, is set beside the effects of usury, both alike overthrowing the standards of Nature. Virtue and honour, on the other hand, are identified, as in Castiza's first soliloquy, with the norms of the traditional manorial order, which Tourneur makes to stand for social norms in general. Several of his metaphors are taken from the payment of rents—vengeance, for example, is a 'quit-rent.'

Professor Knights' description of the structure of a Shakespearean play, then, is peculiarly appropriate to *The Revenger's Tragedy* also: it is 'an expanded metaphor, by means of which the original vision has been projected into forms roughly correspondent with actuality, conforming thereto . . . according to the demands of its nature.' The central metaphors, and the technique of presentation, are the products of mediaeval ways of thought, as they had taken shape on the stage in the conventions of the Moralities. With his narrow and hypersensitive mentality, his imperviousness to the psychological make-up of individuals, and his intense preoccupation with ethics, Tourneur could not have written successful drama except by means of their example.

The total impression created by the development of his plot, by the figures of the lecherous old Duke and his court, by the imagery and rhythms of the verse, is that of a hectic excitement, a perverse and over-ripe vitality on the verge of decay; the themes of the danse macabre, suggested in *Hamlet* and *The Malcontent*, dominate *The Revenger's Tragedy*. But the satire is not hysterical; Tourneur maintains an alert sardonic irony which makes its objects grotesque as well as disgusting. The sense of proportion expressed in the style is not that of the Revenge plays; it comes from the Moralities, and from Jonson. Jonson's influence is most apparent in the scene where Vendice tempts his mother and sister; the subject is from *The Malcontent*, the style from Volpone: [7]

Vendice: Would I be poor, dejected, scorned of greatness,
Swept from the palace, and see others' daughters
Spring with the dew o' the court, having mine own
So much desired and loved by the duke's son?
No, I would raise my state upon her breast;
And call her eyes my tenants; I would count
My yearly maintenance upon her cheeks;
Take coach upon her lip; and all her parts
Should keep men after men, and I would ride
In pleasure upon pleasure . . .

Vendice: How blessed are you! you have happiness alone;
Others must fall to thousands, you to one,
Sufficient in himself to make your forehead
Dazzle the world with jewel, and petitionary people
Start at your presence . . .

These passages are not mere echoes of Jonsonian phrasing: they have the energetic hyperbole and the finely measured scorn of Jonson's best manner. The scene continues with a passage of brilliant extravaganza:

Vendice: O, think upon the pleasures of the palace!
Secured ease and state! the stirring meats,
Ready to move out of the dishes, that e'en now
Quicken when they are eaten!
Banquets abroad by torchlight! music! sports!
Bareheaded vassals, that had ne'er the fortune
To keep on their own hats, but let horns wear 'em!
Nine coaches waiting–hurry, hurry, hurry–
Castiza: Ay, to the devil,
Vendice: Ay, to the devil! (*Aside*) To the duke, by my faith.
Gratiana: Ay, to the duke: daughter, you'd scorn to think o'
the devil, an you were there once. (II, i.)

The excitement of these passages is hardly the product of a nightmare vision. On the contrary, it is controlled and directed by a sense of the crude realities underlying the court's fantastic behaviour. The source and character of Tourneur's grotesquerie is indicated, again, by Spurio's soliloquy:

Faith, if the truth were known, I was begot
After some gluttonous dinner; some stirring dish
Was my first father, when deep healths went round,
And ladies cheeks were painted red with wine,
Their tongues, as short and nimble as their heels,
Uttering words sweet and thick; and when they rose,
Were merrily disposed to fall again. (I, ii).

The nervous and sinister tones of the mockery are balanced by the 'primitive' realism.

Nevertheless, Tourneur does not escape from his cycle of decay; there is nothing in the play, in its scheme of moral and social values, to compensate for Vendice's fall. In the process of commercial development, which had brought new hopes and possibilities to the middle classes, Tourneur saw only that the court had been uprooted from the people and the soil, while the old-fashioned gentry were left to their honour, their poverty, and their discontent. As, throughout the sixteenth century, landlord and ploughman alike had been submitted to a growing dependence on money, and their customary incomes had proved inadequate to meet rising costs and a rising standard of living, the stability of the old hierarchy had broken down. Many of the nobility and gentry were forced to give up their 'hospitality' or to sell their estates; and their successors and survivors, knowing, with Burghley, that 'gentility is nothing else but ancient riches,' had acted accordingly. The nobility themselves had become enclosers, joint-stock-holders, company-promoters, monopolists; the court, at the turn of the century, was the happy-hunting-ground for adventurers and profiteers. Until the end of Elizabeth's reign, this commercialization of the nobility was in harmony with the main economic and political needs of the middle classes: but when the latter had outgrown their royal tutelage, the powers of the court became obstructive; and when titles were sold and honours conferred on irresponsible favourites, it became clear that the system of court privileges opened the way to the machiavellian and the sycophant. The fount of honour was poisoned at the source. While 'the disproportion between honour and means' became more glaring, large numbers of the lesser gentry, deprived of the security of the old order, found themselves landless men, dependent on an uncertain or an insuffcent patronage, men without 'vocations.' Tourneur's Vendice is one of the dramatic spokesmen of these malcontents. His independence belongs to the past; the present is contaminated by the values of 'gold.' On the basis of this contrast, which is extended to society as a whole, Tourneur's poetry formulates an exceptionally coherent response to the life of his time. But the business of buying and selling, the accumulation of wealth without social responsibility, which has hoisted sensuality to its evil eminence in his court, is accepted as normative and final; it becomes a process by which the values of Nature and the impulses which go to maintaining a civilized life are inevitably decomposed into their opposites. This conception forms the organizing principle in Vendice's second speech to the skull, where the complex themes and symbols of the whole play are concentrated into a single magnificent passage.

The irony of this speech is reinforced by the dramatic situation: 'all the betrayed women are in a sense represented by the poisoned skull of Vendice's mistress—not only she herself, but Antonio's wife,

Castiza, who would have been betrayed, and the imaginary "country lady" whom the Duke thought he was about to seduce.' [8] Similarly, 'yon fellow' is the imaginary profligate turned highwayman, the approaching Duke, and the Duchess's youngest son, who has already appeared under judgment for rape, and is ironically despatched in the next scene. Thus the skull becomes the fitting symbol, as it is the final result, of the process represented by the action and the imagery, by which solid realities are exchanged for treacherous appearances. The metaphor of 'exchange' is important; Vendice's irony turns, in this speech, on the ambiguities of the word 'for,' referring both to equivalence in exchange and to purpose or result. In the first lines, a complex group of relationships are associated in the image contrasting the 'labours' of the worm—physically present in 'expend' and 'undo'—with the silken bedizement of the lady for whom they are undertaken, a contrast which appears, at the same time, as one between the silk and the skeleton it covers; it is for the skull that the labours are ultimately intended. The 'silkworm' is also the worm of the grave; it suggests, too, the poor weaver, 'undone' for the sake of the wealthy—the contrast between rich and poor is made explicit in the next speech;—and the colours of the silk and of the gold which is paid for it are made flat and wan by the suggested comparison with her 'yellow' face. The speech is developed round a further series of exchanges:

> Does the silkworm expend her yellow labours
> For thee? for thee does she undo herself?
> Are lordships sold to maintain ladyships
> For the poor benefit of a bewitching minute?
> Why does yon fellow falsify highways
> And put his life between the judge's lips,
> To refine such a thing, keeps horse and men
> To beat their valours for her?
> Surely we're all mad people, and they
> Whom we think are, are not; we mistake those,
> 'Tis we are mad in sense, they but in clothes. (III, v.)

In the third and fourth lines, the process of commercial exchange is again ironically invoked; the social stability implied by 'lordships' and 'maintained' is undermined in the colloquial sarcasm of 'ladyships,' and the 'bewitching minute' of lust is a 'poor benefit' to exchange for an inherited estate—'poor,' too, in the sense that procreation is made futile. 'Bewitching' recalls the earlier scene in which it was suggested that Gratiana's attempt to prostitute her daughter was due to diabolic possession; it detaches Vendice from the dissolution he contemplates and yet implies that it is inescapable. "Yon fellow" implicates the Duke and his stepson as well as the broken gallant, so that 'falsify' attaches to the royal justice itself together with the royal highway. There is also a suppressed pun on counterfeit coinage, which, with the corrosive impression of 'falsify,' is carried on in the next lines: by his emphasis on the root senses of the verbs ('maintain,' 'falsify,' 'refine'), Tourneur sets up a characteristic tension between the imagined activities and the ideal relationships to which they ought to conform. In the old dispensation—as in Medwall's play—Nature had appointed Reason to govern Sensuality; here, Reason has been overturned. It takes its revenge, against the irrationality of the 'bewitching minute,' in the contrast between the life and the moment of sentence. The judgment is also the Last Judgment. As before, the mounting rhythm then returns, after a pause, to the slow, heavy syllables referring to the skull, the final cause, it is suggested, as it is the final stage, of the whole movement—'to refine such a thing.' The phrase, coming at this point, implies both that the overlay of 'refinement' on her 'ladyship' is as futile, and as deathly, as the poisoned cosmetic on the skull, and that this comparison actually clarified a state of affairs present wherever bones are clothed with flesh. The next phrase again catches in its puns the self-destruction of a powerful stimulus; 'keeps' relates it to 'maintains,' four lines above; 'beat their valours' refers primarily to the fierce courage of the highwaymen, but 'beats' also means 'abates,' and 'valors' are 'values'—once again the purchase of death for life. Thus the perversion of the impulses making for life finds its culminating expression in the image of violent action, and the activity is simultaneously nullified by means of the puns. The last three lines generalize what has already been revealed to the senses. Just as the great lady of the first lines has dissolved into her 'ladyship,' so all seeming realities have been reduced to the skull; so that to murder the Duke with the poisoned skull is a fully appropriate revenge.

Tourneur's symbols, then, are organized by applying to the contemporary world the standards of the mediaeval social tradition, as it had survived through the sixteenth century. But *The Revenger's Tragedy,* with its alternation between finely wrought passages of high mental and nervous tension and passages of clumsy sententious generalization, represents an emotional equilibrium which Tourneur evidently could not maintain. He had profited by the example of Jonson, who had remodelled the Morality drama, with its barely delineated types and its sparse, loosely connected incidents, into something solid and closely-knit; but Jonson's mind was the more elastic, more confident of the permanent validity of his standards, more independent and detached. His dramatic structures allow of a varied interplay of motives and experiences; Tourneur's do not. In *The Revenger's Tragedy* he succeeded in directing the response to his situation by presenting Morality figures who express, or arouse, acute and powerful, but narrowly restricted emotions. When, instead of dealing with types, he tried to examine individual motives, and to argue out the reasons for his judgments, he failed. By comparison with the earlier play, *The Atheist's Tragedy* is abstract and forced. The best passages, such as the description of Charlemont's supposed death at Ostend, are set speeches, almost independent of their dramatic contexts; the symbolism is mechanical, the poetic theorising lame and unconvincing. Charlemont, who, unlike Vendice, leaves his revenge to heaven, is an uninteresting paragon; and D'Amville's villainy and Castabella's innocence are so naively paraded that Tourneur defeats his purpose—if Castiza's shrill chastity were emphasized in the same way, so that the puppet became a person, she would be nauseating. Charlemont and his father have some of the virtues Tourneur attributed to Vere and Salisbury; but when he comes to offer his positive values, they are formal and, dramatically, lifeless.

With Jonson and *The Revenger's Tragedy*, the influence of the mediaeval tradition virtually came to an end. None of the Stuart dramatists whose main work came later—with the partial exception of Massinger, in his comedies—attempted to revive it; the trend of dramatic writing was towards semi- or pseudo-naturalism. Webster fumbled with the Revenge conventions in the effort to develop something relatively new to the stage—to excite varied or conflicting sympathies for individuals at odds with their surroundings. His picture of society resembles Tourneur's; but the Morality elements, which had represented for the latter the dramatic equivalents for a central core of judgments and feelings, have disappeared; and Webster, unable to come to rest on any attitude, from which to value his people, more stable or more penetrating than a pose of stoical bravado, could not write coherent drama at all. Where they are not simply melodrama, his plays depend on exploiting immediate sensations, disjointed from their dramatic contexts; and this applies not only to his stagecraft, but to his verse, which works by analogous means, and which gains, as Tourneur's loses, from quotation in short passages. His plays, with their unrealized 'sense of tragic issues' in the individual, point towards a dramatic reorientation, a development from Shakespeare, which they do not themselves achieve. After Shakespeare, the only dramatist to achieve such a reorientation was Middleton.

NOTES

1. See *Drama and Society in the Age of Jonson,* p. 188; and *cf.* M. C. Bradbrook, *Themes and Conventions of Elizabethan Tragedy,* p. 70.

2. The Moralities afforded a vehicle for moral and social criticism to Catholic humanists like Medwall, writing at the end of the fifteenth century, and to Protestant reformers like Lupton, writing in the middle of Elizabeth's reign. They themselves drew on the earlier mediaeval drama. The later Moralities have been unduly neglected; there is an excellent account of them by Louis B. Wright in *Anglia,* Vol. LIV.

3. *Themes and Conventions,* Chapter VII.

4. Cf. Bradbrook, *op. cit.*, pp. 66–72, 166–167. The speech in which he describes his motives (at the end of Act I, iv) makes it clear that they belong to the situation, not his character. Similarly, his behaviour in his second disguise would be ridiculous if it were really addressed to Lussurioso; but it is addressed primarily to the audience, on the assumption that every stage disguise is successful.

5. On the hostility of early puritanism towards 'usury,' and the relation between this and the economic position of the yeomanry and the small traders, see R. H. Tawney, *Religion and the Rise of Capitalism* (p. 159 and *passim*), and his *Introduction* to Wilson's *Discourse Upon Usury,* especially pp. 24, 30.

6. E. Troeltsch, *The Social Teaching of the Christian Churches,* Vol. I, p. 249. By the end of the sixteenth century, it was felt that social changes and scientific thought had together altered the standards of Nature for human conduct—in Ralegh's words, 'there [was] a confused controversy about the very essence of nature.'

7. Compare the wooing of Celia in *Volpone;* and *cf.* L. C. Knights, *op. cit.,* pp. 185–188. *Volpone* was produced in 1606, *The Revenger's Tragedy* published in 1607.

8. I have again made use of Miss Bradbrook's analysis (*op. cit.,* pp. 169–172).

HEREWARD T. PRICE

The Function of Imagery in Webster

FOR MANY generations symbolism has dominated the poetry of America and Europe. In time, of course, the critics found out what was happening and they began to investigate the movement. They have carried their investigations further and further afield over the literature of the last four centuries and in the process they have enormously widened our knowledge of poetry. Through their labors we read with clearer eyes and a deeper enjoyment than before.

Shakespeare has, naturally, received a great deal of attention. He is indeed the center of a lively controversy about the exact function which he intended imagery to perform. One body of critics sees the Shakespearian play as a symbol at large made up of many smaller symbols. Such integration into a coherent form does not, of course, constitute for this school the whole truth about a play. They do not ignore the other structure of plot or of characterization. But they assert that a study of the elaborate interdependence of Shakespeare's images will afford us a valuable key to his meaning. Other critics refuse to recognize in Shakespeare any planned and complex correlation of imagery. Some even treat the idea with scorn.

We ought to approach this problem not as if it were something peculiar to just one writer but from the viewpoint of general Elizabethan practice. Not enough work has been done on other Elizabethans. We may perhaps obtain some light on Shakespeare by studying the technique of his contemporaries. Possibly, by establishing likeness or difference, by comparison or contrast, we shall come to see Shakespeare's characteristic tendencies more clearly. I have chosen Webster to investigate because in the depth, the subtlety, and the complexity

From *PMLA,* LXX (September 1955), pp. 717–39. Reprinted by permission of the author and the Modern Language Association of America.

of his imagery he comes nearer than any other Elizabethan dramatist to the power of Shakespeare. Moreover his sombre rendering of life's terrors provides something that our generation can respond to immediately and with perfect comprehension.

While Webster approaches Shakespeare in many aspects of his imagery, there can be no comparison between them in range. Shakespeare wrote a large number of plays over a long period of time. Webster, on the other hand, is known chiefly for the *White Devil* and the *Duchess of Malfi*, which were written fairly close together. They resemble one another in the nature of the symbols used. In fact, the *Duchess of Malfi* even takes over symbols from the *White Devil*. The resolute consistency with which Webster elaborates an extended sequence of diverse but interrelated images distinguishes the *White Devil* and the *Duchess of Malfi* not only from Webster's other work but also from the rest of the Elizabethan drama. It is because of their unique quality that I single out these two plays for discussion and ignore all else that Webster wrote. I say unique because the other plays, either alone or in partnership, do not display that contexture of imagery which we find in the *White Devil* and the *Duchess of Malfi*. Except in the two plays I have chosen for discussion there is no chain of related imagery that is in itself a form of construction and that reinforces the construction of action.

Before we begin, we must first point out that there was a stock of images common to all Elizabethan drama. We must, for instance, train ourselves to recognize proverbs.[1] Elizabethan critics regarded them as an ornament of style, readers delighted in them, and poets would try to give pleasure by interweaving proverbs or reminiscences of proverbs into their work. Many figures that appear to be brilliant inventions turn out on inspection to be old proverbs. When Bosola says: 'Thou sleep'st worse, then if a mouse should be forc'd to take up her lodging in a cats eare' (*Duchess of Malfi* IV.ii.135–136),[2] he appears to have hit upon a striking figure. In reality he is only employing a proverb well known to the Elizabethans. They would approve of the passage because Webster gave to an old saw a novel application.

I pass over shortly the question of Webster's debts to contemporary authors. He notoriously lifted his images from a large number of writers, especially from Sidney and from Montaigne. But it is also true that he rarely borrows without improving on his source. His mind was a sieve through which only the essential elements passed.

He trims his borrowings so closely as to achieve the utmost economy and sharpness of phrase. At other times Webster uses what in his source is flat or merely logical in order to show his characters turning to passion or violence, and in Webster it sounds like the grinding of teeth in a curse. Or elsewhere by a slight change in rhythm or wording he transforms the prosaic into haunting poetry. When he conveyed other people's bright ideas, Webster was following the conventional Renaissance practice of imitation, and he could plead the conventional justification that he put his imitation to very good use. Whatever he took he worked into the essential substance of the play.

If we then ask what really distinguishes Webster from other Elizabethans, we find it in his consistent use of a double construction, an outer and an inner. He gives us figure in action and figure in language. These he fuses so intimately as to make the play one entire figure. Now it is possible to say that this would be true of all drama. But, if we except Shakespeare, no other dramatist works so resolutely as Webster at making figure in action and figure in word conform to one another all the way through. Most Elizabethan dramatists tend to use figure for its power of enhancing a speech, a scene, or a particular moment in a play. But in the *White Devil* and the *Duchess of Malfi* a figure is usually one of a series of figures, all of which are focussed on the same control point. The verbal images dovetail into one another exactly as they closely parallel the figure in action, rising and falling with it, inseparable from it. Webster is important in the history of English dramatic art just because of this exact and sustained correlation. The severe self-discipline necessary to achieve Webster's superb uniformity of effect is most unusual among writers in England. It might almost be called un-English; it is certainly un-Elizabethan.

For Webster the figure-in-words appears at first sight to be the more important. The action gives the impression of being loose, and while it leads up to violent explosions, as for instance, murders, Webster does not primarily exploit such happenings for their value as sensation. Like every dramatist he keeps us hanging in fear and hope about the thing that is to happen, but he interests us far more in what moves the minds of his characters. He works up to a sudden speech or perhaps only to a sudden line to reveal as by lightning the essential quality of a life or even the meaning of the whole play. That is his *grand coup*. In his two great plays a cruel villain plans to destroy a group of people. The event interests us, of course, but we are much more deeply occupied in watching Webster turn inside out the minds of good and bad characters in a successive, deep, and rich revelation. It is only after inspecting the play very carefully that we discover how much our interest in character has been kept up and repeatedly stimulated by Webster's skilful manipulation of action, his use of contrast, and especially by his superb timing.

The general function of imagery in Webster is of course the same as in all other drama. It is the most pregnant expression of truth. It reveals character, it does the work of argument, it emphasizes mood, and it prefigures the events to come. In Webster the foreshadowing is typically ironical. The good that is promised turns out to be evil. Webster especially uses imagery to convey the basic conflict of his drama, the conflict between outward appearance and inner substance or reality. He gives us a universe so convulsed and uncertain that no appearance can represent reality. Evil shines like true gold and good tries to protect itself by putting on disguise or a false show. What is hidden rusts, soils, festers, corrupts under its fair exterior. The devil is called the 'invisible devil.'

Most powerfully of all Webster uses poison to express the relation between fair show and foul truth. Poison kills all the more certainly because it is not seen or even suspected. In the *White Devil* Webster weaves into his lines about thirty references to poison. Parallel to this the action itself contains a number of notable poisonings. In addition Webster uses *devil* as a key-word. In the *White Devil* it occurs twenty-six times. The relentless repetition of the same kind of figure, the heaping up of the same words, time and again, cannot be accidental. Such frequency of occurrence shows that there must be method, conscious and deliberate.

I begin with the *White Devil.* Lucas explains the meaning of the title, 'a devil disguised under a fair outside' and he backs up his definition by many quotations (I.193–194). The *N.E.D.* gives the following meanings for *white:* morally pure, stainless, innocent; free from malignity, beneficent; propitious, auspicious, happy; highly prized, pet, darling; fair-seeming, specious, plausible. In the conflict between these meanings lies the irony of the title. Probably Webster also had in mind two Elizabethan proverbs, *The White devil is worse than the black* (D 310 in Tilley) and *The devil can transform himself into an angel of light* (D 321 in Tilley). The very title of the play, then, is a figure of the sort we have been discussing. Vittoria is the white devil: white to outside view, inside the black devil.

Lodovico opens the play with a series of figures that express the relation between deceptive appearance and the bitter reality. (He is to end the play by sacrilegiously putting on the disguise of a friar in order to commit a series of murders.)

> *Lodo.* . . . Fortun's a right whore.
> If she give ought, she deales it in smal percels,
> That she may take away all at one swope.
> This tis to have great enemies, God quite them:
> Your woolfe no longer seemes to be a woolfe
> Then when shees hungry. *Gas.* You terme those enemies
> Are men of Princely ranke. (I.i.4–10)

Here we have two themes at which Webster labors persistently, both pertaining to the difference between seeming and being. First we have Fortune that makes a show of favor in order to deceive. Secondly, the rich and powerful are not regarded as wolves, however wolfish they may be. Only the penniless and hungry adventurer is looked upon as a beast of prey. The magnificence of rank covers a multitude of sins. The unrelenting repetition of this kind of figure binds all the scenes of the play into a whole of the highest possible unity. Webster varies the figure to include hidden disease or indeed any kind of rottenness that develops unseen.

Webster then introduces that particular theme of hidden corruption, of magnificent rank covering sin, that is the overt subject of the play. Brachiano now lives in Rome, 'And by close pandarisme seekes to prostitute/The honour of Vittoria Corombona' (I.i.41–42). Close pandarism is, of course, hidden pandarism, pandarism that is kept close. Act I.ii is concerned most of all with the *close pandarisme.* Here is corruption of the vilest sort. Vittoria's brother, Flamineo, undertakes to corrupt his sister's honor. He asks Brachiano to conceal himself, using an ominous word that foretells the end: 'Shrowd you within this closet, good my Lord' (I.ii.33). He then goes on to seduce Vittoria from her husband Camillo and win her over for Brachiano. At the same time Camillo is tricked into believing that Flamineo is persuading Vittoria to come back to him. The scene that follows may appear to be the ordinary stuff of Elizabethan drama. Flamineo tricks Camillo, and the trick is everywhere in Elizabethan comedy and tragedy. Camillo stands apart, watching Flamineo and Vittoria talking, and commenting on what he sees. That also is common form in Elizabethan drama. Camillo's most important comment is: 'A vertuous brother, a my credit' (145). The difference between Webster and other Elizabethans lies in the exact correspondence between his figures-in-word and figures-in-action. Camillo is entirely deceived by appearances, the seeming good cloaks horrible evil. Webster uses the old tricks of the stage but he fills them with his own meaning.

And now Webster follows up with figures that promise happiness, only to deceive. Flamineo foretells for Vittoria the delights which the affair with Brachiano will bring to her: 'Thou shalt lye in a bed stuft with turtles feathers, swoone in perfumed lynnen like the fellow was smothered in roses—so perfect shall be thy happiness, that as men at Sea thinke land and trees and shippes go that way they go, so both heaven and earth shall seeme to go your voyage. Shalt meete him, tis fixt with nayles of dyamonds to inevitable necessitie' (148–153).

These lines contain one of the main ironies of the play. Webster grants Brachiano and Vittoria no happiness. While for a brief moment 'heaven and earth *seem* to go their voyage,' only Flamineo's last prophecy comes true. Necessity binds them all together in a way Flamineo did not foresee. And what horror and revulsion Webster conveys in the one word *happy,* coming from the mouth of the brother and pander and used of the sister he is seeking to prostitute.

For the rest of the scene Webster pursues the difference between appearance and reality in a long series of figures. He piles up these figures especially to describe the fair outside of Camillo that covers only a 'lousy slave' (45–48, 100–102, 125 f).

Then Webster makes Vittoria narrate a dream in which she suggests to Brachiano how he may murder her husband and his own wife. She invents the figure of a yew tree to represent the marriages of Vittoria to Camillo and of Brachiano to Isabella. Vittoria speaks of the *eu* to Brachiano and of course she means *you.* As we shall see Webster repeats the figure of the *yew* later on (IV.iii.123–126). The marriages represented by the yew were rooted in decay and could not prosper.

In connection with the dream Webster identifies Vittoria for the first time as the devil. Flamineo says: 'The divell was in your dreame' (240) and follows almost at once: 'Excellent Divell./Shee hath taught him in a dreame/To make away his Dutchesse and her husband' (246–248).

A little later Cornelia introduces the first mention of poison:

O that this faire garden,
Had [with] all poysoned hearbes of Thessaly,

At first bene planted . . . rather [then] a buriall plot,
For both your Honours. (264–268)

Flamineo sums up the scene by speaking of the ways of policy as winding and indirect, flowing like rivers with 'crooke bendings' and imitating 'the suttle fouldings of a Winters snake.' (346) 'Subtle' implies deceit, and a snake, 'anguis in herba,' strikes from concealment and kills by poison.

The happiness they are all so confident of turns out to be Dead Sea fruit. In the case of Vittoria and Brachiano Webster defers the ironic event, but in the next scene (II.i) with Isabella he makes it follow upon the too confident forecast at once. Isabella is certain she can win back Brachiano:

I do not doubt
As men to try the precious Unicornes horne
Make of the powder a preservative Circle
And in it put a spider, so these armes
Shall charme his poyson, force it to obeying
And keepe him chast from an infected straying.
(II.i.13–18)

Notice the themes of *poison* and *infection*. Poison kills without being seen, infection corrupts long before its effects are visible—here are the two most frequent themes of the play. Of course, Isabella's attempt to recover Brachiano is a complete failure.

Isa. You are as welcome to these longing armes,
As I to you a Virgine. *Brac.* O your breath!
Out upon sweete meates, and continued Physicke!
The plague is in them. *Isa.* You have oft for these two lippes
Neglected Cassia or the naturall sweetes
Of the Spring-violet. . . . (165–170)

She fails, and notice that Brachiano in this speech can no longer see her as she is. Not only does Webster show evil disguised, he shows us also that Brachiano's foulness prevents him from seeing the good.

Brachiano curses his marriage and cruelly casts Isabella off. But she, in her love for her husband, pretends that it is she who has broken up the marriage. She 'puts on an act' of spiteful jealousy and rage and convinces her brother the Duke that she is but a 'foolish, mad, and jealous woman.' Here again Webster gives us the appearance that deceives. But this time it is purest goodness that cloaks itself in evil.

Webster's world is so corrupt that goodness itself works to deceive. No appearance is true.

The next scene is full of figure-in-action. In two dumb-shows a conjurer reveals how the Duchess and Camillo are murdered. In the one show villains lay poison on the picture of Brachiano–and depart laughing. The Duchess kneels before the picture, does three reverences to it, kisses it thrice, and the poison on it kills her. Brachiano, watching the dumb show, exclaims, 'Excellent.' Such pitiless confrontation of opposites is the strongest of irony. In the second dumb-show Flamineo, Camillo, and others drink healths. Flamineo and Camillo 'compliment' one another as to who shall first use the vaulting-horse, and then Flamineo breaks Camillo's neck.

And now that Brachiano has lost his wife and Vittoria her husband, the way seems clear for the promised happiness. But Flamineo and Vittoria are arrested immediately. Here is Webster's method. Vittoria is promised happiness if she submits to Brachiano, Isabella thinks she can 'charm the Duke's poison,' 'keep him from an infected straying.' Both are deceived by the event. Isabella dies of Brachiano's poison, Vittoria is arrested even before she sees Brachiano. Webster builds his figures into the construction of the play, the whole of the play is in them, and that gives them their power.

But there is more in this scene. Here we see the characteristic polarity of Webster's method in the extreme. The murderers 'depart laughing,' Isabella is all humility, devotion, and love, and even in her dying agony manages to prevent anyone else from being poisoned by the picture. Brachiano sees his wife's supreme love and the tortures of her death, and remarks, 'Excellent, then shee's dead.' The principle of polarity is clear.

This polarity is seen in the figures of appearance and reality all through the play.

In the famous trial-scene (III.ii) Vittoria faces her accuser with superb intellectual resource. Judge and defendant fight one another with figure, and for every figure the Cardinal hurls at Vittoria, she immediately retorts with another. The Cardinal proceeds to strip her of her fair-seeming in order to show the foul heart inside. He will point out her follies in more 'natural red and white' than that upon her cheek. She seems to be goodly fruit but is like the apples of Sodom and Gomorrah, so that when he touches her, she will fall to soot and ashes. Night by night she counterfeited a prince's court. Again and again he comes back to that word *counterfeit*. 'This whore, forsooth, was holy,' 'Ha,' exclaims Vittoria, 'whore, what's that?' It is her only blunder. In twenty lines the Cardinal informs her with abundant detail:

> They are first,
> Sweete meates which rot the eater: In mans nostrill
> Poison'd perfumes. They are coosning Alcumy,
> Shipwrackes in Calmest weather . . .
> . . . conterfetted coine . . .
> You, gentlewoman!
> Take from all beasts, and from all mineralls
> Their deadly poison. (83–106)

Again Webster's figures show the polarity—or the irony—he loves. Sweatmeats which rot, shipwrecks in calmest weather, the stretch between these opposites is the source of Webster's strength.

The Cardinal also fixes on Vittoria the name of devil.

> I am resolved
> Were there a second Paradice to loose
> This Devell would betray it. *Vit.* O poore charity!
> Thou art seldome found in scarlet. (71–74)
> *Card.* You know what Whore is; next the devell, Adultry,
> Enters the devell, Murder. (112–113)
> If the devill
> Did ever take good shape behold his picture. (224–225)

That is, she is the White Devil.

She retorts with spirit and throws back at him the reproach of falseness: 'These are but faigned shadowes of my evels./Terrify babes, my Lord, with *painted* devils' (150–151). But this only strengthens Webster's theme of appearance and reality. She displays a splendid spirit, she is magnificent in intellect and courage, and she is—a whore and a murderess.

The Cardinal in passing sentence again insists on her rottenness: 'Such a corrupted triall have you made/Both of your life and beauty . . .' (269–270). Vittoria raves at him and leaves the court with a figure that reverses the ideas of appearance and reality in Vittoria's favor: 'Through darkenesse Diamonds spred their ritchest light' (306). Again we see the polarity of Webster's figure, the stark contrast of darkness and rich light. This line also shows Webster's habit of summing up a movement in its closing words. The light will become rich through the darkness, in adversity Vittoria's character will show its richest light.

In the next scene (III.iii) Webster continues to harp on the theme of corruption. Flamineo is the chief speaker: 'A Cardinall . . . theres nothing so holie but mony will corrupt and putrifie it' (23–24). 'Religion; oh how it is commeddled with policie. The first bloudshed in the world happened about religion' (36–37).

In the next scene (IV.i) the Cardinal and the Duke play at fence, trying to deceive one another. The Cardinal preaches dissimulation, the false front, the concealed intrigue: 'We see that undermining more prevailes/Then doth the Canon' (15–16). He lends the Duke a black book in which he has collected the names of notorious offenders in the city. The list is so large that it demonstrates the immense rottenness of Society. And again Webster rams into us his idea of corruption concealed by outward show: 'See the corrupted use some make of bookes:/Divinity, wrested by some factious bloud,/Draws swords, swels battels, and orethrowes all good' (99–101).

In the next scene the Duke sends a love-letter to Vittoria, suggesting that she should elope with him. He hopes it will be played into Brachiano's hands. This is exactly what happens. Brachiano believes Vittoria has been unfaithful and his rage with her brings insight.

> Your beautie! ô, ten thousand curses on't.
> How long have I beheld the devill in christall!
> Thou hast lead mee, like an heathen sacrifice,
> With musicke, and with fatall yokes of flowers
> To my eternall ruine. (IV.ii.88–92)

The *devill in christall* is the White Devil. Music and flowers lead to ruin. Here again the principle of polarity is clear. Vittoria answers Brachiano:

> What have I gain'd by thee but infamie?
> Thou hast stain'd the spotlesse honour of my house . . .
> I had a limbe corrupted to an ulcer,
> But I have cut it off; and now Ile go
> Weeping to heaven on crutches. (IV.ii.109–123)

A stain on honor, corruption, the ulcer: here Webster pursues relentlessly the same themes.

But the letter has a second effect. Brachiano and Vittoria make up their quarrel and then resolve to adopt the suggestion in the letter and run away to Florence. Again the trick succeeds, appearances deceive, they deceive most dangerously when they flatter. The suggestion to elope to Florence seemed wonderful. It promised to Vittoria and Brachiano liberty and the enjoyment of their love. But when the Duke hears that they have fled, he exclaims that is exactly what he has been aiming at. 'Thy fame, fond Duke,/I first have poison'd; directed thee the way/To marrie a whore; what can be worse?' (IV.iii. 57–59).

The word *poison'd* links this piece of treachery with the other poisonings in the play. The Duke has destroyed by means of something whose apparent sweetness concealed its deadliness. He has really taken the Cardinal's hint and 'undermined' the lovers.

Meanwhile the Cardinal has been elected Pope. He sees Lodovico talking with the Duke and warns him to conjure from his breast that cruel devil. He especially warns him against his plan to kill Brachiano: 'Like the blacke, and melancholicke Eugh-tree,/Do'st thinke to root thy selfe in dead mens graves,/And yet to prosper?' (IV.iii.123–125). Here, as we have already mentioned, Webster recalls Vittoria's fable of the ewe-tree in I.ii and this links the beginning with the end of the play, one murder with the other. But after the Pope has left, the Duke sends a servant to Lodovico with a thousand crowns. Lodovico can only think that they come from the Pope. He soliloquizes on the art of great ones in concealing their designs. Here again Webster gives us the figure of false show in action. Such a trick may be common enough in Elizabethan drama, but the sharp irony of it has an intricacy that is peculiar to Webster. Lodovico believes that the holy churchman is dissembling with him. In reality it is the Duke who is fooling him. This world is so full of false shows that we deceive ourselves even when we recognize that trickery is afoot.

The deceitfulness of appearances dominates the close of the play. Villainy is cloaked under a show of holiness, and again events that seem to promise happiness turn to disaster. In IV.iii Lodovico takes the sacrament to prosecute the murder of Brachiano and Vittoria in their palace, i.e., he uses the false show of holiness for murder. Webster opens V.i. by a magnificent wedding procession of Brachiano, Vittoria, and their household. Flamineo remains on the stage. He speaks: 'In all the weary minutes of my life,/Day nere broke up till now. This mariage/Confirmes me happy.' *Hortensio*. ' 'Tis a good assurance./Saw you not yet the Moore that's come to Court?' (V.i.1–4). Even at the first moment of Flamineo's happiness, Webster shows him about to be destroyed. The Moor is the Duke in disguise and he has brought with him the murderers Lodovico and Antonelli disguised as holy men, as Capuchins. Disguise is not, as it may be elsewhere, merely a convention, something to be expected in a play of blood. It is the meaning of the play that these murderers use the mask of holiness to kill.

Again we see the polarity of Webster's method. The brilliant marriage-procession and Flamineo's assurance of happiness are immediately followed by a dialogue between the three disguised murderers. Flamineo, with unconscious irony, sums up this passage with a commonplace about the deceitfulness of appearances: 'Glories, like glowwormes, afarre off shine bright/But lookt to neare, have neither heat nor light' (38–39). The couplet has many facets. The glow-worm may point at the marriage, at the happiness so soon to be blasted. It may also refer, as Mr. Lucas's note shows, to 'persons of paltry eminence.' But it all illustrates Webster's method. The situation is figure-in-action reinforced by figure-in-words.

Act v.ii opens with a typical mixture of figure-in-action and figure-in-word. Cornelia enters with her son Marcello. She is wearing a crucifix. Marcello says: 'I have heard you say, giving my brother sucke,/Hee tooke the Crucifix betweene his hands,/And broke a limb off.' *Cor.* 'Yes: but 'tis mended' (v.ii. 11–13). At this point Flamineo enters and runs his brother Marcello through. This incident, again, shows Webster's characteristic polarity. The mother is giving suck to her child: he breaks the crucifix. Since the crucifix has been mended, she is entirely without fear: at that very moment: Enter Flamineo. *Flamineo runnes Marcello through.* The thought is mirrored twice, in the language, and in the action.

Cornelia is at first deceived by appearances. She cannot believe that Marcello is dead, 'he is not dead, hee's in a trance' (v.ii.29). There is a tragic chasm here between appearance and reality. Brachiano enters and Cornelia, in a moment of superb greatness, lies to him in order to save Flamineo's life. She is torn between two emotions, love for the murdered son and love for the son that murdered him. The only thing that could come out of these twisted emotions was the lie. And now to illustrate the sharpness of Webster's irony, we are compelled to reproduce the text as it stands.

> *Fla.* [to the Duke]. At your pleasure.
> *Lodovico sprinckles Brachiano's bever with a poison.*
> Your will is law now—Ile not meddle with it. (75–76)

Webster mingles many figures in this short passage, all focussed on the falseness of appearances. Brachiano's will is law *now*, in a few seconds he will be dead. At the same time Lodovico secretly sprinkles poison into the strong helmet that Brachiano will put on his head in order to protect his life. And of course there is the treachery of Lodovico, disguised as a monk, and therefore honored as a guest, evil concealed under a robe of religion.

At the moment of death Brachiano repeats the actions of his wife as she was dying. She had prevented those about her from touching the poisoned picture. Brachiano says to Vittoria: 'Do not kisse me, for I shall poyson thee' (v.iii.27). In this repetition there is terror. The moral law has not been mocked, it has vindicated itself with a resolute exactness. 'An eye for an eye . . .' But further, Brachiano speaks the horrible truth about his love. It was poison for Vittoria.

At the end of Brachiano's life he sees the false show dissolve and he is confronted with the terrible reality. He is made to see the full horror of his life and of death. In death, 'horrour waights on Princes' (35). His agonized ravings seem to be nonsense but they make grim sense. He speaks of quails (i.e., loose women) who feed on poison. He sees the Devil come to visit him. And when Vittoria says 'heer's nothing,' he answers: 'Nothing? rare! nothing! when I want monie,/Our treasurie is emptie; there is nothing,/Ile not bee us'd thus' (v.iii.107–109). So far as he is concerned, this answer sums up the play. His adventure with Vittoria promised happiness and he has had nothing.

And then comes the last false show. The two assassins enter, disguised as friars. They hold up the crucifix to him. Then they throw off their disguise and reveal themselves to him. They add to his torments by piling reproaches on him, they call him devil, they say his art was poison. They glory in detailing to him the poisons that are melting his brains. But on the very threshold of death Brachiano's love finds its final great expression. He shouts 'Vittoria! Vittoria!' His love is still undefeated and in his extremity he calls to her for help. It reminds one of 'Pompilia, will you let them murder me.'

Here Webster achieves a level of greatness in understanding the depth of a man's soul which he sustains throughout the play. Brachiano has murdered his wife and the husband of his mistress, but he is yet capable of a deep and selfless love for the woman he dishonors. Appearances deceive in two ways; they disguise the good as well as the evil. It would appear that two people so debased and ruthless as Vittoria and Brachiano must be incapable of a great love. But in Webster no one is thoroughly evil. After Vittoria and Brachiano have committed all their crimes and their expectations have turned against them, this love, a source of so much evil and suffering, remains a thing of strength and beauty. Probably in his final cry 'Vittoria! Vittoria!' Brachiano transcends his crimes and brings salvation upon himself. Webster shows the same transfiguration in Vittoria, who, on learning of Brachiano's death, exclaims, 'O well! this place is hell!'

Vittoria comes running in but the pretended friars push her out of the room. 'What! will you call him againe/To live in treble torments? *for charitie,/For Christian charitie,* avoid the chamber.' (172–174). Once more the grim irony, the fairest of appearances is used to conceal the foulest of crimes. As quickly as possible, to prevent any more interruptions, Lodovico strangles Brachiano with 'a true love-knot' sent from the Duke of Florence.

In the concluding scenes Webster rings the changes on the figures he has been employing throughout the play. Lodovico and Gaspero enter, still disguised as churchmen, and confront Vittoria and Flamineo with the horrible truth that they are to die. Vittoria pleads:

> O your gentle pitty:
> I have seene a black-bird that would sooner fly
> To a mans bosome, then to stay the gripe
> Of the feirce Sparrow-hawke.
> *Gas.* Your hope deceives you. (v.vi. 184–187)

This is a terrible speech, fundamental to the play. Man, made in the image of his Creator, is false to this image. He is viler in his cruelty than the beasts. And hope in this play always deceives.

Webster repeats the idea of false show when he makes Vittoria appeal to Lodovico: 'You, my Deathsman!/Me thinkes thou doest not looke horrid enough,/Thou hast to[o] good a face to be a hang-man' (210–212). But Lodovico is as pitiless as Gaspero. In his turn he calls her 'thou glorious strumpet,' that is, she is still the white devil, her glorious beauty covering only foulness. But the truth is, she is now really glorious. Both she and Flamineo are great in death. Webster plays on the word *glorious*. Flamineo says:

> Th'art a noble sister,
> I love thee now . . .
> Know many glorious woemen that are fam'd
> For masculine vertue, have bin vitious,

> Onely a happier silence did betyde them.
> Shee hath no faults, who hath the art to hide them.
>
> (241–247)

Part of this problem of appearance and reality arises from the greatness of soul which is revealed or uncovered in the 'devils' of the play. Strip some veils of appearance from them and they are foul, strip those other veils from them and their hearts are seen to harbor an inviolable greatness.

Webster does not leave us without reverting to another principal figure—the deceitfulness of fortune.

> *Vit.* My soule, like to a ship in a blacke storme,
> Is driven I know not whither. *Fla.* Then cast ancor.
> Prosperity doth bewitch men seeming cleere,
> But seas doe laugh, shew white, when Rocks are neere.
>
> (248–251)

Finally the end of the play curiously echoes the beginning. Giovanni has the last word: 'Let guilty men remember their blacke deedes,/Do leane on crut[c]hes, made of slender reedes.' To the last bitter word of the play men's trust is deceived. In *The White Devil* Webster was something of a pioneer. Rich as Elizabethan drama is in imagery, nobody before Webster had elaborated a system of figure so intricately linked and so profound.

In the *Duchess of Malfi* Webster brings the system to perfection. In his first speech Webster gives to Antonio a long figure comparing by implication the French court with the Italian. The French court is kept clean of infamous persons, however,

> [in] a Princes Court . . . if't chance
> Some curs'd example *poyson't* neere the head,
> 'Death, and diseases through the whole land spread.'
>
> (I.i.12–16)

Bosola enters and Antonio characterizes him as 'the onely Court-gall,' [sore or ulcer] (24).

Webster now gives us the figures-in-action. The Cardinal and the Duke begin their work. The Cardinal, who years ago suborned Bosola to murder, advises the Duke: 'Be sure you entertain that Bosola/For your Intelligence: I would not be seene in't' (235–236). 'I would not be seene in't'—Webster introduces here the motif of hidden corruption that is to pervade the play. Bosola thus describes the Cardinal and the Duke: '[They] are like Plum-trees (that grow *crooked* over standing-pooles [i.e., stagnant],) they are rich, and ore-laden with Fruite, but none but Crowes, Pyes, and Catter-pillers feede on them' (50–54). Then Antonio closes this movement by an analysis of Bosola, saying that he is very valiant, but his melancholy will poison his goodness, and as immoderate sleep rusts the soul, his want of action will eat him up, like moths in cloth. Thus in the first eighty-four lines of the play Webster has done far more than introduce certain characters, he has established the idea of treachery, poison, and slow corruption working in individuals and in the state.

Antonio goes on to characterize the Cardinal and the Duke in the same way. The Cardinal is a brave fellow, but 'such flashes hang superficially on him, for forme: but observe his inward Character . . . The Spring in his face, is nothing but the Ingendring of Toades . . .' (157–160). Of the Duke it is the same, 'What appeares in him mirth, is merely outside' (170). The two brothers are twins 'in qualitie.'

Webster then turns to the other corrupt characters. Like Fortune, the Court promises and deludes. Bosola complains that his service at Court has been badly rewarded: 'What creature ever fed worse, then hoping Tantalus? . . . places in the Court, are but beds in the hospitall, where this mans heade lies at that mans foote' (I.i.57–68).

After Bosola's exit Delio reveals that Bosola had served seven years in the galleys for the murder which the Cardinal had suborned him to commit.

Ferdinand now sets about corrupting Bosola anew. He persuades him to be a spy in the household of the Duchess by procuring for him the Provisorship of the Horse to the Duchess. Bosola accepts: 'For the good deed you have done me, I must doe/All the ill man can invent: Thus the Divell/Candies all sinnes [o'er]' (298–300), and later, 'What's my place?/The Proviso[r]-ship o'th horse? Say then my corruption/Grew out of horse-doong: I am your creature' (311–313).

Then the Cardinal and Ferdinand take the Duchess in hand and in a string of metaphors hint strongly at the dangers of her marrying again. They warn her against a honey-dew of the court that is poison and especially against hypocrisy, against making her face belie her heart. In the behavior of the two brothers we see the figure-in-action, fair seeming never covered falser hearts.

They make no impression on the Duchess. As soon as they leave, she proclaims her intention of essaying this dangerous venture of marriage. She tells her secret to Cariola, who answers: 'I'll conceale this secret from the world/As warily as those that trade in *poyson*,/Keepe *poyson* from their children,' (394–396). In the famous wooing-scene that follows, Webster shows the Duchess, in contrast to her brothers, as a candid and open nature. Webster uses the figures of falseness and deception to show that they do not apply to the Duchess or Antonio. The Duchess says to Antonio:

> You were ill to sell your selfe,
> This darkning of your worth, is not like that
> Which trades-men use i'th' City—their false lightes
> Are to rid bad wares off. (496–499)

Again speaking of those born great, she says:

> We are forc'd to . . . leave the path
> Of simple vertue, which was never made
> To seeme the thing it is not. (508–514)

When at last the Duchess and Antonio pledge their troth, Webster shows the falseness of their hopes by the irony of the words he chooses. When the Duchess kisses Antonio, she says 'I signe your *Quietus est*' (532), a double-edged phrase significant of death. When she speaks of danger from her brothers, she lightheartedly challenges her fate: 'time will easily/Scatter the tempest' (539–540). As we shall see, this prophecy will be terribly reversed. When she proclaims their absolute marriage, she adds: 'Blesse (Heaven) this sacred Gordian, which let violence/Never untwine' (549–550). But the Gordian knot was not untwined; Alexander severed it with a blow of his sword. And to celebrate their contract, Antonio and the Duchess sing their loves in the sweetest music and the most delicious figures Webster can invent (551–561). The whole love-scene is so strong because the image in word is completely fused with the image in action. The ironic hints leave no doubt that the trust in Fortune, which both the words and the action show, would in time be cheated. In order to make his irony quite clear Webster concludes the scene with a speech by Cariola:

> Whether the spirit of greatnes, or of woman
> Raigne most in her, I know not, but it shewes
> A fearefull madnes. I owe her much of pitty. (576–578)

Thus from this one scene we see how Webster shifts his kaleidoscope round about, displaying in many different patterns the irony of specious appearance hiding bitter reality. An inexorable logic links the figures, giving the scene its unity and making it a most powerful intellectual construction. All the persons in the play, their every word, everything they do, are symbols of one idea.

In the next scene Webster invents a conversation between Bosola, Castruchio, and an Old Lady, apparently in order to lead up to the speech:

> What thing is in this outward forme of man
> To be belov'd? . . .
> Though we are eaten up cf lice, and wormes,
> And though continually we beare about us
> A rotten and dead body, we delight
> To hide it in rich tissew. (II.i.47–60)

Webster follows this up with an image-in-action. Bosola, suspecting the Duchess to be pregnant, offers her some apriccts, they are 'wondrous faire ones.' Bosola says that the knave gardener 'did ripen them in horsedoung' (150). Notice the echo of I.i.312 where Bosola says his corruption grew out of horse-dung.[3] The Duchess eats the apricots greedily and they bring on the pangs of labor. She bears a son and Bosola sends the news to Rome to her brothers Ferdinand and the Cardinal, who now begin to plan her death. The interconnection of events is clear from the fruit, ripened out of horse-dung, that was so 'wondrous fair' but so disastrous in effect, right along to the wild rage of Ferdinand in Rome. Through these scenes Webster scatters images continuing the idea of secret corruption and false show. Antonio says of Bosola 'This Moale do's undermine me' (II.iii.15). Bosola ends the scene with the couplet: 'Though Lust doe masque in ne'r so strange disguise,/She's oft found witty, but is never wise' (II.iii.92–93). He misunderstands the Duchess completely. Appearances deceive in many ways. They prevent us from seeing the good as well as the evil. But immediately the next scene shows us the Cardinal with Julia, his mistress, and the Cardinal says to her: 'Thou art a witty false one' (II.iv.7), and the application of Bosola's words is clear.

Delio, at the end of the scene, speaking of Antonio, says 'unfortunate Fortune' (107). In this oxymoron he expresses the chief irony of the play.

With Act III Ferdinand moves upon the Duchess. Antonio is afraid:

> He is so quiet, that he seemes to sleepe
> The tempest out (as Dormise do in winter)—

> Those houses, that are haunted, are most still,
> Till the divell be up. (III.i.24–27)

Here there is a double echo: the 'tempest' linking this speech with the words of the Duchess, and 'Dormise' echoing Ferdinand's admonition to his spy, Bosola, to be 'like a pollitique dormouse' (I.i.307). Then Webster invents the figure-in-action. Ferdinand completely deceives the Duchess about his intentions and she exclaims *aside:* 'O bless'd comfort—/This deadly aire is purg'd' (67–68). Again the irony of too confident hope that will be defeated.

Webster continues this figure-in-action in the next scene where he shows the Duchess, Antonio, and Cariola harmlessly laughing and making fun of one another. The Duchess exclaims: 'When were we so merry? my haire tangles' (61), and then: 'Doth not the colour of my haire 'gin to change?/When I waxe gray . . .' (III.ii.66–67).

The next minute she turns and sees Ferdinand with a poniard, which he gives her, saying: 'Die then, quicklie:/Vertue, where art thou hid? What hideous thing/Is it, that doth ecclipze thee?' (80–82). That is to say, while in other parts of the play the good do not see the vice hidden by hypocrisy, Webster twists the idea of appearance and reality to show that Ferdinand, on the other hand, cannot recognize virtue when it stands before him in its most beautiful form.

At the end of the scene Webster invents the image-in-action again when Bosola's defense of Antonio sounds so genuine and warm that he dupes the Duchess into confiding in him and learns that Antonio is her husband. He advises her to go 'to faigne a Pilgrimage' to Loretto so that her flight may *seem* a princely progress. Cariola is against this jesting with religion, 'Tis faigned Pilgrimage' but the Duchess will not listen to her. The virtuous Duchess is not good at feigning; that is Bosola's job, and by making her feign Bosola sends her to her doom.

In III.iii Webster leads up by a series of concentrated images to a new climax of power. The two brothers have just heard that the Duchess is going on a feigned pilgrimage, and Webster uses his favorite method of describing them through bystanders.

> *Sil.* He [the Cardinal] lifts up's nose, like a fowle Por-pisse before
> A storme. (III.iii.63–64)

Notice the link with the Duchess's carefree contempt for any storm the brothers could raise (I.i. 539–540).

It is difficult for us to recapture the effect of this figure of the porpoise on Webster's audience. It is built up on the proverb, 'The porpoise plays before the storm.' Since we have lost contact with proverbs, we can no longer feel their power.

Pes. These are your true pangues of death,
The pangues of life, that strugle with great states-men—
Del. In such a deformed silence, witches whisper
Their charmes. (68–71)

Surely this figure is so tremendous because it bears the weight of the whole play.

Card. Doth she make religion her riding hood
To keepe her from the sun, and tempest? (72–73)

Notice Webster's consistency in the characterization by figure. He gives the Cardinal figures strong by reason of their conciseness. Notice he repeats the idea of *tempest*.

Ferd. That: that damnes her: Me thinkes her fault, and beauty
Blended together, shew like leaprosie—
The whiter, the fowler: I make it a question
Whether her beggerly brats were ever christned.
(III.iii. 74–77)

It is part of Webster's irony that the Duchess, by allowing herself to be duped into feigning a pilgrimage, has outraged the deepest religious feelings of those two pillars of the Church, the Cardinal and Ferdinand. They are both murderers, and the Cardinal keeps his mistress, but to go on a feigned pilgrimage they regard as utterly unpardonable. Webster brings it home to us that their religion is entirely external, a matter of show, without inner depth. Again, when Ferdinand speaks of her fault and beauty showing like leprosy, the whiter the fouler, we have the same twisted irony as before. Ferdinand sees her whiteness and imagines it is evil. He cannot see the reality and he misjudges the appearance.

Ferd. *Antonio!* A slave, that . . . nev'r in's
li[f]e, look'd like a Gentleman,
But in the audit time. (III.iii.87–89)

The irony of this is obvious. He misjudges Antonio by his appearance as certainly as he does the Duchess. The line is rich in its sardonic humor because it states with such a cutting edge the typical attitude of the conventional aristocrat towards the middle class. Thus in these few figures Webster has shown us that these two brothers are base, formidable through their treachery, and contemptible through their littleness of soul and mind.

The dumb-show in III.iv. is another figure-in-action. The Pope has appointed the Cardinal to be a general in his wars and so the Cardinal comes to the shrine of Our Lady of Loretto to lay aside his vestments as a man of God and to put on the armor of a soldier. To the same shrine come Antonio, the Duchess and their family. Choirs of priests sing to solemn music the praises of the Cardinal. The Duchess and her party, however, are banished from the shrine, and we are told the Pope has seized her dominions into his protection. The Church blesses the priest who goes out to kill but to the good it denies the consolations of religion and robs them of their property. To go back to I.i. 'the curst example,' poisoning the state and the church 'near the head,' is spreading disease through the whole land.

In III.v. Bosola brings the Duchess a letter from the Duke, promising as he avers 'All love and safetie.' The Duchess answers:

> Thou do'st blanch mischiefe–
> Wouldst make it white: See, see; like to calme weather
> At Sea, before a tempest, false hearts speake faire
> To those they intend most mischiefe.
> [Reads] A Letter.
> *Send* Antonio *to me; I want his head in a busines:*
> A politicke equivocation–
> He doth not want your councell, but your head;
> That is, he cannot sleepe till you be dead.
> And here's another Pitfall, that's strew'd ore
> With Roses . . . (III.v.33–42)

Eternal repetition of the same theme of evil hidden by fair show. Bosola retires and the Duchess and Antonio take their eternal farewell of one another.

In IV.i. Bosola pretends to offer the Duchess comfort, she answers. 'I will have done:/'Pray-thee, why do'st thou wrap thy poysond Pilles/In Gold, and Sugar' (IV.i.22–24). In the ensuing passage Ferdinand tries to break her spirit by a series of horrors. He first insists on seeing the Duchess in a completely darkened chamber. He offers her apparently his hand to kiss, it turns out to be a dead man's hand which he has brought with him. Then 'is discover'd (behind a Traverse) the artificial figures of Antonio, and his children; appearing as if they were dead.' Finally there is a dance of madmen with 'music answerable.'

All these are figures-in-action, attempts to deceive and to strike down by false show. In contrast to this, Bosola can torture her still more by pointing to reality.

Dutch. I could curse the Starres . . .
And those three smyling seasons of the yeere
Into a Russian winter: nay the world
To its first Chaos.
Bosola. Looke you, the Starres shine still. (IV.i.115–120)

He points to the stars, indifferent to her curses, pitiless, terrible—surely this line is among the greatest ever written.

In the next scene Webster goes even further. In a famous passage, marked by his characteristic polarity, confronting character with character, he makes the Duchess say:

Who am I?
Bos. Thou art a box of worm-seede, at best, but a salvatory of greene mummey: what's this flesh? a little cruded milke, phantasticall puffe-paste . . .
Dutch. Am not I, thy Duchesse?
Bos. Thou art some great woman sure, for riot begins to sit on thy forehead (clad in gray haires) twenty yeares sooner, then on a merry milkemaydes. Thou sleep'st worse, then if a mouse should be forc'd to take up her lodging in a cats eare . . .
Dutch. I am Duchesse of Malfy still.
Bos. That makes thy sleepes so broken:
'Glories (like glowe-wormes) afarre off, shine bright,
But look'd to neere, have neither heate, nor light.
(IV.ii.122–142)

Here we see Webster's technique. No speech, however glorious, is allowed to stand without its swift riposte. And again the same motif in a different figure, appearance and reality still quarrel, the beautiful body is but a box of worm-seed. And he takes over a couplet from the *White Devil* to show that as the great lady grows grey, the glories of the Duchess have neither heat nor light.

A little later executioners enter and Bosola sings a dirge for the Duchess in which he brings together two motifs in a couplet: 'Their life, a generall mist of error,/Their death, a hideous storme of terror'

(190–191). The executioners strangle her and Ferdinand enters. Fate has given him what he demanded of her. Bosola points to the dead Duchess and says: 'Shee is what/You'll'd have her' (271–272). And now that Ferdinand has achieved what he has planned, he exclaims: 'Cover her face: Mine eyes dazell: she di'd yong' (281). I do not wish to rush in where angels fear to tread and endeavor to improve on this famous line. But I am obliged to point out that it is not 'merely' superb 'poetry.' It is strong because it is built into the construction of the play. Ferdinand has never known his sister, and only now, when he has murdered her, and she is lying dead at his feet, does reality strike him and he sees her for the first time. William Archer will have none of this line. He says: 'It is not difficult to hit upon sayings which shall pass for highly dramatic simply because they are unforeseen and unlikely.'[4] It is curious that a famous critic who spent his life in writing about plays should know nothing about the construction of a play. Webster has taken infinite pains to lead us up to this line. He foresaw it and when it comes, we recognize it was inevitable that it should come. It is the climax of the play, the watershed, the dividing line.

Bosola now claims his reward from Ferdinand, but in vain. Again hope is completely deluded. Bosola sums up:

> Your brother, and your selfe, are worthy men;
> You have a paire of hearts, are hollow Graves,
> Rotten, and rotting others . . .
>   I stand like one
> That long hath ta'ne a sweet, and golden dreame.
> I am angry with my selfe, now that I wake.
>
> (IV.ii.344–351)

Bosola is converted and turns from evil, but he can do no good. He desires more than anything to help Antonio and then—another figure-in-action—by mistake he stabs Antonio in the dark. In dying Antonio repeats the constant theme: 'In all our Quest of Greatness . . . /(Like wanton Boyes, whose pastime is their care)/We follow after bubbles, blowne in th' ayre' (V.iv.75–77).

Webster continues his figures-in-action. The Cardinal gives order to his retinue not to come to his aid if they hear calls for help. Such calls will probably come from the mad Ferdinand. When Bosola attacks him, he does cry for help, but his retinue only exclaim, 'Fye upon his counterfeyting!' (V.v.28). And for his counterfeiting the

Cardinal dies. Bosola stabs him repeatedly at his ease—no one interferes. Ferdinand, who has gone mad, now enters. In his madness he thinks the Cardinal is the enemy and he therefore helps Bosola. He stabs the Cardinal and in the scuffle gives Bosola his death-wound. Bosola still has strength before he dies to kill Ferdinand. All this the Cardinal might have prevented but for his 'feigning.' Their lives are a 'mist of error.'

In a final figure Delio sums up the theme of empty show that runs through the play.

> These wretched eminent things
> Leave no more fame behind 'em, then should one
> Fall in a frost, and leave his print in snow—
> As soone as the sun shines, it ever melts,
> Both forme, and matter: I have ever thought
> Nature doth nothing so great, for great men,
> As when she's pleas'd to make them Lords of truth:
> 'Integrity of life, is fames best friend,
> Which noblely (beyond Death) shall crowne the end.
>
> (v.v.138–146)

I have given these figures in such detail, as they occur, in order to make quite clear the nature of Webster's structure. Figure-in-action and figure-in-word reinforce one another. He repeats his theme tirelessly, spinning innumerable variations with his figures of the magnificent outer show and the inner corruption, of life, fortune, hopes that look so fair and delude us utterly, of the many bitter, twisted ironies of the difference between appearance and reality.

Webster's coordination of the figure-in-word with the figure-in-action makes his position in drama unique. Marlowe's figure runs parallel to his action; he rarely fuses the two. Ben Jonson devotes his attention to developing the action, to which figure is subsidiary. Chapman is neither clear-headed nor patient enough to work out an elaborate pattern like Webster's. The only possible comparison is with Shakespeare. There can be no doubt that Webster profited by Shakespeare's example. But even Shakespeare could in his turn have learned something from Webster's skill in interlacing long chains of figure and action in order to express an irony so varied, so subtle, and so profound.

But to come back to where we started from, it is extremely important that all students of Shakespeare's art should familiarize themselves with Webster's technique. Perhaps if modern critics recognized the stern consistency with which Webster developed his elaborate imagery, they would be able to see that Shakespeare was doing very much the same sort of thing. They would no longer refuse to believe that Shakespeare coordinated his images. They might even come to admit that Shakespeare used plan and system in the development of his imagery, and that while he appears on the surface to be more simple than Webster, he plumbs to depths that Webster never reached.

NOTES

1. See Morris Palmer Tilley, *A Dictionary of Proverbs in England in the Sixteenth and Seventeenth Centuries* (Ann Arbor, 1950).

2. I take all my quotations and the numbering of the lines from F. L. Lucas's edition of Webster (London, 1928). I have occasionally italicized words in quotations for emphasis.

3. Charles Williams has already called attention to this echo, pp. xviii–xix. He also calls attention to the use of the word *dung-hill* (IV.i.76).

4. *The Old Drama and the New* (New York, 1926), p. 61.

INGA-STINA EKEBLAD

The 'Impure Art' of John Webster

> The art of the Elizabethans is an impure art. . . . The aim of the Elizabethans was to attain complete realism without surrendering any of the advantages which as artists they observed in unrealistic conventions.[1]

OBVIOUSLY *The Duchess of Malfi* is an outstanding example of the 'impure art' of the Elizabethans. Here, in one play, Webster plays over the whole gamut between firm convention and complete realism: from the conventional dumb-show—

> *Here the Ceremony of the Cardinalls enstalment, in the habit of a Souldier: perform'd in delivering up his Crosse, Hat, Robes, and Ring, at the Shrine; and investing him with Sword, Helmet, Sheild, and Spurs: Then* Antonio, *the* Duchesse, *and their Children, (having presented themselves at the Shrine) are (by a forme of Banishment in dumbe-shew, expressed towards them by the Cardinall, and the State of* Ancona) *banished*[2] (III. iv)—

to the would-be realistic pathos of

> I pray-thee looke thou giv'st my little boy
> Some sirrop, for his cold . . . ; (IV. ii. 207–8)

or from the horror-show of '*the artificiall figures of* Antonio, *and his children; appearing as if they were dead*' (IV. i. 66–67) to the realization of a character's psychological state, in such lines as Ferdinand's much-quoted 'Cover her face: Mine eyes dazell: she di'd yong' (IV. ii. 281) or Antonio's 'I have no use | To put my life to' (V. iv. 74–75).

From *Review of English Studies,* N.S. IX (1958), pp. 253–67. Reprinted by permission of The Clarendon Press, Oxford, and the author.

So Webster's dramatic technique needs to be understood in relation to the 'confusion of convention and realism' which Mr. Eliot speaks of; and indeed many critics would in this 'confusion' see the key to Webster's alleged failure as a dramatist. They would say that Webster's method of mixing unrealistic conventions with psychological-realistic representation leads to lack of structure in his plays as wholes.[3] It seems, in fact, to have become almost an axiom that when Webster uses conventional dramatic material—such as the various Revenge play devices—it is for show value, 'for effect,' and not because the progress of his dramatic action, and the meaning of the play, are vitally tied up with that convention—as they are, for example, in *The Revenger's Tragedy* or *The Atheist's Tragedy*. While Tourneur's 'bony lady' is simultaneously an incentive to revenge and a tool for moralizing, the *memento mori* and centre of meaning of the play, Webster's wax figures seem to have no other function than Madame Tussaud's. And while Tourneur's famous speech, 'Do's the Silke-worme expend her yellow labours | For thee? . . . ,' is closely dependent on, and interacts with, the skull on the stage, Webster's dramatic meaning would appear to inhere in his poetry—such as Bosola's '. . . didst thou ever see a Larke in a cage?'—irrespective of the dramatic devices employed. Is it, then, only when his poetry fails to do the trick that Webster 'falls back on showmanship,'[4] such as 'all the apparatus of dead hands, wax images, dancing madmen and dirge-singing tomb-makers in *The Duchess of Malfi*'?[5]

Now, while recognizing that in other Elizabethans than Webster (for example Tourneur) the dramatic form is more firmly and consistently controlled by established conventions, we must, on the other hand, not blind ourselves to the richness which may inhere in the very 'confusion' of convention and realism. The two can be confused; but they can also be fused. And I hope to show that Webster—though he often leaves us in confusion—does at his most intense achieve such a fusion, creating something structurally new and vital. This something, however, is very much more elusive to analysis than the more rigidly conventional structures of Tourneur, or the more clearly 'realistic' structure of Middleton (as in *The Changeling*).

I wish to examine *The Duchess of Malfi*, IV. ii—the Duchess's death-scene. It is a part of the play to which no critic of Webster has been indifferent; it stirred Lamb's and Swinburne's most prostrate praise and Archer's most nauseated denunciation, and later critics have only less ardently condemned or lauded it. Its complexity has been sensed, but hardly satisfactorily analysed.[6]

No one, I think, would deny that this scene contains Webster's most penetrating piece of character-analysis. Through language where juxtaposition of sublime and lowly suggests the tremendous tension in her mind:

> Th'heaven ore my head, seemes made of molten brasse,
> The earth of flaming sulphure, yet I am not mad:
> I am acquainted with sad misery,
> As the tan'd galley-slave is with his Oare (IV. ii. 27–30)

we follow the Duchess's inner development towards the acceptance of her fate; till finally, though 'Duchesse of *Malfy* still,' she humbly kneels to welcome death. And yet, in the midst of this representation of human experience, Webster introduces a pack of howling madmen, to sing and dance and make antic speeches; and as they leave the stage, the whole apparatus of 'dirge-singing tomb-makers,' &c., is brought in. How are we to reconcile such apparently opposed elements? The commonly accepted answer is that this is only one more instance of Webster's constant letting us down, his constant sacrifice of unity of design, in order to achieve a maximum effect. But, in a scene which is so clearly the spiritual centre of the play, which verbally—through poetic imagery—gathers together all the chief themes of the play and thus becomes a kind of fulcrum for the poetry, ought we not to devote particular attention to the dramatic technique used, before we pronounce it as grossly bad as the answer suggested above would indicate?

In fact, if we pursue the question why Webster inserted a masque of madmen in a would-be realistic representation of how the Duchess faces death, we shall find that the madmen's masque is part of a larger structural unit—a more extensive masque. Within the scene, this larger masque is being developed on a framework of 'realistic' dramatic representation—the framework itself bearing an analogous relationship to the masque structure. The action of the scene is grasped only by seeing both the basic framework and the masque structure, and the progressive interaction of the two. It is this structural counterpointing of 'convention' and 'realism,' this concentrated 'impurity' of art, that gives the scene its peculiar nature; indeed, it contains the meaning of the scene.

By 1613–14, the years of the composition of *The Duchess of Malfi*, the introduction of a masque in a play was a long-established dramatic device. In the Revenge drama, from Kyd onwards, masques were traditionally used to commit revenging murder [7] or otherwise resolve the plot. Furthermore, in the years around the writing of *The Duchess of Malfi* the leading dramatists show a strong interest in the marriage-masque—we need only think of the elaborate showpiece inserted in *The Maid's Tragedy*, or the masques of *The Tempest* and *The Two Noble Kinsmen*. During these years, any play which includes a marriage seems also almost bound to contain a marriage-masque.[8]

Now, in *The Duchess of Malfi* it is the Duchess's love and death, her marriage and murder, which are the focal points of the dramatic action. And in IV. ii Webster has, by the very building of the scene, juxtaposed—counterpointed—the two. He has done so by drawing on masque conventions. To see how, and why, we must proceed to a detailed analysis of the scene-structure.

The essence of the masque, throughout its history, was 'the arrival of certain persons vizored and disguised, to dance a dance or present an offering.' [9] Although the structure of the early, Tudor, masque had become overlaid with literature (especially, of course, by Ben Jonson) and with show (by those who, like Inigo Jones, thought of the masque primarily in terms of magnificent visual effects), the masques inserted in Jacobean plays—if at all elaborated on—stay close to the simpler structure of the Elizabethan masque. That structure, we may remind ourselves, is as follows:

1. Announcing and presenting of the masquers in introductory speeches (and songs).
2. Entry of masquers.
3. Masque dances.
4. Revels (in which the masquers 'take out' and dance with members of the audience).

   A further contact between masquers and audience—especially common when the masque is still near to its original form: groups of disguised dancers suddenly intruding into a festive assembly—can be the presenting of gifts by the masquers to the one, or ones, to be celebrated.
5. Final song (and speeches).

These features all appear in *The Duchess of Malfi,* IV. ii.

As the scene opens, the 'wild consort of Mad-men' is heard offstage as a 'hideous noyse.' The verbal imagery is preparing for the consciously scenic quality of what is to come. The Duchess turns immediately from her both ominous and ironic remark,[10] 'And Fortune seemes onely to have her eiesight, | To behold my Tragedy,' to the question, 'How now, what noyce is that?' Here a Servant enters, to perform the function of the Announcer of the masque: 'I am come to tell you, | Your brother hath entended you some sport,' and the Duchess answers, by a phrase which in terms of the plot only would seem absurd—for what is her power to give or refuse entry?—but which is natural when coming from someone about to be 'celebrated' with a masque: 'Let them come in.' The arrival of the masquers in *Timon of Athens*, I.ii, may serve to show that the opening of the scene follows the traditional pattern for the reception of unexpectedly arriving masquers:

TIM. What means that trump?

Enter Servant.

SERV. Please you my lord there are certain ladies most desirous of admittance.

TIM. Ladies? What are their wills?

SERV. There comes with them a forerunner my lord which bears that office to signify their pleasures.

TIM. I pray let them be admitted.

Now the Servant in IV. ii becomes the Presenter of the masque and delivers a speech introducing each of the eight madmen-masquers:

There's a mad Lawyer, and a secular Priest,
A Doctor that hath forfeited his wits
By jealousie: an Astrologian,
That in his workes, sayd such a day o'th'moneth
Should be the day of doome; and fayling of't,
Ran mad: an English Taylor, crais'd i'th'braine,
With the studdy of new fashion: a gentleman usher
Quite beside himselfe, with care to keepe in minde,
The number of his Ladies salutations,
Or 'how do you,' she employ'd him in each morning:
A Farmer too, (an excellent knave in graine)
Mad, 'cause he was hindred transportation,
And let one Broaker (that's mad) loose to these,
You'ld thinke the divell were among them.

This product of Webster's grim comico-satirical strain is, of course, in terms of realistic plot totally out of place here. Not so, however, if seen in the relevant tradition. From 1608 to 1609 practically every court masque was preceded by an antimasque, often danced by 'antics': 'O Sir, all de better, vor an antick-maske, de more absurd it be, and vrom de purpose, it be ever all de better.' [11] In each of the earlier antimasques, the antic figures were all of a kind, and there was no attempt to differentiate them. It is in the masques performed at the Princess Elizabeth's wedding, in February 1613,[12] that individualized comic characters first appear. It is worth noting that Campion's 'twelve franticks . . . all represented in sundry habits and humours' in *The Lords' Masque*—such as 'the melancholicke man, full of feare, the schoole-man overcome with phantasie, the overwatched usurer . . .' —as well as Beaumont's various figures in the second antimasque of *The Masque of the Inner Temple and Gray's Inn,* are described in much the same manner as Webster's eight madmen. Webster is here working in an antimasque tradition which was to have many uses in the drama after him. We see it, for instance, in Ford's *The Lover's Melancholy* (1628), which in III. iii has a masque of the same shape as the madmen's interlude in *The Duchess of Malfi:* six different types of Melancholy are described and present themselves; their antic talk is given; and then the Dance, 'after which the masquers run out in couples.'

After the presentation, the masquers themselves appear—'*Enter Madmen*'—and one of them sings a song to what the stage directions describe as 'a dismall kind of Musique.' [13] Even without the music, there is plenty of dismalness in the jarring jingle of the words:

O let us howle, some heavy note,
some deadly-dogged howle,
Sounding, as from the threatning throat,
of beastes, and fatall fowle.

Webster's audience had the benefit of the musical setting, which, according to Mr. Cutts, 'makes a vivid and forceful attempt to convey the horror of the imagery of owls, wolves and harbingers of death.' The antimasquers at the court of James frequently appeared in the shape of animals; [14] and it seems that, for example, the madmen-masquers ordered for the wedding of Beatrice Joanna in *The Changeling* were to wear animal disguises. Stage directions in *The Changeling* tell us: '*Cries of madmen are heard within, like those of birds and beasts,*' and the explicit comments on this are:

Sometimes they [madmen] imitate the beasts and birds,
Singing or howling, braying, barking; all
As their wild fancies prompt 'em. (III. iii. 206–8)

Here, then, is another antimasque tradition drawn upon in *The Duchess of Malfi*. The bestiality of these madmen comes out chiefly in the imagery of the song:

> As Ravens, Scrich-owles, Bulls and Beares,
> We'll bell, and bawle our parts.

But we may be helped by other madmen-antimasquers to imagine, visually and aurally, how the song, and indeed the whole interlude, was executed.

Directly after the song various madmen speak for themselves, in a series of disjointed speeches which verbally link this episode with main themes of the whole play. Images of hell-fire, of madness and bestiality (preparing, of course, for Ferdinand's lycanthropy)—to mention only the most important—are concentrated here. After the speeches follows '*the Daunce, consisting of 8. Mad-men, with musicke answerable thereunto.*' It is left to us to imagine the lumbering movements and discordant tunes which this passus must have contained; yet we should not forget that, though there is only a bare reference to it in the stage directions, the dance must have been the climax of the madmen's interlude. Now, it is not 'from the purpose,' but truly meaningful, that in the centre of *The Duchess of Malfi* there should be this antic dance, accompanied by these incoherent words and discordant tunes. We know that to the Elizabethans the unity and coherence of macrocosm and microcosm alike was naturally expressed as a dance:

> Dancing, the child of Music and of Love,
> Dancing itself, both love and harmony,
> Where all agree and all in order move,
> Dancing, the art that all arts do approve,
> The fair character of the world's consent,
> The heavn's true figure, and th'earth's ornament.[15]

And so the climactic dance would be particularly significant in the marriage-masque, the purpose of which was to celebrate the union brought about by the power of Love. Ben Jonson built his *Hymenaei* (1606) round this idea,[16] and the central dance of that masque is a 'neate and curious measure,' accompanied by the following chorus:

> Whilst all this *Roofe* doth ring,
> And each discording string,
> With every varied voyce,
> In Union doth reioyce. (306–9)

The dance in *The Duchess of Malfi,* on the contrary, acts as an ideograph of the *dis*-unity, the *in*-coherence, of the Duchess's world. It acts as a visual and aural image of what the action of the play has led to, the difference between the happiness and unity of the wooing-scene, imaged as the most perfect movement and melody:

> ANT. And may our sweet affections, (like the Sphears)
> Be still in motion.
> DUCH. Quickning, and make
> The like soft Musique. (I. i. 551–4)

and this scene where the Duchess herself has found that

> ... nothing but noyce, and folly
> Can keepe me in my right wits. (IV. ii. 6–7)

By now it should be possible to say that the madmen's masque is not just 'Bedlam-broke-loose,' as Archer, and with him many, would have it. Nor do we need to excuse this interlude, as has been done, by saying that Webster is not alone in it; that there are plenty of madmen in Elizabethan drama, and Webster's Bedlam stuff is as good as any. Such an excuse does not save the scene, as a piece of dramatic art, from damnation. But we are beginning to see the masque as peculiarly functional in the play. We have seen its connexions with anti-masque conventions; now we must see how it is related to the events that are represented on the stage.

In fact, there are reasons to believe that in this masque there is a nucleus of folk tradition, the bearing of which on the action of the play justifies the inclusion of the masque.

The widowhood of the Duchess is much stressed throughout the play—from the brothers' interview with her in the very first scene, around the motto, 'Marry? they are most luxurious, | Will wed twice' (I.i. 325–6). It is well known that objections to second marriages were still strong at the beginning of the seventeenth century. We need go no farther than Webster's own *Characters,* 'A Vertuous Widdow' and 'An Ordinarie Widdow,' [17] to get a notion of how strong they were. Early in 1613 Chapman's satiric comedy *The Widow's Tears* (1605–6), in which the 'luxury' of two widows provided the plot, had had a successful revival. The general attitude to widows' marriages was to see them as 'but a kind of lawful adultery, like usury permitted by the law, not approved; that to wed a second was no better than to cuckold the first.' [18] And in Webster's source, Painter's translation of Belleforest's story of the Duchess of Malfi, the Duchess is an *exemplum horrendum* to all women contemplating a second marriage:

> You see the miserable discourse of a Princesse loue, that was not very wyse, and of a Gentleman that had forgotten his estate, which ought to serue for a lookinge Glasse to them which be ouer hardy in makinge Enterprises, and doe not measure their Ability wyth the greatnesse of their Attemptes . . . foreseeing their ruine to be example for all posterity. . . .[19]

Webster's Duchess, newly widowed, marries again, and marries a man in degree far below her—in fact one of her servants. Those are the facts on which the plot of the play hinges; they comprise her double 'crime.' But they also explain the point of the mental torture which, in the coming of the madmen, Ferdinand has devised for his sister.[20] For the madmen's interlude—such as we know it from Webster's stage directions, and such as we divine it from the sung and spoken words —is strikingly similar to a kind of *ludus,* one of the predecessors of the masque proper, namely the *charivari.*

Du Cange defines *charivarium* thus: 'Ludus turpis tinnitibus & clamoribus variis, quibus illudunt iis, qui ad secundas convolant nuptias,' and *O.E.D.* refers to Bayle's *Dictionnaire:* 'A Charivari, or Mock Music, given to a Woman that was married again immediately after the death of her husband.' The *charivari* as such was a French *ludus,* or marriage-baiting custom, dating from the latter part of the Middle Ages,[21] 'originally common after all weddings, then directed at unpopular or unequal matches as a form of public censure.'[22] But the practice which the word stands for was not limited to France. English folk-customs and folk-drama knew the equivalent of the French *charivari*[23]—indeed a descendant of it was still known when Hardy put his skimmington-ride into *The Mayor of Casterbridge.* In the early seventeenth century a widow in an English village, marrying one of her late husband's servants, might well be visited by a band of ruffians, showing their disapproval through clamour and antic dances. Often we can trace the antimasque of a courtly masque back to village *ludi.* Clearly the connexion between the grotesque dances of antimasques and various popular celebrations was, as Miss Welsford says, 'still felt, if not understood, in the seventeenth century' (*Court Masque,* p. 29). And so I do not think it too far-fetched to assume that the spectators at the Globe and the Blackfriars would have seen in the 'clamoribus variis' of Webster's madmen a kind of *charivari* put on to 'mock' the Duchess for her remarriage. They would then have seen a meaning in

Ferdinand's (and Webster's) device which totally escapes us when we see it as just one Bedlam episode among many. For, if seen as related to the *charivari* tradition, the madmen's masque becomes a contrivance of cruel irony on the part of Ferdinand: in a sense, the Duchess is here being given her belated wedding entertainment. The Duchess is of 'royall blood,' and the wedding of such an elevated person would have had to be celebrated with some show allegorically bearing on the occasion. The year 1613, because of the spectacular celebrations of the Princess Elizabeth's wedding, was, above all years in the period, a year of marriage festivities. So the audience would be particularly prepared to respond to the masque-features of this Webster scene. And in that response would be the realization of the dissimilarities of this masque from such masques as did honour to the Princess and her Count Palatine, or the one Prospero put on for Miranda. The Duchess's masque, as far as we have followed it, is all antimasque, all a grotesque mockery; but that is not in itself the point. It is the cruel twist of this mockery, as the madmen's interlude turns out to be merely the antimasque prelude to a kind of main masque, which strikes home.

Traditionally, after the masquers had danced 'their own measure,' they would be ready to 'take out' members of the audience to dance. It is this feature—the involving of the spectators in the proceedings—which more than anything else distinguishes the masque as an art form from the drama. And now the Duchess is indeed 'taken out.' For directly upon the madmen's 'own measure,' Bosola, masqued *'like an old man,'* enters, and his 'invitation,' or summons, to the Duchess is as conclusive as could be: 'I am come to make thy tombe.' The Duchess has for a while been as much a passive spectator as anyone in the audience. Now, with a sudden change, she takes part in what is happening. Bosola's disguise is like that of the traditional masque image of Time,[24] and his appearance, while again focusing our attention on the Duchess, turns the mock wedding-masque into what reminds us of a Dance of Death. The text of this 'dance' is Bosola's words:

> Thou art a box of worme-seede, at best, but a salvatory of greene mummey: what's this flesh? a little cruded milke, phantasticall puffe-paste: our bodies are weaker then those paper prisons boyes use to keepe flies in: more contemptible: since ours is to preserve earth-wormes. . . .

From the point of view merely of plot this is a rather extravagant way of saying: 'Like all men, you are a worthless creature,' or something of the kind. But we see now that this speech is as much fed with meaning by the masque structure around it as is Tourneur's skull-speech by the presence of the *memento mori*. Webster's practical joke is not as spectacular as Tourneur's, and there is none of the grotesque fun of the 'bony lady' in it; but it has some of the effect of Mutability entering into an Epithalamium, or of the skeleton Death joining the masque-dancers at the Jedburgh Abbey marriage-feast.[25] In the lines just quoted there is all the medieval sense of the perishable nature of all things, and this sense deepens as Bosola's focus widens:

> ... didst thou ever see a Larke in a cage? such is the soule in the body: this world is like her little turfe of grasse, and the Heaven ore our heades, like her looking glasse, onely gives us a miserable knowledge of the small compasse of our prison.

There is a pointed consistency in the movement of thought, through associatively linked images,[26] from the nothingness of the Duchess's body to the despicableness of all flesh, to the plight of the soul in the body and of man in the universe—the correspondence between microcosm and macrocosm enabling Webster to move from one to the other in the last image. All that remains is to be absolute for death.

But the end of the masque is not yet reached. In the course of Bosola's and the Duchess's dialogue, horrible life is given to the masque convention of presenting gifts:

> Here is a present from your Princely brothers,
> And may it arrive wel-come, for it brings
> Last benefit, last sorrow.

The gifts are 'a Coffin, Cords, and a Bell,' presented by the Executioner. One is reminded of a passage in *The White Devil* where Brachiano, who is about to be strangled—also for a love-crime—is told, 'This is a true-love knot | Sent from the Duke of Florence' (v. iii. 175–6). The parallelism is such that it is tempting to see in the earlier image the seed of an idea worked out more fully in *The Duchess of Malfi*.[27]

By this time we are ready for a change of guise in Bosola. He becomes 'the common Bell-man' (who used to ring his bell for the condemned in Newgate on the night before their execution), and accompanied by the bell he sings his dirge: 'Hearke, now every thing is still.' The situation has turned like that threatened by the King in *Philaster*, v. iii:

I'll provide
A masque shall make your Hymen turn his saffron
Into a sullen coat, and sing sad requiems
To your departing souls.

The dirge would answer to the concluding song of the masque; and it is here part and conclusion of the Duchess's masque. In fact, through the death-imagery of Bosola's song, we hear epithalamic echoes. The invocation,

The Schritch-Owle, and the whistler shrill,
Call upon our Dame, aloud,

refers, of course, to the harbinger of death so often mentioned in Elizabethan-Jacobean drama and poetry. But it also stands out as the very reverse of the traditional epithalamic theme of averting evil in the shape of birds [28]—as in Spenser's *Epithalamion*, 345–6:

Let not the shriech Oule, nor the Storke be heard:
Nor the night Rauen that still deadly yels,

or the last stanza of the marriage-song in *The Two Noble Kinsmen*, I. i:

The crow, the slanderous cuckoo, nor
The boding raven, nor chough hoar,
Nor chattering pie,
May on our bridehouse perch or sing,
Or with them any discord bring,
But from it fly.

Further, the Duchess is bidden to prepare herself:

Strew your haire, with powders sweete:
Don cleane linnen, bath your feete.

Preparation for death, this is; and the strewing of her hair could be taken as a penitential act, or simply as referring to the new fashion [29] —a cruel echo of her happy chatting in the bedchamber scene, just before disaster descends:

Doth not the colour of my haire 'gin to change?
When I waxe gray, I shall have all the Court
Powder their haire, with Arras, to be like me. (III. ii. 66–68)

But one may also hear an echo of Ben Jonson's *Hymenaei* where the 'personated Bride' has her haire 'flowing and loose, *sprinckled with grey*' (my italics) [30]—an idea which was to be taken up by Donne in the fourth stanza of his *Epithalamion* on the Earl of Somerset's wedding on 26 December 1613, to be made the basis of a witty conceit:

> Pouder thy Radiant haire,
> Which if without such ashes thou would'st weare,
> Thou which to all which come to looke upon,
> Art meant for Phoebus, would'st be Phaeton.

So the Duchess's preparations for the 'laying out' of her dead body have cruel reminiscences of those connected with the dressing of the bride. And, finally, the end and climax of the dirge,

> 'Tis now full tide, 'tweene night, and day,
> End your groane, and come away,

strongly suggests the traditional exhortation at the end of the epithalamium, referring to the impatiently awaited night of the bridal bed: Catullus's lines 'sed abit dies: | perge, ne remorare' (*Carmen,* lxi. 195–6) and their echo through practically every Elizabethan-Jacobean epithalamium, as—to give only one example—the final lines in Campion's *The Lords' Masque:*

> No longer wrong the night
> Of her Hymenean right,
> A thousand Cupids call away,
> Fearing the approaching day;
> The cocks already crow:
> Dance then and go!

And so the Duchess goes, not to an ardent bridegroom, but to 'violent death.' [31] It is the culminating irony of the scene.

There is clearly a close kinship between IV. ii and the wooing-scene in Act I. While the death-scene is interwoven with marriage-allusions, Death is very much there in the scene where the marriage *per verba de presenti* takes place. We hear, for instance, of the Duchess's will (playing, of course, on the two senses of 'testament' and 'carnal desire'), of winding-sheets, and of a kiss which is a *Quietus est;* of the 'figure cut in Allablaster | Kneeles at my husbands tombe,' and of a heart which is 'so dead a peece of flesh.' There is, however, one crucial difference between the two scenes. In the wooing-scene, the counterpointing of marriage and death is entirely verbal: it is through 'uncomical puns' and apparently irrelevant images that sinister associations are fused with the dramatic situation. In IV. ii, on the other hand, Webster has used the very building of the scene to express something of that typically Jacobean paradox which is contained in the two senses of the word 'die.' The masque elements in the Duchess's death-scene, then, are truly functional. Unlike, say, the masque in *The Maid's Tragedy*, which is a self-contained piece of theatre (it is justified in the play as a whole by acting as an ironic foil to the actual wedding-night which follows), the masque in *The Duchess of Malfi* gathers into itself all the essential conflicts of the play. And it does so on all levels: from the pure plot conflict between the Duchess and her brothers, involving questions of revenge and persecution, to the deep thematic clashes of love and death, man and Fate, which much of the poetry of the play is nourished by.

So Act IV, scene ii of *The Duchess of Malfi* gives an insight into Webster's 'impure art.' The scene as a whole neither fits into a realistic scheme of cause and effect or psychological motivation, nor does it consistently embody convention. It balances between those two alternatives. It is a precarious balance, and at other points we see Webster losing it. But in this scene he holds the tension between the two and draws strength from both sides—the kind of strength which tempts one to suggest that Webster's art is most 'impure' at the centres of meaning in his plays; that his peculiar skill, not only as a dramatic poet but as a poetic dramatist, lay in the ability to utilize the very impurity of his art.

But when, finally, we try to see how Webster holds the balance between convention and realism, we seem to find that it is by poetic means: within the scene, the masque is related to the 'realistic' dramatic representation of what happens, in the manner of a poetic analogy. That is, the Duchess's marriage, leading to her murder, is like a marriage-masque turned into a masque of Death. The two chief structural components of the scene are: (1) the plot situation—the Duchess imprisoned and put to death, because she has remarried, and (2) the *charivari*-like antimasque of madmen, developing into a masque of Death. In pursuing the interconnexion between these two, we have come to see that they are best understood as two halves of one metaphor, certainly 'yoked by violence together,' but in the end naturally coming together, to give the full meaning of the scene. Conventional masque elements—such as Webster's original audience would have known from other plays—have helped to give Webster a structure on which to build up the most pregnant irony. The irony is there in the basic analogy between the represented human situation and the masque. It is clinched at individual points, when the analogy is most forcible—that is, at each new stage in the masque. And the irony culminates when the two parts of the analogy become interchangeable: the Duchess becomes 'involved' in the masque, and her fate becomes one with the progress of the masque. Also, as in any effective metaphor, the implications reach beyond the immediate situation: in Bosola's worm-seed speech not only the Duchess but—in the manner of the *Danse Macabre*—all flesh and all things are involved. What Webster wanted to say here he could say in no other way. What he does say we can understand only by grasping the technique of the scene.

NOTES

1. T. S. Eliot, *Selected Essays* (New York, 1950), pp. 96, 97.

2. I quote from *The Complete Works of John Webster*, ed. F. L. Lucas (London, 1927).

3. Cf. M. C. Bradbrook, *Themes and Conventions of Elizabethan Tragedy* (2nd edn., Cambridge, 1952), pp. 187, 194, 211.

4. *The Age of Shakespeare*, Pelican Guide to English Literature (London, 1955), p. 352.

5. W. A. Edwards, 'John Webster,' *Scrutiny*, ii (1933), 20. Cf. also Ian Jack, 'The Case of John Webster,' ibid., xvi (1949), 38–43.

6. Miss Bradbrook sees this scene as largely symbolical: it represents the Duchess's Hell or Purgatory (*Themes and Conventions*, p. 197).

7. Cf. Vendice's words: 'A masque is treasons licence, that build upon; | Tis murders best face when a vizard's on' (*The Revenger's Tragedy*, v. i. 196–7).

8. The two traditions of revenging-murder masque and marriage-masque sometimes meet. See, for example, Middleton's *Women Beware Women* (1625?), where the cupids' arrows are literally deadly, and Hymen himself carries and presents a poisoned cup.

9. Welsford, *Court Masque*, p. 7. In discussing the masque I also draw on R. Brotanek, *Die englischen Maskenspiele* (Wien, 1902); P. Reyher, *Les Masques anglais* (Paris, 1909); E. K. Chambers's chapter on 'The Masque' in *The Elizabethan Stage* (Oxford, 1923), i. 149–212; the chapter on the masque in C. H. Herford and Percy Simpson's edition of Ben Jonson (Oxford, 1925), ii. 249–334; and Allardyce Nicoll, *Stuart Masques and the Renaissance Stage* (London, 1937).

10. Ironic because it echoes back to the wooing-scene, where the Duchess tells Antonio, 'I would have you leade your Fortune by the hand | Unto your marriage bed' (I. i. 567–8). She is here thinking of the traditionally blind figure of Fortune and merely making a playful conceit. Yet unwittingly she is expressing her own blindness to the consequences of her action. And when the image is repeated in IV. ii it is to make the tragic irony explicit. Now Fortune is no longer blind, nor is the Duchess; but what they see is only suffering and death. The Fortune image is used so as to point the almost literal opening of eyes that the action has brought about.

11. Vangoose in Ben Jonson's *The Masque of Augures. With the Severall Antimasques Presented on Twelfe-Night, 1622.*

12. Three masques, by Campion, Beaumont, and Chapman respectively, were performed on the occasion. The possibility that Webster directly imitates Campion's masque of madmen has been pointed out; and John P. Cutts, 'Jacobean Masque and Stage Music,' *Music and Letters,* xxxv (1954), 193, suggests that 'it is Robert Johnson's music which is involved in the transference . . . of the madmen's antimasque from *The Lords' Masque* to *The Dutchesse of Malfy.*' What I am concerned with here, however, is not imitation or adaptation as such, but the fact of a common tradition.

13. The setting, which had been broken in two in B.M. Add. MS. 29481 and wrongly catalogued, has recently been reassembled by John P. Cutts. He ascribes it, conjecturally, to Johnson. See *Music and Letters,* xxxiii (1952), 333–4.

14. Cf. A. H. Thorndike, 'Influence of the Court-Masque on the Drama, 1608–15,' *P.M.L.A.,* xv (1900), 114–20.

15. Sir John Davies, *Orchestra,* ll. 666–71.

16. There is an admirable discussion of the theme of Union in *Hymenaei* in D. J. Gordon's *Hymenaei:* Ben Jonson's 'Masque of Union,' *Journal of the Warburg and Courtauld Institutes,* viii (1945), 107–45. See esp. pp. 118–19.

17. *Works,* ed. Lucas, iv. 38–39.

18. *The Widow's Tears,* II. iv. 28–31 (in Chapman's *Comedies,* ed. T. M. Parrott, London, 1911).

19. William Painter, *The Palace of Pleasure,* ed. J. Jacobs (London, 1890), iii. 43.

20. One meaning of the device is, of course, to drive the Duchess mad, the irony of the scene being that it has exactly the opposite effect: it leads to terrifying clearness of vision and composure of mind in the Duchess. See Ferdinand's motivation in IV. i. 151–6: 'And ('cause she'll needes be mad) I am resolv'd . . . .' But this still does not explain why the scene was given just the form it has.

21. The most famous *charivari* of all is the one at the French court on 29 January 1393. A wedding was taking place between 'un jeune chevalier de Vermandois' and 'une des damoiselles de la reine,' who was a widow. Disguised as 'hommes sauvages,' King Charles VI and five of his lords suddenly entered the hall of the festivities, making queer gestures, uttering horrible wolfish cries, and performing an antic dance. (Cf. Welsford, *Court Masque,* p. 44.) In the end the masquers caught fire; and though the King himself survived, he never quite recovered from the shock. See Froissart's

account in *Collection des Chroniques Nationales Françaises* . . ., ed. J. A. Buchon (Paris, 1825), xiii. 140–9, particularly Buchon's note, p. 142: 'Le moine anonyme de St. Denis dit que "C'était une coutume pratiquée en divers lieux de la France, de faire impunément mille folies *au mariage des femmes veuves* et d'emprunter avec des habits extravagants la liberté de dire des vilenies au mari et à l'épousée."' (My italics.)

22. Funk and Wagnall, *Standard Dictionary of Folklore, Mythology and Legend* (New York, 1949), i. 212.

23. See E. K. Chambers, *The Medieval Stage* (Oxford, 1903), i. 393.

24. Cf. for example Time in Jonson's masque *Time Vindicated;* or Queen Elizabeth's coronation, when in a pageant 'issued one personage, whose name was Tyme, apparayelled as an olde man, with a scythe in his hand . . .' (J. Nichols, *The Progresses of Queen Elizabeth* (London, 1823), i. 50).

25. Alexander III of Scotland in 1285 married Joleta, daughter of the Count de Dreux. At their marriage-feast in Jedburgh Abbey, 'while a band of maskers danced before the king and queen, Death in the form of a skeleton appeared in their midst and struck terror into spectators and performers alike' (P. Hume Brown, *History of Scotland* (Cambridge, 1902), i. 128–9). Cf. R. Withington, *English Pageantry* (Cambridge, Mass., 1918–20), i. 103.

26. The box containing worm-seed (the pun on the two senses of 'anthelmintic medicine' and 'seed producing maggots' should be noticed, for in the sense of 'medicine' the image is parallel to the subsequent 'salvatory of greene mummey') becomes the paper prison with flies in it, the flimsiness of which was prepared for by the intervening 'puffe-paste.' The paper prison becomes the birdcage (which image has an extra layer of meaning because of its connexion with the actual dramatic situation of the imprisoned Duchess). Each image derives from, but adds to and develops, a preceding image.

27. Cf. also the notion of masque in the last scene of *The White Devil:* Lodovico and Gasparo, 'disguised,' entering to murder Flamineo and Vittoria, introduce themselves ironically: "We have brought you a Maske' (v. vi. 170).

28. See J. A. S. McPeek, *Catullus in Strange and Distant Britain* (Harvard, 1939), ch. vii.

29. Powdering the hair was just coming into fashion in England at this time (F. L. Lucas in *Works,* i. 255).

30. That Jonson had most likely misinterpreted his source-books and made a mistake when he described the Roman bride as having her hair strewn with grey does not alter the argument (see my note on *Hymenaei, N. & Q.,* cci (1956), 510–11).

31. It need hardly be said that the parallel death-bed/bridal-bed is often drawn on in the drama of these years. The most spectacular instance is perhaps in *The Maid's Tragedy,* II. i, where the deserted Aspatia helps to put Evadne to bed, the two women being played off against each other as 'bed' against 'bier.' It was such exquisite horror that was inherited from the Jacobeans by Beddoes—see, for example, *Death's Jest Book,* IV. iii. 230–57

(ed. H. W. Donner, London, 1950), where Athulf sings a song intended to be simultaneously his own dirge and his beloved's epithalamium:

A cypress-bough, and a rose-wreath sweet,
A wedding-robe, and a winding-sheet,
A bridal-bed and a bier.

. . . . . .

Death and Hymen both are here.

But one might note that the parallel, or contrast, could also be used in the most matter-of-fact manner:

Lift up thy modest head,
Great and fair bride; and as a well-taught soul
Calls not for Death, nor doth controul
Death when he comes, come thou unto this bed.

(Sir Henry Goodere, 'Epithalamion of the Princess' Marriage,' 1613; in *English Epithalamies,* ed. R. H. Case, London, 1896.)

JOHN DANBY

Beaumont and Fletcher: Jacobean Absolutists

After all, Beaumont and Fletcher were but an inferior sort of Shakespeares and Sidneys.

C. LAMB, *Specimens of an English Dramatic Poetry*. Note on *Maid's Tragedy*

CHARLES LAMB's judgment is not likely to be reversed however much the plays of Beaumont and Fletcher are re-read or re-assessed. But something less than justice is done them if the Shakespeare comparison is made prematurely or in the wrong way. In any such comparison they will naturally come out on the wrong side; and they have rarely been read without the motive of comparison in mind. Coleridge, for example, wrote:

> The plays of Beaumont and Fletcher are mere agregations without unity; in the Shakespearian drama there is a vitality which grows and evolves itself from within—a key-note which guides and controls the harmonies throughout.[1]

And Lamb:

> Fletcher's ideas moved slow; his versification, though sweet, is tedious; it stops every moment; he lays line upon line, making up one after the other, adding image to image so deliberately that we see where they join: Shakespeare mingles everything, he runs line into line, embarrasses sentences and metaphors; before one idea has burst its shell another is hatched and clamours for inclusion.[2]

From *Poets on Fortune's Hill* (London: Faber and Faber, 1952), pp. 152–83. Reprinted by permission of the publisher and the author.

The more recent reports on their work are in much the same vein. On the question of dramatic workmanship generally Miss Ellis-Fermor repeats Coleridge's charge: Beaumont and Fletcher sacrifice everything to situation and immediate effect.[3] Lamb's criticism of their verse has been made again, in other words, by Mr. T. S. Eliot: imagery in the Beaumont and Fletcher verse amounts merely to dead flowers of speech planted in sand.[4] Neither as dramatists nor as poets do they seem to have the roots that clutch. Yet at the beginning of this century Shakespeare's last plays were commonly regarded as having been strongly influenced by Beaumont and Fletcher.[5] And at any time after the death of James I (Fletcher too died in 1625) something like the following comparisons would be made by the polite and instructed reader:

When Jonson, Shakespeare, and thyself did sit,
And sway'd in the triumvirate of Wit,
Yet what from Jonson's oil and sweat did flow,
Or what more easy Nature did bestow
On Shakespeare's gentler muse, in thee full grown
Their graces both appear; yet so, that none
Can say, here Nature ends and Art begins;
But mixt, like th'elements, and born like twins.[6]

Denham need carry no authority, but he is a reminder of the Caroline rating which, as a phenomenon of taste and choice, calls for understanding. There was a time when Beaumont and Fletcher seemed the universal geniuses, combining qualities which avoided on the one hand Jonson's laboured calculation of effect and on the other Shakespeare's merely random happiness:

Manners and scenes may alter, but not you;
For yours are not mere humours, gilded strains;
The fashion lost, your massy sense remains.[7]

The judgment is no doubt a mental aberration. But it was broadspread in the seventeenth century, typical of a class and a time.

I propose now to look at the position Beaumont and Fletcher occupied in their contemporary world; then, to examine what they actually did in one of their serious plays; finally, bearing in mind their present-day neglect, when practically all the other Jacobeans have had their vogue, to hazard a fresh placing of their work from the point of view of a modern observer.

I

The social positioning of Beaumont and Fletcher has often been noticed. So has the timing of their appearance. The provenance of what they put into their plays has also been commented on. What is most lacking, in their case, would seem to be that which is most needed—the linking of these things significantly, so as to make possible the right groupings and the appropriate comparisons.

Professor A. Harbage has pointed to their special position among dramatists of their time:

> In the reign of James a greater number of the writers seem to have been gentlemen by birth, but there is no change in the status of their occupation. Typical of this group was John Fletcher, well-born, and well-nurtured but *déclassé*; he lacked patrimony, his father had died in debt and in royal disfavour. Most dedicatory epistles . . . were suggestive of mendicancy, and could scarcely be written by the gentle according to the strictures of the day. The one true exception to our rule is Francis Beaumont, his father a judge in a family still prospering. But Francis was a younger son. . . .[8]

The best sketch of Bishop Fletcher and son (Harrington only portrays the father) is given by Bishop Goodman, that anxious whitener of sepulchres wherever possible:

> Doctor Fletcher, dean of Peterborough, he was made almoner and Bishop of Bristol . . . he was afterwards preferred to London; and there he married my Lady Baker, a very handsome, beautiful woman. . . . Here many libels were made against him: I remember part of one of them:
>
> *We will divide the name of Fletcher;*
> *He, my Lord F.; and she, my Lady Letcher.*
>
> I think he had a check from the Queen, and died for sorrow. His son was a poet to a playhouse.[9]

Bishop Goodman's professional charity was apt to fail when confronted with failure. He obviously regarded the son's career as a fitting appendage to the father's disgrace. Harington is kinder to the man by including in his contempt most of the courtier-Bishop's contemporaries:

> What shall I say for him? *Non erat hoc hominis vitium sed temporis?* [10]

The original judgment of Lamb at the head of this chapter may be more fully understood in a social than in a literary sense (though it has the literary implication too). It is important either way that Beaumont and Fletcher had a Bishop and a Judge for their fathers and not a bricklayer or a small country-tradesman. The Great House, however, was not around them, as it was around Sidney: they were, after all, an inferior sort of Sidneys. The Great House was some distance away behind them, or, as an ambition, some distance in front of them: Beaumont actually did marry well and retire from the stage; Fletcher had to be content with the playhouse and the Mermaid. These he maybe succeeded in converting into something agreeable to the court *élite*—an urban substitute for Wilton and Penshurst.

The precise social placing of Beaumont and Fletcher carried with it specific differences of endowment and interest and intention as compared with those with which the popular dramatist worked. Something more, however, must be added. Beaumont and Fletcher were inferior Sidneys of the second generation. The work done within the Great House itself is different from that work which is based on it (as 'literature') but which is actually done outside its walls by persons whose right of admittance might be a matter for conjecture, for a public that would certainly, in most cases, be excluded. The distinctions are not merely snobbish. The declension is real. In Sidney's day the Great House had been a centre of culture in its own right, independent of the Court. Sidney draws a picture of it in the opening pages of the *Arcadia*—itself a typical achievement of the Great House in literature. There Lord Kalander can comment critically and with sharp detachment on the sillinesses of King Basilius, who, in leaving his palace and shirking his responsibilities, has fallen away from the standards the Great House expected the Palace to uphold. The Great House and its literature (the *Arcadia, The Faerie Queene*, the Pastorals, and the petrarchan sonnet-sequences) belonged to the polite Renaissance and to something consciously European. Its works were to stand comparison with those of Greece and Rome, France and Italy; epics in prose or verse compendiously analysing love and the ideal man. Beaumont and Fletcher take over from this tradition the matter of the Arcadian and pastoral and petrarchan, together with the conscious intention of the Great House to achieve literature—the intention, as it becomes with them in fact, to make the popular drama literary. In their case, however, the declension has to be reckoned in: a twofold degeneration, what Harrington would see as *vitium hominis et temporis*.

The Jacobean phase can best be seen, as the Victorians saw it, in a sinister light. In both politics and letters the Court asserted itself disastrously, to upset a precarious balance. James's claim to the kingly prerogative was not the attempt to retain something which had been granted Elizabeth. It was a bid for something Elizabeth herself had never pretended to, and which (on the terms maintained by James) had never existed. The structure behind Elizabeth's rule had been a confederation of Great Houses. Her power was merely the exertion in a single person of the reason, the competence, the influence, and the desert upon which this confederation (ideally) based itself. In the person of James the Court usurped the place the Great House had occupied. Thereby what Greville called 'the strong middle wall' was broken. Looking at the disgusting shambles of James's dramatic entertainment for the King of Denmark, Harrington remarked that it was different 'in our Queen's days.'[11] Commenting more widely, a Lord Kalander could have noted almost item by item how James was behaving like Basilius in his dotage. This political depression of the Great House and the values it represented is paralleled in the literary field by James's taking over the Chamberlain's men and making them King's Players, and by his attaching other of the actors' companies to the Queen and the Prince. The influence of the Court seems to have vulgarized both the politics and the literature of the Great House. It coarsened the technique of government and perverted taste.

It is this that makes the timing of Beaumont and Fletcher as important as the placing. The *déclassé* son of the Bishop and the younger son of the Judge are James's unconscious agents. They are capturing the Great House literature for the courtier, writing for adherents of a Stuart king rather than for Tudor aristocrats. Their work, from one point of view, represents a snobbish vulgarization and a sectional narrowing of the great tradition.

In this Beaumont and Fletcher are not alone, nor are they unrespectable. They occupy very much the same social and literary position as Donne. Donne himself was a marginal beneficiary of the Great House tradition, who survived, depressed and now utterly dependent, to write subserviently under the conditions inaugurated by James.

Donne in his *Satyres* can claim rightly:

> *With God and with the Muses I conferre.*[12]

Or again:

On a huge hill,
Cragged, and steep, Truth stands...
Keep the truth which thou hast found; men do not stand
In so ill case here, that God with his hand
Sign'd Kings blanck-charters to kill whom they hate,
Nor are they Vicars but hangmen to Fate.[13]

This has the tone and independence of Kalander and the Great House. In *The Sunne Rising* (still in the pre-Jacobean period) Donne can also write:

If her eyes have not blinded thine,
Looke, and tomorrow late, tell mee,
Whether both th'India's of spice and Myne
Be where thou left'st them, or lie here with mee.
Aske for those Kings whom thou saw'st yesterday,
And thou shalt heare, All here in one bed lay.
She is all States, and all Princes, I,
Nothing else is.
Princes doe but play us; compar'd to this,
All honor's mimique; All wealth alchimie.[14]

It is the same Donne that writes the *Satyres* and *Songs and Sonets.* In the *Satyres* he takes his stand on truth and his own independent experience, on a kind of dignity which he feels due both to God and the Muse. In *Songs and Sonets,* in spite of the different content, there is a similar tone. *The Sunne Rising* gets an immediate sanction. It has tenderness, playfulness, impatience, and pride, vigorous courage and tough reasonableness. Its components, matched with hyperbole and conceit, lie well together with each other and with the form in which they are expressed. One feels confident that the poet would put things in right order of priority. Even the final hyperbole is not a lie, or a merely poetic truth. Hyperbole will eventually become one of the main Jacobean vehicles of self-persuasion: here it is the witty stretching of plain sense in order to take in more truth:

She is all States, and all Princes, I,
Nothing else is.

—'She is all the States I care about and am a loyal member of; and I am sole ruler as well as subject in this State, complete servant and complete King. Nothing else is—is important, is as much, is so completely known.'—The 'over'-statement that is presented to a first glance as an extravagance resolves itself, on a second glance, into an interesting exploration of what is generally accepted and acceptable. The effect is carried by the rich ambiguities of 'is,' itself capable of meaning everything or nothing: everything if we regard it as saying 'has real Being,' nothing if we see it as needing always an extension before it can mean anything; everything and nothing as it means 'is' or 'seems.'

'Is' and 'seems' and the ambiguities playing through them set up a frame that contains what immediately follows—with its almost unnoticeable inversion of what Dr. Richards has called *vehicle* and *tenour:*

Princes doe but play us; compar'd to this,
All honor's mimique; All wealth alchimie.

—Love is both an assertion and a surrender of the will, a resolved belief and a rapture. Rule, honours, and token currency are secondary phenomena, social shadows or derivatives or a language for or an expression of the primary society which two lovers form. None of them can stand in their own right, or can be so immediately known, as love can, to be more than provisionally true. They are means not ends. Their usurpation of the central position in the world would be a perverse tyranny. They command not belief, but, at the most acquiescence; their claim over us is felt not as a rapture but as coercion. Again the hyperbole is on the surface only: the direction in which it works is towards an interesting exploration of sense.

In all this Donne is in the great tradition of Sidney. He writes as the poet above the need or the desire to sing at doors for meat, as the poet exploring truth and investigating the metaphysic of love: love not as a petrarchan convention but as the key to what conventions are about. Within ten years the tone and truth of Donne's verse change. The 'truth' he was dedicated to in the *Satyres* becomes the fabrication of the compliments he there despised. The mistresses of the *Songs and Sonets* become the patronesses of the *Verse Letters.* There the riches of 'mine' and 'India,' 'America' and 'coins,' become suddenly concretized to the moneys he desperately needed:

She that was best and first originall
Of all fair copies, and the generall
Steward to Fate; she whose rich eyes, and breast,

Guilt the West Indies, and perfum'd the East;
Whose having breath'd in this world, did bestow
Spice on those Isles, and bade them still smell so,
And that rich Indie which doth gold interre,
Is but as single money, coyn'd from her:
She to whom this world must itself refer,
As Suburbs, or the Microcosme of her,
Shee, shee is dead; shee's dead: when thou knowst this,
Thou knowst how lame a cripple this world is.[15]

Donne here is adding image to image rather than writing poetry; and the imagery is repetitious, commercial, mercenary. What he says, furthermore, is now felt as only poetically true. The hyperboles do not extend sense: they balance permissively on a convention or a fashion of compliment.

Beaumont and Fletcher provoke comparison with the later Donne. *Non erat hoc hominis vitium sed temporis.* They are involved in the same degeneration of a tradition, impelled by similar bread-and-butter needs. It was economic pressure that deflected Donne from the metaphor of *Songs and Sonets* to the conceits of the *Anniversaries.* It was the urge of the younger son to exploit the India of the stage, the desire of the *déclassé* to rehabilitate himself in court circles (the memory and the ambition of the Great House still working in each of them) which drove Beaumont and Fletcher to descend on the popular theatre and wrest it from its popular way to something they could approve of and make their social equals applaud. This of course makes their descent on the playhouse much more consciously a social strategy than in all likelihood it was. There is, however, the fact that two of the earliest plays they wrote were, first, a burlesque of what the popular audience approved, *The Knight of the Burning Pestle* which was not well received, and second, *The Faithful Shepherdess,* a literary pastoral of which Fletcher wrote to one of James's new baronets:

This play was never liked, unless by few
That brought their judgments with 'em. [16]

Compared with the tradition digested naturally into the drama of Shakespeare the Sidneian world is itself a narrow thing. It is conscious and classical and avoids contacts with what in the *Arcadia* would be called the Helots. The world of Beaumont and Fletcher is still narrower. The difference is that between Penshurst and Wilton and the Court or Blackfriars. The former were European and national at the same time. The latter became something local and sectional.

Beaumont and Fletcher's social affiliations, then, are the same as Donne's; their literary tradition goes back on one side, but on the new Jacobean terms, to the Elizabethan Great House. They operate at a time when the tradition is already degenerating; they are themselves, in fact, prime agents in the degeneration—in the adaptation of platonism and petrarchanism to an inferior end and audience. Their ambition and their strategy can be represented as being a twofold invasion. On the one hand they will capture the popular playhouse, on the other they will gate-crash court society. The Sidneian matter supplied protective colouring for the latter; their dramatic facility ensured success in the former. Their work is brilliantly opportunistic. They are quick to catch and reflect back the lights of their social and literary environment. But they are not to be regarded solely as followers of fashions and tastes. Their social significance in the early Jacobean period goes deeper. They had the power to be formers of attitudes, initiators rather than mimics. They supplied the basis of what will later develop into the Cavalier mentality. In this respect their work can be compared with that of Byron. Later people—not in literature but in actual life—play out Beaumont-and-Fletcherism in their own biographies. Kenelm Digby is one of their heroes in the flesh. The early part of Herbert of Cherbury's autobiography reads like one of their plays.

It is evasive, therefore, to regard their art as merely the creation of a 'fairy world.' [17] Their plays strike roots deep into a real world—the world of their time and of the embryonic Cavalier. Their 'unreality' for us amounts to a criticism of much more than the two dramatists concerned. It is a judgment too of the habits of mind of an actual section of a historical society—a world, in spite of its heritage of charity from the Middle Ages and of instructed reason from the Great House, soon to be confronted with the situation of dictated choice in the midst of civil conflict, a world of radical self-division and clashing absolutes: the world ready to split in every way which Beaumont and Fletcher's serious plays symbolize.

We might turn now to one of these serious plays. Our purpose will be to look for signs of consistency and method. Our leading idea will be, they are not organized, as Shakespeare's plays are, by metaphor—'a key-note which guides and controls the harmonies throughout'—

but rather by that which organizes Donne's *Anniversaries*, the hyperbole and the conceit. And it is the experience organized by hyperbole and conceit which strikes the roots that clutch Beaumont and Fletcher's time. What these roots were we shall also attempt to say.

II

The central situation in *Philaster* involves three people. Arethusa, the princess, is the only child of the King. Philaster, legitimate heir to part of the Kingdom, is in love with her. Bellario is Philaster's 'page,' sent by him to Arethusa to serve as their means of communication. The events of the play are set in motion by the arrival, at the Court, of Pharamond, the Spanish prince, who comes seeking the hand of Arethusa. This touches off, first, the rebellion story: the group of courtiers led by Dion are unwilling for Philaster's legitimate claims to be put on one side, as Philaster himself is too. Secondly, Pharamond's incontinence while at the Court (the reverse side, as in *Songs and Sonets*, of the idealistic petrarchan woman-worship) leads to the calumny which will start rotating the relations between the three in the central triangle. Pharamond is discovered early in his stay with a loose waiting-woman who avoids publicity by accusing Arethusa of similar looseness with Bellario, and thus blackmails the King into silence. This lie is repeated to Philaster by Dion. Dion is intent on Philaster's leading the popular revolt and breaking with Arethusa.

A larger frame is sketchily suggested for the central happenings in the play: the King, like Henry IV, is aware of the guilty means whereby he has come to the throne and is depriving Philaster of his just inheritance. He sees his misfortunes as part of a providential punishment for his sins. Arethusa too feels that providence is at work—in her case, a providence working through romantic love for the restoration of justice.

The retention of this traditional providence supervising the working out of the plot might be significant. It is not what we think of as the typically Beaumont-and-Fletcherian. It seems rather to be a gesture in the direction of something Shakespearian. (Philaster is moved by the spirit of his 'father' as Hamlet was, and the King's guilty conscience is reminiscent of Claudius as well as Henry IV.) Though the King, Arethusa, and the courtiers more than once underline it in their speeches, it might be intended merely as a familiar colouring for the story, the better to insinuate what was essentially new. The references to providence, in any case, belong to the outer shell of the play. The inner core, wherein the novelty consists, and in which the main seriousness of the dramatists is displayed, is the platonic or petrarchan triangle of the lovers. It is the happenings here that I propose to concentrate attention on. These provide almost all the 'situations' and 'dramatic effects' to which Beaumont and Fletcher are said to sacrifice everything: coherence of character, moral integrity, artistic unity.

The basis of the emotional attitudes throughout is a prevailing disposition to wilful belief, belief as an all-or-nothing reaction, consciously directed, an absolute self-commitment. The typical Beaumont and Fletcher situations turn on the divisions that such rival absolutes bring about when the central characters find themselves between two or more of them.

In *Philaster* (as in the plays generally) one of these absolutes is the King. At one point in the play the King's absoluteness is given a satiric or comic turn. The princess Arethusa is lost in the forest and her father is commanding that she shall be found:

KING. *I do command you all, as you are subjects,*
To show her me! What! am I not your King?
If ay, then am I not to be obeyed?
DION. *Yes, if you command things possible and honest.*
KING. *Things possible and honest! Hear me, thou,*
Thou traitor, that do'st confine thy King to things
Possible and honest! show her me,
Or let me perish if I cover not
All Sicily with blood.
DION. *Indeed I cannot,*
Unless you tell me where she is. (IV. ii.)

But brute facts call the King's bluff and he is forced at length to realize his limitations:

Alas! What are we Kings!
Why do ye gods place us above the rest,
To be served, flattered, and adored, till we
Believe we hold within our hands your thunder,
And when we come to try the power we have
There's not a leaf shakes at our threatenings?
I have sinned, 'tis true, and here stand to be punished
Yet would not thus be punished: let me choose

My way, and lay it on!

DION. *He articles with the gods. Would somebody would draw bonds for the performance of covenants betwixt them.* (IV. ii.)

We have said that this passage is comic or satiric. To be so definitive is maybe over-precipitate. There seems, rather, to be a mixture, or a confusion, or a wavering between intentions in its treatment. Clearly, however, the scene cannot be claimed for full seriousness. The King is not Lear, and Dion is neither Kent nor the Fool. The significant thing is the way the characters fling themselves into disparate roles, adopting one extreme stance after another with all-or-nothing wilfulness. The roles have nothing in common except the wilfulness behind them. The King will be absolute King, the King will be patient sinner suffering the strokes of the gods. Dion (who could have been made a Lord Kalander or a Kent) remains the debunking commentator on both, not disinterested but uninterested in what he says. Neither Dion nor the King seem to have anything in common, not even common humanity, nor the common relationship of King and subject. Instead, they both seem to be embodiments, as it were, of the attitudes they voice—attitudes, again, that the romantics would accuse of having no organic interconnection, and between which transition can only be made by violent self-galvanizations of the will.

If the scene itself is not to be taken seriously, the frequent occurrence of such scenes in the plays must be. It is profoundly symptomatic of Beaumont. Though he is not being clearly satirical or comic, and while the total effect is too confused for full artistic seriousness, there is no doubt that seriousness is intended. The point is that Beaumont's mind works like the minds of his characters, and he is involved in quandaries similar to theirs. He lacks the supporting strength of an independent position from which to see with detachment what he is writing about. Sidney had this strength and support through membership of the Great House: his portrait of Basilius, therefore, is steady and unequivocal. Jonson and Shakespeare had the strength and independence of yet another tradition which enabled them to comment on Kingship, in plays like *Sejanus* or *King Lear,* with equal unmistakeability. Beaumont has no steady ground to stand on. His attitude to the King, therefore (to take the single example of this scene) inevitably wavers. Beaumont himself is surrounded by the clamorous absolutes which have to be chosen among and which it is nonsense to choose among. But choice is dictated for him. He is himself deeply engaged in the attitudes he is writing about, and in the attitude of mind which makes 'attitudes' important. He is responding deeply to something in his environment. He is a part of his contemporary situation in a pejorative sense.

There is also the fact of Beaumont's adolescence which is relevant here. His concern with attitudes and choice is adolescent—the adolescent as the parvenu to the adult world who brings with him all the virgin will to be convinced, but who has not yet had the time to acquire the wisdom that would illuminate what he is choosing and bring relevant order to his convictions. Beaumont and Fletcher's work indicates the collapse of a culture, an adult scheme is being broken up and replaced by adolescent intensities. It is this which makes the Caroline rating of their work, as compared with that of Jonson and Shakespeare, such a bad augury.

The scene with Dion and the King is about as bad as Beaumont and Fletcher can be. It does, however, reveal the kind of forces among which even their good scenes are set, and the kind of 'situation' we have to deal with in reading them. These 'situations' have much to do with 'psychology,' but little to do with the naturalism of consistent character-portrayal. The psychology is that of a blind compulsion to be certain and to be convinced. It is the psychology, too, of a time when action was demanded on the basis of the conviction entertained; and when loyalties were being solicited by widely different authorities.

Kingship is only one of the absolutes in the general Beaumont and Fletcher environment. They are not interested in assessment of any of the absolutes separately, and are weakest when they pretend to be. Their best work is done where their main interest lies—in the conflict of the absolutes and the contortions it imposes on human nature.

In Act I, Scene i, this typical inner setting is swiftly arranged. Philaster comes into the Presence to challenge Pharamond's right to replace him as heir to the throne. He begins by making his obeisances to the King:

Right noble sir, as low as my obedience,
And with a heart as loyal as my knee
I beg your favour.

The King gives him permission, within the bounds proper to a subject, to say what he will. Philaster then immediately turns on Pharamond, and threatens him with hyperbolical rebellion if ever he should take the throne. The King intervenes to check him; Philaster's defiance collapses:

I am dead, sir; you're my fate. It was not I
Said I was wronged.

The King thinks Philaster must be possessed. Philaster rejoins that he is possessed—and with his father's spirit:

It's here, O King,
A dangerous spirit! now he tells me, King,
I was a King's heir, bids me be a King,
And whispers to me, these are all my subjects . . .
But I'll suppress him; he's a factious spirit,
And will undo me. Noble sir, your hand;
I am your servant.
KING. *Away! I do not like this:*
I'll make you tamer, or I'll dispossess you
Both of your life and spirit. For this time
I pardon your wild speech, without so much
As your imprisonment.

There is no suggestion of satire here. The King is one of the absolutes Philaster recognizes. The demands of justice (the 'spirit' of his father) are another. But there is no moral conflict in Philaster. He can live absolutely in either the one loyalty or the other. It is a law of the Beaumont world that absolute committal removes the need for moral deliberation, and supervenes on conflict by suppression of one of the warring terms. The courtiers, Philaster's friends, for example, are bent on revolt:

shrink not, worthy sir,
But add your father to you; in whose name
We'll waken all the gods, and conjure up
The rods of vengeance, the abused people,
Who, like raging torrents . . .

But Philaster does not so much as feel the pressure of their rhetoric:

Friends, no more;
Our ears may be corrupted; 'tis an age
We dare not trust our wills to.

The audience is left, at the end of this first scene, with an exciting sense of an either-or world, and of a hero who will be all-or-nothing whichever way he is thrown: for it is obvious he won't (in the normal sense of the word) decide. There is this, and a further sense besides—something that comes through in Philaster's words last quoted: the sense that this is not only literary entertainment, but literature aware of itself as a symptom rather than a reflection of the dangerous reality surrounding it—aware of a world that cannot be trusted, and in which the mind is forced back upon itself to make a world of its own, by belief, or resolve, or art:

> *'tis an age*
> *We dare not give our wills to.*

The other sphere in which the absolutes manifest themselves for the Beaumont hero we are introduced to in the scene immediately following. Arethusa sends for Philaster. Up to now neither he nor the audience have had any inkling of what is to take place. But Arethusa is in love with Philaster. The scene is a minor example of the stunts with situation which characterize all the Beaumont and Fletcher plays: the subject cannot woo the princess, so the princess will declare her love to the subject. More than this, it is an interesting example of Beaumont's technique exerting itself on a more serious level. Its congruency with what has gone before it and with what will follow after helps to credibilize the incredibles later to be handled.

Arethusa's inversion of propriety is justified by invoking the overruling power of the gods. She is driven by forces larger than human:

> *'tis the gods,*
> *The gods that make me so; and, sure, our love*
> *Will be the nobler and the better blest,*
> *In that the secret justice of the gods*
> *Is mingled with it.* (I. ii.)

But this divine sanction is in fact supererogatory: love itself is an absolute for the Beaumont and Fletcher lovers.

Secondly, there is the teasing way in which the proposal is made. Philaster assumes (the audience is already aware of what is in Arethusa's mind) that a declaration of love is the last thing that will be made in the interview. And Arethusa's first words seem to bear out his fears. Why, she asks, has he laid scandal on her in a public place, and called the great part of her dowry in question? Philaster's reply is similar to his original reaction to the King:

Madam, this truth which I shall speak will be
Foolish; but for your fair and virtuous self,
I could afford myself to have no right
To anything you wished.

Notwithstanding, Philaster confesses he is loath to give

His right unto a sceptre and a crown
To save a lady's longing.

He is still unaware that Arethusa is in love with him. Arethusa then says she must have both kingdoms, and even more. Philaster must turn away his face while she tells him the full length of her demands. At this Philaster flies into heroics:

I can endure it. Turn away my face!
I never yet saw enemy that looked
So dreadfully but that I thought myself
So great a basilisk as he; or spake
So horribly but that I thought my tongue
Bore thunder underneath, as much as his;
Nor beast that I could turn from: shall I then
Begin to fear sweet sounds? a lady's voice
Whom I do love? Say, you would have my life;
Why, I will give it you; for 'tis to me
A thing so loathed, and unto you that ask
Of so poor use, that I will make no price:
If you entreat I will unmovedly hear.

This is wit according to Dr. Johnson's formula: contrary ideas yoked together by violence. It is witty in that what the audience knows is love on Arethusa's part, Philaster takes to be hate; what he thinks is a demand about to be made on him the audience knows is an offer about to be made to him. Philaster's misapprehension has been successfully raised at this point to hyperbolical proportions. And in one and the same speech we see his heroism and his helplessness, his worth and his sense of worthlessness asserted.

But a measure of depth and seriousness can be recognized in the admittedly adolescent mood in which the hero and the scene are conceived. The part somehow seems to become greater than the whole, the contortions of the hero more important than the forces that produce them. The fact that Philaster is labouring under a misapprehension does not make for complacency in the spectator; and the heroics—on a fair reading—are not received as ridiculous. From this point of view the scene works like a joke that has been pushed too far: except that it never has been a joke. Arethusa's apparently teasing lack of straightforwardness is in keeping with her situation. She must be assured that Philaster would in any case give himself utterly before she can offer herself utterly to him. The point is in that 'utterly'—the adolescent all-or-nothing terms in which the commitments are conceived.

The scene in any case works two ways. There is the joke that it will all have a happy ending. There is also the sense, fatal to our taking the joke at its face value, that happiness as a conclusion to what the scene reveals is an irrelevance. Philaster's heroic and pathetic self-contortion, his insistent readiness to give himself utterly (misapprehension or no) to love or death, are part of a tragi-comedy that cannot really be happy.

There is a final aspect of the Beaumont and Fletcher manner which this scene illustrates, a factor which still further assists belief in Philaster's reactions later. This is the monadic self-enclosure of the characters—part of the petrarchan convention of love, or a part of the native adolescence of Beaumont's mind. The lover can be completely insulated within his love, regardless of the beloved. Love is not necessarily a mutual contract, it can be a private direction of the will, like prayer; or a service, like virtue, that justifies itself by being its own reward. This quality comes out in the scene when Arethusa has finally confessed her love to Philaster, and he replies:

Madam, you are too full of noble thoughts
To lay a train for this contemned life,
Which you may have for asking: to suspect
Were base, where I deserve no ill. Love you!
By all my hopes, I do, above my life!
But how this passion should proceed from you
So violently, would amaze a man
That would be jealous.

The world of Beaumont is a violent, extreme, arbitrary, sudden, and wilful thing, ready at any moment to be inverted, or to swing from one contrary to another. We have seen how the external plot is arranged so that opposite pulls can be exerted at any minute on the main characters, and how—with Philaster in the first scene—the loyalty of the subject is absolute but never complete, since it can only be maintained by an actively willed suppression of the disloyalty he also shares in. Here, the opposites are introjected into the heart of what might seem the only single certainty and purity the Beaumont lovers can find. Love itself, in the moment of its most open and utter declaration, is recognized to be an incalculable force, ambivalently sinister in its possibilities: binding and yet disruptive:

> *how this passion should proceed from you*
> *So violently, would amaze a man*
> *That would be jealous.*

Philaster sees the chaste and hitherto inaccessible model of womanhood suddenly proposing to him. He is overwhelmed, but of course ready to accept. In the midst of his confusion he is able to note the possible ambiguity of Arethusa's behaviour for an interpreter that '*would* be jealous.' His 'amazement' is another stroke of wit, and an oddly serious one. He loved Arethusa apart from any hope of reciprocation: in spite of her impossibility and almost because of it. (The 'psychology' is the same here as in Marvell's poem.) Now that the Impossible She is so possible, the possibility might itself argue an imperfection. Philaster will love her, of course, on the new terms still. But these will require suppression of the interpretation just glimpsed. A fresh tension is thereby introduced. And when Arethusa is calumniated, as she is soon to be, the scales will tilt again, the disruption will begin, and inverted pertrarchanism show itself in near-obscenity and disgust of life. The conception in this scene prepares us to accept Philaster's subsequent misbelief of Arethusa.

It is a scene well contrived within the limits of the initial sonneteerish postulates. It might even be claimed to carry more conviction then Leontes' jealousy, or the somersault of Posthumus; though, it must be added, Shakespeare was not really interested in the postulates Beaumont adopted, and does not seem to have bothered overmuch with the mechanics appropriate to them.

Act II springs the trap which has been prepared for Philaster's love. Arethusa is accused of intimacy with Bellario, the Viola-like page Philaster sent her. (In justice to Beaumont's workmanship it might be pointed out that again we have been prepared for the sort of thing the calumniators report: In Act II, Scene iv, misconduct with pages is represented as almost habitual in court circles.) Act III is devoted to Philaster's reception of the report, his interview with Bellario (who is in love with him) and his encounter with Arethusa herself.

Close analysis of this act (a most effective one) would not carry insight into Beaumont's technique much further. There is no increment of growing wisdom in the situation as it develops. Beaumont's plays, in fact, have no developing revelations, crowded as they are with surprises and fresh turns. For all the increasing violence and cleverness of their movement they seem to get nowhere. The return is always to the original starting-point: the petrarchan nexus, the adolescent all-or-nothingness, the willed and rigid stance on one set of assumptions maintained by the resolved suppression of another, the sense of an arbitrary outer world and a dissociated inner one, of rifts that cannot be bridged but must be desperately overleapt, the mêlée of absolute claims and exaggerated postures—an agony of self-scission based on misapprehension and brought back (by the external contrivances of the plot) to a 'happy' conclusion: a curious sense, typical of decadence, of something at once more primitive and more sophisticated than the normal.

But while it does not further insight into the essential Beaumont situation Act III is a good example of what we have called the 'extended conceit.' This is particularly true of the scene between Philaster and Bellario.

Philaster has just received his friend Dion's account of Arethusa's scandalous behaviour. He is soliloquising on the theme 'What the eye doesn't see'; how, for animals, nothing is but what is seen; but for man, nothing is (at times) but what is not:

O that like beasts we could not grieve ourselves
With what we see not! Bulls and rams will fight
To keep their females, standing in their sight:
But take 'em from them and you take at once
Their spleens away; and they will fall again
Unto their pastures; growing fresh and fat;
And taste the waters of the springs as sweet
As 'twas before, finding no start in sleep;
But miserable man— (III. i.)

—and at this point Bellario enters. The rest of the speech (it can be imagined well enough) will be demonstrated in action on the stage rather than compressed into metaphor. Philaster is amazed that Bellario, the monster of lust and ingratitude, should still look outwardly the same as he has always done:

See, see, you gods,
He walks still; and the face you let him wear
When he was innocent is still the same,
Not blasted! Is this justice? do you mean
To intrap mortality, that you allow
Treason so smooth a brow? I cannot now
Think he is guilty.

The speech carries on the ruminations of the soliloquy. It works too a kind of trick with intellectual mirrors, animating all the confusions between 'is' and 'seems' in which mortality can so easily entrap itself, precipitating Philaster into the midst of these confusions, where he finds himself choosing again—hurling himself on the desperate other side of the gulf he has opened out before himself: he cannot now think Bellario is guilty. The volte-face is well executed, and restores both sides of Philaster's self-division to equal status; the prerequisite for Beaumont's strongest occasions.

The remainder of the scene is constructed wittily along similar lines. Beaumont exploits fully the device of double-consciousness (or even double-talk) which is expressive of something central in his conception. The divided man confronts the integral, and mistakes it. Bellario is really innocent. Philaster thinks instead he is the consummate actor of innocence. Philaster will therefore act the part to compete with this, and hoist the engineer with his own petard. The mirror effects begin to multiply.

Philaster inquires how Bellario has been treated while with Arethusa:

Tell me, my boy, how doth the princess use thee?
For I shall guess her love to me by that.

Bellario gives his innocent account of all Arethusa's favours. Philaster is caught by the reviving shock of his love and disgust. He recovers and presses Bellario harder. We are shown the familiar reverse side of petrarchan idealism. The catastrophic overthrow of his love (only possible by reason of his 'noble' mind and the 'virtue' it would espouse) releases an unmanageable and compulsive evil within him. Philaster is as much bound now to the most squalid prurience as he was formerly to the chastest adoration. And the agent of his overthrow, whom he would make the pander to his itch for obscenities, is the innocent 'page' he regards as his greatest friend, and who (beneath it all) is really a girl faithfully in love with him—and thus doubly incapable of disloyalty. It is easy to see what the generation which produced the metaphysicals saw in such scenes as this. It is the 'conceit' perfectly stage-managed, without the overt imagery of conceit:

PHIL. *She kisses thee?*
BEL. *Not so, my lord.*
PHIL. *Come, come, I know she does.*
BEL. *No, by my life.*
PHIL. *Why then she does not love me. Come, she does:*
I bade her do it; I charged her by all charms
Of love between us, by the hope of peace
We should enjoy, to yield thee all delights
Naked as to her bed; I took her oath
Thou should'st enjoy her. Tell me, gentle boy,
Is she not parallelless? is not her breath
Sweet as Arabian winds when fruits are ripe?
Are not her breasts two liquid ivory balls?
Is she not all a lasting mine of joy?
BEL. *Ay, now I see why my disturbed thoughts*
Were so perplexed: when first I went to her
My heart held augury. You are abused;
Some villain hath abused you: I do see
Whereto you tend. Fall rocks upon his head
That put this to you! 'tis some subtle train
To bring that noble frame of yours to nought.
PHIL. *Thou think'st I will be angry with thee. Come,*
Thou shalt know all my drift; I hate her more
Than I love happiness, and placed thee there
To pry with narrow eyes into her deeds.
Hast thou discovered? is she fallen to lust,
As I would wish her? Speak some comfort to me.
BEL. *My lord, you did mistake the boy you sent:*
Had she the lust of sparrows or of goats,
Had she a sin that way, hid from the world,
Beyond the name of lust, I would not aid
Her base desires: but what I came to know
As servant to her, I would not reveal,
To make my life last ages.

The code of Honour sets a final and inescapable trap for its observers. Absolute loyalty forbids any telling of tales, even when a friend or a lover commands. Honour itself can thus ally with deception. Philaster has to proceed to threats:

oh, my heart!
This is a salve worse than the main disease.
Tell me thy thoughts; for I will know the least
(Draws his sword)
That dwells within thee, or rip thy heart
To know it: I will see thy thoughts as plain
As I do now thy face.

At the climax of his rage he returns to the thought with which he began on first seeing Bellario.

The rest of the scene solves the problem of Philaster's transition from threatening Bellario's life to sending him away still loved but still thought to be the deceiver. The moves are worked with the same skill, but still continuing within the narrow and violent compass of the petrarchan and adolescent postulates. The note on which Philaster ends is the second return to the dilemma of what things are and what they seem. This time the resolution seems magnanimous:

Rise, Bellario:
Thy protestations are so deep, and thou
Dost look so truly when thou utter'st them,
That, though I know them false as were my hopes,
I cannot urge thee further. But thou wert
To blame to injure me, for I must love
Thy honest looks, and take no revenge upon
Thy tender youth: a love from me to thee
Is firm, whate'er thou dost...
...But, good boy,
Let me not see thee more: something is done
That will distract me, that will make me mad
If I behold thee.

The mood, however, is not one of firm resolve. It is rather the passing stability of exhaustion in the midst of fever. All the items of Philaster's self-division are still present. Only the informing energies that usually stir them to conflict are absent. The verse moves to the rhythm of a relaxed exhaustion. In the lull of the violent fit Philaster is at length able to hold together all the opposites. He can call up again the absolute of his affection for the page, and recognizes too that it will be overthrown at any moment by 'distraction.' Occasions like this show how firmly Beaumont has hold on what he is doing, and how consistent is his conception.

What is it that Beaumont is doing? To analyse the serious scenes that ensue would tell us little more than is already apparent from those examined so far. Philaster sees Arethusa, in a subdued mood he confesses himself her slave, her

> *creature, made again from what it was*
> *And newly-spirited.* (III. ii.)

Then, stirred again, he reviles both himself and her. He echoes Donne's *A Lecture upon a Shadow:*

> *all the good you have is but a shadow,*
> *I' the morning with you, and at night behind you.*

He goes off into the forest which provides a fitting back-drop for the Beaumont and Fletcher worlds, both inner and outer. Here the court hunts, and court ladies disappear into convenient brakes. Here the normal countryman can comment on his betters in much the same vein as Harrington commented on the hunting parties of James and the King of Denmark. Here a brute creation seems to pursue the rational.[18] Lovers wound themselves and wound each other, and seek death in the pastoral environment they otherwise long for as the asylum from their conflicts and confusions. At times the Beaumont vision strikes through the verse. There is resonance, for example, in Arethusa's cry at the end of Act III, Scene ii, when Philaster has left her and she is called to join her father's hunting:

> *I am in tune to hunt!*
> *Diana, if thou canst rage with a maid*
> *As with a man, let me discover thee*
> *Bathing, and turn me to a fearful hind,*
> *That I may die pursued by cruel hounds,*
> *And have my story written in my wounds.*

The forest, above all, is where the heroes and heroines get lost, with the lostness that is recurrent in Beaumont:

> *Where am I now? Feet, find me out a way,*
> *Without the counsel of my troubled head:*
> *I'll follow you boldly about these woods,*
> *O'er mountains, through brambles, pits, and floods,*
> *Heaven, I hope, will ease me: I am sick.* (IV. iii.)

And in the same forest where all seems confused, the feet of the plot somehow find a way, and bring everything to a happy ending. The fourth act is as clever in its transitions from the climaxes of the third as it is in its preparation for the surprises and dénouement of the fifth.

III

We have concentrated our commentary on the petrarchan part of the play, and on only a part of that. There is much else in Beaumont and Fletcher that has received more attention. It is, however, the treatment of the love-triangle which, it seems to me, belongs particularly to their seriousness both as conscious analysts and unconscious symptoms of a particular human plight. The dramatists (or Beaumont alone, if he was solely responsible) attain in their handling of the petrarchan a personal inflection which is both distinctive and distinguished. The main roots that clutch in their work strike down through this into the heart of their time.

The petrarchan matter indicates their derivation. They are in the tradition which began with the Great House, the source of the Arcadian, Heroic, and Pastoral, as well as of the sonnet sequences, the literature of the Elizabethan *élite.* Their derivation is important from the social as well as from the literary point of view. Or rather, the literary importance does not exist apart from the social. That both Shakespeare and Beaumont and Fletcher went to the same Arcadian and Romance sources at about the same time means two things, not one. Different interests were involved, and different intentions, and these were in part the result of differences in their respective social placings. On a superficial glance alone, it is obvious that Beaumont and Fletcher, as 'inferior Sidneys,' the shabby genteel of the Great House, cannot usefully be compared with Shakespeare until the important prior distinctions between the two have first been made. Their prime affiliations are not with the tradition in which Shakespeare wrote but with the tradition—however degenerate—of the Sidneians and the metaphysicals.

A close examination of *Philaster* only brings out more clearly the difference in content and conception between their romances and those of Shakespeare's last period. On their own ground Shakespeare could not compete with them. Nor would he, one can suppose, have been minded to. The intensely narrowed world in which they are at home is one which Shakespeare's maturity cannot be conceived as entering. At the same time it is evident that Beaumont and Fletcher could have learnt nothing to their essential purposes from Shakespeare's last plays. Their own romances are a genre peculiar to themselves, in spite of the surface lights from *Antony, Lear, Othello, Hamlet,* and possibly *Troilus,* which they reflect. If it is a case of influence one on another it would seem likely that the Victorians were right, and that Shakespeare was the debtor. Paradoxically, in a case like this it is easier to imagine the greater taking a cue from the lesser—and then going off on its own. *The Winter's Tale* and *Cymbeline* do resemble the Beaumont romances. Structural resemblance we should not expect, but resemblance in the incidentals and externals there certainly is. However, Shakespeare's last plays, internally, belong to the body of his own writing, and through that to the tradition in which they were produced. Their framework is the large metaphor his work had established for him before Beaumont and Fletcher began to write.

Beaumont and Fletcher are dramatic opportunists. *Philaster,* besides its petrarchan core, has quick and successful utilizations of the large themes of the maturer drama; the theme of rebellion, of the guilty King on the throne, the theme of the King John who turns to a Falconbridge in time of trouble. (Philaster gathers up the roles of Falconbridge, Hal, and Hamlet as ancillary to his main role of lover-hero.) But it is the petrarchan core which is important for the final assessment of the two dramatists.

We have said that it is by reason of the petrarchan matter, as they treat it, that their work strikes roots into their time. Petrarchanism is an important aspect of the Renaissance. It held out the opportunity to concentrate on a territory sealed off from the other realities, social, ethical, or religious. It hinted seductively that a social code, the basis of morality, the effects of religious discipline, could all be found in the ceremonial cult of Stella or Astrea. Ideal love would be in itself a liberal education. It would be open, also, only to such as had the leisure and the facilities of the Great House around them. Petrarchanism was both insulated and aristocratic. In the case of Beaumont the insulation works to make the large traditional themes marginal, reducing them to convenient plot-ingredients.

The roots of petrarchanism, however, strike deeper than this, particularly in the Beaumont and Fletcherian drama. Its real importance there is that the central love-triangle, conflict and self-contortion in the setting of the absolutes, presented a small-scale model and a disguise for the larger situations of real life: situations of dictated choice, of self-commitment, of wilful belief that looks like headstrong denial—situations suited to the extremities of the emotional partisan. (The reign of James brought the question of partisanship to the forefront in almost every sphere.) In the person of Philaster the embryonic Cavalier could live through in pantomime what he would later have to live through in fact except that the terms would be changed. The Beaumont hero feels himself already 'fated.' He is cut off from the social past and the neighbourly present and his future includes only death. He is absolved from the need to exert rational control, and incapable of compromise. He is self-enclosed in the splintering world of the contending absolutes, and all the violence of activity these call out can only end in self-destruction. The fated lover-hero of the Beaumont drama is one of the great premonitory symbols of the seventeenth century.

Thus plays like *Philaster* are not merely passively addressed to the tastes of their audience. They play an active role. They catch at the half-felt or the unconscious and give it expression. Beaumont and Fletcher do not cater superficially, they shape for their audience the attitudes and postures the audience is not wholly aware yet that they will need. On a most cursory view, of course, as we have tried to show, Beaumont and Fletcher clearly aimed at a two-level appeal. Their plays could easily compete with the popular theatre in dramatic stir and skill; they had something to offer, too, to the aristocrat whose poetic reading was Donne, whose private pastime was the Sonnet, and whose connoisseurship was reserved for 'wit.'

The main poetic feature of Beaumont and Fletcher is their adaptation to the stage of the sonneteer's material and the sonneteer's 'conceit.' The primary affiliation of their drama is with the Sidneians and the metaphysicals. That this should have been overlooked may be a result of the recent concentration, in criticism, on the *imagery* of poetry: the fashion for what Dr. I. A. Richards has called 'metaphor-hunting.' Clearly, poetry is not to be limited to the devising of *imagery* narrowly conceived. Our indifference to the poetry of Sidney, Spenser, and Jonson, with its accompanying exaltation of Donne, Herbert, and Marvell, may eventually be recognized as a by-product of Mr. T. S. Eliot's personal pamphleteering for what—even in him—was to be merely a chapter in his own poetic development. In any case, the absence of 'verbal texture' in Beaumont and Fletcher's verse is not decisive. Their words are stretched in the frame of their situations, and it is the frame which gives them the manifoldness of 'wit.' Their achievement was to make dramatic situation perform the work of metaphysical conceit.

A play like *Philaster,* we have said, further, leaves one with a sense of something at once more sophisticated and more primitive than the normal, of something we associate with decadence. Each of the operative words here can bear fuller expansion.

The world they construct is a product of sophistication. Sophistication implies immediate viability within a restricted circle; a degree of knowledgeability in the extreme, which yet never reaches as far as wisdom; a specialness of insight and an extreme localization of field; an intensity that fails to bring breadth of view, and which breadth of view would render impossible. Beaumont's work has this sophistication. It comes, I have argued, from his concentration on the petrarchan matter, with interests even more circumscribed than those of Sidney. And even Sidney's tradition was narrower, less mixed, and less ancient than that of Shakespeare. It would be wrong, however, to think of Beaumont and Fletcher as deliberately constructing a 'fairy world.' Their artefact is more sinister and more serious than that. It is more like the *Anniversaries* than Hans Anderson.

The world into which Beaumont and Fletcher fit, as the Victorians used to insist, however clumsily and vaguely, is the world of James I and fermenting civil war. They can be regarded from one point of view as unconsciously fighting a rearguard action on behalf of the Court, compensating with advances in Blackfriars for the retreats in Westminster. The importance of Philaster is that he foreshadows figures in real life: figures of the same class and temper as Kenelm Digby, who married, *ad maiorem gloriam amoris,* an alleged courtesan.

In history as in the Beaumont drama the setting for the main actors was one in which all-or-nothing and either-or, were continually presented as the alternatives for choice. The absolutes of Justice for the subject, Loyalty to the King, Faith in God, Obedience to Church Discipline—a medley of incompatible demands surrounded the individual. Behaviour could no longer be regulated by agreed social habits, or by decent mutualizations of differences as between souls naturally Christian. The outer world and the inner world were beginning to exhibit the phenomena of fissure. In such a situation belief does tend to become wilful and hyperbolical, resting on suppressions and assertions combined. The Philaster hero focusses all this, and becomes the kind of Byron-model for his generation. In him the conflicts, self-divisions and desperate stands, the distraction and the longing for certainty, the bewildered lostness and the violence which will destroy what it loves and finally turn on itself—pathetically and comically jumbled, all the agonies and irresponsibilities meet.

And yet Lord Falkland can be seen as part of Beaumont's world, as well as Kenelm Digby. He too was one who did not want civil war, and yet was confronted with it. He did not wish to take sides, yet when all were fighting he must fight too, and only one side could be taken. And the story goes that on the eve of Newbury he prepared himself as if for his own burial, went out to battle in clean linen, was lost at the head of his cavalry among the opposing ranks, and was discovered next day dead on the field—the kind of suicide without self-slaughter a Philaster would have willed for himself, or Arethusa wished:

> *I am in tune to hunt!*
> *Diana . . . let me discover thee*
> *Bathing, and turn me to a fearful hind,*
> *That I may die pursued by cruel hounds,*
> *And have my story written in my wounds.*

The primitive quality in the play is what we should expect from a decaying or collapsing culture. It is congruent, too, with what we have called the adolescent in Beaumont's conception. Both the primitive and the adolescent indicate a reversion to the premature imposed on a civilization by the new and unmanageable developments taking place inside it. Beaumont was only twenty-four when *Philaster* was written. It is not likely that he should have become maturer as he got older. His adolescence lent itself to the requirements of the time more than Jonson's detached satire could do, or Shakespeare's socially unuseable inclusiveness of comprehension. What we call the modern world was about to launch on a phase when the adolescent and the wilful had special survival value. Since Beaumont's day our society has become increasingly partisan, increasingly juvenile in its wilfulness and its unwisdom. Beaumont and Fletcher are, in an unfortunate sense, the first of the moderns. Their counterpart in the nineteenth century, we suggested, was Byron. A contemporary parallel to their work might be that of Graham Greene. The decadence they reflect has been a condition permanent since their time, and, if anything, apt to be aggravated.

NOTES

1. S. T. Coleridge, *Lectures on Shakespeare* (Bohn Edition), p. 400.
2. Charles Lamb, *Specimens of English Dramatic Poetry:* Note on *Two Noble Kinsmen.*
3. Una Ellis-Fermor, *Jacobean Drama*, p. 207.
4. T. S. Eliot, *Selected Essays*, p. 155.
5. A. H. Thorndike, *The Influence of Beaumont and Fletcher on Shakespeare, passim.*
6. John Denham, 'On Mr. Fletcher's Works.' See *The Works of Francis Beaumont and John Fletcher* (Ed. A. R. Waller), Vol. I, p. xxiii.
7. J. Berkenhead, 'On the Happy Collection of Master Fletcher's Works.' See Beaumont and Fletcher's *Works*, Vol. I, p. xli.
8. Alfred Harbage, *Cavalier Drama*, p. 22.
9. Bishop Goodman, *Court of King James* (Ed. John S. Brewer), p. 134.
10. Sir John Harington, *Nugae Antiquae* (Arr. by Rev. H. Harington, 1779), Vol. I, p. 134.
11. *Op. cit.*, Vol. II, p. 129.
12. John Donne, *Complete Poems*, etc. (Nonesuch Edition), p. 122.
13. *Op. cit.*, p. 129.
14. *Op. cit.*, p. 6.
15. *Op. cit.*, p. 203.
16. 'To that Noble and true Lover of Learning, Sir Walter Aston Knight,' *Works*, Vol. II, p. 520.
17. *Op. cit.*, p. 207.
18. *Nugae Antiquae*, Vol. II, p. 130.

MURIEL BRADBROOK

Thomas Middleton

MIDDLETON's tragedies are as similar in their methods of construction as they are different from the plays already considered. Rowley's name appears on the title page of *The Changeling*, but it is difficult to see the possibility of his sharing in the main plot, for its unity is of a kind which not even the most sympathetic collaboration could achieve.

The connection between the two plots of this play is, however, very carefully worked out. It is indicated even in the title, 'The *Changeling*,' which describes both Antonio, the innocent, and Beatrice-Joanna, the inconstant woman (a usual meaning—*vide Anything for a Quiet Life*, 2. 1. 71, and *N.E.D. sub verb.*).

The construction of the play is masked by the greater naturalism of the treatment. Compared with the characters of earlier plays, Middleton's are fuller, more natural and human. Their motives and actions may be conventionally 'Italianate' (they have vestigial remains of the Revenge code in the melancholy of Tomazo the revenger and the appearance of the ghost), but their feelings and responses are normal. Beatrice-Joanna's famous outburst, when the murderer demands possession of her as a reward:

> Why 'tis impossible thou canst be so wicked
> Or shelter such a cunning cruelty
> To make his death the murderer of my honour—
> (3. 4. 121 ff.)

is only the most obvious illustration of Middleton's interest in the

From *Themes and Conventions of Elizabethan Tragedy* (Cambridge University Press, 1935), pp. 213–39. Reprinted by permission of the publisher and author.

way the mind works. Deflores' brief plea to the man he has cuckolded, when he hears Beatrice-Joanna crying out in futile anger:

Let me go to her, sir— (5. 3. 112)

is so assured of his right to calm her that the husband can but send him in.

The construction of the play is, however, partly dependent on themes: briefly it may be described as a study in the conflict of passion and judgment, and of the transforming power of love. All the characters (save Alsemero) are entirely at the mercy of their feelings, which are instinctive and uncontrollable. Judgment is blinded, so that the characters practise all kinds of deception and self-deception to gain their ends. Love is 'a tame madness,' a kind of possession which seizes upon a man and 'changes' him so that he is no longer recognisable. In the main plot the themes are worked out naturalistically; in the subplot the use of the madmen, and of more literal transformations, as well as more farcical action, makes a kind of phantasmagoria. The key words are 'change,' 'judgment' and 'will' (in the sense of instinctive desire, often of sensual desire, as in Shakespeare). The connection between plot and subplot is summed up in the final scene where the structure of themes is explained.

Alsemero. What an opacous body had that moon
That last changed on us! here is beauty changed
To ugly whoredom; here servant-obedience
To a master-sin, imperious murder;
I, a supposed husband, changed embraces
With wantonness—but that was paid before—
Your change is come too from an ignorant wrath
To knowing friendship. Are there any more on's?
Antonio. Yes sir I was changed too from a little ass as I was to a great fool as I am: and had like to ha' been changed to the gallows, but that you know my innocence always excuses me.
Franciscus. I was changed from a little wit to be stark mad
Almost for the same purpose.
Isabella (*to her husband*). Your change is still behind,
But deserve best your transformation. (5. 3. 199 ff.)

'Transformation' is a useful word to describe the character changes in the play: people are changed in the eyes of others, and they are also changed radically in themselves by the power of love.

The play opens with Alsemero falling in love. It was 'in the Temple' which he instinctively feels to be an omen (the use of omens as what would now be called promptings of the unconscious mind plays a large part in the play). In any case he is already transformed; from an ardent traveller he becomes a loiterer, from a woman hater a courtier so that his friend cries:

> How now: the laws of the Medes are changed sure: salute a woman: he kisses too: wonderful! (1. 1. 60)

This sense of shock and discovery is the same in kind (though not in intensity of course) as the 'discoveries' of Beatrice-Joanna, of Isabella and of Alsemero.

The dialogue which follows states the main theme. Alsemero roundly declares his love, to which Beatrice-Joanna replies:

> Be better advised, sir:
> Our eyes are sentinels unto our *judgments*
> And should give certain *judgment* what they see;
> But they are rash sometimes and tell us wonders
> Of common things, which when our *judgments* find
> They can then check the eyes and call them blind.
> (1. 1. 73 ff.)

Alsemero has seen her twice, however, and this he considers amply sufficient for the co-operation of eyes and judgment.

Deflores is then introduced, and Beatrice-Joanna's instinctive hatred of him. 'She knows no cause for't but a peevish *will.*' Beatrice-Joanna and Alsemero have a long discussion on the idiosyncratic character of the will (compare *The Merchant of Venice,* 4. 1. 44–62) and its instinctive precritical judgments. Beatrice-Joanna's father then appears and a conversation, in which asides and equivocations are frequent, shows to what extent Beatrice-Joanna's 'will' is already transforming her. She says:

> I shall *change* my saint, I fear me: I find
> A giddy turning in me— (1. 1. 158–9)

an echo of Alsemero's 'I keep the same church, same devotion' which points the contrast between them. Her father explains to Alsemero that she is betrothed to Alonzo de Piracquo: immediately his plans change, he must go away. The father will have her married at once, 'I'll want my *will* else.' Beatrice-Joanna adds aside, 'I shall want mine if you do it.' Finally Deflores, remaining to soliloquise, reveals his plight as the same one:

I know she hates me
Yet cannot choose but love her: no matter,
If but to vex her, I will haunt her still:
Though I get nothing else, I'll have my will.
(1. 1. 237–40)

The second act opens with Beatrice-Joanna busily deluding her own judgment. Alsemero's friend has just arranged an assignation, and she catches at his discretion as a justification for herself.

How wise is Alsemero in his friend,
It is a sign he makes his choice with *judgment:*
Then I appear in nothing more approved
Than making choice of him. . . . (2. 1. 6 ff.)

She loves 'with intellectual eyesight' as Alsemero thought he did.

Instead of Alsemero, Deflores arrives. He describes his own infatuation coolly (he is well aware of his ugliness, so that only 'intellectual eyesight' could ever endure him) yet he does not despair, and when Beatrice-Joanna turns on 'this ominous ill-faced fellow' he endures her patiently. He has a certain self-knowledge which sets him above the others, if it does not give him self-mastery.

Why am I not an ass to devise ways
Thus to be railed at? I must see her still,
I shall have a mad qualm within this hour again
I know't. (2. 1. 77 ff.)

When he is gone Beatrice-Joanna enlarges on the feeling of danger he inspires in her. The scene concludes with an interview with her unwelcome lover, Piracquo. He refuses to recognise her very plain dislike of him, since love has overpowered his judgment too. His brother comments on his incredulity:

Why, this is love's tame *madness,*

a significant link with the subplot.

All this interweaving of self-deception and self-awareness is supported by dialogue of the greatest ease and naturalness. There is no sustained heroic pitch as in Tourneur or Webster; the climaxes of feeling are simply expressed, not in obviously rich and poetic language.

I have within my eyes all my desires. . . . (2. 2. 8)
Here was a course

Found to bring sorrow on her way to death
The tears would ne'er have dried till blood had
choked 'em. (2. 2. 37–9)

The scene in which Deflores is given the commission to kill Piracquo is one of ironic comedy. Having seen her secret interview with Alsemero he has hopes for himself and when Beatrice-Joanna seems more friendly he is really deceived into thinking her judgment is changed.

Beatrice-Joanna. You've pruned yourself, methinks:
you were not wont
To look so amorously.
Deflores. Not I—
'Tis the same phisnomy to a hair and pimple
Which she called scurvy scarce an hour ago.
How is this?
Beatrice-Joanna. Come hither; nearer, man.
Deflores. I'm up to the chin in heaven! (2. 2. 74 ff.)

At first he coaxes her into speaking because he half believes she is in love with him. She is trying to get her request out naturally and he makes things easy by importuning her.

Beatrice-Joanna. Oh my Deflores!
Deflores. How this? she calls me hers?
Already, my Deflores—You were about
To sigh out somewhat, madam? . . .
Beatrice-Joanna. Would creation—
Deflores. Ay well said, that's it.
Beatrice-Joanna. Had made me man.
Deflores. Nay that's not it. (2. 2. 97 ff.)

He may be ironical, but it is hardly likely. They part mutually deceived, Beatrice-Joanna rejoicing at being rid of him and he in having won her.

The murder is quickly done and the great discovery scene follows. Beatrice-Joanna is congratulating herself on her judgment

So wisdom by degrees works out her freedom. (3. 4. 13)

Deflores is something more than complacent as he enters and shows her the severed finger of Piracquo. She is horrified, for she had not visualised the murder; Deflores the hired assassin was to stand between her and the dirty business of the stabbing. He is quite calloused physically, and cannot understand her qualms at sight of the ring—'the first token my father made me send him.' When she tells him to keep the jewel, however, her coarseness is exposed in turn by his retort:

> 'Twill hardly buy a capcase for one's conscience though
> To keep it from the worm, as fine as 'tis. (3. 4. 45–6)

His anger rises as he realises her attitude towards himself. The barriers of her modesty, dignity and stupidity are not easily broken; she only thinks of him as a servant and at first actually appeals to him on those grounds.

> Think but upon the distance that creation
> Set 'twixt thy blood and mine and keep thee there.
> (3. 4. 131–2)

Deflores' reply suggests that she has become 'transformed': she is no longer the woman she was, since her love has altered.

> 'Twas chang'd from thy first love, and that's a kind
> Of whoredom in the heart, and he's chang'd now
> To bring thy second on, thy Alsemero. (3. 4. 144–6)

She is 'the deed's creature,' and one with him. It will be seen that later both Beatrice-Joanna and Alsemero acknowledge her transformation.

Deflores' speeches have also a naturalistic interpretation. The pain of his disillusion can be felt behind his violence; it breaks out finally in an appeal to her pity, as direct as hers to him:

> I live in pain now: that shooting eye
> Will burn my heart to cinders. (3. 4. 152–3)

When she submits he drops to a tenderness heard again in the final scene. It is one of Middleton's most daring and most perfectly managed modulations of feeling:

> Come rise and shroud your blushes in my bosom:
> Silence is one of pleasure's best receipts:
> Thy peace is wrought for ever in this yielding.
> (3. 4. 167–9)

The last two acts are worked out in the same manner as the first three. Beatrice-Joanna makes the same mistake with Diaphanta as she did with Deflores. ''Tis a nice piece gold cannot purchase,' and so she bribes her maid to take her place on the marriage night.

Diaphanta's lust nearly wrecks the plan, as Deflores' had done. He arrives and suggests an alarm of fire, but Beatrice-Joanna is as slow now as heretofore to see the point of his proposals.

> *Beatrice-Joanna.* How, fire, sir? that may endanger the whole house.
> *Deflores.* You talk of danger when your fame's on fire? (5. 1. 33–4).

The trick of the 'magic' glass of water by which Alsemero tests her virginity is not out of place, for it belongs with the 'omens' and other irrational elements rather than with the naturalism of character and speech; it is also reinforced by the stronger suggestion of 'magic' in the subplot.

Alsemero is the only character whose 'will' does not overpower his judgment. Beatrice-Joanna fears his clear sight (4. 1. 1–17). He is contrasted with Piracquo who would not hear a word against his betrothed:

> Were she the sole glory of the earth,
> Had eyes that could shoot fire into Kings' breasts
> And touched, she sleeps not here. (4. 2. 106–8)

The quarrel with Tomazo de Piracquo seems 'ominous' to him; but his innocence relieves him. At the moment of discovery he remembers his early scruples:

> O the place itself e'er since
> Has crying been for vengeance! the Temple. . . .
> (5. 3. 73–4)

Beatrice-Joanna now appears hideous to him, even physically hideous, and in that is akin to Deflores. Her transformation is complete, through the discovery of her deceit.

> The black mask
> That so continually was worn upon't
> Condemns the face for ugly ere't be seen. (5. 3. 3–5)

> O thou art all deformed. (5. 3. 78)

Beatrice-Joanna miscalculates a third time: she confesses murder but denies adultery, thinking Alsemero will pardon the greater crime, since it was done for his sake. She knows him no better than Deflores or Diaphanta; he rejects her with horror and it is left for Deflores' resolution to cut the thread, by murder and suicide. Beatrice-Joanna recognises her transformation, at first indirectly: of the word 'whore' she says:

> It blasts a beauty to *deformity*
> Upon whatsoever face that breath falls
> It strikes it ugly. (5. 3. 33–5)

Finally she recognises her union with Deflores, and the significance of her first 'will' to dislike him (5. 3. 157–60).

The revenge of Tomazo de Piracquo is also a matter of will. At first he likes Deflores, but later he feels an inexplicable recoil from him.

The subplot is connected with the main plot chiefly by implication. It acts as a kind of parallel or reflection in a different mode: their relationship is precisely that of masque and antimasque, say the two halves of Jonson's *Masque of Queens*. The direct links at the end have already been mentioned: there is also a scene of parallel action, first noted by Mr. Empson, in which Isabella, the wife of the madhouse keeper, is detected with her lover by a servant Lollio. He proceeds to exact the same price from Isabella that Deflores did from Beatrice-Joanna:

> Come, sweet rogue: kiss me, my little Lacedemonian: let me feel how thy pulses beat: thou hast a thing about thee would do a man pleasure, I'll lay my hand on it. (3. 3. 247–50)

Her reply is an inversion of Beatrice-Joanna's. She threatens in turn:

> Be silent, mute,
> Mute as a statue, or his injunctions
> For me enjoying, shall be to cut thy throat,
> I'll do't, though for no other purpose. (3. 3. 253–6)

Deflores enjoyed Beatrice-Joanna in return for cutting a throat.

Isabella has two lovers, who are disguised as a fool and a madman in order to gain access to her. Antonio, the fool, throws off his hideous disguise, which he calls a *deformity* (3. 3. 195) and appears as her lover suddenly:

> This shape of folly shrouds your dearest love,
> The truest servant to your powerful beauties,
> Whose *magic* had the force thus to *transform* me.
> (3. 3. 127–9)

It is parallel to Deflores' appearance as the lover of Beatrice-Joanna. The quality of the surprise is similar (not, of course, the intensity). The other lover never actually encounters her, but sends a letter in which he says:

> Sweet Lady, having now cast off this counterfeit cover of a madman, I appear to your best *Judgment* a true and faithful lover of your beauty . . . (Love) shapes and transhapes, destroys and builds again. . . .

In the same scene Isabella puts on the disguise of a madwoman to meet the fool; but she is only temporarily transformed. Her speeches are full of references to Dedalus and Icarus, which suggest the dangerous nature of their secret and the preciousness of the reward. But the fool does not recognise her, and so she returns to her former state, and is never actually unfaithful to her ridiculous husband.

The chorus of madmen depict the bestial element in man, rather as Caliban does, or the rout in *Comus*. At the climax of the subplot, when Isabella is hard pressed by Antonio, Lollio cries 'Cuckoo! cuckoo!' and there is the direction:

> *Madmen above, some as birds, others as beasts.*

Bullen and other editors rearrange this, but it clearly means that the madmen appear on the upper stage in the masquing habits which they are to wear at their entertainment at Beatrice-Joanna's wedding. They are a symbolic presentation of evil. Isabella explains:

> They act their fantasies in any shapes [i.e. costumes]
> Suiting their present thoughts.

Already they have been heard within crying at the game of barley-break:

> Catch there: catch the last couple in hell! (3. 3. 173)

The old worn pun gains in horror when Deflores echoes it to Alsemero in the final scene:

> I coupled with your mate
> At barley-break: now we are left in hell. (5. 3. 165–6)

Vermandero adds, 'It circumscribes us here,' thinking of the actual chalk ring.

The supernatural element in the main plot is veiled: it depends on the omens and the 'magic' effects of Alsemero's chemistry. The subplot is fantastic and pictorial. The masque of madmen, ostensibly prepared for the wedding, is actually given in rehearsal before Isabella at the end of Act 4. She is summoned to it:

> Away then, and guide them in, Lollio:
> Entreat your mistress to see this sight.

The importance of this masque can be gauged by the comparison with that in Ford's *The Lover's Melancholy* (3. 3). Here the doctor Corax has a masque of melancholy men to cure the melancholy of the Prince. The different types of the disease are taken from Burton, and each is symbolically dressed. For instance, Lycanthropia has 'his face whited, with black shag hair, and long nails and with a piece of raw meat.' The wanton melancholy is 'a Sea-Nymph big-bellied, singing and dancing,' the point of this being of course that *mermaid* was slang for prostitute.

The Prince remaining unmoved, Corax adds:

> One only kind of Melancholy
> Is left untouched: 'twas not in art
> To personate the shadow of that fancy:
> 'Tis named love-melancholy . . .
> Love is the tyrant of the heart: it darkens
> Reason, confounds discretion: deaf to counsel
> It runs a headlong course to desperate madness.

The Prince, like Claudius in *Hamlet*, breaks off the revels abruptly. The significance of this passage with its symbolic treatment of madmen and the connection between love and madness involved in the symbolism is perhaps all the stronger for there being no trace of any direct influence of Middleton.

Throughout the scenes of the subplot of *The Changeling*, riddling games and tableaux keep up the bizarre horror.

> Here's a fool behind a knave, that's I: and between us two fools there is a knave, that's my master: 'tis but we three, that's all.
> We three, we three, cousin. (1. 2. 202 ff.)

This is the husband posed between Lollio, his servant, and Antonio, his 'patient,' both of whom are deceiving him at the moment when they so firmly assert that he is the knave and they the fools. So Isabella is posed between her husband and her two lovers throughout the play. So Beatrice-Joanna is posed between her husband and her two lovers, Piracquo and Deflores, in the one scene where the supernatural is allowed to intrude overtly into the main plot, and the silent ghost of Alonzo appears to Deflores and Beatrice-Joanna as they plot the second murder, that of the waiting woman Diaphanta. Yet even here the tone is kept quiet: to Deflores the ghost is only a 'mist of conscience,' while Beatrice-Joanna does not even see it clearly enough to recognise it: it felt an 'ill thing' that left a shivering sweat upon her. So firmly does each half of the play retain its own proper atmosphere, and yet so closely are they interwoven with each other.

Women, Beware Women is a slighter play than *The Changeling*. Its themes are nearer to a thesis; the moralising is sharply cut off and put into the mouth of the Cardinal in Act 5. But this play is, however, also a study in the progressive deterioration of character. The first part of the play is much more natural than the latter half; here the writing is full of little observations of daily life, not sharpened like Webster's epigrams, but entering easily and unobtrusively. The characters are humble; consequently their speech is often quite near to that of Middleton's comedies. Yet at the end the catastrophe is achieved through the old convention of murder in a masque, though this is varied by making the masquers attack each other—a method not used since *The Spanish Tragedy*.

Plot and subplot are contrasted in their action: in the main plot a love-marriage is wrecked by ambition; in the subplot a marriage of convenience cloaks an infamous love affair. They are united by the schemes of Livia who is the pander in both cases. Bianca stands between her lover, the Duke, and her husband, as Isabella does between Hippolito and the ward. Both have the innocence of ignorance at first, like Beatrice-Joanna; but the larger part played by mercenary calculations in this play (even Deflores was not mercenary) lowers the tone of it.

At the beginning Leantio introduces his new wife to his mother. His renunciation of riches (after stealing an heiress) is a little too smug; his sentiments do not sound as if they had ever been tested by experience; he is jauntily didactic.

> I find no wish in me bent sinfully
> To this man's sister or to that man's wife;
> In love's name let 'em keep their honesties
> And cleave to their own husbands: 'tis their duties.
>
> (1. 1. 28 ff.)

Bianca is equally sure of herself:

> I'm as rich as virtue can be poor. (1. 1. 128)

The mother's strictly practical remarks pass unheeded, yet they are shrewd enough. Leantio has wronged Bianca by bringing her to poverty, and may expect to hear of it. The scene is written in a tone of *naïveté;* all the characters have the same accent, and even the mother hardly ventures to question the enthusiastic idealism of her son.

In the next scene the contrast is evident; a marriage is being arranged. The tone is more dignified, especially in the protests of Isabella, the unfortunate subject of the bargain.

> O the heartbreakings
> Of miserable maids when love's enforced!
> Their best condition is but bad enough.
> When women have their choices, commonly,
> They do but buy their thraldoms, and bring great portions
> To men to keep them in subjection. (1. 2. 169 ff.)

Even her affections are betrayed; for her uncle Hippolito, whose love she had valued, reveals that

> Blood, that should be love, is mixed with lust— (1. 2. 231)

and Isabella vows to see him no more.

The next scene shows the ingenuous lovers taking leave of each other. It is chiefly their affection which is stressed, yet the purely sensuous nature of it is significant. Leantio's debate with himself, however, is virtuous simplicity itself, though this in itself is ominous, for such an innocence is ill-armed against 'policy.'

The next scene opens with an equally friendly and easy discourse between Livia and her brother Hippolito; but the upshot of this affectionate exchange is that she promises to procure their niece for him. Livia's affection is sincere; but, since she is simply without moral scruples of any kind, the very kindness of it becomes horrible, and suspicion is cast over all frankness and love when it can lead to such a speech as:

> You are not the first, brother, has attempted
> Things more forbidden than this seems to be.
> I'll minister all cordials now to you
> Because I'll cheer you up, sir; (2. 1. 46 ff.)

and it is underlined by the short soliloquy which follows (beginning

'Beshrew you, would I loved you not so well!'). In the scene of seduction which follows Livia falsely tells her niece that she is not bound to obey her father, and accept the unpleasant marriage, because she is not really his child. Not a word is said of Hippolito, but there are indirect hints.

> What a largeness in your will and liberty
> To take or to reject or to do both!
> For fools will serve to father wise men's children
> All that you've time to think on. (2. 1. 160 ff.)

This refers in the first place to her 'father' Fabricio, but also as a suggestion that marriage with the foolish ward may be wisdom. Isabella is completely deceived; she receives Hippolito willingly; and still the simple, unsophisticated accent is preserved in her speech, even while she plots the covering marriage, making the whole thing seem more pitiful than criminal, and quite effectively debarring any heroics, any idea of 'magnificence in sin.'

> So discretion love me,
> Desert and judgment, I've content sufficient.
> She that comes once to be a housekeeper
> Must not look every day to fare well, sir,
> Like a young waiting gentlewoman in service,
> For she feeds commonly as her lady does,
> No good bit passes her but she gets a taste on't
> But when she comes to keep house for herself
> She's glad of some choice cates then once a week
> Or twice at most, and glad if she can get 'em. . . .
> (2. 1. 215 ff.)

This scene is immediately followed by the masterly seduction of Bianca. Livia's methods are precisely the same as before. Her friendly accents are those of Isabella, the old mother, or Bianca.

> Widow, come, come, I've a great quarrel to you:
> Faith, I must chide you that you must be sent for:
> You make yourself so strange, never come at us. . . .
> (2. 2. 142 ff.)

The courteous interchange is heightened when Bianca appears to something more polished; but when Guardiano has finally enticed away and brought her to the Duke, the tone changes abruptly. The Duke is absolutely hard; to her pleas for release, he replies:

I think
Thou know'st the way to please me. I affect
A passionate pleading 'bove an easy yielding:
But never pitied any—they deserve none—
That will not pity me. (2. 2. 363 ff.)

He is completely mercenary too:

Come, play the wise wench and provide for ever.
(2. 2. 387)

Bianca's virtue simply collapses. It seems to be the Duke's determination at this point rather than any ambition which wins her, just as Livia, having warned Hippolito, turns round and 'cheers him up.'

Guardiano's comment sums up the satirical attitude of the whole scene, during which the old mother has been innocently engaged in her game of chess.

It's a witty age;
Never were finer snares for women's honesties
Than are devised in these days. (2. 2. 401 ff.)

It is an attitude wholly devoid of the 'pity' and 'affection' which has been shown between Bianca, Leantio and the mother, or between Livia and Hippolito or Hippolito and Isabella, but Guardiano from the first has been frankly mercenary; that was his motive here:

Advancement,
I venture hard to find thee. (2. 2. 409–10)

This new, hard, mercenary, ironical tone is to become increasingly prevalent and infect all the simpler characters as ambition gains a hold on them. Their 'affections' are shown to be without roots.

Bianca enters again, but she is now changed. The Duke has opened her eyes to horror. 'Infections, mists and mildews hang at's eyes.' In a bitter aside she upbraids Guardiano, which he counters with one of the familiar, good-tempered speeches, which from now onwards are to sound only hollow and insincere.

Well, so the duke love me,
I fare not much amiss then: two great feasts
Do seldom come together in one day,
We must not look for't. (2. 2. 449 ff.)

(Compare Isabella's words, quoted above. The 'practical' tone of their worldly wisdom again takes from the horror and makes the villainy seem petty.) Livia prophesies that even this resentment will not last long: '' Tis but a qualm of honour, 'twill away.'

In the third act Bianca fulfils exactly her mother-in-law's prophecies in Act I, Scene 1. Her 'affections, wills and humours' are so commonplace in their form that the scene has the same air of ironic comedy as the preceding one: it reflects back to the seriousness of Isabella's pleas for freedom in marriage.

> Wives do not give away themselves to husbands
> To the end to be quite cast away: they look
> To be the better used and tendered rather
> Highlier respected and maintained the richer:
> They're well rewarded else for the free gift
> Of their whole life to a husband. (3. 1. 47 ff.)

This is directly connected with the mother's words in Act I, Scene 2; and Leantio's soliloquy which follows, on the delights of wedlock, in its unctuous morality and its sensuality is a malicious preparation for his cool reception, and almost justifies the demonstration of humours which Bianca gives.

> She'll be so greedy now and cling about me . . . (3. 1. 107)

is met with

> No matter for a kiss, sir: let it pass:
> 'Tis but a toy, we'll not so much as mind it.
> (3. 1. 150–1)

The messenger from the Duke soon arrives and makes his danger clear to Leantio, but at first he fears only the consequence of his having stolen Bianca, and imagines that if he keeps her in hiding, all will be well; her indignant refusal to be 'rude and uncivil' disillusions him. The abrupt collapse of the mother's virtue is a minor ironic underlining of the situation; a few sweetmeats are sufficient to overcome her, and Leantio is left to soliloquise again. His two soliloquies are exactly parallel. In the first:

> Honest wedlock
> Is like a banqueting house built in a garden
> On which the spring's chaste flowers take delight
> To cast their modest odours. (3. 1. 89 ff.)

The second opens:

> O thou, the ripe time of man's misery, wedlock,
> When all his thoughts, like overladen trees
> Crack with the fruits they bear, in cares, in jealousies.
> (3. 1. 271 ff.)

In the following scene Leantio is bribed with an office by the Duke and forced to watch the courtship of his wife. Hippolito also is forced to display the graces of Isabella by leading a dance with her, for the benefit of the ward. The similarity of their situations is suggested in their asides.

> *Leantio.* I'm like a thing that never yet was heard of
> Half merry and half mad: much like a fellow
> That eats his meat with a good appetite
> And wears a plague sore that would fright a country. (3. 2. 52 ff.)

> *Hippolito.* Come, my life's peace—I've a strange office here . . .
> Like the mad misery of necessitous man,
> That parts from his good horse with many praises
> And goes on foot himself. (3. 2. 193 ff.)

The gaiety of the scene, with its dancing, music and feasts, has the same ironic contrast with the misery of Leantio, Isabella and Hippolito, as the quietness of the chess scene with its rapid intrigue. More than a third of the scene is taken up by asides in which these characters explain their feelings, while the action all the while remains animated. Leantio's soliloquy at the departure of the Duke and Bianca is one of the finest pieces of writing in the play, expressing this time not moral indignation but the agony of outraged feelings. It is the last time that such feelings are to be heard in the play. For Livia, the bawd, has fallen in love with him and approaches him with the familiar poisonous suggestions of wealth, the attack upon such feelings.

> Young gentlemen that only love for beauty
> They love not wisely: such a marriage rather
> Proves the destruction of affection;
> It brings on want, and want's the key of whoredom.
> (3. 2. 282 ff.)

Leantio's sense of values is not immediately overthrown; he cries out:

> O my *life's wealth,* Bianca! (3. 2. 307)

For money is not yet all-prevailing with him. It is during the course of one of those soliloquies which seem to telescope a lengthy mental process that worldly values conquer, and he accepts Livia's offer.

Do but you love enough, I'll give enough.
Troth then, I'll love enough and take enough.

So he sinks to Bianca's level; and in the scene where they bandy insults over one another's advancement (4. 1) this equality is explicitly set forth. Her fine lodgings and his fine clothes are set against each other; and her conscience is seen to be wholly dead, while his is still in the stage of ineffective stirring as hers had been earlier (2. 3, *ad fin.*).

It is at this point, however, that a new theme is introduced, which is to swell during the last two acts: that of death and judgment. More powerfully than in *The Changeling* it is given as the 'punishment' and inevitable end of sinners. Leantio threatens Bianca in a whisper:

I speak softly now
'Tis manners in a noble woman's lodging
But come I to your everlasting parting once
Thunder shall seem soft music to that tempest.
(4. 1. 86 ff.)

This, conveyed to the Duke, brings about his own death. But the note of doom is struck again in the lengthy speech of the Cardinal, when he points to the Duke's body and says:

There's but this wall between you and destruction
When you're at strongest, poor thin clay— (4.1.242–3)

and, for Bianca:

Is she a thing
Whom sickness dare not visit or age look on
Or death resist? doth the worm shun her grave?
(4. 1. 248–50)

It is a note which curiously enough had been sounded by Leantio (with apparent irrelevance) in the opening speech in 1. 1:

To have the toil and grief of fourscore years
Put up in a white sheet, tied with two knots:
Methinks it should strike earthquakes in adulterers
When even the very sheets they commit sin in
May prove, for aught they know, all their last garments.
(1. 1. 20 ff.)

Except as a prelude to the later passages, this appears an excrescence. It will be noted how these references make man seem something pitiable and puny, confirming the impression of the intrigue.

In the very next scene, death comes sharply. Leantio is struck almost unawares, and in dying feels his wife's curse on him, as Livia feels the punishment for her sins. Pity is dead. She reveals the incest: Guardiano will 'listen to nothing but revenge and anger'; Isabella's revenge will be 'acted without pity.' The masque is arranged: the bawd plays the marriage goddess and the adulteress a nymph wooed by two swains.

The wedding procession of the Duke is interrupted by the Cardinal, whose speech would apply equally well to the other marriage. His attack rouses pitiless revenge in Bianca; and so the scene is set for the masque.

Here the ironic casting is supplemented by action. Isabella is killed by a shower of gold:

> Bright eyed prosperity which all couples love,
> Ay and makes love. (5. 1. 156–7)

'Prosperity,' or ambition of it, has undone Bianca, Leantio, Isabella, and the rest.

The ironical series of deaths follows quickly. Guardiano is caught in his own trap; Livia and Isabella kill each other; Hippolito commits suicide; the Duke is poisoned by mistake, and Bianca commits suicide, recalling her marriage vow, as Leantio had recalled her curse (5. 1. 252–3; cf. 4. 2. 43–5).

'Measure for measure' is recognised by Hippolito and Bianca, and it is she who speaks the real epilogue:

> Pride, greatness, honour, beauty, youth, ambition,
> You must all down together, there's no help for it.
> (5. 1. 260–1 ff.)

The huddle of murders may be improbable, but the overhanging atmosphere of mortality in the last act makes all the method of narrative of subsidiary importance. Death in some form is felt to be inevitable. Bianca, Leantio, Hippolito, Isabella and Livia have destroyed themselves already by destroying all moral sense,[1] and physical death has been pronounced upon them by the Cardinal who speaks with the voice of Heaven (*vide infra*).

It need hardly be added that the subsidiary figures have usually something to contribute to the atmosphere of the play. The ward, like the madmen of *The Changeling*, represents the completely bestial, as Caliban does in *The Tempest*. His lustfulness is continually stressed: it is lust at its coarsest, but only there as a commentary on the lust of the Duke and Hippolito, so that although too much space may seem to be given to his obscenities they are necessary as a ground-base for the consort of themes. Guardiano's cunning and Fabricio's foolishness serve similar ends; and the Cardinal's speeches are nearly all impersonal comments on the total situation. There is not a scene in the play which is really superfluous or divorced from the pattern as a whole, which may be summed up as the conflict between love and mercenary selling of love, with self-destruction envisaged as the inevitable result of the spiritual suicide of lust and ambition.

The imagery of the two plays is not systematised to the same extent as Chapman's or Webster's, yet there are certain dominating images in the Shakespearean manner which give a distinct tone to the play. For example Deflores is constantly referred to as a 'poison,' implying I think the natural antipathy which the good people in the play feel for him, marking him out as opposed to the healthful and life-giving associations of food and feasts. The discussion of instinctive likes and dislikes in Act 1 centres round food: Alsemero's 'poison' is 'a cherry.' When Beatrice-Joanna first thinks of using Deflores, she exclaims:

> Why men of art make much of poisons:
> Keep one to expel another. . . . (2. 2. 46–7)

And when she is forced to submit to him she thinks of him as a poisonous snake who has seized her (with a hidden reflection on the legend that vipers devoured their parents, for she is the employer of Deflores):

> Was my creation in the womb so curst
> It must engender with a viper first? (3. 4. 165–6)

Alsemero knows that Beatrice-Joanna so hated Deflores that 'the very sight of him is poison to her,' and therefore does not credit Jasperino's suspicions. Tomazo suspects him of having poisoned his brother; he is

> so most deadly venomous
> He would go near to poison any weapon. . . .
> (5. 2. 17–18)

Nevertheless he challenges Deflores:

I'd rather die like a soldier by the sword
Than like a politician by thy poison. . . .
(5. 2. 28–9)

And when Beatrice-Joanna finally confesses, she cries:

I have kissed poison for it, stroked a serpent.
(5. 3. 67)

It is not fortuitous, I think, that Alsemero is a physician and Alibius too. There is also a significant number of images dealing with the appetite and with food and drink. Miss Spurgeon has shown how in *Troilus and Cressida* such images give a certain coarseness to the sexual feelings in that play, by equating one appetite with the other. Here the images belong chiefly to Deflores and reinforce the suggestion that his feelings for Beatrice-Joanna are essentially gross. He is even eager for the murder, as a means to an end, and says:

I thirst for him. . . . (2. 2. 134)

Beatrice-Joanna comments on his eagerness:

Belike his wants are greedy: and to such
Gold tastes like angels' food. (2. 2. 127–8)

It is this grossness of feeling which makes him imagine Beatrice-Joanna attracted to himself:

Hunger and pleasure they'll commend sometime
Slovenly dishes and feed heartily on 'em,
Nay, which is stranger, refuse daintier for them.
Some women are odd feeders. . . . (2. 2. 152 ff.)

And when he returns after the murder he cries, in anticipation:

My thoughts are at a banquet. . . . (3. 4. 18)

His final triumphant assertion of his dominance over Beatrice-Joanna is in the same form:

it is so sweet to me
That I have drunk up all, left none behind
For any man to pledge me. (5. 2. 172 ff.)

Tomazo's melancholy is at once a thirst for blood (4. 20) and an inability to 'taste the benefits of life' with 'relish.' The madmen in the subplot are clamorous for food (1. 2).

The images of food are much more frequent in *Women, Beware Women,* however, as fits the coarser quality of the feelings in that play. I have counted a total of twenty-two passages where this imagery is used, some of which are of a considerable length; and there are continual direct references to feasting (especially in 2. 2, 3. 1 and 3. 2). The coarsest characters are gluttonous; for instance, the ward wants some of Isabella's sweetmeats and says, with a reference which makes the symbolism apparent,

> These women when they come to sweet things once
> They forget all their friends, they grow so greedy,
> Nay, often times their husbands. (3. 2. 75 ff.)

And the mother is ready to condone adultery for the sake of a feast.

> I'll obey the duke
> And taste of a good banquet, I'm of thy mind
> I'll step but up and fetch two handkerchiefs
> To pocket up some sweetmeats and overtake thee.
> (3. 1. 265–8)

Bianca comments on this:

> Why here's an old wench would trot into a bawd now
> For some dry sucket or a colt in marchpane.
> (3. 1. 269–70)

It is reminiscent of the christening scene in *A Chaste Maid in Cheapside* (3. 2).

In the first scene Bianca compares her varied fortunes to a feast where all classes of people mingle. In the next scene Livia talks of a husband's privileges—'obedience, forsooth, subjection, duty and such kickshaws'—as dishes prepared for him by his wife. She 'ministers cordials' to her brother and bids him 'taste of happiness,' describing him in the curious lines:

> Thou art all a feast
> And she that has thee a most happy guest. (1. 2. 152 ff.)

She tells the false tale to Isabella with:

> You see your cheer, I'll make you no set feast.

Isabella compares her former cruelty to Hippolito with an *apéritif,* and goes on to describe her love in terms of feasting (*vide supra,* p. 227). In the seduction scene the pictures are 'a bit to stay the appetite.' Guardiano endures Bianca's anger, since two feasts do not come together, and Livia thinks she only dislikes sin because its flavour is new to her.

In the feasting scene (3. 2) the references become thicker. The ward is 'coarse victuals' to Isabella while she smells 'like a comfit maker's shop' to him. (In the next scene she consoles herself that he has only 'a cater's place' in choosing her.)

Leantio feigns mirth like someone whose appetite hides disease (*vide supra,* p. 230). His place is 'a fine bit to stay a cuckold's stomach.' To the end he 'eats his meat with grudging' and cannot reconcile himself to the loss of Bianca. He, like the ward, has only a cater's place; it is largely through this kind of imagery that the link between plot and subject is kept. Bianca, like Deflores, dies 'tasting my last breath in a cup of love.' The other chief images of the play are those drawn from plagues and diseases, from treasure and jewels, and from light and darkness. The metaphors of disease are nearly always applied to lust, reinforcing the connection between spiritual and physical death. It is like 'destruction' worn in a man's bosom; a 'plague' which a man brings home to his own house. Livia's love for Leantio is 'a diseased part' which Hippolito must cut off. Bianca finds the Duke diseased (perhaps this is meant to be taken literally) but:

> Since my honour's leprous why should I
> Preserve that fair that caused the leprosy?
> (2. 2. 429–30)

And she dies recognising her foulness in words which recall those of *The Changeling:*

> My *deformity* in spirit's more foul
> A blemished face best fits a leprous soul. (5. 2. 246–7)

The metaphors of wealth need hardly be considered; their functions will be evident. Affection is the wealth of the good. Bianca, while she is chaste, is Leantio's 'treasure,' his 'jewel,' his 'life's wealth.' He in turn is Livia's 'riches.' The use of light and darkness occurs in the last two acts only: it is symbolised in the action in the scene where the Cardinal brings two candles on to the stage and shows his brother the darkness of his own life. Bianca is called 'brightness' and 'bright Bianca' by the Duke: Leantio's life was such that 'flames were not nimbler,' though to Hippolito the crown of his sin is that he is 'an impudent daylight lecher.' The atmosphere of darkness thickens to the close (all the revels would be by torchlight) and is mingled with imagery of blood.

It is not absolutely necessary to grasp the scheme of imagery or even the themes, in order to appreciate the plays. They are not completely dependent upon this scheme in the way in which the plays of Tourneur are: a great deal can be got from them on the level of narrative-and-character alone. But it is difficult to grasp the connection of plots and subplots in any other way, without which Middleton must seem to combine an exceptional power of construction and a wanton disregard of its elementary principles in the most curious way. It remains true, however, that the stress which should fall upon themes and imagery is much lighter in Middleton's plays than in those of most of his contemporaries. This is not to say that Middleton's language is less poetic or less important than that of the other poets, but that he also relies upon action and characterisation in a way which no one else did (except Shakespeare). His language too gains its effects by different methods from those of the majority of the Elizabethans; he does not rely upon explicit statement or direct speech but upon implication; nor upon a gorgeous and elaborate vocabulary, but upon a pregnant simplicity which is perhaps more difficult to achieve, and is certainly found more seldom.

NOTE

1. See Leantio's words, I. I. 47–8: 'If it be known, I've lost her: do but think now What that loss is—life's but a trifle to it.'

HELEN GARDNER

The Tragedy of Damnation

WE ARE all familiar with the progeny of Milton's Satan and the effort of most recent criticism has been directed towards clearing the Satan of Milton's poem from his associations with the Promethean rebel of romantic tradition. But the question whether Satan had any ancestors has hardly been raised, or has been dismissed by reference to the devil of popular tradition, or by an allusion to the heroic figure of the Old English *Genesis B.* The late Mr. Charles Williams, in an essay on Milton which seems likely to become a classic, and Mr. C. S. Lewis, building, as he delighted to own, on Mr. Williams, destroyed, one hopes for ever, the notion that Satan had grounds for his rebellion.[1] But when we have agreed that Satan's 'wrongs' which 'exceed all measure' exist only in Shelley's generous imagination, and that it is easier to draw a bad character than a good, and have assented to the statement that Satan's career is a steady progress from bad to worse and ends with his complete deformity, we still have no explanation of why the Romantic critics stood *Paradise Lost* on its head, or why the 'common reader' finds the imaginative impact of the first books so much more powerful than that of the last, or why, as one re-reads the poem, the exposure of Satan's malice and meanness seems curiously irrelevant. There remains always, untouched by the argument, the image of enormous pain and eternal loss. It is out of key with the close of the poem, which does not drive it from our memory, nor absorb it.

'From hero to general, from general to politician, from politician to

From *Essays and Studies,* I (1948), pp. 46–66. Reprinted by permission of the author. The title of this essay has been changed from its original form, 'Milton's "Satan" and the Theme of Damnation in Elizabethan Tragedy.'

secret service agent, and thence to a thing that peers in at bedroom or bathroom windows, and thence to a toad, and finally to a snake—such is the progress of Satan,' writes Mr. Lewis, and he rightly declares that there is no question of Milton's beginning by making Satan too glorious and then, too late, attempting to rectify the error. 'Such an unerring picture of "the sense of injured merit" in its actual operations upon character cannot have come about by blundering and accident.' We can parallel this account of the career of Satan, but not from Iago and Becky Sharp, whom Mr. Lewis cites as examples of bad characters who are more interesting than their virtuous opposites. From a brave and loyal general, to a treacherous murderer, to a hirer of assassins, to an employer of spies, to a butcher, to a coward, to a thing with no feeling for anything but itself, to a monster and a 'hell-hound': that is a summary of the career of Macbeth. From a proud philosopher, master of all human knowledge, to a trickster, to a slave of phantoms, to a cowering wretch: that is a brief sketch of the progress of Dr. Faustus. With varying use of mythological machinery, this theme of the deforming of a creature in its origin bright and good, by its own willed persistence in acts against its own nature, is handled by Shakespeare and Marlowe, and with great power, but in a purely naturalistic setting, by Middleton and Rowley in *The Changeling*. It is on the tragic stage that we find the idea of damnation in English literature before *Paradise Lost*. 'Satan,' writes Mr. Williams, 'is the Image of personal clamour for personal independence.' He is in rebellion against 'the essential fact of things.' The same can be said of Faustus, of Macbeth, and of Beatrice-Joanna, and it is particularly interesting to notice that in *Macbeth* and *The Changeling* the dramatists have altered their sources to bring out the full implications of the theme.

The devil was a comic character in the medieval drama; in the Elizabethan period he virtually disappears in his own person from the greater plays. But what Mr. Lewis calls 'the Satanic predicament' is there, and it appears in the tragic, not the comic mode of vision. The terrible distinction between devils and men in popular theology lay in the irreversibility of the fall of the angels. Unlike men the fallen angels were incapable of repentance and so for them there was no pardon. As Donne puts it: 'To those that fell, can appertaine no reconciliation; no more then to those that die in their sins; for *Quod homini mors, Angelis casus;* The fall of the Angels wrought upon them, as the death of a man does upon him; They are both equally incapable of change to better.' [2] Donne recognizes that some of the Fathers thought that 'the devill retaining still his faculty of free will, is therefore capable of repentance, and so of benefit by this comming of Christ'; [3] but this is exactly the point which Aquinas denies and Donne assents to his view. Aquinas decides that the fallen angels cannot repent, since, though they know the beginnings of penitence in fear, their free-will is perverted: 'Quidquid in eis est naturale, totum est bonum et ad bonum inclinans, sed liberum arbitrium in eis est in malo obstinatum; et quia motus virtutis et vitii non sequitur inclinationem naturae, sed magis motum liberi arbitrii; ideo non oportet, quamvis naturaliter inclinentur ad bonum, quod motus virtutis in eis sit, vel esse possit.' [4] In the tragic world of Faustus and Macbeth we find presented to us in human terms this incapacity for change to a better state. It never occurs to us that Macbeth will turn back, or indeed that he can; and though Marlowe, in this more merciful, as he is always more metaphysical, than Shakespeare, keeps before us the fact of Faustus's humanity by the urgings of the Good Angel, yet to the Good Angel's 'Faustus, repent; yet God will pity thee,' comes at once the Bad Angel's response: 'Thou art a spirit; [5] God cannot pity thee'; and to Faustus's

> Who buzzeth in mine ears, I am a spirit?
> Be I a devil, yet God may pity me;
> Yea, God will pity me, if I repent.

comes the confident statement of the Bad Angel: 'Ay, but Faustus never shall repent'; to which Faustus gives a despairing assent: 'My heart is harden'd, I cannot repent.' [6]

In the three plays mentioned, along with this incapacity for change to a better state, or repentance, go two other closely related ideas. The initial act is an act against nature, it is a primal sin, in that it contradicts the 'essential fact of things,' and its author knows that it does so. It is not an act committed by mistake; it is not an error of judgment, it is an error of will. The act is unnatural and so are its results; it deforms the nature which performs it. The second idea is the irony of retributive justice. The act is performed for an imagined good, which appears so infinitely desirable that the conditions for its supposed satisfaction are accepted; but a rigorous necessity reigns and sees to it that though the conditions are exacted literally, the desire is only granted ironically, and this is inevitable, since the desire is for something forbidden by the very nature of man.[7]

We are unfortunate in possessing Marlowe's greatest play only in an obviously mutilated form; but in spite of possible distortion and some interpolation in the centre, the grandeur of the complete reversal stands out clearly. Apart from its opening and concluding choruses, which provide an archaic framework, and the short closing scene in the 1616 text, where the scholars find the mangled body of Faustus, the play begins and ends with the hero in his study. In the first scene Faustus runs through all the branches of human knowledge and finds them inadequate to his desires. Logic can only teach argument; medicine stops short where human desire is most thwarted, since it cannot defeat death; law is a mercenary pursuit, and divinity, which he comes to last, holds the greatest disappointment: it is grounded in the recognition of man's mortality and his fallibility. The two texts from Jerome's Bible insult his aspiration: *Stipendium peccati mors est,* and *Si peccasse negamus, fallimur, et nulla est in nobis veritas.*[8] He turns instead to magic because it is

> a world of profit and delight,
> Of power, of honour, and omnipotence.

He decides to 'tire his brains to get a deity.' The sin of Faustus here is presumption, the aspiring above his order, or the rebellion against the law of his creation.

But when he is last seen alone in his study it is the opposite sin which delivers him to damnation: the final sin of Faustus is despair.[9] However much he may call in his fear on God or Christ, it is the power of Lucifer and the bond with Lucifer which he really believes in. It is to Lucifer he prays: 'O, spare me, Lucifer!,' and 'Ah, rend not my heart for naming of my Christ!' Donne gives presumption and despair as one of the couples which the Schoolmen have called sins against the Holy Ghost because naturally they shut out those meanes by which the Holy Ghost might work upon us . . . for presumption takes away the feare of God, and desperation the love of God.'[10] They are the two faces of the sin of Pride. Faustus tormented by devils is obsessed by their power; but the Old Man is safe from them, because of his faith. The great reversal from the first scene of *Dr. Faustus* to the last can be defined in different ways: from presumption to despair; from doubt of the existence of hell to belief in the reality of nothing else; from a desire to be more than man to the recognition that he has excluded himself from the promise of redemption for all mankind in Christ; from haste to sign the bond to desire for delay when the moment comes to honour it; from aspiration to deity and omnipotence to longing for extinction. At the beginning Faustus wished to rise above his humanity; at the close he would sink below it, be transformed into a beast or into 'little water drops.' At the beginning he attempts usurpation upon God; at the close he is an usurper upon the Devil.[11]

As for the reward Faustus obtains, it is difficult to argue from the play as it has come down to us, and one should not in fairness say that Faustus appears to sell his soul for the satisfaction of playing practical jokes. But there are two episodes of some significance near the beginning, in which Marlowe's hand is clearly apparent, which it is possible to argue from. Faustus takes Mephistophilis as his servant; he demands twenty-four years of 'all voluptuousness'

> Having thee ever to attend on me,
> To give me whatsoever I shall ask,
> To tell me whatsoever I demand,
>
> . . . . . .
>
> And always be obedient to my will.

As the play proceeds it is clear what happens with the last clause of the agreement: the obedient servant becomes the master. It is Mephistophilis who speaks with authority as representative of 'great Lucifer' and it is Faustus who obeys. But it is the same with the other two clauses. Immediately after the bond is signed Faustus begins to ask questions, and he asks about hell. He receives what are in the context of the play true answers, but he does not believe them. He thinks hell a fable, and Mephistophilis with melancholy irony leaves the subject: 'Ay, think so, till experience change thy mind.' Then Faustus makes his first request: he asks for a wife. Here the text is plainly defective; the verse breaks down into half-lines and prose, a devil enters dressed as a woman with fireworks attached which explode. But after this horseplay, Mephistophilis resumes in dignified Marlovian verse:

> Marriage is but a ceremonial toy:
> And if thou lovest me, think no more of it.
> I'll cull thee out the fairest courtesans,
> And bring them ev'ry morning to thy bed:
> She whom thine eye shall like, thy heart shall have.

If we turn to the source, the English Faust Book, we can, I think, see the implications of the scene and conjecture why Marlowe set it here.

> Doctor *Faustus* . . . bethinking himself of a wife called *Mephistophiles* to counsaile; which would in no wise agree: demanding of him if he would breake the couenant made with him or if hee had forgot it. Hast thou not (quoth *Mephistophiles*) sworne thy selfe an enemy to God and all creatures? To this I answere thee, thou canst not marry; thou canst not serue two masters, God, and my Prince: for wedlock is a chiefe institution ordained of God, and that hast thou promised to defie, as we doe all, and that hast thou also done: and moreouer thou hast confirmed it with thy blood: perswade thy selfe, that what thou doost in contempt of wedlock, it is all to thine owne delight.

When Faustus persists in his demand, an ugly devil appears and offers himself as a bride. On his vanishing Mephistophilis re-appears to say: 'It is no iesting with us, holde thou that which thou hast vowed, and wee will perform as wee haue promised.' [12] The point of the scene is clear even in the play as we have it: Faustus's first request is met with a refusal. The source gives the full implications of that refusal, which may have been cut out to allow for more fireworks: marriage and 'the fairest courtesans' are incompatibles. Faustus has not exchanged limitations for freedom; he has merely exchanged one kind of limitation for another. Marriage belongs to the world he has left. He cannot have all he wants, for the satisfaction of some desires involves the thwarting of others.

It is the same with knowledge soon after. Faustus disputes with Mephistophilis of 'divine astrology.' The answers he gets he dismisses with contempt; he knew them already. But then he goes on to ask the great question:

> *Faust.* Well, I am answer'd. Now tell me who made the world.
> *Meph.* I will not.
> *Faust.* Sweet Mephistophilis, tell me.
> *Meph.* Move me not, Faustus.
> *Faust.* Villain, have I not bound thee to tell me any thing?
> *Meph.* Ay, that is not against our kingdom.
> This is: thou art damn'd; think thou of hell.

Some kinds of knowledge, like some kinds of experience, Faustus has shut himself off from. He has not escaped the necessity of choice. It is a chosen path he follows to the end. Marlowe does all he can by the device of the two angels to keep before us that Faustus is still a man, and that repentance is open to him, if he will only

> Call for mercy, and avoid despair.

But he persists. His rewards are the delights of the imagination, sweet and terrible fantasies, culminating in the vision of Helen,[13] and the exercise of what power Mephistophilis allows him, for the practical jokes probably represent a debasing rather than an alteration of Marlowe's intention. But knowledge and felicity he has exchanged for shadows, and for power he gets slavery.

The theme of damnation was explicit for Marlowe in the story he dramatized. Shakespeare reads it into the story of Macbeth, or rather he shapes his material to bring out the same fundamental conceptions as are embodied in the Faustus myth. The story is fully developed in terms of human beings and their relations to each other. Macbeth's crime is a crime against his fellow men, against society, and this provides Shakespeare with what Marlowe found so difficult to construct, a proper middle to his play. But even so *Macbeth* is by far the shortest of the great tragedies, in spite of having far the longest exposition, and, as Bradley noted, its minor characters are singularly lifeless and uninteresting. The interest is concentrated almost wholly on Macbeth and his wife.

The crime that Macbeth commits is, as has been pointed out, without any of the excuses which the source offered. A quite different play could have been made out of Holinshed's narrative; Shakespeare might have written the tragedy of a brave and able man, impatient at misgovernment, killing a weak and ineffective king, and being corrupted by the evil means he had chosen to a supposedly good end. There is a rational motive too in the other story from which Shakespeare took the details of the murder, for Donwald, who slew King Duff, was avenging his kinsfolk, who had been barbarously punished by the king. But Shakespeare's Duncan is blameless and kingly, and he has paid all honour to Macbeth. The deed is committed with the fullest knowledge of its wickedness, and, indeed, of its folly. Macbeth knows, until the moment when his judgment is overpowered by his wife, that, whether or not there is retribution in the life to come, some crimes are so outrageous that they cannot escape vengeance here. Macbeth himself analyses for us the nature of his deed: it defies the ties of blood and loyalty, the trust between man and man on which society is built, the primitive sacredness of the guest, and the reverence that is due to virtue and innocence. Macbeth knows that the act is inhuman, that it does not 'become a man.' Lady Macbeth knows this too: she knows the deed is a violation of her womanhood; she must become 'unsexed,' become a monster to do it.

The close of *Macbeth* shows the same deadly ironic justice as the close of *Dr. Faustus.* Macbeth and his wife expel pity and remorse from their natures, and they find themselves confronted by a world that has no pity for them. In the last act, nobody says a word of Macbeth that is not inspired by a cold hatred. He is 'this dead butcher,' and he is allowed no death speech of exculpation. There is no restoration of the original image of the hero in this play as there is in *Othello.* To point the full horror of his hunting down we are shown, just before, the death of Young Siward, 'God's soldier.' For as Faustus is shown to us first and last in his study, so Macbeth is shown first and last as a soldier, and Young Siward's is the death he might have died. Macbeth did more than 'does become a man' and becomes, as he himself knew he would, 'none.' At the end of the play he is simply a wild beast to be destroyed. 'Turn, hell-hound, turn,' cries Macduff to him, and he himself compares himself to a baited bear. His head is borne in like a monster's. He put aside feeling and he finds himself at the end incapable of feeling. He threw away 'golden opinions' and he gets curses; he broke the laws of hospitality and friendship, and he finds himself solitary in a world united against him.

Just as Shakespeare blackened the deed, so he refused to Macbeth any satisfactions upon earth. The ten years of just and prosperous reign in Holinshed are suppressed. The first words we hear Macbeth utter when we see him alone after his crowning are: 'To be thus is nothing.' The great central scene of the play impresses this on us by a vivid visual image: Macbeth wears the crown, but we do not see him seated among his lords; the murdered Banquo sits in his place. Like Faustus Macbeth desires incompatibles: he wants to overleap morality and law to achieve his ambition and at the same time to have the security that only obedience to the law can bring, the 'honour, love, obedience, troops of friends' which he realizes at the close he 'must not look to have.'

In both *Dr. Faustus* and *Macbeth* what astounds our imagination is the spectacle of the hero's suffering, the exploration of the nature of separation, intermittent in *Dr. Faustus,* but sustained throughout the play in *Macbeth.* Macbeth never loses that horror at himself which made him gaze upon his 'hangman's hands' as if they were not his. What he does is a perpetual offence to what he is, and he never ceases to feel it. The horror implicit in the exact Latin of Aquinas is here made vivid to the imagination: 'ideo non oportet, quamvis naturaliter inclinentur ad bonum, quod motus virtutis in eis sit, vel esse possit.'

At first sight *The Changeling* appears a very different play from either *Dr. Faustus* or *Macbeth*, though Beatrice-Joanna has sometimes been compared with Lady Macbeth because of the lack of imagination she shows when she incites to murder. The supernatural, which broods over *Macbeth* and is essential to the story of *Dr. Faustus*, becomes here only a perfunctory acknowledgment of the popular taste for ghosts of murdered men. Beatrice-Joanna makes her choice and instigates to crime, prompted only by her passion for Alsemero, with no 'supernatural solicitings' to disturb her judgment. But though this is true literally, Middleton gains an effect that is beyond the natural by the wonderful invention of De Flores.[14]

The alterations that Middleton made in his source are very remarkable; all the play's most memorable situations are invented. The story as told by Reynolds is flat and pointless, as the following summary shows.[15]

> The opening situation is the same as in the play: Beatrice-Joanna, who meets Alsemero at Mass by chance, is being urged by her father to marry Alonzo Piracquo. She has never liked Piracquo and is at once attracted by Alsemero. The story develops slowly with Beatrice-Joanna removed to the country, and corresponding clandestinely with Alsemero, who at last comes secretly to see her, admitted by her waiting woman, Diaphanta. Beatrice-Joanna tells him 'before *Piracquo* be in another World, there is no hope for *Alsemero* to inioy her for his wife in this'; whereupon Alsemero proposes to send him a challenge. But Beatrice-Joanna makes him promise not to meddle, and swears she can manage her father. The secret meeting is reported to her father, and she realizes that he is set upon her match with Piracquo, and so 'after shee had ruminated, and runne ouer many bloody designes: the diuell, who neuer flies from those that follow him, proffers her an inuention as execrable as damnable. There is a Gallant young Gentleman, of the Garrison of the Castle, who followes her father, that to her knowledge doth deepely honour, and dearely affect her: yea, she knowes, that at her request he will not sticke to murther *Piracquo:* his name is *Signiour Antonio de Flores.*'
>
> Beatrice-Joanna then sends for de Flores and 'with many flattering smiles, and sugered speeches, acquaints him with her purpose and desire, making him many promises of kindenesse and courtesies.' De Flores is so 'intangled in the snares of her beautie, that hee freely promiseth to dispatch *Piracquo;* and so they first consult, and then agree vpon the manner how.' The murder is committed just as in the play, except that de Flores cuts off no finger for proof. He then tells

Beatrice-Joanna what he has done, 'who doth heereat infinitly reioyce, and thankes him with many kisses.'

Piracquo's disappearance is accepted as a mystery; Beatrice-Joanna hints to her lover that Piracquo is dead 'but in such palliating tearmes, that thereby shee may delude and carry away his iudgement, from imagining, that shee had the least shadow, or finger heerein.' Her father withdraws his objections and 'heere our two Louers, to their exceeding great content, and infinite joy, are vnited, and by the bond of marriage of two persons made one.'

But after three happy months, Alsemero suddenly becomes jealous, and begins to restrain his wife's liberty. She complains to her father, but his remonstrances are useless, and Alsemero carries her off to the country. Her father sends de Flores to her with a letter, and de Flores 'salutes and kisseth her, with many amorous embracings and dalliances.' She bids him visit her often as her lover. Alsemero is told of the *liaison* by Diaphanta, and accuses Beatrice-Joanna of infidelity. She, 'in seeking to conceale her whoredome, must dicouer her murther,' and tells Alsemero that she has to show courtesy to de Flores, because he got rid of Piracquo for her. Alsemero, who is unaffected by the revelation of the murder, charges her to admit de Flores no more; but she continues with the affair, and being caught is killed with her paramour by Alsemero. At the trial Alsemero is acquitted of murder, when Diaphanta swears to the fact of adultery. But the author regards him as guilty of concealing the murder of Piracquo, and arranges a fit punishment for him too. He is challenged by Piracquo's younger brother, Tomaso, and by using treachery in the duel kills him. For this he is seized, and after confessing the truth is executed.

The power of Middleton's play lies in something which is quite absent from the source: the absolute contrast at the beginning and the identity at the close of Beatrice-Joanna and De Flores. She is young, beautiful, a virgin, and of secure rank; he is no 'Gallant young Gentleman,' but a despised serving-man, an 'ominous ill-fac'd fellow,' one of those broken soldiers of fortune who are so common in Jacobean tragedy, and he bears the marks of a dissolute life on his face. Middleton is usually praised and praised rightly for the intense realism of his characterization, and particularly for the two studies of Beatrice-Joanna and De Flores; but there is more than realism here. What Mephistophilis is to Faustus, what the 'supernatural solicitings' and the horror of the deed are to Macbeth, De Flores is to Beatrice-Joanna. He is repulsive and she has a strong instinctive loathing of him. She too sins against her nature, when she accepts the thing her nature most loathes as the instrument of her will. The deed comes to her mind through him, because she recognizes him as a suitable instrument. She is horrified when Alsemero suggests a challenge. She is afraid he may be killed, or that the law may step in and seize him. Her instinct tells her that he is an innocent man, and so she remembers another who is not:

> Blood-guiltiness becomes a fouler visage;—
> And now I think on one; I was to blame,
> I ha' marr'd so good a market with my scorn.[16]

It has been said that Beatrice-Joanna has no moral sense: that she is irresponsible, and only develops a sense of responsibility at the close of the play. This is true in a sense; but it might be truer to say that she develops a moral consciousness through her violation of what is fundamentally a moral instinct and a very deep one: the instinct which tells her that De Flores is her opposite.

Middleton's handling of the centre of his play is just as striking. In the centre of *Macbeth* we have the banquet, the concrete image of a hollow kingship; in the centre of *The Changeling* is the marriage that is no marriage. On her wedding night, Beatrice-Joanna has to send her waiting-woman to her husband's bed; we see her outside the door in a frenzy of jealousy and impatience. She too has given away her 'eternal jewel' and got nothing in exchange. The three months of happiness in the source have disappeared, as did the ten years of prosperous kingship in Holinshed. Beatrice-Joanna might say of her married state as Macbeth does of his kingship: 'To be thus is nothing.' She employs De Flores to get Alsemero. She loses Alsemero and gets De Flores. She becomes 'the deed's creature.' In the end she recognizes her link with him and what she has become and sees herself as defiled and defiling. Like Faustus, who continues to affirm his bargain, like Macbeth who adds murder to murder, she too is involved in repetition of the original act; she has again to employ De Flores for her safety; he becomes to her 'a wondrous necessary man' and she comments: 'Here's a man worth loving,' as he makes his preparations for the dispatch of Diaphanta.

With the same sense of the implications of his theme, Middleton makes Alsemero absolutely innocent of any complicity. Beatrice-Joanna and De Flores tower over the play, as Macbeth and Lady Macbeth, and Faustus and Mephistophilis do. Alsemero's function is not to interest us in himself, but to be a standard by which we see what has happened to Beatrice-Joanna. He was to be her reward, and so, in an ironic sense, he is, when he turns upon her with horror and cries: 'O, thou art all deform'd!' She makes a last despairing effort with a lie: 'Remember, I am true unto your bed'; to which Alsemero replies:

> The bed itself's a charnel, the sheets shrouds
> For murder'd carcasses.

As last she tells the truth, and the truth of the play emerges.

> *Beatrice-Joanna.* Alsemero, I'm a stranger to your bed;
> Your bed was cozen'd on the nuptial night,
> For which your false bride died.
> *De Flores.* Yes, and the while I coupled with your mate
> At barley break; now we are left in hell.
> *Vermandero.* We are all there, it circumscribes us here.[17]

It is not suggested that there is any direct relation between these three plays, in the sense that one was inspired by the others; nor is it suggested that when Milton drew his Satan he had these great tragic figures in mind. What is suggested is that Satan belongs to their company, and if we ask where the idea of damnation was handled with seriousness and intensity in English literature before Milton, we can only reply: on the tragic stage. Satan is, of course, a character in an epic, and he is in no sense the hero of the epic as a whole. But he is a figure of heroic magnitude and heroic energy, and he is developed by Milton with dramatic emphasis and dramatic intensity. He is shown, to begin with, engaged in heroic and stupendous enterprises, and again and again in moments of dramatic clash; rousing his supine followers, awaiting his moment in the great debate, confronted with Sin and Death and Chaos itself, flinging taunt for taunt at his angelic adversaries. But most strikingly he is presented to us by the means by which the great Elizabethan dramatists commended their tragic heroes to our hearts and imaginations: by soliloquy. Milton gives to Satan no less than five long soliloquies in Eden, three in the fourth book and two in the ninth.[18] In them he reveals to us 'the hot Hell that alwayes in him burnes,' and recalls again and again

> the bitter memorie
> Of what he was, what is, and what must be
> Worse.

It is in them that the quality which makes Satan a tragic figure appears most strikingly, and it is the quality Mr. Lewis makes weightiest against him: his egoism.

'Satan's monomaniac concern with himself and his supposed rights and wrongs is a necessity of the Satanic predicament,' says Mr. Lewis. The same is true of the great tragic heroes of Shakespeare, and this capacity of theirs to expose relentlessly the full horror of their situations is just what makes them the heroes of their plays.[19] The predicament of Claudius is direr than Hamlet's, but Shakespeare pays little attention to it; Malcolm is the righteous avenger of a horrible crime, but the sympathy we feel for him we take for granted. We are held enthralled instead by the voice of Hamlet, defining for us his 'bad dreams' or that of Macbeth telling us of solitude. If we are to complain that wherever he goes, and whatever he sees, Satan finds nothing of interest but himself, and to compare him unfavourably with Adam, who can converse on topics of general interest such as the stars, what should we say of Lear, who finds in the majesty of the storm or the misery of the naked beggarman only fresh incentives to talk about the unkindness of his daughters? If we can say of a speech of Satan's that 'it fails to be roaring farce only because it spells agony,' we can say the same of Macbeth, complaining at the close of a career of murderous egoism that he has no friends, or of Beatrice-Joanna, 'a woman dipp'd in blood' talking of modesty. Satan is an egoist and Satan is a comic character in exactly the same way as Hamlet, Macbeth, Othello, and Lear are egoists and comic characters. 'O gull! O dolt!' cries Emilia to Othello. We do not pity him the less because we assent.

The critical problem of *Paradise Lost* seems to me to lie here. We are concerned with Satan in a way that is quite different from the way we are concerned with Adam and Eve. In Mr. Lewis's treatment this is quite clear. He uses all his skill to make us regard Satan as a despicable human being, discussing him in terms of 'children, film-stars, politicians, or minor poets'; but he uses equal skill to make us realize we must not regard Adam in this way. If he is right, as I think he is, in pressing a distinction between our attitudes to the two figures, he poses an acute problem for the reader of *Paradise Lost,* and appears to convict Milton of the artistic failure involved in a mixture of kinds.

The distinction I feel I would express in rather different terms. Adam and Eve are representative figures, and the act they perform is a great symbolic act. The plucking of the apple is not in itself imaginatively powerful; its power over us springs from its very triviality; the meaning and the consequences are so much greater than the image of a hand stretched out to pluck the fruit. The temptation and fall of Eve is profound in its psychological analysis, but it lacks the shock of dramatic situation. As Mr. Lewis says: 'The whole thing is so quick, each new element of folly, malice, and corruption enters so unobtrusively, so naturally, that it is hard to realize we have been watching the genesis of murder. We expect something more like Lady Macbeth's "unsex me here".' In other words the situation is not dramatically exploited, lingered on. The scenes between Adam and Eve are deeply human, but they lack the terror, and the dreadful exaggeration of tragedy. The quarrel is only too sadly life-like, but it does not appal us, as does the spectacle of Othello striking Desdemona. In the ninth book and the books that follow, Milton is tracing with insight, with humanity and with humility the process in man through sin to repentance. The progress is steady and ordered; what is said is fully adequate to the situation, appropriate but not astounding. But Satan's defiance of God is not expressed by a symbolic gesture; in his rebellion the act and its meaning are one. And in the earlier books, and indeed wherever Satan appears, what is said goes beyond the necessities of the narrative, because Milton was writing as a tragic artist obsessed by his imagination of a particular experience, and exploring it with the maximum intensity. The experience might be called 'exclusion.' Wherever he goes, whatever he looks at, Satan is perpetually conscious of this. His exclusion is self-willed, as is the exclusion of Faustus, Macbeth and Beatrice-Joanna. Like them he gazes on a heaven he cannot enter; like them he is in the end deformed; like them he remains in the memory with all the stubborn objectivity of the tragic.

If it can be accepted that Satan as he is conceived and presented to us is a tragic figure, it is possible to suggest another explanation for the Romantic misconception of the poem than a dislike of Milton's theology. The early nineteenth century was greatly concerned it would seem with tragic experience; its great poets wanted to be 'miserable and mighty poets of the human heart.' All of them attempted to write tragedy, but, with the possible exception of *The Cenci,* they produced nothing that is admitted to be fully tragic. It was also a period remarkable for penetrating and subtle Shakespearian criticism, but for a criticism which lost a sense of the play in its discussion of the psychology of the characters, and which tended to minimize in the tragic heroes the very thing that made them tragic and not pathetic, the evil in them. In the criticism of the period Hamlet is 'a sweet prince,' Lear 'a man more sinned against than sinning.' Hamlet's savagery and Lear's appalling rages are overlooked. Lamb turned from the stage because he could not bear the cruel comedy of *King Lear*, nor the sight of Desdemona in Othello's arms. Realized intensely in the mind, divorced from his action in the play, the tragic hero was reshaped. It is of the essence of tragedy that it forces us to look at what we normally do not care to look at, and have not invented for ourselves.[20] The failure either to write or to appreciate tragedy in the Romantic period springs from the same cause: the Romantic poets' pre-occupation with themselves, and their lack of capacity to submit themselves to the 'mystery of things.' The famous passage in which Keats defined Shakespeare's quality as 'Negative Capability' goes to the root of the matter. But 'Negative Capability' is as necessary to the spectator and critic of tragedy as to its creator. The tragic is destroyed when we identify the hero with ourselves. Just as the Romantic critics tended to see the heroes of Shakespeare's tragedies as more admirable, more tender, more purely pathetic than they are, so feeling Satan's kinship with the tragic hero they sentimentalized him and made him conform to their limited conception of tragedy. Because he was to be pitied, they minimized the evil in him, inventing wrongs to explain and excuse it.[21]

The present age is also not an age of great tragic writing, though there are some signs of a revival of the tragic spirit. Its best poetry is symbolic, and its criticism, in reviving for us the medieval tradition of allegory, tends towards an allegorical interpretation of all art. Mr. Lewis, in exposing Shelley's misconceptions, has inverted the Romantic attitude, for the effect of his chapter on Satan is to make us feel that because Satan is wicked, and wicked with no excuse, he is not to be pitied, but is to be hated and despised. Shelley saw in Satan the indomitable rebel against unjust tyranny, and while regretting the 'taints' in his character excused them. Mr. Lewis, who thinks more harshly of himself and of human nature than Shelley did, exposes Satan with all the energy and argumentative zeal which we used to hear our European Service employing in denouncing the lies of Goebbels and revealing the true nature of the promises of Hitler. Both Shelley's passionate sympathy and Mr. Lewis's invective derive from the same fundamental attitude: 'It is we who are Satan.' As often happens with plural statements, this is a merely verbal extension of the singular; that is to say it is infected by an egoism that distorts the proper function of the tragic. When we contemplate the lost Archangel, we should not be seeing ourselves in heroic postures defying tyrants, nor weighing up our chances of ending in Hell, any more than, while we watch the progress of Lear, we should be thinking how ungrateful other people are to us for our goodness to them, or resolving to think before we speak next time. Though Shelley and Mr. Lewis are on different sides, they agree in taking sides. Neither of them accepts the complexity of the emotion which Satan arouses.

The tragic is something outside ourselves which we contemplate with awe and pity. Aristotle began the perversion of tragic theory when he suggested that the terror we feel is a terror that the same fate may befall us. Aristotle was a philosopher and a moralist, and, like many of his kind since, wanted to make tragedy safe and useful. But tragedy does not exist to provide us with horrid warnings. 'Pity,' said Stephen Dedalus, expanding the cryptic Aristotelian formula, 'is the feeling which arrests the mind in the presence of whatsoever is grave and constant in human sufferings and unites it with the human sufferer. Terror is the feeling which arrests the mind in the presence of whatsoever is grave and constant in human sufferings and unites it with the secret cause.' [22] We accept the justice by which the tragic hero is destroyed. Indeed if it were not for the justice we should have no pity for him. The acceptance of the justice makes possible the pity, and the pity calls for the justice without which it would turn to loathing. But the cause must be secret in tragedy; it must be felt within the facts exposed; what is hateful in the tragic world is that Eternal Law should argue.

The unity of tragedy is destroyed if the critic makes himself either the champion of the hero or the advocate of Eternal Law. Tragedy 'arrests the mind' as the sufferings of others do, but as our own do not. But in life the arrest is short, for we are involved in the necessity of action. As spectators of tragedy we are released from our perpetual burden of asking ourselves what we ought to do. To use tragedy either as a moral example or as a moral warning is to destroy the glory of tragedy, the power it has to release us from ourselves by arousing in us the sense of magnitude and the sense of awe. Wordsworth, the most untragic of great poets, saw something of the nature of tragedy when he wrote,

> Suffering is permanent, obscure and dark,
> And shares the nature of infinity.

Tragedy may present us with a 'false infinite' but it has that nature. It is permanent 'with such permanence as time has.' Like the rock in Mr. Eliot's *The Dry Salvages,*

> Waves wash over it, fogs conceal it;
> On a halcyon day it is merely a monument,
> In navigable weather it is always a seamark
> To lay a sudden course by: but in the sombre season
> Or the sudden fury, is what it always was.

The figure of Satan has this imperishable significance. If he is not the heroic rebel of Shelley's imagination, neither is he merely an 'unerring picture of the "sense of injur'd merit" in its actual operations upon character.'

But if Mr. Lewis's view seems like an inversion of Shelley's, Mr. Williams's is not very unlike Blake's. What Blake perceived in *Paradise Lost* was a radical dualism, which was perhaps the inevitable effect of treating the myth in epic form. Among the many difficulties inherent in the subject was the difficulty of knowing how much to include in the direct action and how much to put into relations. It was impossible for Milton to begin where his tragedy *Adam Unparadised* was to have begun, in Paradise; the direct action would have been insufficient to fill the epic form. Even as it is, *Paradise Lost* is overweighted with relations. Epic tradition forbade him to begin at the beginning with the exaltation of the Son. Possibly his decision to begin with the moment when Satan lifts his head from the burning waves was inevitable once he had decided against the dramatic form in which he first conceived the subject. But the effect of beginning there, and of the whole of the 'Prologue in Hell' is to make the action of the poem seem to origin in Hell, and to make the acts of Heaven seem only the response called out by the energies of Hell. However much Milton contradicts this later and asserts the overriding Will, the structure and design of his poem contradict and fight against his intention. The parallel, so often praised, between the silence in Hell, and the silence in Heaven reinforces the feeling of dualism, since *contraria sunt aequalia,* and Satan and the Son seem balanced against each other, as Blake saw them to be, while the priority of the scene in Hell seems to make Heaven parody Hell rather than Hell Heaven. Mr. Williams's statement that 'the Son is the Image of Derivation in Love, and Satan is the Image of personal clamour for personal independence' is not unlike Blake's assertion of 'the contraries from which spring what the religious call good and evil.' It suggests at least that Milton made Satan too important in the scheme of his poem.

Perhaps the problem which *Paradise Lost* presents to the critic has its origin in Milton's own change of mind over the form in which he was to write his masterpiece. He first chose the subject of the Fall of Man as suited to a tragedy, and we know that he not only planned the disposition of his material in dramatic form, but actually began the writing. His draft *Adam Unparadised* provides Lucifer with two soliloquies: in the first he was to 'bemoan himself' and 'seek revenge upon man'; in the second he was to appear 'relating and consulting on what he had done to the destruction of man.' The first soliloquy was therefore to have been mainly expository, and in the second Lucifer was to take over the duty of the classical messenger and relate the catastrophe. The strict concentration of classical tragedy would have prevented Lucifer from usurping on the main interest, and his predicament, however much he 'bemoaned himself,' would have been subordinated to the whole design. Why Milton changed his mind we do not know, and he set himself a problem of extraordinary difficulty in choosing to treat this particular subject in epic form. He had somehow to fill the large epic structure, and it is difficult to see how else he could have done it than by expanding Satan's rôle. But it is possible that he turned away from tragedy because his interest had radiated out from the true centre of the action, the Fall itself, and his imagination demanded the larger freedom of the epic. Certainly the fact that Phillips remembered seeing the opening lines of Satan's first soliloquy as part of the projected tragedy suggests that Milton's conception of Satan began to form early, and it may have been that the writing of this first soliloquy showed Milton that the tragic form would not allow him to develop his conception as fully as he wished to. But whether the decision to begin his poem with Satan in Hell was simply the inevitable result of enlarging his action to make it sufficient for an epic, or whether it was Milton's interest in Satan that led him to abandon tragedy for epic, and he therefore naturally began with Satan, the figure of Satan, originally conceived dramatically, is developed dramatically throughout, and Milton expended his creative energies and his full imaginative power in exploring the fact of perversity within a single heroic figure. In this, as in much else, he is what we loosely call an Elizabethan, sacrificing simplicity of effect and strength of design to imaginative opportunity; creating the last great tragic figure in our literature and destroying the unity of his poem in doing so. The dualism which Blake found in the poem's thought, and which in Mr. Williams's analysis seems to dictate its design, is certainly there in its manner. The strong emotions of pity and terror do not mix well with the interest, sympathy and 'admiration' which we feel for the heroes of what Mr. Lewis has called 'the secondary epic,' and, with the possible exception of Hazlitt, no critic of note has done justice to both Satan and Adam as artistic creations. The subject demanded an 'infernal Serpent'; instead Milton has given us 'a lost Archangel.' There would be no difficulty if Satan were simply an Iago; the difficulty arises because he is a Macbeth.

NOTES

1. See *The English Poems of Milton*, with a preface by Charles Williams, (World's Classics) 1940, and C. S. Lewis, *A Preface to Paradise Lost*, 1942.

2. *LXXX Sermons*, 1640, p. 9. A recent reading of Donne's *Sermons* for another purpose has impressed upon me how often Donne provides the comment of a theologian or a moralist upon the tragedies of his contemporaries.

3. *Ibid.*, p. 66.

4. *S.T.*, Supplement, Q. XVI, Art. 3.

5. *Spirit* here as elsewhere in the play means evil spirit, or devil.

6. All quotations from *Dr. Faustus* are from the edition of Dr. F. S. Boas, 1932. The point that Faustus is presented to us as incapable of real repentance, though like the devils he knows the beginnings of penitence in fear and 'believes and trembles,' is obscured if we accept, as Dr. Boas does, the suggestion of Mr. H. T. Baker (*Modern Language Notes*, vol. XXI, pp. 86–7) and transfer to Faustus the close of the Old Man's speech in Act v, scene i (p. 161). In this most touching scene the Old Man makes a last appeal to Faustus to remember his humanity:

> Though thou hast now offended like a man,
> Do not persever in it like a devil;
> Yet, yet, thou hast an amiable soul,
> If sin by custom grow not into nature.

7. Donne supplies us with a comment on the 'omnipotence' of Faustus, the 'kingship' of Macbeth and the 'marriage' of Beatrice-Joanna, when he says: 'For small wages, and ill-paid pensions we serve him (Satan); and lest any man should flatter and delude himselfe, in saying, I have my wages, and my reward before hand, my pleasures in this life, the punish-

ment, (if ever) not till the next, The Apostle destroyes that dreame, with that question of confusion, *What fruit had you then in those things, of which you are now ashamed?* Certainly sin is not a gainfull way; . . . fruitlesness, unprofitableness before, shame and dishonor after.' *LXXX Sermons,* p. 65.

8. It is worth noting that Faustus does not complete the text, which is familiar from its use as one of the Sentences. 'If we say that we have no sin, we deceive ourselves, and the truth is not in us: but, if we confess our sins, he is faithful and just to forgive us our sins, and to cleanse us from all unrighteousness.'

9. The word *despair* or its derivative *desperate* occurs thirteen times in the play. See i. 3. 91; ii. 1. 4 and 5; ii. 2. 25 and 31; iv. 5a, 31; v. 1, 64, 68, 72 and 79; v. 2. 11, 92 and 101.

In *The Conflict of Conscience* by Nathaniell Woodes, Minister of Norwich, published 1581 (Hazlitt-Dodsley, vol. VI) in which we can see the old morality play of wrongful choice, punishment, repentance and forgiveness turning into the Elizabethan tragedy of sin and retribution, the whole struggle in the final act is between the hero's despair and the efforts of his friends to convince him that he is not beyond God's mercy. One can commend the enterprise if not the success of the Minister of Norwich in trying to put the finer points of the doctrine of justification by faith into fourteeners. Poor as his play is, it shows in a most interesting way the great debate of the sixteenth and seventeenth centuries on the freedom of the will being turned into drama. In *The Conflict of Conscience,* at the very last moment, faith conquers, and the happy ending of the old morality is preserved. In *Dr. Faustus,* which retains formally much of the old morality, despair triumphs. Our understanding of some of the tragedies of Shakespeare and his contemporaries might be enriched if we thought more in terms of

> Providence, Foreknowledge, Will, and Fate,
> Fixt Fate, free will, foreknowledge absolute,

and less in terms of 'fatal flaws' and 'errors of judgment.'

10. *LXXX Sermons,* p. 349.

11. 'The greatest sin that ever was, and that upon which even the blood of Christ Jesus hath not wrought, the sin of Angels was that, *Similis ero Altissimo,* to be like God. To love our selves, to be satisfied in our selves, to finde an omnisufficiency in our selves, is an intrusion, an usurpation upon God.' Ibid., p. 156. 'Did God ordain hell fire for us? no, but for the Devil and his Angels. And yet we that are vessels so broken, as that there is not a sheard left, to fetch water at the pit, that is, no means in our selves, to derive one drop of Christs blood upon us, nor to wring out one tear of true repentance from us, have plung'd our selves into this everlasting, and this dark fire, which was not prepared for us: A wretched covetousness, to be intruders upon the Devil; a wretched ambition, to be usurpers upon damnation.' *XXVI Sermons,* 1660, p. 273.

12. *Dr. Faustus,* ed. cit., Appendix I, pp. 181–2.

13. Dr. Greg has recently recovered for us the full mingling of horror

and beauty in the scene in which Faustus embracing Helen cries: 'Her lips suck forth my soul: see where it flies!' He points out that Helen is a 'spirit' and that in this play a spirit is a devil. 'Faustus commits the sin of demoniality, that is bodily intercourse with demons.' See W. W. Greg, 'The Damnation of Faustus,' *Modern Language Review*, April, 1946, pp. 97–107.

14. Since the problem of authorship does not affect my argument, I use Middleton's name for brevity, instead of speaking of Middleton and Rowley.

15. John Reynolds, *God's Revenge against Murder*, 1621, Book I, History IV, pp. 105–46.

16. Quotations from *The Changeling* are from *The Works of Thomas Middleton* edited by A. H. Bullen, 1885–6, vol. VI.

17. The echo from *Dr. Faustus* can hardly be accidental.

> Hell hath no limits, nor is circumscrib'd
> In one self place; but where we are is hell,
> And where hell is, there must we ever be.

18. In spite of the explanatory and anticipatory element in these soliloquies, their general effect, particularly in the two longest, IV, 32–113 and IX, 99–178, is quite different from the effect of the soliloquies of villains such as Richard III or Iago. In them we are conscious of activity of intellect and atrophy of feeling; here, as in the soliloquies of Hamlet or Macbeth, the plans announced are less important than the analysis of the hero's predicament.

19. Henry James puts this well in the preface to *The Princess Casamassima,* London, 1921, p. viii. 'This in fact I have ever found rather terribly the point—that the figures in any picture, the agents in any drama, are interesting only in proportion as they feel their respective situations; since the consciousness, on their part, of the complication exhibited forms for us their link of connection with it. But there are degrees of feeling—the muffled, the faint, the just sufficient, the barely intelligent, as we may say; and the acute, the intense, the complete, in a word—the power to be finely aware and richly responsible. It is those moved in this latter fashion who 'get most' out of all that happens to them and who in so doing enable us, as readers of their record, as participators by a fond attention, also to get most. Their being finely aware—as Hamlet and Lear, say, are finely aware —*makes* absolutely the intensity of their adventure, gives the maximum of sense to what befalls them.'

20. It may be suggested that the success of *The Cenci,* compared with other tragedies of the period, is partly due to the fact that the story was not invented by Shelley. He plainly felt some of the 'superstitious horror' which he tells us the story still aroused in Italy, and was fascinated by the portrait of Beatrice.

21. In the preface to *Prometheus Unbound,* Shelley compared Satan with Prometheus and declared that Prometheus is the 'more poetical character' since he is 'exempt from the taints of ambition, envy, revenge, and a desire for personal aggrandisement, which, in the Hero of *Paradise Lost,* interfere with the interest.' He thought that the character of Satan 'engenders in the mind a pernicious casuistry which leads us to weigh his faults with his

wrongs, and to excuse the former because the latter exceed all measure.' When he wrote the preface to *The Cenci,* Shelley had abandoned the notion that moral perfection made a character poetically interesting, and acknowledged that if Beatrice had been 'wiser and better' she would not have been a tragic character, but he speaks again of the 'casuistry' by which we try to justify what she does, while feeling that it needs justification. When he compared Milton's God and his Devil in *A Defence of Poetry,* Shelley declared Satan was morally superior on the grounds that his situation and his wrongs excused in him the revengefulness which is hateful in his triumphant Adversary. In all three passages one can see Shelley's feeling that the Hero is a person whose side we take. The theme of a nature warped by suffering injustice, and repaying crime with crime, is certainly tragic when handled with seriousness and moral integrity as in *The Cenci,* though it slides all too easily into the sentimental absurdities of the Byronic outcast, and it is always in danger of shallowness. It is the tragic formula of an age which does not believe in original sin, and thinks of evil as not bred in the heart, but caused by circumstances.

22. James Joyce, *A Portrait of the Artist as a Young Man,* chapter v.

T . S . ELIOT

Philip Massinger

MASSINGER has been more fortunately and more fairly judged than several of his greater contemporaries. Three critics have done their best by him: the notes of Coleridge exemplify Coleridge's fragmentary and fine perceptions; the essay of Leslie Stephen is a piece of formidable destructive analysis; and the essay of Swinburne is Swinburne's criticism at its best. None of these, probably, has put Massinger finally and irrefutably into a place.

English criticism is inclined to argue or persuade rather than to state; and, instead of forcing the subject to expose himself, these critics have left in their work an undissolved residuum of their own good taste, which, however impeccable, is something that requires our faith. The principles which animate this taste remain unexplained. Canon Cruickshank's book [1] is a work of scholarship; and the advantage of good scholarship is that it presents us with evidence which is an invitation to the critical faculty of the reader: it bestows a method, rather than a judgment.

It is difficult—it is perhaps the supreme difficulty of criticism—to make the facts generalize themselves; but Mr. Cruickshank at least presents us with facts which are capable of generalization. This is a service of value; and it is therefore wholly a compliment to the author to say that his appendices are as valuable as the essay itself.

The sort of labour to which Mr. Cruickshank has devoted himself is one that professed critics ought more willingly to undertake. It is an important part of criticism, more important than any mere expres-

---

sion of opinion. To understand Elizabethan drama it is necessary to study a dozen playwrights at once, to dissect with all care the complex growth, to ponder collaboration to the utmost line. Reading Shakespeare and several of his contemporaries is pleasure enough, perhaps all the pleasure possible, for most. But if we wish to consummate and refine this pleasure by understanding it, to distil the last drop of it, to press and press the essence of each author, to apply exact measurement to our own sensations, then we must compare; and we cannot compare without parcelling the threads of authorship and influence. We must employ Mr. Cruickshank's judgments; and perhaps the most important judgment to which he has committed himself is this:

> Massinger, in his grasp of stagecraft, his flexible metre, his desire in the sphere of ethics to exploit both vice and virtue, is typical of an age which had much culture, but which, without being exactly corrupt, lacked moral fibre.

Here, in fact, is our text: to elucidate this sentence would be to account for Massinger. We begin vaguely with good taste, by a recognition that Massinger is inferior: can we trace this inferiority, dissolve it, and have left any element of merit?

We turn first to the parallel quotations from Massinger and Shakespeare collocated by Mr. Cruickshank to make manifest Massinger's indebtedness. One of the surest of tests is the way in which a poet borrows. Immature poets imitate; mature poets steal; bad poets deface what they take, and good poets make it into something better, or at least something different. The good poet welds his theft into a whole of feeling which is unique, utterly different from that from which it was torn; the bad poet throws it into something which has no cohesion. A good poet will usually borrow from authors remote in time, or alien in language, or diverse in interest. Chapman borrowed from Seneca; Shakespeare and Webster from Montaigne. The two great followers of Shakespeare, Webster and Tourneur, in their mature work do not borrow from him; he is too close to them to be of use to them in this way. Massinger, as Mr. Cruickshank shows, borrows from Shakespeare a good deal. Let us profit by some of the quotations with which he has provided us—

Massinger:

> Can I call back yesterday, with all their aids
> That bow unto my sceptre? or restore

My mind to that tranquillity and peace
It then enjoyed?

Shakespeare:

Not poppy, nor mandragora,
Nor all the drowsy syrops of the world
Shall ever medicine thee to that sweet sleep
Which thou owedst yesterday.

Massinger's is a general rhetorical question, the language just and pure, but colourless. Shakespeare's has particular significance; and the adjective 'drowsy' and the verb 'medicine' infuse a precise vigour. This is, on Massinger's part, an echo, rather than an imitation or a plagiarism—the basest, because least conscious, form of borrowing. 'Drowsy syrop' is a condensation of meaning frequent in Shakespeare, but rare in Massinger.

Massinger:

Thou didst not borrow of Vice her indirect,
Crooked, and abject means.

Shakespeare:

God knows, my son;
By what by-paths and indirect crook'd ways
I met this crown.

Here, again, Massinger gives the general forensic statement, Shakespeare the particular image. 'Indirect crook'd' is forceful in Shakespeare; a mere pleonasm in Massinger. 'Crook'd ways' is a metaphor; Massinger's phrase only the ghost of a metaphor.

Massinger:

And now, in the evening,
When thou should'st pass with honour to thy rest,
Wilt thou fall like a meteor?

Shakespeare:

I shall fall
Like a bright exhalation in the evening,
And no man see me more.

Here the lines of Massinger have their own beauty. Still, a 'bright exhalation' appears to the eye and makes us catch our breath in the evening; 'meteor' is a dim simile; the word is worn.

Massinger:

What you deliver to me shall be lock'd up
In a strong cabinet, of which you yourself
Shall keep the key.

Shakespeare:

'Tis in my memory locked,
And you yourself shall keep the key of it.

In the preceding passage Massinger had squeezed his simile to death; here he drags it round the city at his heels; and how swift Shakespeare's figure is! We may add two more passages, not given by our commentator; here the model is Webster. They occur on the same page, an artless confession.

Here he comes,
His nose held up; he hath something in the wind,

is hardly comparable to

The Cardinal lifts up his nose like a foul porpoise before a storm,

and when we come upon

as tann'd galley-slaves
Pay such as do redeem them from the oar

it is unnecessary to turn up the great lines in the *Duchess of Malfy*. Massinger fancied this galley-slave; for he comes with his oar again in *The Bondman*—

Never did galley-slave shake off his chains,
Or looked on his redemption from the oar . . .

Now these are mature plays; and *The Roman Actor* (from which we have drawn the two previous extracts) is said to have been the preferred play of its author.

We may conclude directly from these quotations that Massinger's feeling for language had outstripped his feeling for things; that his eye and his vocabulary were not in co-operation. One of the greatest distinctions of several of his elder contemporaries—we name Middleton, Webster, Tourneur—is a gift for combining, for fusing into a single phrase, two or more diverse impressions.

> . . . in her strong toil of grace

of Shakespeare is such a fusion; the metaphor identifies itself with what suggests it; the resultant is one and is unique—

> Does the silk worm expend her yellow labours? . . .
> Why does yon fellow falsify highways
> And lays his life between the judge's lips
> To refine such a one? keeps horse and men
> To beat their valours for her?
>
> Let the common sewer take it from distinction . . .
> Lust and forgetfulness have been amongst us . . .

These lines of Tourneur and of Middleton exhibit that perpetual slight alteration of language, words perpetually juxtaposed in new and sudden combinations, meanings perpetually *eingeschachtelt* into meanings, which evidences a very high development of the senses, a development of the English language which we have perhaps never equalled. And, indeed, with the end of Chapman, Middleton, Webster, Tourneur, Donne we end a period when the intellect was immediately at the tips of the senses. Sensation became word and word was sensation. The next period is the period of Milton (though still with a Marvell in it); and this period is initiated by Massinger.

It is not that the word becomes less exact. Massinger is, in a wholly eulogistic sense, choice and correct. And the decay of the senses is not inconsistent with a greater sophistication of language. But every vital development in language is a development of feeling as well. The verse of Shakespeare and the major Shakespearean dramatists is an innovation of this kind, a true mutation of species. The verse practised by Massinger is a different verse from that of his predecessors; but it is not a development based on, or resulting from, a new way of feeling. On the contrary, it seems to lead us away from feeling altogether.

We mean that Massinger must be placed as much at the beginning of one period as at the end of another. A certain Boyle, quoted by Mr. Cruickshank, says that Milton's blank verse owes much to the study of Massinger's.

'In the indefinable touches which make up the music of a verse [say Boyle], in the artistic distribution of pauses, and in the unerring choice and grouping of just those words which strike the ear as the perfection of harmony, there are, if we leave Cyril Tourneur's *Atheist's Tragedy* out of the question, only two masters in the drama, Shakespeare in his latest period and Massinger.'

This Boyle must have had a singular ear to have preferred Tourneur's secondary work to his *Revenger's Tragedy,* and one must think that he had never glanced at Ford. But though the appraisal be ludicrous, the praise is not undeserved. Mr. Cruickshank has given us an excellent example of Massinger's syntax—

> What though my father
> Writ man before he was so, and confirm'd it,
> By numbering that day no part of his life
> In which he did not service to his country;
> Was he to be free therefore from the laws
> And ceremonious form in your decrees?
> Or else because he did as much as man
> In those three memorable overthrows,
> At Granson, Morat, Nancy, where his master,
> The warlike Charalois, with whose misfortunes
> I bear his name, lost treasure, men, and life,
> To be excused from payment of those sums
> Which (his own patrimony spent) his zeal
> To serve his country forced him to take up!

It is impossible to deny the masterly construction of this passage; perhaps there is not one living poet who could do the like. It is impossible to deny the originality. The language is pure and correct, free from muddiness or turbidity. Massinger does not confuse metaphors, or heap them one upon another. He is lucid, though not easy. But if Massinger's age, 'without being exactly corrupt, lacks moral fibre,' Massinger's verse, without being exactly corrupt, suffers from cerebral anaemia. To say that an involved style is necessarily a bad style would be preposterous. But such a style should follow the involutions of a mode of perceiving, registering, and digesting impressions which is also involved. It is to be feared that the feeling of Massinger is simple and overlaid with received ideas. Had Massinger had a nervous system as refined as that of Middleton, Tourneur, Webster, or Ford, his style would be a triumph. But such a nature was not at hand, and Massinger precedes, not another Shakespeare but Milton.

Massinger is, in fact, at a further remove from Shakespeare than that other precursor of Milton—John Fletcher. Fletcher was above all an opportunist, in his verse, in his momentary effects, never quite a pastiche; in his structure ready to sacrifice everything to the single scene. To Fletcher, because he was more intelligent, less will be forgiven. Fletcher had a cunning guess at feelings, and betrayed them; Massinger was unconscious and innocent. As an artisan of the theatre he is not inferior to Fletcher, and his best tragedies have an honester unity than *Bonduca.* But the unity is superficial. In *The Roman Actor* the development of parts is out of all proportion to the central theme; in *The Unnatural Combat,* in spite of the deft handling of suspense and the quick shift from climax to a new suspense, the first part of the play is the hatred of Malefort for his son and the second part is his passion for his daughter. It is theatrical skill, not an artistic conscience arranging emotions, that holds the two parts together. In *The Duke of Milan* the appearance of Sforza at the Court of his conqueror only delays the action, or rather breaks the emotional rhythm. And we have named three of Massinger's best.

A dramatist who so skilfully welds together parts which have no reason for being together, who fabricates plays so well knit and so remote from unity, we should expect to exhibit the same synthetic cunning in character. Mr. Cruickshank, Coleridge, and Leslie Stephen are pretty well agreed that Massinger is no master of characterization. You can, in fact, put together heterogeneous parts to form a lively play; but a character, to be living, must be conceived from some emotional unity. A character is not to be composed of scattered observations of human nature, but of parts which are felt together. Hence it is that although Massinger's failure to draw a moving character is no greater than his failure to make a whole play, and probably springs from the same defective sensitiveness, yet the failure in character is more conspicuous and more disastrous. A 'living' character is not necessarily 'true to life.' It is a person whom we can see and hear, whether he be true or false to human nature as we know it. What the creator of character needs is not so much knowledge of motives as keen sensibility; the dramatist need not understand people; but he must be exceptionally aware of them. This awareness was not given to Massinger. He inherits the traditions of conduct, female chastity, hymeneal sanctity, the fashion of honour, without either criticizing or informing them from his own experience. In the earlier drama these conventions are merely a framework, or an alloy necessary for working the metal; the metal itself consisted of unique emotions resulting inevitably from the circumstances, resulting or inhering as inevitably as the properties of a chemcial compound. Middleton's heroine, for instance, in *The Changeling*, exclaims in the well-known words—

> Why, 'tis impossible thou canst be so wicked,
> To shelter such a cunning cruelty
> To make his death the murderer of my honour!

The word 'honour' in such a situation is out of date, but the emotion of Beatrice at that moment, given the conditions, is as permanent and substantial as anything in human nature. The emotion of Othello in Act v is the emotion of a man who discovers that the worst part of his own soul has been exploited by some one more clever than he; it is this emotion carried by the writer to a very high degree of intensity. Even in so late and so decayed a drama as that of Ford, the framework of emotions and morals of the time is only the vehicle for statements of feeling which are unique and imperishable: Ford's and Ford's only.

What may be considered corrupt or decadent in the morals of Massinger is not an alteration or diminution in morals; it is simply the disappearance of all the personal and real emotions which this morality supported and into which it introduced a kind of order. As soon as the emotions disappear the morality which ordered it appears hideous. Puritanism itself became repulsive only when it appeared as the survival of a restraint after the feelings which it restrained had gone. When Massinger's ladies resist temptation they do not appear to undergo any important emotion; they merely know what is expected of them; they manifest themselves to us as lubricous prudes. Any age has its conventions; and any age might appear absurd when its conventions get into the hands of a man like Massinger—a man, we mean, of so exceptionally superior a literary talent as Massinger's, and so paltry an imagination. The Elizabethan morality was an important convention; important because it was not consciously of one social class alone, because it provided a framework for emotions to which all classes could respond, and it hindered no feeling. It was not hypocritical, and it did not suppress; its dark corners are haunted by the ghost of Mary Fitton and perhaps greater. It is a subject which has not been sufficiently investigated. Fletcher and Massinger rendered it ridiculous; not by not believing it, but because they were men of great talents who could not vivify it; because they could not fit into it passionate, complete human characters.

The tragedy of Massinger is interesting chiefly according to the definition given before; the highest degree of verbal excellence compatible with the most rudimentary development of the senses. Massinger succeeds better in something which is not tragedy; in the romantic comedy. *A Very Woman* deserves all the praise that Swinburne, with his almost unerring gift of selection, has bestowed upon it. The probable collaboration of Fletcher had the happiest results; for certainly that admirable comic personage, the tipsy Borachia, is handled with more humour than we expect of Massinger. It is a play which would be enjoyable on the stage. The form, however, of romantic comedy is itself inferior and decadent. There is an inflexibility about the poetic drama which is by no means a matter of classical, or neoclassical, or pseudo-classical law. The poetic drama might develop forms highly different from those of Greece or England, India or Japan. Conceded the utmost freedom, the romantic drama would yet remain inferior. The poetic drama must have an emotional unity, let the emotion be whatever you like. It must have a dominant tone; and if this be strong enough, the most heterogeneous emotions may be made to reinforce it. The romantic comedy is a skilful concoction of inconsistent emotion, a *revue* of emotion. *A Very Woman* is surpassingly well plotted. The debility of romantic drama does not depend upon extravagant setting, or preposterous events, or inconceivable coincidences; all these might be found in a serious tragedy or comedy. It consists in an internal incoherence of feelings, a concatenation of emotions which signifies nothing.

From this type of play, so eloquent of emotional disorder, there was no swing back of the pendulum. Changes never come by a simple reinfusion into the form which the life has just left. The romantic drama was not a new form. Massinger dealt not with emotions so much as with the social abstractions of emotions, more generalized and therefore more quickly and easily interchangeable within the confines of a single action. He was not guided by direct communications through the nerves. Romantic drama tended, accordingly, towards what is sometimes called the 'typical,' but which is not the truly typical; for the *typical* figure in a drama is always particularized —an individual. The tendency of the romantic drama was towards a form which continued it in removing its more conspicuous vices, was towards a more severe external order. This form was the Heroic Drama. We look into Dryden's 'Essay on Heroic Plays,' and we find that 'love and valour ought to be the subject of an heroic poem.' Massinger, in his destruction of the old drama, had prepared the way for Dryden. The intellect had perhaps exhausted the old conventions. It was not able to supply the impoverishment of feeling.

Such are the reflections aroused by an examination of some of Massinger's plays in the light of Mr. Cruickshank's statement that Massinger's age 'had much more culture, but, without being exactly corrupt, lacked moral fibre.' The statement may be supported. In order to fit into our estimate of Massinger the two admirable comedies—*A New Way to Pay Old Debts* and *The City Madam*—a more extensive research would be required than is possible within our limits.

II

Massinger's tragedy may be summarized for the unprepared reader as being very dreary. It is dreary, unless one is prepared by a somewhat extensive knowledge of his livelier contemporaries to grasp without fatigue precisely the elements in it which are capable of giving pleasure; or unless one is incited by a curious interest in versification. In comedy, however, Massinger was one of the few masters in the language. He was a master in a comedy which is serious, even sombre; and in one aspect of it there are only two names to mention with his: Those of Marlowe and Jonson. In comedy, as a matter of fact, a greater variety of methods were discovered and employed than in tragedy. The method of Kyd, as developed by Shakespeare, was the standard for English tragedy down to Otway and to Shelley. But both individual temperament, and varying epochs, made more play with comedy. The comedy of Lyly is one thing; that of Shakespeare, followed by Beaumont and Fletcher, is another; and that of Middleton is a third. And Massinger, while he has his own comedy, is nearer to Marlowe and Jonson than to any of these.

Massinger was, in fact, as a comic writer, fortunate in the moment at which he wrote. His comedy is transitional; but it happens to be one of those transitions which contain some merit not anticipated by predecessors or refined upon by later writers. The comedy of Jonson is nearer to caricature; that of Middleton a more photographic delineation of low life. Massinger is nearer to Restoration comedy, and more like his contemporary, Shirley, in assuming a certain social level, certain distinctions of class, as a postulate of his comedy. This resemblance to later comedy is also the important point of difference between Massinger and earlier comedy. But Massinger's comedy differs just as widely from the comedy of manners proper; he is closer to that in his romantic drama—in *A Very Woman*—than in *A New Way to Pay Old Debts;* in his comedy his interest is not in the follies of love-making or the absurdities of social pretence, but in the unmasking of villainy. Just as the Old Comedy of Molière differs in principle from the New Comedy of Marivaux, so the Old Comedy of Massinger differs from the New Comedy of his contemporary Shirley. And as in France, so in England, the more farcical comedy was the more serious. Massinger's great comic rogues, Sir Giles Overreach and Luke Frugal, are members of the large English family which includes Barabas and Sir Epicure Mammon, and from which Sir Tunbelly Clumsy claims descent.

What distinguishes Massinger from Marlowe and Jonson is in the main an inferiority. The greatest comic characters of these two dramatists are slight work in comparison with Shakespeare's best—Falstaff has a third dimension and Epicure Mammon has only two. But this slightness is part of the nature of the art which Jonson practised, a smaller art than Shakespeare's. The inferiority of Massinger to Jonson is an inferiority, not of one type of art to another, but within Jonson's type. It is a simple deficiency. Marlowe's and Jonson's comedies were a view of life; they were, as great literature is, the transformation of a personality into a personal work of art, their lifetime's work, long or short. Massinger is not simply a smaller personality: his personality hardly exists. He did not, out of his own personality, build a world of art, as Shakespeare and Marlowe and Jonson built.

In the fine pages which Remy de Gourmont devotes to Flaubert in his *Problème du Style*, the great critic declares:

> La vie est un dépouillement. Le but de l'activité propre de l'homme est de nettoyer sa personnalité, de la laver de toutes les souillures qu'y déposa l'éducation, de la dégager de toutes les empreintes qu'y laissèrent nos admirations adolescentes;

and again:

> Flaubert incorporait toute sa sensibilité à ses oeuvres. . . . Hors de

> ses livres, où il se transvasait goutte à gouette, jusqu'à la lie, Flaubert est fort peu intéressant.

Of Shakespeare notably, of Jonson less, of Marlowe (and of Keats to the term of life allowed him), one can say that they *se transvasaient goutte à gouette;* and in England, which has produced a prodigious number of men of genius and comparatively few works of art, there are not many writers of whom one can say it. Certainly not of Massinger. A brilliant master of technique, he was not, in this profound sense, an artist. And so we come to inquire how, if this is so, he could have written two great comedies. We shall probably be obliged to conclude that a large part of their excellence is, in some way which should be defined, fortuitous; and that therefore they are, however remarkable, not works of perfect art.

This objection raised by Leslie Stephen to Massinger's method of revealing a villain has great cogency; but I am inclined to believe that the cogency is due to a somewhat different reason from that which Leslie Stephen assigns. His statement is too *apriorist* to be quite trustworthy. There is no reason why a comedy or a tragedy villain should not declare himself, and in as long a period as the author likes; but the sort of villain who may run on in this way is a simple villain (simple not *simpliste*). Barabas and Volpone can declare their character, because they have no inside; appearance and reality are coincident; they are forces in particular directions. Massinger's two villains are not simple. Giles Overreach is essentially a great force directed upon small objects; a great force; a small mind; the terror of a dozen parishes instead of the conqueror of a world. The force is misapplied, attenuated, thwarted, by the man's vulgarity: he is a great man of the City, without fear, but with the most abject awe of the aristocracy. He is accordingly not simple, but a product of a certain civilization, and he is not wholly conscious. His monologues are meant to be, not what he thinks he is, but what he really is: and yet they are not the truth about him, and he himself certainly does not know the truth. To declare himself, therefore, is impossible.

> Nay, when my ears are pierced with widows' cries,
> And undone orphans wash with tears my threshold,
> I only think what 'tis to have my daughter
> Right honourable; and 'tis a powerful charm
> Makes me insensible of remorse, or pity,
> Or the least sting of conscience.

This is the wrong note. Elsewhere we have the right:

> Thou art a fool;
> In being out of office, I am out of danger;
> Where, if I were a justice, besides the trouble,
> I might or out of wilfulnss, or error,
> Run myself finely into a praemunire,
> And so become a prey to the informer,
> No, I'll have none of 't; 'tis enough I keep
> Greedy at my devotion: so he serve
> My purposes, let him hang, or damn, I care not...

And how well tuned, well modulated, here, the diction! The man is audible and visible. But from passages like the first we may be permitted to infer that Massinger was unconscious of trying to develop a different kind of character from any that Marlowe or Jonson had invented.

Luke Frugal, in *The City Madam,* is not so great a character as Sir Giles Overreach. But Luke Frugal just misses being almost the greatest of all hypocrites. His humility in the first act of the play is more than half real. The error in his portraiture is not the extravagant hocus-pocus of supposed Indian necromancers by which he is so easily duped, but the premature disclosure of villainy in his temptation of the two apprentices of his brother. But for this, he would be a perfect chameleon of circumstance. Here, again, we feel that Massinger was conscious only of inventing a rascal of the old simpler farce type. But the play is not a farce, in the sense in which *The Jew of Malta, The Alchemist, Bartholomew Fair* are farces. Massinger had not the personality to create great farce, and he was too serious to invent trivial farce. The ability to perform that slight distortion of *all* the elements in the world of a play or a story, so that this world is complete in itself, which was given to Marlowe and Jonson (and to Rabelais) and which is prerequisite to great farce, was denied to Massinger. On the other hand, his temperament was more closely related to theirs than to that of Shirley or the Restoration wits. His two comedies therefore occupy a place by themselves. His ways of thinking and feeling isolate him from both the Elizabethan and the later Caroline mind. He might almost have been a great realist; he is killed by conventions which were suitable for the preceding literary generation, but not for his. Had Massinger been a greater man, a man of more intellectual courage, the current of English literature immediately after him might have taken a different course. The defect is precisely a defect of personality. He is not, however, the only man of letters who, at the moment when a new view of life is wanted, has looked at life through the eyes of his predecessors, and only at manners through his own.

NOTE

1. *Philip Massinger*, by A. H. Cruickshank (Oxford: Blackwell, 1920).

R. J. KAUFMANN

Ford's Tragic Perspective

I

Ford has not been altogether fortunate in his critics. They have been attentive, but perhaps Ford, like children, would have fared the better for a little healthy neglect. His reputation has been refracted into a grotesque pattern of distorted and partial images, largely, one supposes, because there is much distracting foreign matter in his canon, many invitations to irrelevancy in his historical position. As the last of the great Elizabethan tragic writers on the one hand and as the somewhat bookish exploiter of these great predecessors' visions on the other, he is set either too high or too low by standards quite external to his manifest performance.[1] It is time we accord Ford his proper status as a minor classic writer on the scale of Emily Brontë, E. M. Forster, Hawthorne, and Scott Fitzgerald—writers typically obsessive in theme, deeply constrained personally, and nervously unresponsive to all save their main concerns. Such writers share in consequence a tendency to self-parody which is the underside of their splendid local intensities. The critic of great minor writing is obliged to enjoin his readers to observe decorum, not to ask too much of these writers, lest in so doing they miss the exquisite psychological disclosures which are the hallmark of such art.

It is one's initial sensitivity to the obsessive quality of Ford's art which provokes resistance to T. S. Eliot's accusation that Ford's plays are marred by 'the absence of purpose' and that, more particularly, *'Tis Pity She's a Whore* 'may be called meaningless' since the 'characters of the greatest intensity' are not seriously related to 'an action

From *Texas Studies in Literature and Language* I (Winter 1960), pp. 522–37. Reprinted by permission of the journal and the author.

or a struggle for harmony in the soul of the poet.[2] In this essay I am attempting to show the insufficiency of this judgment. Ford struggles purposively with humanity's genius for self-deprivation, with its puzzling aspiration to be the architect of its own unhappiness. He does this with the kind of persistence that argues 'an action of the soul.'

Recent years have been fruitful in the kind of cruel experience which makes Ford's anxious world imaginatively accessible—specifically, our acquaintance with thc plays of the modern French theater has taught us to read him better. The sophisticated fairy tales of Anouilh, the geometry of neat but not portentous spiritual encounter in Giraudoux, the studies in the lonely and gifted man's search for a sufficient identity as we find it in Sartre's *Flies* and Camus' *Caligula*—all variously can instruct us in the tonal qualities and special intellectual mode of Ford's plays. Ford, too, is the type of intellectual who is humanly restive under the tyranny of mind and yet artistically dependent upon its more rigid formulations. Hence the neatly logical surface *and* the sense of inchoate emotion in these plays. All such playwrights share an insight into the self-defining quality of individual human action. If the root of existential thought is the conviction that each man 'makes himself' through a qualifying series of choices, then Ford is as surely and as interestingly an existentialist as Sartre. But there is, I think, a more direct route to the analysis of Ford's tragic perspective.

In this essay I follow a set of interrelated themes through three plays: *The Queene, Love's Sacrifice,* and *'Tis Pity She's a Whore.* My narrower aim is to show Ford discovering more and more adequate means to project and analyze the central psychological motive which animates his protagonists. It will be initially sufficient to call this quality *jealousy,* though thereby we merely apply a label of convenience to a complex set of mental actions which Ford gradually explores. More broadly, I hope to reveal the special meaning of tragic jealousy for Ford, through examination of his key obsessive themes. These themes of *misalliance,* of the psychology of *vows,* of *counterfeiting,* all relate to Ford's heightened awareness of the *arbitrary* in human life. In fact it is as a student of the arbitrary that I see Ford and will seek to present him.

The core situation in Ford is one of misalliance, of natures subtly mismatched and progressively at odds with themselves and with received social sanctions. This central situation applies to external misalliance, as to marriages of persons of different social derivation in *Love's Sacrifice,* to unnatural extensions of social bonds, as in the incestuous love of *'Tis Pity,* and to the sad mismatching of youth and age in *The Broken Heart.* It can also apply without distention to the misalliance of the inner and the outer self in a single character. It is the most special quality of the Fordian hero that he 'calls' himself to a role that his residual nature (conscience and shaping habits) will not permit him to fulfill. The protagonist misidentifies himself through a too arbitrary choice,.disregards too much in himself, and tragedy results. It is this troubled contest between overt resolve and inner need, between what we demand and what we are free to accept, that makes for the tension of tragic experience.

Ford does not write simply about 'problems,' as his critics seem to wish; he slowly learns to write about irreducible *situations* in which the qualities of the participants necessarily harden into tragic contours *through* their relations with each other. It is just this concession that Ford implicitly exacts of us as his readers: that the human entanglements he writes about are precisely *not* problems, and the minute we literal-mindedly seek solutions, we collapse the delicately achieved balance of his plays. Ford is like Henry James in this. As a writer of terminal tragedy, he starts with the assumption of the good breeding and dignity of defeat. He denies us any vulgar 'escape' from disaster (which is, after all, what a solution is). This preference for the noble identity secured in defeat Ford shares with the late Stoics and with the modern existentialist writers of the literature of extreme situations. The Sartre of *The Flies* would recognize a brother in the Ford of *'Tis Pity.*

Once this combined necessity for dignity in defeat and for triumph over misalliance in the self through the costly beauty of the kept vow is accepted, there is a marvellous, subdued consistency to Ford's plays. Only through constructive exertions of the protagonist's will is tragedy then possible. In effect, we watch Ford's heroes counterfeit an adequate heroic stature through equating of the self with an arbitrary vow, and, since these choices are never prudent or circumspect, rich opportunities are thereby earned for a death of dramatic intensity. The key phrase to Ford could well be Juliet's 'If aught else fails myself have power to die.' A powerful and personally organized death is the resolution of the soul's misalliance in Ford. But such deaths are no more perfect in their isolation than are the people who contrive them—there is the costly imperfection of jealousy which guarantees that the most stoical tragedy is still a social experience. We can watch Ford's insight and technical mastery grow together as he learns to organize adequately complex dramatic statements of these themes from the unformed but promising *The Queene,* through the halfway house of *Love's Sacrifice* to proper fullness in *'Tis Pity She's a Whore.*[3]

II

The Queene is an imaginatively amphibious play, for if in its language it is halfway onto the cool strand of Ford's detached and attentive mature manner, it is also washed by the billowing falsities of Fletcher's tragicomic trickery. It bears no date.[4] It seems to me clearly the sort of work a dramatist writes who is just discovering his proper personal themes but has yet to work free of the prevailing 'correct' way to dramatize them. It is the test of Caroline originality to be able to transcend the facilities of Fletcher.

The Queene is a sort of sophisticated, theatrical fairy tale that does not quite maintain itself. Ford, whose interest in the type of gifted man still ludicrously open to flattery (and hence a candidate for *Ātē* is lifelong), has here in the central masculine role, Alphonso, an imperfectly convincing combination of Chapman's Byron and Shakespeare's King Ferdinand of Navarre, with a special vice of jealous misogyny. It is this seemingly paradoxical latter quality that will interest us, for I agree with Oliver that the play is a kind of preliminary attempt at the central action of *Love's Sacrifice,* 'each of the plays treating a husband's baseless suspicion of the chastity of his wife.'[5] Ford being of analytical mind, he only slowly learned to do what a more spontaneously gifted writer does directly. He did not seem to work from a central core of fable. His plays have the quality always of being built up from separately conceived parts. This fact is useful to us in *The Queene,* for here we find in disjunction elements that mature reflection will fuse. I hardly want to do more than enumerate them, for Ford barely does more than that with them himself.

We will need the bones of the plot. It is double and rests, typically for Ford, on the Queen's unqualified love for the vain, intolerant, woman-hater and political revolutionary, Alphonso, whom she repeals from execution at the outset in order to place him on the throne as King. This is paralleled by the equally unreasoning love of Velasco, the heroic military commander, for a widow. Both infatuated characters are made violently unhappy by their passion. Both are laid under the most arbitrary injunctions by their loved ones. The Queen is asked, immediately after the wedding, to establish separate households and to forego the privileges of marital love until Alphonso is satisfied of her purity and fidelity. Velasco is ordered to surrender his valiancy and to earn the title of coward, before his love will be acceptable. These could be dismissed as the rather arch postulates of sophisticated theater from Euripides to Anouilh, but such generic leveling obscures the peculiar tone of this play. We can see that Ford, the young man from the provinces, the puritan of *Christes Bloodie Sweat,* will always be an imperfect recruit to this sort of unanchored moral world. He will not be able to forget that the capricious love-game rests on an ennui which 'is a metaphysical emotion' stemming from an unappeasable sense of inner emptiness. This emptiness provokes a sense of unworthiness which is the seedbed for jealousy and sterile manipulation of others whose regard or love must always seem ulterior to one who cannot value himself. An analytical anthology of key assertions in the play will make this clearer.

Critics have made the sense of honor a key emotion in Ford. Perhaps—but as Velasco says, 'Ide rather loose my honor then my faith,' [6] and later, 'passions at their best are but sly traytors / To ruin honour.' (2728–30) It can be put almost syllogistically, this basic logic of Ford's world: Passion is able to dominate all men; Honor (reputation) is a frequent casualty of such passion; therefore, to cling to honor alone is unavailing. However, the logic of extreme situations is to join forces with the passions you cannot overcome. If you have an undeniable attraction, the intelligent recourse, then, is to place not only your love but your converted virtue there. This means narrowing your sense of honor or self-esteem deliberately, for the pleasing of the loved object. Hence the arrogant indifference to the rest of the world of a Giovanni, an Orgilus, even a Perkin Warbeck. I am as certain as one can be of anything conjectural that Ford thrilled to Othello's 'My life upon her faith,' and that slowly he learned that this statement contains one of the most profound ironies in Shakespeare's masterpiece of irony, for it can be better read 'Her life upon my faith.' The faith being defective in a Giovanni as it is in an Othello, desperate tragedy results.

The main action of *The Queene* is the unconvincing homeopathic cure of Alphonso, who is 'most addicted to this pestilence of jealousy,' (3593) but not before Alphonso has mindlessly conjured up visions of adultery and has sent his Queen towards the scaffold to answer for it. He even praises her beauty as she is being prepared for execution, till one of the lesser characters anticipates the reader: 'Heer's a medley love / That kills in Curtesie.' (3425–26) His real reason for having his Queen killed (as opposed to his public reasons) forms one of those psychic outcroppings which are the real basis for our insights in literature as well as in life:

> ...had she bin still
> As she was, mine, we might have liv'd too happily
> For eithers comfort (3372–76)

This Calvinistic sentiment is, I think, a revealing one. Ford's characters are terrified by the threat of happiness which saps identity. They are forever controlling themselves, narrowing their characters down to monomaniacal attachments and pursuits which in turn they find more demanding than they can sustain. When we return to what we started from—Alphonso as a violent misogynist whose jealousy is stifling—we can see the full curve of the key theme. The Fordian hero fears women too much to have the faith in them which alone can save him. In *The Queene* we are far from the rarely subtilized jealousy and imperfect faith of a Giovanni, but the very inchoate quality of this earlier play provides a family of critical clues.

III

In *Love's Sacrifice,* we ask at once whether the title speaks of the sacrifices made *to* love or the very sacrifice *of* love itself through needless entertainment of passions destructively incompatible with it. It is this richer meaning that Ford pursued here, and only realized in later works. The grounds for believing the former are readily indicated. Clear cases can be made for all three characters in the triangle: the wronged husband Caraffa, the Duke, who has condescended to marry beneath him; his superficially errant Duchess, Bianca; and the troubled true lover, true friend, Fernando. Bianca is carried past herself into a real desire for Fernando, a desire which his courtly scruple and loyalty to the bonds of friendship will not permit him to gratify. Trapped in a relationship which cannot mature, she eagerly incites her shocked husband to murder her when he discovers and misinterprets this unperfected liaison. She asks to be and succeeds in becoming a sacrifice to her awakened sense of a love she is unable to obtain. Her problem is routine. Ford's handling of her development is sketchy, but promising. What in effect he shows us is that her character is decent but thin, lacking in the deeper compunctions we call nobility, and hence her undernourished sense of abstract honor would not alone have been sufficient to prevent adultery once she had put herself regularly in the way of temptation. It is one of Ford's distinctions that he understands the emotional process of the essentially feminine mind—the sluggish but impressive logic of radical emotion. We can say then at the outset that Bianca is a somewhat conventional self-elected martyr for love—her *sacrifice* is the standard romantic one of a now useless life *to* an unobtainable ideal of love.

Fernando, her lover, is at once passionate and scrupulous. His finer self is aroused by Bianca's confession of helplessness against her need for his love; he voluntarily imposes upon himself a restraint whereby he renounces ready physical gratification in the interests of her supposed welfare. We could say that he is able to sublimate his passion through the agency of his excited sense of honor. What he turns to in this renunciation is the rather melodramatic compensatory pleasure of a grand death, in which he can speak scornful words of the Duke's failure to have trust in the perfection of Fernando's talent for friendship. There is something priggish about Fernando, and a good bit of as yet undeveloped Fordian *hybris*. Or, better, there is something close to *Ātē*—to tragic infatuation with one's own sufficiency. There is a nice distinction here: the man fraught with *hybris* believes himself invulnerable to the gods; the man seized with *Ātē* thinks he already *possesses* a full vision of himself and of the consequent interpretation that must be put on his actions by all observers. *Hybris* teaches one to say, 'Nothing can *happen* to me.' *Ātē* persuades one to think, 'Since I know what I am doing, no one else can misunderstand.' Ford understood what confers significance in the world of events. Others do shape notions; we are misunderstood. His tragedies are mainly ones of *Ātē*, of misguided and passionate attempts to deny not only the right of the world to judge (the tenet of romantic individualism), but the very ability of the world to assign values where the ego of the protagonist has established prior claims. The strange silences which attend the movements of Ford's heroes have been remarked by critics. They are silent because their private reasons are sufficient; the world's claims are thus not opposed and equal, but negligible and incommensurate.[7] Fernando courts martyrdom in his own gently contemptuous fashion, refusing the moral canons of 'life-hugging slaves.' He is a sacrifice to a somewhat abstracted notion of love, one not perfectly separable from chillier Stoic notions of self-consistency.

The Duke sacrifices himself at the end of the play, largely because he must preserve his precarious dignity. He cuts a poor figure throughout, and his final theatrical self-execution before the dead 'lovers'' tomb (in which he then assigns himself a place—a troublesome *ménage à trois* in perpetuity) is self-described as performed

> . . . for Bianca's love
> Caraffa, in revenge of wrongs to her,
> Thus on her altar sacrificed his life. (V, iii) [8]

Were it not for the fact that, as Robert Ornstein has most interestingly pointed out,[9] we tend to accept as true the self-evaluations spoken by stage characters not manifestly villainous and hypocritical, we would not find much in this remark at all. The simple, sub-theatrical fact is that the Duke has thoroughly botched everything, has displayed no hint of understanding or love or character. We find his final act gratuitous, his joining the dead lovers (whose relationship possesses at least a shred of validity) an intrusion.

Why does the play seem so centerless? Why do its well-phrased passions seem so stagey and false? I think the answer lies not in putative ethical confusion in the play which 'preserves in the separate fates of the main protagonists a consistent ethical scheme.' [10] Rather, it lies in the disastrously wrong point of view from which Ford chooses to 'narrate' or project his play. It has been noted by earlier critics that the play resembles *Othello.* I point out now that it is a very oblique *Othello,* and that the uselessly novel obliquity of Ford's vision is what subtracts from tragic concentration and spoils his dramatic scheme. Let me briefly indicate how this off-center view of the action affects the play.

What Ford omits in imitating Shakespeare's great play on the theme of misalliance is precisely the indispensable feature—the massive centrality of Othello himself. Shakespeare puts us squarely behind Othello, whose mighty figure steadily gains control over our imagination. By something very close to expressionist techniques, the latter part of the play becomes for us more and more a vision of the world as Othello mistakenly sees it; we are swept up and hurried to his dreadful, misconceived, and yet inevitable destiny. We are very precisely *with* Othello as he chooses and acts. Anyone who doubts this must not have felt the shocked recall to reality that Emilia's knock at the death-chamber door constitutes, nor noted how strange the intrusion of commonplace language seems, after the rhythms of Othello's spacious and noble misconception. It almost makes one weep to read prim critical reductions of this terrible error which we are never asked to approve, only *to understand in process.* The precise poetic quality of this tragic fantasy as it usurps the world is what we are asked to see—what we do see. Jealousy is what we call it before Shakespeare has brought us within it; afterwards we know how a violent 'purity' of faith in Othello has been used by Shakespeare to raise an otherwise uncomprehended indignity of life to the level of tragedy. The tragedy is made out of the patient contemplation of one man's reactions to torment, his consequent re-editing of reality, and his subsequent conduct.

In Ford's hands the theme of misalliance is apparently abstracted, and the Duke is given a set speech or two early in the play to let us know that he dotes on his wife's beauty and that he realizes that he has gone against custom in marrying beneath his rank:

> Though my gray-headed senate . . .
> Would tie the limits of our free affects [affections]—
> Like superstitious Jews,—to match with none
> But in a tribe of princes like ourselves . . .
> But why should princes do so, that command
> The storehouse of the earth's rich minerals? (I, i)

As superficially similar as this is to the standard plot-postulates of Fletcherian tragicomedy, I think we would be wrong to follow the current fashion and reduce the play to mechanical, problem-play exploration of the consequences of the Duke's foolish disregard of custom in making this wilful misalliance. The truth seems to be rather that Ford is troubled by the Duke's presence and can supply him with no real interior function. Now and then he is recalled to the stage, to watch from a position of bemused detachment the apish deformations of behavior visible, as usual, in Ford's minor characters. Ford makes a gesture at the theme of 'authority,' which orders Shakespeare's play, when he has the Duke exclaim,

> How we
> Who sway the manage of authority
> May be abused by smooth officious agents! (I, ii) [11]

The critical significance of Ford's quandary is detectable right here. If one's authority is to be abused with tragic (rather than comic or merely didactic) consequences, then the authority must be *conveyed,* not merely assumed as an artistic convenience. Ford's Duke appears on the stage only spasmodically, and merely to be manipulated by his embittered sister and the purportedly fiendish servant, D'Avolos, who together perform Iago's dark functions. The effect is of a goodly catalogue of officious agents, of much intended malice and much *cause* for suffering of which we see little convincing evidence. One senses a deeply insufficient engagement of Ford's imagination. What he *really* wanted to write about here, I think, is how the fineness of the lovers was a product of the Duke's jealousy. The Duke's presence as a lens for conventionally evaluating their acts, however, is a technical embarrassment not to be overcome. Either the Duke is right, in which case the lovers are morally swamped; or he is as irrelevant as Soranzo in *'Tis Pity*, a person whose claims are negligible and whose sufferings have no dramatic assertion whatsoever. Ford, by borrowing the half-remembered authority of Othello's compelling figure, has deepened his artistic predicament. It makes it harder to ignore the Duke, a thing we must do if we are to feel the effect of what is viable in the play. What he has yet to learn is that the noble lover and the jealous lover must be one and the same. Ford, the student of misalliance, has misallied themes in this play. As a result, the whole play has a dreamlike quality, and an uninvited irony of tone playing over its surface.

There is much to interest us in the crisscross pattern of true and counterfeit loves, of true and counterfeit reports, of true honor and its deceptive likeness, of false sacrifice as a self-relieving act and true sacrifice as giving up what you want most for reasons of Conradian delicacy. There is a real dignity in the lovers' acceptance of the roles they wish to play and then act out to their logical and terrible conclusion. The Duchess, when accused by her husband before he sacrifices her, makes no excuses, asks no mercy, but rather, accepts her role gladly; she only demands the right to define it as it really is, not as it seems to be. She has no wish to be a real martyr for counterfeit reasons. Fernando's attraction was physical, a fact she faces without illusion. She will not falsify her own nature to buy life. The heroic self in Ford is one free of illusions about what one intends to be. Fordian heroes can read their own motives, however conventionally base.

The entire play, *Love's Sacrifice*, centers to one side of the issues that characterize a normal adultery-revenge play. Ford's interest is not in what people think happens, what is said to happen, or even in the possibilities for physical action, but in what happens to the sensibilities of the people involved—how those who are apparently wrong achieve dignity and how the one apparently right (the Duke), sacrifices everything, always too late and always without comprehension. The unmodulated descent into terrible self-knowledge, which makes *Othello* the most searing of Shakespeare's plays, is totally lacking here, not because the Duke does not repent of his error, but because he has no artistically achieved character, through empathy with which we can know the quality of this change. The Duke's only recourse at the end is a cold, self-destructive fury, whereby to make a meaningless sacrifice of himself. The Duke has never had the existentialist opportunity that confers privilege in Ford's world; he has had no chance to choose a role, to counterfeit a true self. Ford does not make the same mistake with Giovanni in *'Tis Pity.*

IV

'Tis Pity She's a Whore has all the assurance *Love's Sacrifice* lacks. The first act has such a neat economy of attack, such a rare directness, that it argues Ford's confident impatience to give body to a world he sees rising before him. The writing blooms with certitude. It is worth the trouble to state how Ford builds the telling structure of his first act. It has four parts: Giovanni's incestuous compulsion is presented through an argument, entered *in medias res,* between the Friar and Giovanni. This stands apart like Euripides' prologue to *Hippolytus*, where the causal agency is announced, so that we are free to concentrate on the human consequences.

Next we see Annabella beleaguered by suitors whose characteristics are venality, cowardice, and corrupt worldliness. By their defects of quality these suitors create a predisposition in favor of the girl's need for love; we grow sensitive to her isolation and learn to justify her despair of beauty and dignity in her life. Ford's strategy throughout is here prefigured. The carefully contrived world of the play is one in which marriage is debased, sacraments are violated, vows are disregarded, churchly and secular sanctions are loosened and enfeebled. Without being baroquely overdrawn, the world of the play is made to act (in its negations of beauty) as a foil to the desperate choices of Giovanni and his sister. This is not, of course, because Ford approves of incest, but it is done to put the unthinkable within access of thought. Not the least of the functions of tragedy is to enlarge our imaginative tolerance.

This necessary climate being indicated, Ford brings the lovers together. They declare their loves, and, in a fashion obligatory in Ford's world, cement a pact, a mutual vow. Vows are important in Ford's world where an aestheticism of morality prevails, with its accompanying distaste for an ignoble and pointlessly frivolous existence distracted by too much meaningless privilege. By a solemn vow, one circumscribes his choices and hence gains a predictable future. Vows are at once the expression of taste and the most arbitrary and compelling form of self-definition—a vow can confer identity. We should pay attention to vows in Ford's plays. The one exchanged between Giovanni and Annabella is like a betrothal, and each repeats the same formula on their 'mother's dust':

> I charge you,
> Do not betray me to your mirth or hate:
> *Love me or kill me.* (I, iii. *Italics mine*)

Contrary to conventional opinion, this is precisely what Giovanni does; his love being corrupted, he kills his sister. Once we credit the literal and sanctified binding force of this vow, much of Giovanni's frenetic behavior in the latter part of the play, his 'mirth or hate,' becomes intelligible. More of that later.

With great rapidity, Ford has shown us the isolation of both Giovanni and Annabella and then brought them together with a resolution quiet and fiercely pure. They now will have significance only in relation to this arbitrary vow whereby they have separated themselves from any hope of unconventional felicity. This counterfeit marriage represents a radical misalliance which is made narrowly sacred by an arbitrary vow. It is the perfect concentrate of Ford. It is also typical of Ford that this scene should be counterpointed immediately with Bergetto's fatuous trivialities, as his prejudicially cheerful inanities are permitted to speak for the world the lovers are denying. But Ford is not content, even with this marvellously compressed total, as his accomplishment in the first act. He makes one other point which invites careful reflection. The uncle of Bergetto, a straightforward sort of man without any illusions but still hopeful, watches the idiotic ineptitude of his nephew (whose suit to Annabella he is trying to forward) and factually observes, 'Ah, Sirrah, then I see there is no changing of nature. Well, Bergetto, I fear though wilt be a very ass still.' (I, iv) There are useful implications in this comical assertion of our fixed natures.

One of the commonest criticisms of Ford as an artist concerns the evident unsuccess of his comic subplots. This is possibly unjustified, since we are beginning to see how funny is the ardent status-seeking of the stupid and unqualified now that we are again socially swamped by it. But by the use of comic characters (required to express unchangeable qualities), Ford can slyly forestall any hesitation we might feel in accepting the inflexible, self-defeating commitments which are the hallmark of his tragic protagonists. Ford's world, in consequence, must often be solemn and pompous, lest its close alliance with the world of comedy—the arbitrary quality of his characters—be too distractingly apparent.

We are led directly from this to the special dilemma of dramatists like Ford (and Euripides, whom he resembles in many ways). Ford centers his dramatic world on fixed and irrevocable commitments which the characters themselves contract. Fernando, Giovanni, Penthea in *The Broken Heart,* Perkin Warbeck—all hold sacred their own declarations of purpose, and their tragedy relates to these openly stated dramatic vows and is displaced from any external agency which can operate only as a secondary cause. Ford's characters are self-defining and nonpolitical. They do not so much defy society as deny its relevance to their lives.

Observing this, we find in Ford's non-dramatic prose the source of a moral contradiction which is latent in the stoical as it is in the extreme protestant ethic. In *A Line of Life* we find him saying, 'where the actors of mischief are a nation, there and amongst them to live well is a crown of immortal commendation.' (p. 396) The difficulty comes in determining what it means 'to live well' when a community standard of intelligible virtue is lacking. One must be his own light. Elsewhere in the same work, Ford opines, 'Let no man rely too much on his own judgment; the wisest are deceived.' (p. 397) Without the guidance of a community whose approbation one seeks and by whose judgments one abides, how is one to avoid the deceptions which lurk even in the choices of the wisest? The Stoic notion of Reason is troublingly like this Humean consensus of the approbation of the best people. The unearned confidence of modern theologues aside, the difficulty in reconciling these two contradictions—that one can no more live by the lights of a corrupt community than he can be the sole sponsor of his own morality—creates the very area in which tragedy is to be found. Ford found it there and Giovanni gives expression to it; he is a martyr to the tragic limitations of the Stoic vision.

It is priggish to suppose that, in times of extreme social dislocation, there is always a better vision than the stoical one available. If a little of this is conceded, then Giovanni is a legitimate tragic figure. Let me conclude my discussion of *'Tis Pity* by indicating precisely in what I think his tragedy consists.

While watching the play, one grows strangely tolerant of the unaccommodated Giovanni, to whom the mindless frivolity of a Bergetto, the casual immorality of a Soranzo, the slack conventional optimism of his father, and the angular traditional arguments of the Friar are alike irrelevant to the passionate central truth of his life—that his sister is good and beautiful. Since he has been educated to prefer the good and the beautiful, he prefers her with a kind of exclusive purity of vision which has at once the narrowness of madness and the cultivated clarity of a splendid sanity. But Ford knows that a vow, a reasoned choice made in the stillness of a moment of seeming truth, must then suffer the tests of a world which impinges on one's acts. A miscalculation of one's purposes, a misalliance of purpose and capacity, can spell corruption. Ford saw, and makes us see, that for Giovanni and for Annabella what has happened is a deeply working denial that others have a reality commensurate to the sense of their own being.

In their ignorance, they overrate themselves. They become coarsened by the necessity they are under to engage in pretenses to preserve the 'utopia for two.' From the moment Giovanni wants more to preserve his rights in his sister than her sense of her own dignity and freedom, he begins to deteriorate morally. We can mark the stages: an embarrassing, callow bravura when speaking of his sexual privileges which (solipsistically) he supposes even the Friar must envy; (II, v) a possessive edginess; (II, vi) an hysterical inflation of language which mounts as he grows less and less capable of crediting any other feelings but his own. (V, ii) In the final murder we can see very clearly that Giovanni is no longer *with* his sister. He acts unilaterally. He no longer possesses the love to share even his plans for a *Liebestod* with her.[12] His selfishness has grown perfect, his love become an abstract and self-oriented thing. He is true only to the negative sanction of their 'marriage' vow,

> Do not betray me to your mirth or hate:
> Love me or kill me. (I, iii)

We watch the monomaniacal workings of his mind as he *does* betray her to 'mirth and hate' and, having done so, having killed all but the gorgeous verbal residue of their love, he kills her.

Giovanni's tragedy is deep and it does provoke terror and pity, for like Othello's, it rests on the most terrible sacrifice of love—not of the object of love only, but of one's ability to give and receive love. *'Tis Pity* is a tragedy of the attrition of dignity and humanity of a man in the possession of *Ātē*. The tragic moral is not readily abstractable, and has nothing to do with incest as such. It is rooted in Ford's profound grasp of the psychological autointoxication which can result from too arbitrary a dedication of one's mysterious humanity. Like Othello, Giovanni is so obviously the dreadfully suffering victim of his own tragic infatuation with phantoms that we are moved closer to the core of our own humanity. The judgment is in the situation; we need not impose one.

Ford's choice of incest as a theme around which to build his greatest play was not itself arbitrary. From it he obtained an intensification of his grasp of the spiritual roots of jealousy that nothing else could have given *him*. A good complementary text for *'Tis Pity* is D. H. Lawrence's study of Edgar Allan Poe, from which I quote two passages:

> The trouble with man is that he insists on being master of his own fate, and he insists on *oneness* . . . having discovered the ecstasy of spiritual love, he insists that he shall have this all the time . . . He does not want to return to his own isolation.

And

> It is easy to see why each man kills the thing he loves. To *know* a living thing is to kill. You have to kill a thing to know it satisfactorily. For this reason, the desirous consciousness, the spirit, is a vampire . . . Keep KNOWLEDGE for the world of matter, force, and function. It has got nothing to do with being.[13]

Ford raised a conventional theme of stage jealousy to a level of comprehension at which I think he would have understood exactly these urgent words of Lawrence's, so instinct with our own aroused sense of the sanctity of being. In brilliantly literalizing the metaphor that the truth of love is written in the heart of the beloved, he has made Giovanni's desperate gouging-out of Annabella's heart more than a piece of sensationalism. It is an act exactly appropriate to Giovanni's austerely curious, intellectual, character; it is also the perfect correlative of the frenzied, higher jealousy to which Ford is giving tragic expression.

To speak one last time in conjunction with Lawrence,

> ... the love is between brother and sister. When the self is broken, and the mystery of the recognition of *otherness* fails, then the longing for identification becomes lust... it is this longing for identification, utter merging, which is at the base of the incest problem.[14]

Listen to the triumphant words of Giovanni as he shows the heart of Annabella,

> 'tis a heart,
> A heart, my lords, in which is mine entombed. (V, vi)

Ford has traced this tragic confusion to its very source. He has answered for himself a question asked by Bianca, importuning Fernando to make love to her in *Love's Sacrifice,* 'what's a vow? a vow? Can there be sin in unity?' This is the radical misalliance–this uncomprehended urge to a unity life does not permit. Aristophanes' comic parable to explain love in Plato's *Symposium* can here be seen as the deep source of human tragedy as well. Giovanni, like Othello, asks for a quality of certitude life does not afford, and hence he 'violates the delicacy' of things. Incest is a model of this–the vehicle of his tragedy; the failure in mutual faith is at once its moral and its cause. After thus tracing Ford's patient exploration of the jealousy that tragically undermines essential faith, it is hard to see in him the purposeless and soulless opportunist of T. S. Eliot's caricature.

NOTES

1. Besides the standard book-length studies by G. F. Sensabaugh (Palo Alto, 1944), Robert Davril (Paris, 1954), H. J. Oliver (Melbourne, 1955), and Clifford Leech (London, 1957), the following modern essays can be recommended: Peter Ure, 'Cult and Initiates in Ford's *Love's Sacrifice,*' *Modern Language Quarterly,* XI (1951), 298–306; G. H. Blayney, 'Convention, Plot and Structure in *The Broken Heart,*' *Modern Philology,* LVI (1958), 1–9; and Alfred Harbage, 'The Mystery of *Perkin Warbeck,*' in *Studies in English Renaissance Drama,* ed. J. W. Bennett, *et al.* (New York, 1959), pp. 125–141.

2. *Essays in Elizabethan Drama* (New York, 1956), p. 139 for first quotation, p. 129 for others.

3. Recent critics have been in disagreement about the chronology of Ford's plays. G. E. Bentley summarizes masterfully: 'For the dating of Ford's later and more distinguished plays the evidence is exasperatingly meagre.' *Jacobean and Caroline Stage* (Oxford, 1956); III, 436–437.

4. The play does not bear Ford's name, but no responsible critic doubts it is his. See Bentley, *op. cit.*, III, 457.

5. H. J. Oliver, *The Problem of John Ford* (Melbourne, 1955), p. 71.

6. Line 580; all quotations from *The Queene* are from W. Bang, ed., *The Queene or The Excellency of her Sex, Materialien,* XIII (Louvain, 1906). There are no scene or act divisions in this text, hence line references alone will be given.

7. Some of the strange stillness which Una Ellis-Fermor found in *The Broken Heart* (*Jacobean Drama,* London, 1936, p. 236) is created by the fact that Orgilus does not make the audience in any way privy to his vengeful designs in the customary way; his reasons are so private as to be not even conventionally shared.

8. For quotations from *Love's Sacrifice* and *'Tis Pity She's a Whore* I have used the Mermaid Series *John Ford,* ed. Havelock Ellis.

9. 'Historical Criticism and the Interpretation of Shakespeare,' *Shakespeare Quarterly,* X (1959), 3–9.

10. Peter Ure, 'Cult and Initiate in Ford's *Love's Sacrifice,' Modern Language Quarterly,* XI (1951), 306.

11. It has never, I think, been remarked that the subplot of this play owes much to *Measure for Measure:* there are strong parallels between Lucio and Ferentes (counterfeiters of vows and tireless sexual athletes), as well as reminiscences of Duke Vincentio as observer of immorality and, indeed, of Shakespeare's concern there for the nature of authority.

12. Oliver's assumption (*op. cit.*, p. 94) that Giovanni 'kills her to save her future torture' seems to me a sentimental reduction of the point.

13. *Studies in Classical American Literature* (New York, 1953), pp. 79–80.

14. *Ibid.*, pp. 85–86.

GALAXY BOOKS

Aaron, Daniel *Men of Good Hope* GB58
Abrams, Meyer H., ed. *English Romantic Poets* GB35
Aquinas, St. Thomas *Philosophical Texts* selected and translated by Thomas Gilby GB29
Barker, Ernest *Reflections on Government* GB15
Bate, Walter Jackson *The Achievement of Samuel Johnson* GB53
Berlin, Isaiah *Karl Marx* GB25
Bowra, C. M. *Ancient Greek Literature* GB30
The Romantic Imagination GB54
Bruun, Geoffrey *Nineteenth-Century European Civilization* GB36
Clark, George *Early Modern Europe* GB37
The Seventeenth Century GB47
Clifford, James L., ed. *Eighteenth-Century English Literature* GB23
Cochrane, Charles Norris *Christianity and Classical Culture* GB7
Collingwood, R. G. *The Idea of History* GB1
The Idea of Nature GB31
The Principles of Art GB11
Cruickshank, John *Albert Camus and the Literature of Revolt* GB43
Dante Alighieri *The Divine Comedy, Vol. 1: Inferno* translated by John D. Sinclair GB65
The Divine Comedy, Vol. 2: Purgatorio translated by John D. Sinclair GB66
The Divine Comedy, Vol. 3: Paradiso translated by John D. Sinclair GB67
Dean, Leonard, ed. *Shakespeare* GB46
Dixon, W. MacNeile *The Human Situation* GB12
Evans-Wentz, W. Y., ed. *The Tibetan Book of the Dead* GB39
Feidelson and Brodtkorb, eds. *Interpretations of American Literature* GB26
Gerould, Gordon Hall *The Ballad of Tradition* GB8
Goethe, Johann *Goethe's Faust* translated by Louis MacNeice GB45
Grierson, Herbert, ed. *Metaphysical Lyrics and Poems of the Seventeenth Century* GB19
Halsband, Robert *The Life of Lady Mary Wortley Montagu* GB44
Heiler, Friedrich *Prayer* translated by Samuel McComb GB16
Herklots, H. G. G. *How Our Bible Came to Us* GB4
Highet, Gilbert *The Classical Tradition* GB5
Juvenal the Satirist GB48
Homer *The Odyssey of Homer* translated by T. E. Shaw GB2
James, Henry *The Notebooks of Henry James* edited by F. O. Matthiessen and Kenneth B. Murdock GB61

GALAXY BOOKS

Kaufmann, R. J., ed. *Elizabethan Drama* GB63
Kierkegaard, Søren *Christian Discourses* GB49
Knox, Ronald A. *Enthusiasm* GB59
Langer, Susanne K., ed. *Reflections on Art* GB60
Lewis, C. S. *The Allegory of Love* GB17
A Preface to Paradise Lost GB57
Malinowski, Bronislaw *A Scientific Theory of Culture* GB40
Matthiessen, F. O. *The Achievement of T. S. Eliot,* third edition GB22
Mills, C. Wright *The Power Elite* GB20
White Collar GB3
Muller, Herbert J. *The Uses of the Past* GB9
Murray, Gilbert *The Rise of the Greek Epic* GB41
Otto, Rudolf *The Idea of the Holy* GB14
Radhakrishnan, S. *Eastern Religions and Western Thought* GB27
Roberts, David E. *Existentialism and Religious Belief* edited by Roger Hazelton GB28
Rostovtzeff, M. *Rome* GB42
Russell, Bertrand *The Problems of Philosophy* GB21
Religion and Science GB50
Schorer, Mark, ed. *Modern British Fiction* GB64
Schumpeter, Joseph A. *The Theory of Economic Development* translated by Redvers Opie GB55
Shapiro, Harry L., ed. *Man, Culture, and Society* GB32
Thucydides *The History of the Peloponnesian War* edited and translated by Richard Livingstone GB33
Tillich, Paul *Love, Power and Justice* GB38
Turberville, A. S. *English Men and Manners in the Eighteenth Century* GB10
Wagenknecht, Edward, ed. *Chaucer* GB24
Weber, Max *From Max Weber: Essays in Sociology* edited and translated by H. H. Gerth and C. Wright Mills GB13
Wedgwood, C. V. *Seventeenth-Century English Literature* GB51
Whitehead, Alfred North *An Introduction to Mathematics* GB18
Woodward, C. Vann *The Strange Career of Jim Crow* GB6
Wright, Austin, ed. *Victorian Literature* GB52
Young, J. Z. *Doubt and Certainty in Science* GB34
Zaehner, R. C. *Mysticism: Sacred and Profane* GB56
Zimmern, Alfred *The Greek Commonwealth* GB62